International Perspectives on Pastoral Counseling

International Perspectives on Pastoral Counseling has been co-published simultaneously as *American Journal of Pastoral Counseling*, Volume 5, Numbers (1/2) (3/4) 2002.

D1711987

The *American Journal of Pastoral Counseling*[TM] Monographic "Separates"

Below is a list of " separates," which in serials librarianship means a special issue simultaneously published as a special journal issue or double-issue *and* as a "separate" hardbound monograph. (This is a format which we also call a "DocuSerial.")

"Separates" are published because specialized libraries or professionals may wish to purchase a specific thematic issue by itself in a format which can be separately cataloged and shelved, as opposed to purchasing the journal on an on-going basis. Faculty members may also more easily consider a "separate" for classroom adoption.

"Separates" are carefully classified separately with the major book jobbers so that the journal tie-in can be noted on new book order slips to avoid duplicate purchasing.

You may wish to visit Haworth's Website at . . .

http://www.HaworthPress.com

. . . to search our online catalog for complete tables of contents of these separates and related publications.

You may also call 1-800-HAWORTH (outside US/Canada: 607-722-5857), or Fax 1-800-895-0582 (outside US/Canada: 607-771-0012), or e-mail at:

getinfo@haworthpressinc.com

International Perspectives on Pastoral Counseling, edited by James Reaves Farris, PhD (Vol. 5, No. (1/2)(3/4), 2002). *Explores pastoral care as practiced in Africa, India, Korea, Hong Kong, the Philippines, Central America, South America, Germany, and the United Kingdom.*

Pastoral Care and Counseling in Sexual Diversity, edited by H. Newton Malony, MDiv, PhD, (Vol. 3, No. (3/4), 2001). *"A balanced and reasoned presentation of viewpoints." (Orlo Christopher Strunk, Jr., PhD, Professor Emeritus, Boston University; Managing Editor, The Journal of Pastoral Care)*

International Perspectives on Pastoral Counseling

James Reaves Farris, PhD
Editor

International Perspectives on Pastoral Counseling has been co-published simultaneously as *American Journal of Pastoral Counseling*, Volume 5, Numbers (1/2) (3/4) 2002.

The Haworth Pastoral Press
An Imprint of
The Haworth Press, Inc.
New York • London • Oxford

Published by

The Haworth Pastoral Press, 10 Alice Street, Binghamton, NY 13904-1580 USA

The Haworth Pastoral Press is an imprint of The Haworth Press, Inc., 10 Alice Street, Binghamton, NY 13904-1580 USA.

International Perspectives on Pastoral Counseling has been co-published simultaneously as *American Journal of Pastoral Counseling,* Volume 5, Numbers (1/2) (3/4) 2002.

The development, preparation, and publication of this work has been undertaken with great care. However, the publisher, employees, editors, and agents of The Haworth Press and all imprints of The Haworth Press, Inc., including The Haworth Medical Press® and The Pharmaceutical Products Press®, are not responsible for any errors contained herein or for consequences that may ensue from use of materials or information contained in this work. Opinions expressed by the author(s) are not necessarily those of The Haworth Press, Inc.

Cover design by Thomas J. Mayshock Jr.

Library of Congress Cataloging-in-Publication Data

Farris, James Reaves
    International Perspectives on Pastoral Counseling / James Reaves Farris editor.
        p. cm.
    ". . . has been co-published simultaneously as American journal of pastoral counseling, volume 5, numbers 1/2/3/4, 2002."
    Includes bibliographical references and index.
        ISBN 0-7890-1922-1 (alk. paper) – ISBN 0-7890-1923-X (pbk: alk. paper)
    1. Pastoral counseling. I. American journal of pastoral counseling. II. Title.
        BV4012.2 .F37 2002
        253.5'09–dc21   2002007981

Indexing, Abstracting & Website/Internet Coverage

This section provides you with a list of major indexing & abstracting services. That is to say, each service began covering this periodical during the year noted in the right column. Most Websites which are listed below have indicated that they will either post, disseminate, compile, archive, cite or alert their own Website users with research-based content from this work. (This list is as current as the copyright date of this publication.)

Abstracting, Website/Indexing Coverage . . . . Year When Coverage Began

- *This periodical is indexed in ATLA Religion Database, published by the American Theological Library Association <www.atla.com>* **2001**
- *BUBL Information Service: An Internet-based Information Service for the UK higher education community <URL: http://bubl.ac.uk/>*. **1997**
- *CNPIEC Reference Guide: Chinese National Directory of Foreign Periodicals*. **1997**
- *Current Thoughts & Trends, "Abstracts Section"*. **1999**
- *e-psyche, LLC <www.e-psyche.net>* **2001**
- *Family & Society Studies Worldwide <www.nisc.com>* **1998**
- *Family Index Database <www.familyscholar.com>* **2001**
- *FINDEX <www.publist.com>* **1999**
- *FRANCIS. INIST/CNRS <www.inist.fr>* **1998**
- *Guide to Social Science & Religion in Periodical Literature*. **1997**
- *Human Resources Abstracts (HRA)* **1998**
- *IBZ International Bibliography of Periodical Literature <www.saur.de>* **1997**
- *Index to Jewish Periodicals <www.jewishperiodicals.com>* **2001**

(continued)

- *International Bulletin of Bibliography on Education* **1998**
- *Orere Source, The (Pastoral Abstracts)* **1997**
- *Referativnyi Zhurnal (Abstracts Journal of the All-Russian Institute of Scientific and Technical Information)* **1997**
- *Religious & Theological Abstracts <http://www.rtabst.org>* **1997**
- *Social Work Abstracts* **1998**
- *Special Educational Needs Abstracts* **1998**
- *Theology Digest (also made available on CD-ROM)* **1997**
- *Zeitschrifteninhaltsdienst Theologie (ZID)* **1998**

Special Bibliographic Notes related to special journal issues (separates) and indexing/abstracting:

- indexing/abstracting services in this list will also cover material in any "separate" that is co-published simultaneously with Haworth's special thematic journal issue or DocuSerial. Indexing/abstracting usually covers material at the article/chapter level.
- monographic co-editions are intended for either non-subscribers or libraries which intend to purchase a second copy for their circulating collections.
- monographic co-editions are reported to all jobbers/wholesalers/approval plans. The source journal is listed as the "series" to assist the prevention of duplicate purchasing in the same manner utilized for books-in-series.
- to facilitate user/access services all indexing/abstracting services are encouraged to utilize the co-indexing entry note indicated at the bottom of the first page of each article/chapter/contribution.
- this is intended to assist a library user of any reference tool (whether print, electronic, online, or CD-ROM) to locate the monographic version if the library has purchased this version but not a subscription to the source journal.
- individual articles/chapters in any Haworth publication are also available through the Haworth Document Delivery Service (HDDS).

ABOUT THE EDITOR

James Reaves Farris, PhD, is Professor of Practical Theology at the Graduate School of Religion at the Methodist University of São Paulo, Brazil. Dr. Farris is an ordained United Methodist Minister in the Southwest Texas Conference, and currently serving as Supervising Pastor of the Methodist Church in Cota 200, Brazil. He is a member of the American Association of Pastoral Counselors, the Society for Pastoral Theology and the Brazilian Counseling Association. He is currently seeking leisure as a Psychologist in Brazil. Dr. Farris is the author of over 25 journal articles in the fields of pastoral care and counseling and the psychology of religion, and is currently co-authoring a book on Pastoral Theology in Brazil.

International Perspectives on Pastoral Counseling

CONTENTS

About the Contributors   xi

Preface   xv
    Howard Clinebell, PhD

Introduction   1
    James Reaves Farris, PhD

Pastoral Counseling in the Philippines: A Perspective
    from the West   5
    Fred C. Gingrich, DMin

Global Issues of Pastoral Counseling: With Particular Attention
    to the Issues of Pastoral Counseling in the Philippines   57
    Louise M. Meeks, BA

Cultural Landscapes of Pastoral Counseling in Asia:
    The Case of Korea with a Supervisory Perspective   77
    Steve Sangkwon Shim, PhD

The Future Landscape of Pastoral Care and Counseling
    in the Asia Pacific Region   99
    Robert Solomon, MD, PhD

Pastoral Counseling in Chinese Cultural Contexts:
    Philosophical, Historical, Sociological, Spiritual
    and Psychological Considerations   119
    Simon Yiu Chuen Lee, DMin

Pastoral Counseling in Indonesia   151
    Aart Martin van Beek, DMin, DTh

Pastoral Care and Counselling: An Asian Perspective   175
    Anthony Yeo, MA

Pastoral Care in Latin America   191
    Sara Baltodano, MPhil

Pastoral Action in the Midst of a Context
    of Economic Transformation and Cultural Apathy   225
    Ronaldo Sathler-Rosa, PhD

Planting Pastoral Counseling Seeds in Brazilian Soil:
    Creating and Recreating Models   239
    James Reaves Farris, PhD

Journeying on the Margins: Moments in Pastoral Care
    and Counselling, from the Inner City of Pretoria   253
    Wilna de Beer, BA
    Stephan de Beer, DD

Complexity and Simplicity in Pastoral Care:
    The Case of Forgiveness   295
    Archie Smith, Jr., MDiv, PhD
    Ursula Riedel-Pfaefflin, PhD

Pastoral Counselling in Multi-Cultural Contexts   317
    Emmanuel Y. Lartey, PhD

Index   329

About the Contributors

Sara Baltodano, MPhil, is Professor of Pastoral Care and Counseling at the Universidad Bíblica Latinoamericana in Costa Rica. She is the author of numerous articles in the areas of Pastoral Care and Counseling and Theology, and is involved in various community action projects related to questions of poverty and justice. Her current areas of interest and research include Liberation Theology, Women's Rights and Contextualizing Pastoral Care and Counseling. She has lectured throughout Central and South America, and is involved in various international organizations.

Howard Clinebell, PhD, is Emeritus Professor, Pastoral Psychology and Counseling, Claremont School of Theology, and is ordained in the United Methodist Church. His current areas of professional interest include counseling for spiritually-centered wholistic wellness, health-nurturing religion and ethics, multi-cultural, bridge-building pastoral care and ecologically rooted counseling. Among other books, he has written *Ecotherapy, Healing Ourselves, Healing the Earth, Understanding and Counseling Persons with Alcohol, Drug, & Behavioral Addictions* and *Anchoring Your Well Being: Christian Wholeness in a Fractured World.* He is a co-founder of The International Pastoral Care Network for Social Responsibility.

Stephan de Beer, DD, is an ordained minister of the United Reformed Church in Southern Africa, and is currently directing an ecumenical inner city community organization, Pretoria Community Ministries, which is involved with women and girls at-risk, homelessness, social housing, economic development, and advocacy work. He is acting Director of the Institute for Urban Ministry, which offers urban theological programmes in conjunction with the University of South Africa. His main areas of research include the church in struggling urban neighbourhoods, the church and urban public policy, urban space, and spirituality. He is co-authoring a series of workbooks on Urban Ministry, and has presented various papers on urban ministry at national and international conferences.

Wilna de Beer, BA, and currently completing her MTh, is a registered social worker, and directs Lerato House, a ministry community working with teenage girls at-risk. Lerato House includes an outreach programme, counselling and therapeutic services, transitional residential housing, educational and health services, and a family reconciliation programme. She is a member of the National Women's Shelter Network and the Gauteng Alliance for Children on the Streets. Her research focuses on the way in which suffering women overcome through participation in community, celebration and ritual.

Fred C. Gingrich, DMin, is Professor of Counseling and Director of counseling programs at the Alliance Biblical Seminary, Manila, Philippines. He is also the Coordinator of the EdD Counseling program for the Asia Graduate School of Theology. His teaching and clinical interests are in the area of marriage and family and he is a Clinical Member and Approved Supervisor of the American Association for Marriage and Family Therapy (AAMFT). He and his wife Heather, PhD candidate, who is also a therapist and counseling instructor, are Canadian missionaries with the Christian Missionary Alliance.

Emmanuel Y. Lartey, PhD, is Professor of Pastoral Theology and Care at Columbia Theological Seminary, Decatur, Georgia, USA. He is also currently President of the International Council on Pastoral Care and Counseling. He was for several years Director of Pastoral Studies at the University of Birmingham, England and has served as Lecturer in Practical Theology at Trinity Theological Seminary in his country of origin, Ghana. His research interests are in inter-cultural pastoral care, counseling and theology. He has authored 2 books and several significant articles and chapters in important books in pastoral care. His most recent book is entitled *In Living Colour: An Inter-Cultural Approach to Pastoral Care and Counselling* (1997).

Simon Yiu Chuen Lee, DMin, is currently Professor of Pastoral Theology (Counseling) at the Alliance Bible Seminary, Hong Kong, where he is head of the Doctor of Ministry Program. He is ordained by the Christian Missionary Alliance of Canada, and currently serving with his wife Lydia as missionary partners in Hong Kong. His main areas of teaching are counseling and spirituality. Currently, his research interests are the integration of theology and psychology and family and crisis counseling. For the past five years, he has been a regular columnist in *The Christian Times*, in Hong Kong. His most recent book is *Care and Cure of the Soul: Integrating Psychological Counseling and Spiritual Direction.*

Louise M. Meeks, BA, is a commissioned missionary of the American Baptist Churches of the USA–International Ministries. She is a graduate of Linfield College, McMinnville, Oregon. Currently, she is assigned to Central Philippine University, Iloilo City, the Philippines and serves as the administrative officer of the Iloilo House of Refuge (formerly Crisis Center for Women & Children) located on the campus of Central Philippine University.

Ursula Riedel-Pfaefflin, PhD, is an ordained Lutheran minister and Professor of Feminism and Theology at the University of Applied Sciences for Social Work, Dresden, Germany. She is Vice President of the ICPCC (International Council of Pastoral Care and Counseling). She teaches in the areas of Practical Theology, Pastoral Care and Counseling, Gender Studies, and Cultural Diversity and is a supervisor in family counseling. She has written *Neue Mütterlichkeit* (*New Mothers*), Gütersloh, 1978, *Frau und Mann*, Dissertation, Gütersloh 1994, *Flügel trotz Allem* (*Feminist Pastoral Care and Counseling*), Gütersloh 2000, and *Displacement and the Yearning for Place* in: *EcoJustice Quarterly*, Vol . 14, Nr. 2, Spring 1994.

Ronaldo Sathler-Rosa, PhD, is an ordained Methodist minister, and has served as Professor of Practical Theology at the Methodist Theological Seminary in Brazil and the Graduate School of Religion of the Methodist University of São Paulo. He is Past President of the International Pastoral Care Network for Social Responsibility. He is currently President of Instituto Bennett, in Rio de Janeiro, Brazil. He has published a wide variety of articles on topics that include Practical Theology, Intercultural Pastoral Care and Counseling and Pastoral Theology. His current areas of interest include Pastoral Theology, Theology and Economy and Justice Issues in Pastoral Care and Counseling.

Steve Sangkwon Shim, PhD, is an ordained clergy member of the PCUSA, and Executive Director of the AAPC-accreditated Korea Christian Institute of Psychotherapy, based in Seoul, South Korea. He is an AAPC-Diplomate and a certified Counseling Psychologist in the Korean Counseling and Psychotherapy Association. He is the founding president of the Korea Association of Spirituality and Psychotherapy, and Visiting Professor at the Presbyterian College and Seminary, Seoul. He is the author of numerous articles relating to the subjects of pastoral psychology, marital therapies, and cross-cultural counseling and supervision.

Archie Smith, Jr., MDiv, PhD, is the James and Clarice Foster Professor of Pastoral Psychology & Counseling at the Pacific School of Religion and Graduate Theological Union, Berkeley, California. He is an ordained American Baptist minister at the McGee Avenue Baptist Church in Berkeley, a diplomat in the American Association of Pastoral Counselors and a

California licensed Marriage Family and Child Therapist–in private practice. He has taught at Clark University, Department of Sociology, and College of the Holy Cross, Department of Religion. He has taught, lectured and consulted in the United Kingdom, Kenya, China, Germany, and Indonesia. In 1999 he gave the GTU distinguished faculty lecture: "Invisible Forces that Determine Human Existence: The Middle Passage." His publications include: *The Relational Self: Ethics & Therapy from a Black Church Perspective*; *Navigating the Deep River: Spirituality in African American Families*; *Tending the Flock: Congregations and Family Ministry* (with B. Lyons); and articles in various journals.

Robert Solomon, MD, PhD, is the bishop of the Methodist Church in Singapore. Prior to that he served as a medical doctor, and later as a pastor in Tamil churches in Singapore. He taught pastoral theology at Trinity Theological College, Singapore, where he was principal. He earned his medical degree in Singapore, his degrees in theology in Manila, and a PhD in pastoral theology from the University of Edinburgh. He has written books such as *Living in Two Worlds*, *The Hurting Heart*, and *Fire for the Journey* and has contributed articles for books and journals. Dr. Solomon is a Fellow of the American Association of Pastoral Counselors, an international advisor for the *Journal of Pastoral Counseling*, and contributing editor of *Dharma Deepika*.

Aart Martin van Beek, DMin, DTh, taught at Satya Wacana Christian University, Salatiga, Indonesia and Jakarta Theology Seminary where he also helped develop local versions of CPE. He is an ordained minister in the PCUSA, a Pastoral Counseling Educator in the American Association of Pastoral Counselors, and is currently the pastor of a Japanese-American Presbyterian Church in California. His present interest is Cross-Cultural Pastoral Counseling. He has published books in English, Dutch and Indonesian that include *Life in the Javanese Kraton* and *Cross-Cultural Counseling*, and a book of short stories and poems about Indonesia, *From the Heart of Java*.

Anthony Yeo, MA, is Clinical Director of the Counseling and Care Center, Singapore, and lecturer in Pastoral Care and Counseling at Trinity Theological College, Singapore, where he works in the areas of pastoral counseling, martial and family therapy, systemic thinking in psychotherapy and clinical supervision. He has been a guest lecturer in Pastoral Counseling in various parts of Asia. He is currently President of the Association of Marital and Family Therapy, Singapore, and is the author of 8 books on counseling, marriage and stress management.

Preface

As I glance back at experiences during the dawning years of modern pastoral counseling after World War II, I rejoice at the hopes that motivated its pioneers. These were hopes for helping to produce a new, exciting chapter in religion's ancient heritage of healing human brokenness. I am also aware of the constrictions that have retarded the full realization of these hopes. The constrictions were rooted in the historical fact that the movement's founders, with all their creativity, imagination and strengths, were predominantly Western, middle-class, individualistic, English-speaking, Protestant Christian males. In recent decades the most enlivening and empowering development has been the rapid enlargement of the movement's constricted horizons of healing and circles of caring. This has occurred as well-trained practitioners have enlarged pastoral counseling's caring concerns with increasingly multi-cultural and multi-racial, as well as multi-faith, gender inclusive, and holistic theories and methods. In North America, African-Americans, Asian Americans, Latinos, Native Americans, Feminists and Womanist pastoral caregivers, thinking and working from their diverse cultural contexts, increasingly have enriched the overall field of pastoral care giving immensely.

On the global scene, it is encouraging, indeed, that the enlarging vision has taken place with accelerating alacrity. In our pluralistic, interconnected world, our field is blessed by widening awareness of other cultures among pastoral caregivers. It is also blessed by the fact that a growing proportion of clergy worldwide, including pastoral counseling teachers and specialists, are women and persons from non-middle class, non-white, and non-Western backgrounds. A horizon-stretching series of six International Congresses on Pastoral Care and Counseling, and the continuing mission of innovative groups like the International Pastoral Care Network for Social Responsibility, are among the many indications of the increasing globalization of the field in many countries and

[Haworth co-indexing entry note]: "Preface." Clinebell, Howard. Co-published simultaneously in *American Journal of Pastoral Counseling* (The Haworth Pastoral Press, an imprint of The Haworth Press, Inc.) Vol. 5, No. (1/2), 2002, pp. xvii-xxi; and: *International Perspectives on Pastoral Counseling* (ed: James Reaves Farris) The Haworth Pastoral Press, an imprint of The Haworth Press, Inc., 2002, pp. xv-xix. Single or multiple copies of this article are available for a fee from The Haworth Document Delivery Service [1-800-HAWORTH, 9:00 a.m. - 5:00 p.m. (EST). E-mail address: getinfo@haworthpressinc.com].

xv

cultures. All the trends support the expectation that continuing movement in this direction will become increasingly rapid as well as crucial
in the decades ahead. The rapidly-growing diversity of care seekers in
many if not most settings bring complex multi-cultural issues that challenge but also can stretch the understanding and healing methods of
pastoral caregivers. The challenging need is to cultivate as much understanding as possible of the different worlds and worldviews in which
human identities–their own and those of care-seekers–are shaped. In
light of these radical changes, this series of papers is a welcome contribution to ongoing multi-cultural bridge building. In this book these authors share important insights from their diverse cultures and
professional experiences. By so doing, they put significant care giving
resources at your fingertips.

In the radically new world of the 21st century, pastoral counselors of
all races and ethnic backgrounds will be challenged by a growing need
that is already prominently evident. This is the need to provide competent help to burdened individuals, couples, families, and communities
of different cultural backgrounds and worldviews than their own. This
need is producing a rising cry for new approaches to healing and wholeness. To respond effectively, caregivers must learn to think outside
many traditional, cultural boxes of theory and practice. They must do
their ministries from multi-cultural and global perspectives such as
those reflected so insightfully in these papers. Clearly these authors are
thinking outside old boxes and, as a result, have created a significant resource for pastoral counselors who are ready to risk thinking in new
ways for new times. In light of their contributions, I feel privileged to
have this opportunity to affirm Professor Farris and the other authors for
sharing their significant learnings in and from a variety of cultures!

Multi-cultural challenges confront us pastoral counselors today more
than ever never before. As I consider these mind-boggling changes, let
me share a personal example of how changes are occurring in the working theories and methodologies of many pastoral counselors around the
world. My own professional journey elicits a flood of vivid images in
my mind. These include images of horizon-stretching privileges I've
had during more than four decades of teaching and practicing pastoral
care and counseling. Many of these images are of graduate students who
came from more than a score of diverse countries and cultures. These
students became their teacher's teacher. Often they opened my eyes by
what they taught me about care giving in their homelands as contrasted
with what I was seeking to teach. I'm very grateful for what these for-

mer students, along with several of the authors of this series, have helped me learn.

I'm also remembering with heart-warming appreciation precious images of learning while teaching in some 30 diverse cultures. The countries that stand out most sharply are those in the impoverished, oppressed, broken-but-birthing two-thirds world. These experiences in other countries and with international students have given me what I now see as gifts-in-disguise. The gifts were moments of learning lessons I often didn't want to learn. The communicators of these lessons have invited, lured, or actively pushed me to move beyond my culturally constricted background. In short, they pushed me to enlarge my own horizons of healing and wholeness. Most often these experiences were gentle confrontations by persons in or from so-called "foreign" cultures. Other such moments of unexpected transformations were mind-shaking experiences in other cultures.

Only when I looked back at them was I able to see that these really were gifts. As they occurred, they shook and shattered provincial but comfortable beliefs and assumptions that together were the foundation of my understanding of pastoral care giving. Usually with some reluctance, I have become more and more aware that I could no longer teach or practice this pastoral art from an ideologically imperialistic, mono-cultural perspective. Increasingly I have become aware of how much the insights of other cultures' care giving perspectives are needed to make Western approaches more healing and effective in today's strange new world. My journey toward multi-cultural competence continues and will (like yours, I suspect), never be more than partially complete.

I recall the mixed feelings I had at a shaking experience during a lecture series at a theological seminary in Buenos Aires, Argentina. It was years ago during the painful struggles for liberation there. A widely published liberation theologian was my interpreter. I asked him to critique my message, after each lecture, in terms of the social and cultural context in that country. When I finished my first lecture, I felt comfortably sure that I had presented a holistic, inclusive perspective. I knew that I had recognized some of the deep differences of my North American context and that of cultures there. After words of generous affirmation of a few things I had said, my interpreter-critic opened my eyes when he did what I had requested–candidly identify what he had found lacking in my lecture. This was my failure to move more than a little beyond "North American individualism in understanding the ministry of pastoral care." In particular, I had failed to recognize that powerful political, economic, and class oppression was complicating everything that pastors confronted when they did care giving with individuals and families. He went on to point out that affluent governments and huge financial institutions (like the World Bank), mainly in the Northern hemisphere, were unwittingly contributing, by their policies, to the widespread poverty, powerlessness, injustice, and landlessness in his as well as many other Latin American countries. These pervasive forces, he said, were at the roots of countless individual, family and community problems with which clergy were asked for help. I reluctantly sensed the validity of his gift of honest criticism. Needless to say, my understanding of what I had believed to be liberating, holistic care giving was shaken deeply. Through the years, this experience reinforced by numerous others, provide incentives to move toward a more radical, systemically oriented, and justice-based understanding of care giving and counseling. From my present viewpoint in today's world, this transforming approach seems much more holistic as well as far more complicated. Most important is the fact that it is also much more effective in cultivating healing and wholeness in all dimensions of peoples' lives.

The need for transformed and transforming multi-cultural perspectives in pastoral care giving is illuminated by a poignant Southeast Asia image. (I am indebted to an outstanding graduate student from a village in what was then called Zaire for citing it in his doctoral dissertation.) Here is the earthy image: "Persons who know only their own culture are like frogs under coconut shells." As you probably know from experience, our human resistances to getting out from under our cultural and religious coconut shells can be fierce. This is because to risk doing so challenges our sense of culturally shaped identity in profoundly anxiety-generating ways. The coconut shells formed by the families and cultures in which we grew up feel much more than just terribly familiar, comfortable, and safe. They also feel "right"–the way things really are or at least should be. But, in the chaotic, interconnected world of the 21st century, such womb-like cultural coconut shells can no longer be really comfortable or truly safe. This is the profound challenge we face, together with all those with whom we have the privilege of doing pastoral care giving.

Leaving one's coconut shell requires an ongoing series of risky leaps of faith. Fortunately, powerful potential benefits can be derived from taking these leaps. Although being under cultural shells gives the illusion of safety, the view is terribly limited. The widening vistas of more multi-cultural perspectives can bring liberating gifts. Persons under their coconut shells, as all of us are and continue to be to some degree, are today hearing the call to enjoy the fresh air of liberation from many voices. These are calls for liberation into the real world–a world that is frightening, violent, and dangerous at times, but also enlivening and empowering with both challenges and opportunities to grow. The illuminating, multi-faceted articles in this symposium are a significant expression of this multi-cultural call to liberation.

As I was struggling to write this preface, the shattering tragedy of September 11th, 2001 in New York City and Washington, D.C. intruded into the process. That human disaster is flooding many hearts around the planet including my own, with tears and prayers. My tears and prayers are for the healing and well being of the country most directed impacted. But, far more importantly, my tears and prayers are for the healing and well being of the whole human family. Listen and respond to the rising volume of collective cries for care giving responses that are healing, reconciling, justice generating, and peacemaking. The cries are at a crescendo level. One thing seems even clearer today than before September 11th. Our world is being hit by tidal waves of collective feelings of shock, rage and existential angst, of collective grief and calls for retribution (often called justice). To respond effectively, pastoral caregivers must be multi-culturally empathetic, aware, and competent. However they must also be more than this. We also must be reconciliation and justice generating as well as holistic peacemaking in our mode of crisis counseling.

May the lessons you eventually draw from this huge global tragedy open new windows of understanding in your sorely needed ministry of pastoral healing and wholeness!

Howard Clinebell
Professor Emeritus
Pastoral Psychology and Counseling
Claremont School of Theology
Claremont, CA
USA

Introduction

James Reaves Farris, PhD

When I pick up a journal or a book the first thing I do is look at the title and the table of contents. What I want to know is whether or not there is anything in the text that interests me, or that speaks to my needs. If the title and table of contents look interesting, I usually thumb through the articles or chapters to see if anything captures my attention. In the case of a journal or text that is a collection of articles I also look to see if I know any of the authors.

This publication is a collection of articles that deal with international perspectives on Pastoral Counseling. That may mean that the title and table of contents will not attract a great deal of attention. Most of us have more than enough to do simply keeping up with current literature dealing with Pastoral Counseling in North American contexts. Further, while many of the authors are widely known and published in their regions of the world, they may not be immediately familiar to readers in the United States.

Taken together, these facts lead to an important question: "Why read a text on international perspectives on Pastoral Counseling written by authors that are not instantly recognizable?" An honest answer to this question is that you should not take the time to read these articles if you are not interested in Pastoral Counseling as it takes place outside of North American and European contexts. However, if you are interested in the wider world of Pastoral Counseling then this text is well worth your time and energy. I know of no other text that offers such an intimate view of Pastoral Counseling as it takes place around the world.

[Haworth co-indexing entry note]: "Introduction." Farris, James Reaves. Co-published simultaneously in *American Journal of Pastoral Counseling* (The Haworth Pastoral Press, an imprint of The Haworth Press, Inc.) Vol. 5, No. (1/2), 2002, pp. 1-3; and: *International Perspectives on Pastoral Counseling* (ed: James Reaves Farris) The Haworth Pastoral Press, an imprint of The Haworth Press, Inc., 2002, pp. 1-3. Single or multiple copies of this article are available for a fee from The Haworth Document Delivery Service [1-800-HAWORTH, 9:00 a.m. - 5:00 p.m. (EST). E-mail address: getinfo@haworthpressinc.com].

1

Steve Sangkwon Shim deals with how Pastoral Counseling models imported from the United States are being adapted to the reality of urban Korea. Emmanuel Y. Lartey deals with Pastoral Care and Counseling in African and multicultural contexts. Wilna and Stephan de Beer address specific issues related to urban realities in Pretoria, South Africa. Ronaldo Sathler-Rosa discusses how globalization and international markets affect Pastoral Theology in Brazil. James Reaves Farris explores the current status of Pastoral Care and Counseling in Brazil. Aart Martin van Beek discusses the importation of Pastoral Care and Counseling models from Holland and the United States in Indonesia. Anthony Yeo presents Asian realities, specifically in Singapore, as they relate to Pastoral Care and therapeutic conversations. Louise M. Meeks discusses the meaning of Pastoral Care and Counseling in the Philippines and the needs of women, while Fred C. Gingrich provides an encyclopedic view of the historical development and current status of Pastoral Counseling in the same culture. Archie Smith, Jr. and Ursula Riedel-Pfaefflin challenge the reader to rethink the meaning of forgiveness from an intercultural perspective. Simon Yiu Chuen Lee details the immense complexities of Chinese cultures from philosophical, historical, sociological, spiritual and psychological perspectives. Sara Baltodano challenges individualistic models of Pastoral Care and Counseling in light of the realities of poverty in Latin America. Robert Solomon provides an overview of the challenges to Pastoral Care and Counseling in Asian-Pacific contexts. Taken together, these texts provide revealing insights into the identity and practice of Pastoral Care and Counseling in diverse cultural contexts.

Taking into consideration these diverse perspectives, it needs to be noted that much of the current literature in the area of Pastoral Care and Counseling is written from North American and European perspectives. The distinct contribution of this publication is to broaden the discussion regarding the identity, nature and uniqueness of Pastoral Care and Counseling by locating it in a variety of cultural contexts. Each article offers a discussion of the identity and distinctiveness of Pastoral Care and Counseling as it takes place in specific cultural contexts.

The reality of the situation is that Pastoral Care and Counseling, as a professional discipline, began in North America and Europe, and has been transplanted into many other contexts. This leads to an almost natural assumption that Pastoral Care and Counseling is more or less the same in every corner of the world. This is simply not true. What the papers presented in this publication clearly show is that imported models and understandings of Pastoral Care and Counseling have been transformed in a variety of ways to fit the needs and realities of different cultural contexts. Pastoral Care and Counseling in Korea, the Philippines and Brazil may share common roots, but they are not the same. Each has developed its own unique identity.

While this is all very interesting, it also has direct implications for persons doing Pastoral Care and Counseling in the United States and Europe because neither are mono-cultural. Offering Pastoral Care and Counseling means, at least to some degree, entering the reality of the person with whom you are working. To enter that reality means to at least understand something of the cultural realities of that person. Each of the texts that follow offer insights into a variety of cultural contexts, and what it means to do Pastoral Care and Counseling in that world.

It is worth noting that several of the papers also deal with influences that directly affect Pastoral Care and Counseling in the United States and Europe. The article by Ronaldo Sathler-Rosa, Brazil, deals with how Globalization and International Markets affect Pastoral Care, Counseling and Theology. Archie Smith, Jr. and Ursula Riedel-Pfaefflin, from Germany and the United States, discuss issues of forgiveness. Sara Baltodano, Costa Rica, explores poverty and Pastoral Care and Counseling. Robert Solomon also deals with how Western influences affect almost every facet of life in Asian-Pacific contexts, and thus challenges pastoral models in this part of the world. It may very well be that one of the underlying themes of this collection is that while there are many differences between cultures, we also share many similar challenges.

Pastoral Counseling in the Philippines:
A Perspective from the West

Fred C. Gingrich, DMin

SUMMARY. This article describes the historical development and current status of Pastoral Counseling in the Philippines. It provides a description of the various influences, historical and current, which influence the identity and practice of Pastoral Counseling within this cultural context. Particular attention is paid to cross-cultural issues and the influence of Western Psychology on the practice of Pastoral Counseling in the Philippines. Interviews are provided and commented upon in order to provide concrete examples. *[Article copies available for a fee from The Haworth Document Delivery Service: 1-800-HAWORTH. E-mail address: <getinfo@haworthpressinc.com> Website: <http://www.HaworthPress.com> © 2002 by The Haworth Press, Inc. All rights reserved.]*

KEYWORDS. Pastoral counseling, the Philippines, psychology, cross-cultural

We arrived in Manila in May 1997 during the aftermath of a typhoon which had flooded the city and closed the Ninoy Aquino International Airport delaying our flight from Vancouver. It was a long flight filled with anticipation, apprehension and our two sleepless boys aged 3 and 4. At the airport we were relieved to be met by the Academic Dean who had recruited us to teach and direct the counseling program at a seminary in Metro Manila. The first few days at the mission guest house, the

[Haworth co-indexing entry note]: "Pastoral Counseling in the Philippines: A Perspective from the West." Gingrich, Fred C. Co-published simultaneously in *American Journal of Pastoral Counseling* (The Haworth Pastoral Press, an imprint of The Haworth Press, Inc.) Vol. 5, No. (1/2), 2002, pp. 5-55; and: *International Perspectives on Pastoral Counseling* (ed: James Reaves Farris) The Haworth Pastoral Press, an imprint of The Haworth Press, Inc., 2002, pp. 5-55. Single or multiple copies of this article are available for a fee from The Haworth Document Delivery Service [1-800-HAWORTH, 9:00 a.m. - 5:00 p.m. (EST). E-mail address: getinfo@haworthpressinc.com].

orientation tours and conversations, the visit to a tropical paradise retreat center all served to introduce us to the multiple contrasts of what one of the Philippine's national heroes, José Rizal, called the "Pearl of the Orient Seas."

Less than a month later I began my full teaching load, and my wife, her half-time load. By this time we had already begun to adjust to some of the obvious contrasts of living in a two-thirds world mega-city: looking for "air-con" (air conditioning) in the midst of tropical heat and humidity; poverty at every street corner as the BMWs drive by; English in formal education settings with the subtle acknowledgment that Tagalog is the real language of Philippine life; massive shopping malls that eclipse anything I'd experienced before alongside the more common "sari-sari" store where you can buy one egg or an ubiquitous "coke." Four years later we still notice these contrasts but we are becoming more aware of the profound contrasts that under gird this post-colonial, Christian, Asian nation.

CULTURAL CONTRASTS:
TWO STORIES

Story One: As part of our counseling program, my wife and I provide small group supervision for students in their counseling internships. Halfway through our 18-week semester, as part of an evaluation of our progress, I asked one of my groups, "How do you feel the cultural aspects of this supervision group are being handled?" I hoped that my well-trained Filipino students would respond with some perceptive analysis of the ways in which my western perspectives as a supervisor impacted them and their clients as Filipinos. However, instead of an in-depth assessment of the cultural chasm between us, in their warm, gentle and respectful way they essentially told me, "This may be a big issue for you, Sir, but it's not for us. We Filipinos are adaptable, flexible and resilient. We can easily take what you teach in class, and say in supervision, and apply it or modify it. Don't worry about it–we're fine!"

On the one hand, I might be tempted to say that these students are being naive about the systemic influences of culture and ethnicity on interpersonal functioning. On the other hand, this is a wonderful example of how sensitive and adaptable Filipinos truly are. The students would not want me, a guest in their country, and their professor, to feel inadequate or badly about anything. Furthermore, they are bright perceptive students, able to maneuver adeptly through the cultural maze of the diverse ethnic mosaic of their own country and the considerable international influence on their society.

Story Two: As part of my research for a previous article I had written (Gingrich, 2000), I had sent out a survey to a number of Christian Filipino psychologists, psychiatrists, and pastoral counselors. In a meeting with two of these colleagues regarding another matter, I was confronted by them in terms of why, as a foreigner, I would agree to write an article about counseling in the Philippines.

The implication was clear and one with which I could only agree. The Philippines has had its history written and re-written by foreigners for centuries. With capable Filipino academics and skilled pastoral counselors, surely this country can write its own history and describe its own approaches to pastoral care and counseling. However, my reply was that I was not intending to write an article from the Filipino perspective for Filipinos; my goal was to write about my perceptions as a foreigner in an attempt to help a primarily western audience understand some of the complexity and diversity of pastoral counseling in another culture.

My intention in writing this article is similar. As an outsider to this culture, yet experienced in training Filipino pastoral counselors, I wish to share my western perspective on pastoral counseling in the Philippines; I do not pretend to understand the depth and richness of the Filipino context or of Filipinos. My hope is that readers, whether western, Filipino or otherwise, will recognize that my attempt to act as a bridge between these worldviews, is from the perspective of a person whose feet are stuck in a western perspective on life, faith and the process of change.

To help provide some additional perspectives, I have included, in Tables throughout the article, a summary of the survey responses to which I referred above. Also, included in Tables are summaries of interviews with four leading Filipino pastoral counselors, representing four Christian denominations, all involved in the training of pastoral counselors in various contexts.

THE PERVASIVE LENS OF CULTURE

With increasing cultural sensitivity in the west, and the globalization of western culture by media and technology, we have all become aware of how culture permeates everything we do, how we think and how we relate. Filipino culture is not so obviously different from the west, but is subtly influenced by a contrasting Asian world-view in the midst of what appears at times to be quite western. Our cultural sensitivities have been sharpened as we strive to move beyond the pleasant accommodation of western values to understand the deeper values that separate the Asian and western worldviews.

The therapeutic literature (e.g., Falicov, 1988; McGoldrick, 1988; McGoldrick & Giordano, 1996) has encouraged me to reflect on the issue of culture, but working primarily in a cross-cultural context, I have come to a new level of awareness regarding how culture fundamentally shapes family functioning and individual identity. The development of cultural competencies as a therapist (Pederson, 1997; Hardy, 1997), and as a supervisor (Wong, 1998), has become a significant component of my interaction with supervisees, despite the issue never being seriously considered in my own training. While I still feel far from really understanding Filipino culture(s), it is encouraging to see that efforts have been made in this direction by Filipinos which have been helpful to me and my Filipino supervisees (e.g., Cimmarusti, 1996; Enriquez, 1989; Santa Rita, 1996).

THE HISTORICAL CONTEXT

Filipino adaptability and interpersonal sensitivity probably has its roots in the pre-colonial tribal cultures. However, it has been the strength of an evolving nation that has had to endure and accommodate to societal control by the Catholic Spanish (16th-19th centuries), the Americans (most of the 20th century) and the Japanese during WWII. Like many third world, post-colonial nations, the society has had to learn to live with those in power and has struggled to form a national identity. What has emerged is a nation which highly values interpersonal harmony, hard work, spirituality, and resilience, all of which nurture the Filipino identity.

The earliest people to inhabit the Philippine islands were likely the Negritos who came from Borneo and Sumatra. Later Malay people came from the south, some arriving in boats called "barangays." They settled in communities also called barangays, and this word is still used to describe the local communities, or neighborhoods in both rural and urban centers throughout the country. Chinese merchants came in the ninth century, and the Arabs in the 14th century. With each group of immigrants came new religions and cultural dynamics that have mutually influenced each other over the centuries. The Malays remained the dominant group until the Spanish arrived.

One could say that in 1521, Magellan discovered the Philippines. However, it may be more accurate to say that on March 16, 1521 Magellan was discovered by the Philippines (Fernandez, 1994, p. 6). Whichever way one describes the event, Spain claimed to control the Philippines for the next 377 years imposing a strong colonial social system, centralized government, and Roman Catholicism. Numerous uprisings occurred under Spanish rule. In 1896, Emilio Aguinaldo led an uprising that ended in a declaration of independence from Spain in 1898. At the same time the Americans defeated the Spanish fleet in Manila Bay as part of the Spanish-American War.

Following the defeat of the Spanish fleet, the United States occupied the Philippines and Revolutionary President Aguinaldo continued resistance against the U.S. Recently this period has been labeled the Philippine-American War (1899-1902) which ended with Aguinaldo's capture and swearing of allegiance to the United States.

The United States always claimed that their occupation of the Philippines was temporary with the purpose of establishing free and democratic government. The first legislative assembly was elected in 1907 and educational and legal systems were put in place. The Catholic Church was disestablished and considerable land was purchased from the church and redistributed. In 1935, under the presidency of Manuel Quezon, the Philippines became a self-governing commonwealth with a transition plan to independence by 1945. The process was interrupted and in 1942 the Japanese at Corregidor Island in Manila Bay defeated the U.S. forces. General Douglas MacArthur began the fight to regain the Philippines in 1944 and about a year later the Japanese surrendered. About one million Filipinos died in the war. The Japanese occupation, guerilla warfare, and battles for freedom resulted in great damage to the country and complete organizational breakdown. Most of Manila was destroyed. However, in July 1946, plans for independence came to fruition with the establishment of the Republic of the Philippines.

The U.S. continued to dominate in the post-war reconstruction era. A communist-inspired rebellion in the late '40s complicated recovery. A series of presidents, including Diosdado Macapagal (1961-65), the father of the current President, Gloria Macapagal-Arroyo, worked to solidify the government, the democratic process, develop and diversify the economy, and build ties with other Asian nations.

President Ferdinand Marcos (1965-1986) is best known for his declaration of martial law in 1972. He reinstituted democracy in 1981 and was re-elected for another six-year term. His government's low regard for human rights, its unlimited power to arrest and detain dissenters, and the corruption and favoritism, resulted in economic decline during his regime. In 1983, Benigno Aquino, a Marcos opponent, was assassinated upon his return to the Philippines. This sparked a "People's Power" uprising that ousted Marcos and installed Corazon Aquino (Ninoy Aquino's widow) as president in 1986.

Aquino's presidency revitalized democracy and civil liberties, but was hampered by political factions resulting in several attempted coups by the military. Economic recovery and development did not progress as hoped. Fidel Ramos was elected in 1992 with an emphasis on "national reconciliation." He legalized the communist party, and began talks with the communist insurgents, Muslim separatists, and military rebels. Amnesty was granted to all groups, and peace agreements signed with some. In 1998, Joseph Estrada was elected with large popular support based on his platform of poverty alleviation and an anti-crime crackdown.

Estrada's presidency came to an end on Jan. 20, 2001, halfway through his term, with a second "People's Power" uprising in response to a stalled impeachment trial of Estrada on corruption charges. His Vice-President, Gloria Macapagal-Arroyo, was sworn in as president to fulfill Estrada's term promising alleviation of poverty, moral recovery and leadership by example.

For the past 100 years or so, the Philippines has had a turbulent history with much political unrest and national disunity. Leaders, both foreign and local, have abused their power and oppressed the people. Economic instability and poverty for large segments of the population persist. In the midst of this turmoil are a people that struggle to define a sense of national identity and rise above the disasters of its history.

THE CULTURAL MOSAIC

The Philippines shares cultural characteristics with many other non-western countries. For instance, Boyd (1993) describes Thailand as "the land of smiles," which for the pastoral counselor prompts the question, What is behind the smile? Another Thai characteristic he discusses is the need in all relationships to establish who is in the superior role resulting in the practice of avoiding the use of first names and the reluctance to self-disclose. In discussing African-Kenyan culture, Rieschick (1993, pp. 39-40) highlights the role of the spirit world in Kenyan ontology, the power of magic and of supernatural beings, and the role of social and familial connections in defining personal identity. In Korea, Kim (1993, p. 114) suggests that Koreans are unlikely to go for counseling because "Asians are reluctant in expressing their feelings, and their family system is utterly authoritarian."

Other examples of similarities between Filipino culture and non-western nations could be cited, but suffice it to say that while many of these characteristics exist, at least in part in the Philippines, the country has in many ways become a mosaic, a composite of many diverse and contrasting influences to the point that what Kim says of "Asians" is no longer entirely true of all Filipinos. The influence of western literature and particularly the media has altered Filipino identity and social relationships especially in the urban centers.

The Philippines is a country of over 7100 islands with a population of 75 million (2000). Though mostly of Malay origin, the cultural diversity in the country is seen in the eight major language/ethnic groups and strong regional identities. Though English and Pilipino (or Tagalog) are the official languages and are widely spoken, 87 other languages/dialects exist. Included in these groups are Muslim people groups numbering about 5% of the population, and living primarily in the south. The American influence is still obvious, as is the European influence, particularly since the Philippines is a popular tourist destination from Europe.

Part of the reason for the strong tie to the rest of Southeast Asia is that the Chinese are the most significant ethnic minority group. They have played an important role in commerce since the ninth century, and because of their high profile economically, they wield considerable influence. Protective of Chinese cultural identity, a significant tension exists between those born in China and the desire of Filipino-born Chinese to assimilate into mainstream Filipino culture. Bond's (1996) edited volume, *The handbook of Chinese psychology,* has over 30 chapters on various dimensions of Chinese culture including language socialization, academic achievement, filial piety, emotions, values and psychotherapy. This resource is particularly helpful in working with Filipino Chinese since in significant ways they differ from the majority culture.

THE DISTINCTIVENESS OF FILIPINO CULTURE

Despite the cultural diversity and openness that exists in the Philippines, many contrasts between Filipino and Western culture can still be made. Table 1 presents a list of these contrasts. Even when in conversation with a Filipino from the educated or economically upper levels of society where many of these distinctions are less obvious, it does not take long for the astute cultural observer to begin to recognize the pervasive influence of Filipino culture. Despite the apparent ease with which a westerner can interact in the Philippines, he/she needs to maintain the stance of a learner, seeking out a "cultural informant" with whom to process cultural issues.

The most striking piece of cultural information that I have read since we have been in the Philippines, is that Filipinos send more than 30 million text messages per day, more than are sent in all of Europe combined (Larmer & Meyer, 2001, p. 11). Considering this is a two-third worlds country and that far from everyone owns a mobile phone, this is a vivid illustration of just how relational a culture the Philippines is. While technology is of course used for business, people I know will receive many non-work related text messages or calls every day. Public meetings will often begin with a reminder to turn off cell phones and beepers, and teachers have had to do the same with students. This need to be in touch and make frequent interpersonal connections is in contrast to the considerable attention given to privacy in the west.

Morais (1979), in commenting on the historical roots of contemporary interpersonal relationships in the Philippines, suggested that Filipinos' loyalty to each other is based on at least four pre-Hispanic values: the patron/client relationship, ritual kinship, "utang na loob" (debt of gratitude), and "suki" relationships (loyalty to market exchange partners). In the Spanish era, these interpersonal dynamics were intensified with social and religious ties like "compadrazzo" (blood brotherhood). Hence, "the ultimate of interpersonal solidarity is a willingness to extend assistance" (p. 47). The logical extension of this is that wealth can be redistributed in an informal social class system, and while this was a characteristic of pre-colonialism, this value is difficult to maintain in the face of western materialism.

The typical Filipino adult has been described as relationship-centered, modest, polite, gentle, friendly, loyal, hospitable, and kind. He or she loves music and dancing, has a high respect for elders and authority, and values personal cleanliness. "Bayanihan" (working together in unity) is also a frequently observed characteristic. Intuitive thinking and symbolic speech are preferred. Negative descriptors might be a sense of inferiority, a tendency to extravagance, lack of discipline and irresponsibility, com-

TABLE 1. Filipino versus Western Values

FILIPINO	WESTERN
Primacy of family and small group affiliation limiting free expression and creativity.	Autonomy, open dissent and creative expression producing social isolation and non-conformity to social norms.
Conceding to the wishes of the group to maintain harmony.	Dissent is seen as intellectually stimulating and broadening.
Gender-role stereotypes and patriarchal family structure.	Egalitarian relationships in family and social relationships.
Smooth interpersonal relationships.	Openness and frankness.
Delicadeza (nonconfrontational communication) particularly evident in females.	Women are encouraged to be assertive and "to fight their own battles."
Optimistic fatalism, *bahala na*, resulting in less stress and anxiety.	Future orientation, careful planning, drive for excellence and economic development through determined effort.
Sensitivity to slights and criticism, *amor propio*, leading to withdrawal and/or vengeance.	Self-confidence, competition and fair play with little concern for the loser.
The dread of *hiya* ("devastating shame") often inhibits competition, but fosters cooperation.	It is all about winning and not losing, though to lose well is not shameful.
Use of ridicule and ostracism to minimize *hiya* in child training.	Use of permissiveness and/or punishment in child training.
Utang nang loob, or reciprocity of favors and gratitude.	Individual rights and the economic "bottom line."

Adapted from: Santa Rita, Emilio (1996). Pilipino families. In McGoldrick, M. et al., *Ethnicity and family therapy*, 2nd ed. New York: Guilford, 324-330.

petitiveness, dependency (on family and others), motivated by "hiya" (shame), tending to resist interfering (sometimes interpreted as indifference), the "mañana habit" (putting off; procrastinating); "bahala na" ("come what may," fatalistic attitude), and "ningas cogon" (unsustained enthusiasm) (De Guzman & Varias, 1967; Bautista, 1988).

Related to counseling, the significant dimensions of Filipino culture that impact my own teaching and counseling are the issues of community versus individualism and the strong social pressure to maintain what has been labeled "Smooth Interpersonal Relationships" (SIR). One of the things I appreciate very much about the Philippines is its emphasis on community. Individual identity is understood only in the context of family and peer relationships. While first world people, in their efforts to establish a sense of personal identity, tend to promote the rights of individuals, assert the power to choose and be self-directed, and fear dependency, Filipinos, along with many other cultures, understand and experience a sense of personal identity only in terms of the relationships of which they are a part. In terms of a theological perspective, western Christians often emphasize personal faith and piety rather than the communal dimension and obligations that appear frequently in biblical passages (e.g., Mt. 5: 23-24, 1 Cor. 12: 12-26 and the "one another" passages).

If the Filipino perspective regarding identity is communal, it follows that SIR would pervade Filipino relationships. Preference for subtlety in communication, indirectness, and "utang na loob" (debt of gratitude) are examples of SIR. Again, this is similar to other non-western cultures. In Rieschick's (1993, pp. 34-35) description of Kenyans, the suggestion was made that while Americans will judge something different in Kenyan culture by saying "that's bad," the Kenyan will describe something different as "that's American." The Kenyan would avoid labeling something bad because even though it may be inappropriate in this context it may be appropriate in another. Similarly, this respect for difference and reluctance to label difference as deficient permeates Filipino interpersonal relationships.

Finally, the contrast between western and Filipino identity has been aptly described with the metaphor of cooked eggs. Westerners think of personal identity much like a hard-boiled egg; we touch each other but there is a clear boundary between where I end and you begin. Filipinos are more like fried eggs where the egg whites flow into one another but the yolks remain distinct (Bulatao, 1979). To extend the analogy, neither culture views scrambled eggs as healthy, which in the western literature would be viewed an example of enmeshment or codependency.

AN EMERGING FILIPINO PSYCHOLOGY

The development of Filipino psychology has also had a struggle to define itself. Early German and Spanish roots were replaced by American behaviorism and a plethora of psychological theories. Many current psychology professors received some of their training abroad. However, a growing number of psychologists are now trained in programs within the Philippines with several well-established, quality doctoral programs in psychology being offered. Publications on Filipino cultural and religious identity and a growing body of research are bringing into the foreground the uniqueness of Filipino psychology.

According to Villar (1997), the development of counseling psychology in the Philippines can be traced back to the introduction of the guidance movement in education in the 1920s. The first psychological clinic was apparently established in 1932 at the University of the Philippines (Salazar-Clemeña, 1993, p.1). In the 1920s and 1930s several prominent Filipinos studied in the U.S. and returned to teach and develop programs at the universities. In 1930 the first psychology department was established at the University of Santo Thomas. By the 1950s formal guidance and counseling programs were being established in the Faculties of Education. The Psychological Association of the Philippines (PAP) was established in 1962, including an accreditation committee to standardize psychology curricula. Its journal, *Philippine Journal of Psychology,* began publishing in 1968. In 1965 the forerunner of the Philippine Guidance and Counseling Association (PCGA) held its first convention. In 1975 the Pambansang Samahan ng Sikolohiyang Pilipno (PSSP), a multidisciplinary group interested in the study of the Pilipino psyche was established, and continues to work toward indigenization of psychology, with conventions and publications in Tagalog. In 1976 the Association of Psychological and Educational Counsellors in Asia (APECA) was established, and in the same year the forerunner of the Philippine Association for Counselor Education, Research and Supervision (PACERS) was established. Over the last twenty years an increasing number of textbooks and books on a variety of topics related to psychology have been published in both English and Tagalog. Collections of articles, such as Ortigas and Carnadang's (1993), provide a valuable insight into the unique topics and approaches to psychology in the Philippines.

The early pioneers in psychology and guidance brought with them the terminology and theoretical perspectives of the predominant counseling approaches in the U.S. Villar (1997) suggests that the earliest approaches were Directive Counseling (Edward Griffith Williamson), Nondirective Counseling (Carl Rogers) and Behavior Modification. In the 1970s, behaviorism was the predominant approach in two of the leading universities. Other approaches made their impact including Reality Therapy, Rational-Emotive Therapy, Logotherapy, Gestalt Therapy, Transactional Analysis, Jungian, Adlerian, Neuro-Linguistic Programming, Multi-modal Therapy, and Brief Therapy. Some of the founders of these approaches (e.g., Victor Frankl) actually visited the Philippines, and advocates and trainers of many of the approaches conducted workshops and seminars, in addition to the American-trained Filipinos.

Several studies of school counselors have been conducted to determine theoretical and technical preferences. Villar's (1997) conclusion is that most counselors do not operate from a consistently applied model. Pragmatic eclecticism seems to predominate. Furthermore, in the research no Filipino counseling approach was mentioned, explaining why Filipino counselors are likely to use Western-based counseling approaches (Villar, 1997, p. 23). However, Villar (1997, p. 33) does hypothesize that "these practitioners, though greatly affected by Western concepts, were trying to utilize whatever were thought to be appropriate to the Philippine context, and build up a Filipino approach." A summary of survey responses addressing these issues appears in Table 2.

As in many developing countries the tension between western psychologies and emerging indigenous psychologies permeates the literature and academic world in the Philippines. "Sikolohiyang Pilipino" (Filipino psychology) represents the desire to develop a Filipino identity and consciousness apart from the colonial heritage. Enriquez (1994), in his already classic work *Indigenous psychology and national consciousness,* using primarily linguistic and field methods, developed a Filipino psychology which rejects the perpetuation of the colonial status of the Filipino mind, opposes the use of psychology for the exploitation of the masses, and resists the "imposition to a Third World country of psychologies developed in industrialized countries" (p. 30). He suggested that the core Filipino value is "kapwa" (shared identity) which of course is in contrast to individualistic western definitions of personhood. "Kapwa" is further described as related to the "pivotal interpersonal value" of "pakiramdan" (shared inner perception). This concept is defined by Villar (1997, p. 208) as a heightened awareness and sensitivity to the feelings of another and appears to be related to the counseling concept of empathy.

Church (1986) and Church and Katigbak (2000) provide thorough summaries of the research on Filipino personality, emphasizing particularly Filipino personality traits and values. A good summary of various perspectives on Filipino values is found in Villar (1997, pp. 203-209). What is interesting, and confusing to the non-Filipino is that different authors describe many of the values in negative, positive or contrasting ways. For instance, Enriquez (1989, p. 54) positively describes the colonial or accommodative surface values of "hiya" (having a sense of propriety), "utang na loob" (showing gratitude or solidarity), and "pakikisama" (companionship or mutual esteem). Using more negative

TABLE 2. Survey Responses

Question: *What do you see as the major differences between western approaches to counseling and counseling in the Filipino context?* **Responses:** • Filipino culture is less time-bound, less directive and less linear. So, counseling here may not always fit neatly into a one-hour time slot, must be less confrontive and cannot dwell on concepts, theories, and ideas; it needs to be more flexible, relational and concrete; counselors need to be more active because the counselee is usually passive. • the counselee prefers to come to a counselor he knows personally than a total stranger. • Filipinos highly value family decision making. Success is a way of bringing honor and financial aid to the family, more than for personal glory. Considering the role of authority figures and family support is essential. • the Filipino spirit world, and deep seated beliefs in 'powers' affecting our lives, is also important to understand. • the Filipino counselor may have to help the counselee "save face" (considering the "hiya" shame dynamic). • the counselor is expected to deliver symptom relief; this is reinforced by the unwillingness to pay the price for more than one session. • there is an absence of awareness that going to the root of the problem is extremely important. • most adults don't have the leisure time to be existential and insightful. The issue for many people is survival, and mental or emotional disorders are another way of draining their already limited economic resources. So one can understand the impatience, anger, pain and very strong sense of powerlessness and helplessness on the part of the client and his relatives. • professionally, there is not much of a difference between western approaches and Filipino approaches since many Filipino counselors were trained abroad or were trained here by professors who were educated abroad.

language, Jocano (1997, p. 10) describes "hiya" as embarrassment, shame or losing face, "utang na loob" as having reciprocal obligations (or more commonly indebtedness), and "pakikisama" as getting along (or as is commonly described "Smooth Interpersonal Relationships"–SIR). The problem appears to be, as Enriquez (1989) points out, that given the colonial past of the Philippines, Filipinos can be very negative in their self descriptions, and there is a great need to restore a positive sense of identity which in turn can form the basis of a unique Filipino psychology and counseling approach.

The cultural differences between west and east emerge in some basic differences in how psychotherapy is conceptualized. In Table 3, Augsburger (1986, p. 364) provides a helpful summary of these dynamics.

As counseling becomes increasingly understood and accepted in Filipino society (see survey responses in Table 4), contextualized Filipino counseling theories are beginning to emerge. Villar (1997, pp. 209-216) makes a preliminary outline of what "Intentional Counseling in the Philippines" should look like. This is an eclectic model that incorpo-

TABLE 3. Comparison of Psychotherapy, West and East

WESTERN PSYCHOTHERAPY	EASTERN PSYCHOTHERAPY
The individual model concentrates on the *text* of psychic disturbance–the decoding of symptoms, the awareness of the person's history, and the analysis of the intrapsychic dynamics–from which the disorder springs.	The relational model concentrates on the *context* of the disturbance–the disordered relationships symbolized in the feelings of despair, shame, guilt, confusion, and isolation–in which the disorder is embedded.
The sources of strength lie in the individual's capacity to be self-directing, to claim autonomy and responsibility, and to use a scientific theory of the self to regain inner direction and control.	The sources of strength lie in the integration of the person in the social and cosmic order, a polyphonic social drama that triggers a ritual restoration of the dialogue with family, community, and tradition.
The individual approach is based on the self-regulating wisdom of the organism of the counselee. The empathy, warmth, and genuineness of the counselor are intense, authentic, but intended to be temporary and, as soon as possible, unnecessary for individual self-determination, definition, and direction.	The relational approach is based on the quality of the relationship the counselor and counselee create: the empathy, support, compassion, nonverbal acceptance, recognition, presence, seeing and being seen, dependency and dependability in an ongoing inclusion in the network of relationships.

rates "elements in the Philippine setting that must be considered for counseling practice" (p. 209).

Salazar-Clemeña (1993) describes her vision for a Filipino counseling model called "Counseling for Peace." Rooted in the experiences of Filipino people who are not at peace, this model proposes a framework of Peace with God, Peace with oneself, Peace with others, Peace in the Nation and Peace in the World.

Decenteceo (1999) proposes a more specific model, the "Pagdadala" (burden-bearing) model of counseling. Filipinos are committed to fulfilling their responsibilities and relationships even though times may be difficult. They derive meaning from their accountabilities and from their sense of belongingness to the community of co-burden bearers. The counselor takes up the burden of helping co-burden bearers. The emphasis of the model is not on solving client problems, but on the struggle in carrying life's heavy burdens. Using intriguing linguistic analysis, Decenteceo (pp. 94-96) describes how the help clients require is to "lighten" the load by: (1) clarifying what their burdens were, why they were carrying them, and where they were taking them; (2) arranging their burdens appropriately so that they are easier to carry; (3) "leaning" on someone for support when about to stagger under the weight; (4) putting the burden down, at least for a while; (5) letting out a breath

TABLE 4. Survey Responses

Question: *How well is counseling understood and accepted in Filipino society (city, urban, socio-economic differences, etc.)?*
Responses:
- there are those who keep things to themselves because of shame, others who think the problem will go away if they try hard enough or if they allow more time, and still others who look into the yellow pages, call their doctor, or ask around for experts.
- counseling is better understood and accepted by the educated people in the city and those belonging to the upper class.
- people from low income groups don't come for counseling if there is a counseling fee; they'd rather buy food than use their money for counseling.
- there are also those who do not know that there are professional counselors in the city.
- most people feel that issues connected to personal life should be shared only with members of the family, close friends or an elder or respected member of the community
- Filipinos are family-oriented; if there is a problem in the family, members are expected to keep this problem a secret. Divulging this 'secret' to a counselor who is not a member of one's family is tantamount to disloyalty to the family.
- if free services, such as those of a priest or nun, a friend, or a "kumare" or "kumpadre" (godparent) are not available or inadequate, they may seek the expert.
- they only go for counseling when the problem has reached the crisis level, e.g., a mental illness needing psychiatric care
- counseling is seldom regarded as "therapy," but more as advice seeking and guidance; a counselee would feel empty-handed if he gets out of the session without the counselor's piece of advice, or a "piece of his mind."
- schools give mainly vocational guidance and disciplinary action.

which makes things lighter (saying "whew" or "catching my breath"); and (6) putting the load down while one tells their story.

Salazar-Clemeña (1993, p. 7) suggests that counseling psychology in the Philippines has developed through an "exploratory phase," then a "boom phase," and is currently undergoing a phase of "critical evaluation." A significant part of the evaluation centers on the issue of culture. Ruiz (2000) critiques the use of "culturally sensitive" approaches which tend to adapt existing theories and methods to new cultural frames, and challenges Filipinos and Asians to develop "culture-specific" approaches, "an alternative counseling framework which best fits our respective cultures" (p. 4). She suggests that this must begin with the target culture's frame of reference. People from the particular culture examine key issues and dimensions of the culture with particular attention focused on the traditional style of helping and the way problems are solved within the culture. Secondly, training materials must be generated emerging from the analysis of the culture. Her challenge is that "We, Asians, have come of age. We are now ready to move on to formulate our very own counseling framework" (p. 5).

THEOLOGIZING IN THE FILIPINO CONTEXT

The Philippines has no official religion though about 83% are Roman Catholic (NSCB, 2000; USDS, 2000) making it the only country in Asia with a Catholic majority. Estimates vary as to the number of Protestants from between 5.4% (NSCB, 2000) to 9% (USDS, 2000). About two-thirds of the Protestants are Evangelical with just over half of the evangelicals being Pentecostal/Charismatic (Johnstone, 1993). The ratio of Filipino Protestants to Catholics is similar to the ratio in Brazil and Chile thirty or forty years ago which leads one church historian to ask the question: "Might it be that the ratio of Filipino Protestants to Catholics in another thirty or forty years will be similar to the ratio in Brazil and Chile today?" (Harper, 2000, p. 277). Harper's analysis of church growth trends in the Philippines concludes that this is the likely direction of the Philippine church.

Overall, it would seem that about 90% of the country is Christian, with about 5% being Muslim, and the remainder from a variety of groups including Buddhism and indigenous groups. In much of Asia, due to the social influence bestowed on Christianity by colonial powers, Christianity's influence is far greater than its numerical strength. "Nevertheless, Christianity suffers from the image of being an alien Western religion not seen to be fully at home in the Asian setting" (Hechanova, 1983, p. 22).

Therefore, as in Latin America and Africa, there has been considerable attention paid to the development of indigenous or contextualized theologies. Koyama (1974) and Song (1979) are examples of early efforts to develop theology from within the Asian context. Mercado (1975, 1982, and 1992), a Catholic theologian, is perhaps the most prolific writer on the enculturation of theology in the Filipino context.

Carino (1992) identifies the following four major emphases in recent theological reflection in Asia which "point to the drawing of an authentic and living Asian theology" (p. 128):

1. Theology as social protest and criticism: theological reflection which emerges from Christian communities that are "critically involved in the vital issues of Asian social and political life." (p. 129)
2. Theology as praxis and advocacy of people: "the challenge to get hold of a new dimension of human freedom." (p. 132)
3. Towards a new theological idiom: "the particular form and mode of expression–by which the people themselves perceived their own sufferings and projected their hopes." (p. 135)

4. Towards a new political vision: providing for "the articulation of alternative visions of political community." (p. 136)

Tano (1981) identifies five Filipino theologians who have attempted, to varying degrees and with varying success, to contextualize theology in the Philippines. Carlos Abesamis, Catalino Arevalo, and Edicio dela Torre are Catholic theologians who along with Emerito Nacpil, a Protestant, present various theologies of liberation. Vitaliano Gorospe attempts a Moral theology based on the Gospel and Filipino values. In summary, he identifies four factors which have significantly influenced the direction of theological reflection in the Philippines. First, the long experience of colonialism under Spain and the U.S. has created a " 'cultural fissure' in the national soul which has made it difficult to for the people to arrive at an indigenous understanding of the world and of themselves" (p. 148). Second, the transitional tensions between traditional values and modernization make it difficult to define Filipino values and integrate them into an indigenized theological framework. Third, socioeconomic polarization makes it difficult to know whose theology one is articulating when theologizing in the Filipino context. Fourth, it is difficult to freely theologize in a society that has experienced the authoritarian rule of martial law during the Marcos regime.

Similarly, Sui (2000) points out a significant difference between western and Asian theology: Whereas western theology is doctrinal in focus, Asian theology is issue-oriented, beginning and ending with people's lived experience. Therefore, Asian theology emphasizes the relationship between theology and culture, theory and praxis, diversity of religious faiths, and social change. Ro (1992, p. 28) commented that the two main theological themes in contemporary Asian theology are liberation theology and religious pluralism.

Thus it is not surprising that a number of Filipino theologians from the Catholic Church, and the Protestant denominations affiliated with the National Council of Churches in the Philippines (1963), have proposed what has been called the Theology of Struggle (e.g., Fernandez, 1994; Institute of Religion and Culture, 1992). Like many countries in Latin America and Africa, the history of the Philippines is one of oppression. The society, government, academic life, social and religious life has been dominated by western influence. As dela Torre (1992, p. 63-64) suggests, however, people who suffer will not struggle if they consider their efforts as futile, or a result of God's will. Also, they will not struggle if the risks are too great, or if their struggle will only result in greater suffering. Martyrdom and the image of the suffering Messiah are common themes in Filipino religious life. In contrast, a theology of struggle is one that emphasizes the liberating themes of the Gospel, of hope, of the possibility of change and a better life.

Overcoming poverty is, therefore, a significant component of the struggle for liberation. This theme is important in Filipino theology as evidenced in books like Beltran's (1987) *The Christology of the inarticulate: An inquiry into the Filipino understanding of Jesus Christ,* Aragon's (1993) *The Theology of Conquest,* and Abesamis's (1999) third edition of his *A third look at Jesus.* In this book, Abesamis suggests that the first look at Jesus is how Jesus looks at himself. The second look is the way Graeco-Roman and Western eyes see Jesus, and the third look is seeing Jesus "by and through the eyes of the poor peoples of the Third World. It is the look at Jesus by the poor and oppressed, the awakened, struggling and selfless poor, who want to create a just, humane and sustainable world. It is also the view of people who themselves are not poor but are in genuine solidarity with the poor" (p. 2).

While much of mainstream Filipino and Asian theology reflects the themes of struggle and liberation, other voices, equally concerned about the contextualization of the Gospel, present biblical critiques of, and alternatives to liberation theologies (e.g., Gnanakan, 1992, 1995; Tano, 1981; Whelchel, 1995). Tano suggests that a theology of liberation is the natural outcome of the socio-political context, but wants to affirm that a Filipino theology must keep the text (Bible) and the context in tension.

Regardless of the particular theological viewpoint, Hechanova's challenge (1983, p. 26-27), though written in the early 1980s, still holds:

> Just as it took centuries for the Church to make the proper distinction between the Christian faith and Western Culture, thus projecting to Asian peoples an alien Christ, so, I predict, it will take a long time for the Christian Churches to make the proper distinction between the Christian faith and many western-inherited ideological stances, thus alienating many Asian people in the process. . . . I see more and more people, including those in clinical education and pastoral care, realizing the need to situate the proclamation of the Christian Gospel within the context of the socio-economic-political realities of Asia.

PASTORAL COUNSELING IN THE PHILIPPINES

The history of pastoral care in the Philippines, and a discussion of pastoral care in other Asian countries, is available in a brief volume entitled *Pastoral Care and Counseling in Asia: Its needs and concerns* (Dumalagan et al., 1983). This book is a summary of the first Asian Conference on Pastoral Care and Counseling, held in Manila, in 1982. In 1997 the 6th Asia-Pacific Congress on Pastoral Care and Counseling was held in Korea with presenters from many Asian countries.

Clinical Pastoral Education began in the Philippines in 1964 when Albert Dalton, an American Episcopal Chaplain Supervisor, came to St. Luke's Hospital in Manila to begin a pilot project on the viability of CPE in the Asian context. The Clinical Pastoral Care Association of the Philippines (CPCAP) was begun in 1965, and its history up to 1982 is described in two articles by Dalton (1983) and Dumalagan (1983). At one point in its history, CPCAP had membership and training centers in both church-affiliated and non-church hospitals and universities, with numerous denominations represented from among Catholic, mainline and evangelical groups, and spread throughout the country. Currently, the Asian Clinical Pastoral Education Association offers CPE training in five locations in Metro Manila and Baguio. The St. Luke's CPE program continues today under the direction of one of Dalton's first group of students, Rev. Narciso Dumalagan (United Churches of Christ in the Philippines). These centers continue to attract students from throughout Asia, thereby having a profound impact not only on the Philippines but also on Pastoral Care and Counseling throughout Asia. See the interviews in Tables 5 and 6 for examples of the impact of these programs on the Philippines.

In many cases, pastoral care and counseling appear in a wide variety of formats and programs. For example, in evangelical circles, Dr. Alfredo Cabrera (see interview in Table 7) serves as the Director of the Greenhills Christian Fellowship's Pastoral Care and Counseling Ministry. As part of this large growing Conservative Baptist church, Cabrera directs the Emmaus Road Counseling Center, a certificate training program in counseling, and a CPE training program.

Another example is seen in the Center for Family Ministry, affiliated with the Loyola School of Theology, Ateneo de Manila University, and directed by Fr. Ruben Tanseco. This organization offers an MA degree in Pastoral Ministry (Family Ministry and Counseling) and a Diploma in Family Ministry. They also offer a wide variety of services: counseling, spiritual direction, seminars, pre-marital and marriage enrichment programs, and lay counseling training programs.

As early as the late 1970s, a group of Christian psychologists/counselors began to meet to share resources and a vision for the development of Christian counseling in the Philippines. Called the *Metanoia Psycho-*

TABLE 5. Interview

Interviewee: Fr. Fernando Boyagan *Position:* Chaplain of Trinity College (Episcopalian) *Training:* Pastoral counseling was not stressed during his training. They studied "Christian Ethics." Member of the Pastoral Care Association of the Philippines. *Experience:* Pastor for twenty years, serving in different parts of the country, primarily in Cotabato, Mindanao. *View of Pastoral Care and Counseling:* • Pastoral care and counseling are synonymous and are expected functions of a minister. • Training for pastoral counseling is usually done through St. Luke's CPE program. • CPE involves three months of supervised training; the daily routine takes two 1-11/2 hr. sessions per day. One session is on interpersonal relations with the sick (listening/caring skills); the other session is for case studies. The rest of the day is spent being with and listening to patients. • The CPE program at St. Luke's was very popular in the '80s; however, the presence of more training options for counseling in the country, and the loss of trainers (who have gone abroad) has decreased attendance in the '90s. • Episcopalian churches in the Philippines do not really have a structure that provides for pastoral counseling. • However, there are women who are actively doing pastoral care in the church. These women are now rising up and asserting their rights as equals with male leaders in the family and in the church. In fact, we now have women ordained as pastors. We have had seminars on gender sensitivity in our churches. Sometimes we see women running the church better. We have members who are resistant to this trend but we have grown. • Usually it is the ministers like us who do most of the pastoral counseling, assisted mostly by women.

logical Foundation, they played a significant role in raising awareness of the need for counseling ministry within the Christian community and were an influential proponent of the integration of culture, Christianity, and counseling.

In 1993, Alliance Biblical Seminary developed the first graduate Christian counseling program. Now at least four seminaries in the country offer counseling majors. Some of the programs have Filipino faculty, while others rely primarily on missionary faculty and ex-pat module instructors. While counseling itself is still not a widely accepted way of dealing with personal problems, the programs have attracted large numbers of students who have an interest in their own personal growth, a desire to integrate psychology and faith, and a passion to help others in their churches, schools, and social service and mission organizations.

THE CONTEXT OF PASTORAL COUNSELING

The Philippines is considered the only Christian country in Asia with 90% of the population affiliated with a Christian group. It has a Catholic

TABLE 6. Interview

Interviewee: Dr. Simplicio Dangawan *Position:* Chief Chaplain of the Philippine Air Force; Professor of Pastoral Counseling at the Union Theological Seminary, Cavite. Experience: Involved in pastoral care for 38 years; supervises 13 Air Force chaplains in the Philippines; has worked with Catholic priests, Muslim religious leaders and was instrumental in the formation of Christian-Muslim religious organizations in the south. Is involved in training of church leaders in the United Church of Christ of the Philippines (UCCP) denomination in the area of pastoral counseling. Developed training/education modules for the military on drug addiction (which is rampant in the military). Was also instrumental in developing workshops on pastoral care for pastors who have not undergone training in CPE or pastoral counseling. With colleagues conducted these seminars/workshops in the provinces so pastors in the rural areas can gather and learn. *View of Pastoral Care and Counseling:* • Pastoral counseling is a part of pastoral care. • In the Philippines, counseling is not properly acknowledged due to the fact that most Filipinos think you are crazy when you go repeatedly to a counselor or pastor; much more so when you go to see a psychiatrist. • Theology and psychology go together. A pastor is conditioned to theologize about the situation. Upon reflection he/she applies skills taken from psychology (especially listening skills) to give the client the opportunity to unburden his/her problems. • In the UCCP, women's and men's associations handle crisis situations and problems with members. There is a faculty/teachers' group that serves as support for these associations. Usually, the pastor directs the pastoral care activities. *Role of the Pastoral Counselor:* • Pastors/priests are the lead counselors in their congregations. To be pastoral means to be caring for people, to lead them to a knowledge of God. • Part of the role of a pastoral care-giver is to be a mediator among warring parties (nationally), and with troubled couples. • The common issues in the Air Force are immorality, drug addiction, abandonment, grief (loss of arms, legs, body parts), death. • In the Air Force, we don't have to look for counselees. The chiefs direct people to the chaplains. We counsel people of different denominations, even Muslims who don't have Muslim chaplains in the military. Counseling is not a denominational matter. *Significant Quote:* • "In this country, many people (even in the church) have yet to see the beauty of counseling as a ministry. Counseling is very time consuming but it is very rewarding in terms of meaning."

majority (65%) with other significant groups represented by Catholic indigenous groups (8.1%), Protestants (7.5%–with 5.1% of that evangelicals), and Muslims (8%) (Johnstone, 1993). Tribal religions have few adherents though the influence of traditional beliefs and syncretistic practices are widespread. *Anitos, nunos, aswangs, lamang lupa* and other spirits, along with *arbularyos* (or *tambalan*), faith healers and representatives of Filipino folk medicine, form a part of many Filipinos' belief system. Some would even claim that Filipinos are only Christian or Muslim externally, not internally: the phrase "split-level" Christianity has been used to describe the Filipinos' magical, traditional beliefs on the one hand, and their fervent adherence to Christian beliefs and

TABLE 7. Interview

Interviewee: Dr. Al Cabrera
Position: Director of the Greenhills Christian Fellowship (GCF) Pastoral Care and Counseling Ministry (including the Emmaus Road Counseling Center)
Training: CPE with Fr. Dumalagan at St. Luke's Hospital; Graduate studies in Dallas; ThD from Philippine Baptist Theological Seminary (PBTS) in Baguio. Member of the Pastoral Care Association of the Philippines.
Experience: After graduating he redesigned the program at PBTS, but was wanting to see pastoral care in action since much of his experience was academic. He said he wanted to see change in people. When GCF invited him to set up the pastoral care program in their church, he saw it as an open door for his vision. He designed the program for GCF, and it is now present in all daughter churches of GCF. The entire Conservative Baptist denomination in the Philippines looks to this program as a model. He provides the training for all pastoral care staff and handles the difficult cases.
Comments on Pastoral Care and Counseling:
• Pastoral care is the task of shepherding.
• Pastoral counseling utilizes insights from psychology; the approach is eclectic; GCF has psychiatrists, psychologists to support the program.
• Church members should be trained in pastoral care and counseling.
• Common issues faced in the church are: abuse, marital problems, conflicts in relationships, trauma, death threats, money problems, depression.
• So far people are very open to the idea of counseling; the counseling center does not run out of counselees.
Significant Quotes:
• "In GCF, counseling is no longer a 'shameful' reality among members"
• "When I was at PBTS, I faced resistance from two directions. One, counseling was a new discipline and people, even in leadership, had to face the change this meant for ministry and the church. Two, nobody wanted to be "investigated"; to be asked about his problems. They'd rather spiritualize their experience. But these resistances did not last long. When people experienced what it meant to be understood, to be listened to, be cared for, the defenses went down."

---

practices on the other. In Mercado's (1977) edited book called *Filipino religious psychology,* he presents valuable descriptions of Filipino medico-religious therapy and counseling, religious experience in popular Catholic devotion, and religious leadership in local indigenous sects.

Though the influence of secularism and the scientific worldview of the modern era have permeated some aspects of society, pastoral counseling inevitably must deal with the issue of "sinapian" (possession or oppression) by the demonic. For Filipinos there is no problem with the continuity between the psychological and the spiritual (Bautista, 2000), and so the need to categorize a symptom as demonic or psychological is not as strong. For evangelicals and charismatics who believe in the role of evil forces who influence people, this is not a difficult aspect of the culture to relate to. However, apart from the role of the Holy Spirit, most Christians will only acknowledge evil spirits. The Filipino worldview, however, encompasses many spirits, both good and bad, friendly and helpful or manipulative and malevolent. Most religious groups have not developed an adequate theology on this topic, and so it rarely is talked about, but continues to significantly influence Filipinos' lives.

The integration of faith and psychology has also been a theme within the Catholic churches. Calpotura's (2000) article describes a model of "psycho-spiritual integration" of counseling and Spiritual Direction, developed at the Emmaus Center since 1981. He refers to Albert Alejo, SJ, who provides a phenomenological description of the Filipino journey into the experience of "ka-loob" (similarity of inferiority) which is at the foundation of a Filipino's relationship with God and others. He writes:

> . . . we begin by knocking on the door of the house, *"Tao po!"* (literally, "A person is here!") We come to announce our personhood wishing to relate with our "kapwa" [unity of self and others–shared identity]. The door is opened, we are ushered in, and we sit down. The *"kuwentuhan"* (storytelling) begins. Food is served to us. We continue our *"kuwento"* (story) as we eat. *"Pagka-nakapanatagang loob na,"* the host shows the person around the house, the yard, introduces him or her to the neighbors and even to their pets. The "kuwentuhan" continues while all of these are happening. *Pagtumagal-tagal na at lumalim na ang pagiisang loob, ang anyaya na ay–"Dumito ka na!" Tuloy ang kuwentuhan hanggang kinaumagahan.* (After a while, when the relationship has deepened, the invitation becomes–"Stay with me!" And then storytelling continues till morning.) The medium of bonding in all this process towards KA-LOOB is the KUWENTO. (p. 89)

The deep sharing of each others' stories requires the reciprocal involvement in each others' lives. Pastors and counselors earn the right to hear the counselee's story by visiting them, getting to know them, their family and their friends, by eating with them, by spending time with them. The western tendency to prefer an anonymous well-boundaried counselor is diametrically opposed to the Filipino need for a recognition of our shared identity.

THE DYNAMICS OF PASTORAL INVOLVEMENT IN PEOPLE'S LIVES

The role of the pastor/priest in the Philippines is quite powerful. Cardinal Jaime Sin, representing the Catholic church in the country, wields considerable political and moral influence. In Protestant circles clergy are regularly addressed with the prefix "pastor," even in informal and non-religious settings. The roots of this considerable social influence likely lie in the hierarchical culture headed by a benevolent father-figure ("datu"), the historic role of the priest in Filipino religious life, and the exalted status of "white" foreign missionaries, both Catholic and Protestant who have dominated religious life in the Philippines for centuries.

As a result, people have high expectations of anyone involved in pastoral ministry. Part of the pastor's role is to provide pastoral care, including visitation in homes, crisis intervention, hospital visits, etc. Parishioners have high expectations for their pastors requiring active involvement in people's lives. Pastoral counseling, which I view as a subset of pastoral care, has equally high expectations. Table 8 summarizes the survey responses regarding how the church perceives pastoral counseling.

The dichotomy between spiritual and other dimensions of human existence (emotional, cognitive, relational) is not as pronounced in the Philippines. Hence, pastors are likely to be involved in all areas of parishioners' lives, and not perceived as only experts in the spiritual. The need to categorize and to assign specializations to different people is not pronounced. Thus, the pastor is an expert in all things. In the west, Spiritual Direction has become widely practiced and sought in both Catholic and Protestant circles. One might expect it to be similar here, however, while there are numbers of Catholic retreat centers and location where one can find a Spiritual Director, it is not prevalent or widely known. Specializations in pastoral care and counseling are only beginning.

Augsburger (1986) identifies eleven metaphors of counseling and uses both western and eastern examples with which to contrast the models. The metaphor which is most clearly reflected in the contemporary Filipino understanding of counseling is that of the "teacher-student" (pp. 353-354). The western therapeutic models which reflect this perspective are the behavioral, social learning, Rational Emotive Therapy, and Reality Therapy approaches. Augsburger describes the eastern version of this relationship as the "guru-chela" relationship in which the guru is active, responsible, directive, advisory and controlling, whereas the chela is more passive, dependent, adaptive, teachable and obedient. While there are many dissimilarities between the teacher-student and guru-chela relationships, the tendency in the Philippines is for the client to approach the pastoral counselor much as they would a teacher—with

TABLE 8. Survey Responses

Question: *How well is pastoral counseling accepted as an important ministry in the churches?* **Responses:** • the Filipino church is not receptive to psychology; the Filipino church understands life problems and psychological problems only from a spiritual perspective. • only recently has there been an admission in certain Christian groups that training in expository preaching and church administration is not adequately preparing our pastors. • in smaller churches, members might approach the pastor, pastor's wife or a trusted deacon for counseling. • in larger churches there might be a counseling department. This is why some pastors and Christian workers are taking up counseling courses in seminary. Counseling seems accepted, but not much effort is done to really promote it as a service to the church members. • at camps and retreats, some person to person counseling is given, but the emphasis is on the spiritual life rather than lifestyle issues. • on the other hand, many church members are hesitant to seek counseling in the church because they are afraid their problem might leak out to the whole church and turn into gossip; the fear exists that if one person in church knows about the problem, other church members will know it too. • people also fear being branded as 'sinful'; they are afraid to reveal their problem to their pastor or deacon as they might be seen as less of a Christian. • people often see counseling as a one time consultation in time of crisis, or a place to go if one has legal problems. • a professional counselor inside or outside the church is not likely to support himself financially; Filipinos expect to get counseling for free.

high respect for their expertise and status, looking for advice and direction, and willing to submit to the counselor's authority.

Parishioners expect to receive advice, direction, and assurance from their pastor. Bautista (n.d., pp. 28-30), a Filipino psychologist, suggests that clients come to counseling with a need to be comforted, a demand for instant solutions, a need for visible proofs of healing, and a need for certainty, all aspects of counseling that traditional western psychotherapy has rejected. The pastor thus has essentially two options: educate the client about what is "proper" counseling and appropriate expectations of the process of change, or respond to their expectations and provide instant reassurance, the "correct" solution, and a promise of healing. For those who have been influenced by western counseling literature, either option leaves the pastor, and often the client dissatisfied and disappointed. The solution is, of course, to develop contextualized approaches to pastoral care that respects the authority invested in the pastor yet allows the pastor to make use of the diversity of paths to healing.

Tan (1989), in discussing psychotherapy with Asian-Americans, refers to this need to have something happen quickly in counseling as the process of giving–"the client's perception that something was received from the therapeutic experience or encounter (e.g., that the client received a 'gift' of some sort or benefit from the therapist and the therapy provided)" (p. 68). Quoting Sue and Zane, Tan (1989) says:

> Gift giving does not imply short-term treatment or even the necessity of finding quick solutions. However, it does imply the need for attaining some type of meaningful gain early in therapy. . . . Our central argument is that therapists should focus on gift giving and attempt to offer benefits from treatment as soon as possible, even in the first session. Some of the gifts (immediate benefits) that the therapist can offer include anxiety reduction, depression relief, cognitive clarity, normalization, reassurance, hope and faith, skills acquisition, a coping perspective, and goal setting. (p. 68)

The success of a pastor's counseling depends on the prior relationship and closeness of the counselor to the client (Castillo, 1999). It is only after the pastor has become a "kaibigan" (friend), and has become relatively close in the client's circle of friends, that counseling is possible. A friend is always available and will be there quickly in time of crisis. The right to counsel depends on the pastor's status (a father-figure, a friend), appropriate behavior (only asking questions which the pastor, given his/her status has the right to ask), and respectful treatment of the parishioner (Castillo, 1999). How much the person is willing to share is an indicator of how far into their friendship circle they have allowed you to come.

Another pastoral counseling dynamic is the need for pastors to approach people whom they think might need counseling or pastoral care. This is a form of preventative counseling in which the pastor identifies a "person with a possible problem" or a "possible problem generating situation or relationship" (Castillo, 1999). Assuming that a relationship is at least at the friendship level, the pastor can identify needs and actively seek to talk to the person about the perceived problem. Western concepts of invasion of privacy and appropriate boundaries in pastoral care do not apply.

Third party counseling is also common (Castillo, 1999). However, coming to the pastor on behalf of a friend is confusing for the pastor because the "friend" may be the client themselves or actually a friend. Pre-counseling is the situation in which the client discusses a little problem to "test the waters" before addressing the real problem. The western desire to get quickly to heart of the matter will offend or frighten the client.

The counseling process tends to be quite short. One session counseling is not uncommon. "Contracting" for an on-going counseling relationship is rare. Limiting a session to an hour, or to a specific time frame, is difficult since "Filipino time" is event oriented. The western emphasis on linear time with a beginning, middle and fixed ending is in contrast to the open-ended, cyclical concept of time (Andres, 1985).

Another dimension of counseling in the Philippines is the perception of truth. Until the advent of postmodernism in the west, truth was seen as objective, or was defined in legal terms. In the Philippines, truth is what the person perceives it to be (Castillo, 1999). This makes marital and family counseling, in particular, easier on the one hand (the participants do not argue as much about what really happened), but harder in that the process of negotiating truth is embedded in the complex layers of status and authority that permeate all relationships.

Related to the issue of the role of the pastor is the role of the laity in pastoral care. Tan (1989, p. 70) suggests that using trained lay counselors within the church context may be a helpful way for people to by-pass the stigma against formal counseling in Asian settings. While the contemporary religious culture in the west is much more inclusive and often actively promotes lay people in helping ministries, this is still relatively new in the Philippines. The Catholic charismatic movement and organizations like "Couples for Christ" have opened the doors for lay involvement. Filipino seminaries, such as my own, actively recruit and encourage lay people to train for counseling ministry. However, the question remains regarding where lay people who graduate from our program will find opportunities for ministry. As well, for all lay-sponsored ministries in the church, the question remains whether they can truly be effective in a culture that invests so much power in the status of the clergy.

THE PASTORAL CARE OF MARRIAGES AND FAMILIES

Another component of the pastoral care ministries of the church, and one that tends to be more lay initiated and led, are the various programs, usually preventative in nature, focusing on pre-marital, marriage enrichment, family life, and parenting. Using primarily psycho-educational and small group modalities, the Philippines has experienced phenomenal growth for the Couples for Christ movement in the Catholic church. Begun in 1981, and now in over 50 countries in the world, it is a Catholic charismatic, evangelistic family ministry focused primarily on the husband-wife relationship but with specific ministries for singles, youth and children (Couples for Christ, 1999). Their strategy makes use of "localised units in different parishes" with publications and large rallies to bring the groups together. In other denominations, no one program has taken root like Couples for Christ.

Counseling in the Philippines is still new with many people hesitant to take advantage of these services even if they are available. However, the observation has been made that people will flock to seminars or workshops, particularly on marriage and family topics. Therefore, training people to respond to personal problems through educational and small group modalities, in addition to counseling relationships, may be very effective and is likely to be a growing approach among churches. The success of such approaches may be in part due the fact that about 90% of the population is functionally literate (USDS, 2000).

Marriage and family counseling, while needed by many, is not frequently requested, and there are few who specialize in it. At the Center for Family Ministry, Ateneo University, courses are taught in Strategic Family Therapy, and since this is an approach that is quite directive, it is likely an appropriate approach for the context. Wat (1998) has made the observation in Hong Kong, that families are resistant to approaches which require the whole family to attend counseling, and to approaches which tend to directly challenge a family's tendency to scapegoat the identified patient (e.g., Structural). Other approaches which require members, in a shame-based culture, to talk openly about their pain (e.g., Satir) are quite difficult for Asian families. He suggests using Bowen's theory which provides structure and direction to help a person differentiate from a dysfunctional family system and allows for individual sessions in marital and family counseling. Indeed, conjoint sessions may not work well in the Philippines because of the initial lack of trust. Individual sessions may be necessary as preparation or rehearsal for conjoint sessions. Openness with each other or an outsider (a therapist) may take time to develop. Consistent with this thinking is the technique of structured separations that may work better in the Philippines than in the west. Separation in the west is often perceived as a prelude to divorce, whereas here the strong sense of duty and other social constraints work to move the couple back together again. The separation may help the couple and the extended family to experience a less enmeshed way of relating (Bautista, 1997).

PASTORAL COUNSELING:
RESPONDING TO SPECIFIC PROBLEMS

Fr. De la Rosa, in his 1996 homily, stated that 50% of Filipino drivers will go through red lights, more than 50% of Filipino couples have separated, 60% of the children are abandoned by their parents, and 60% of the young women are no longer virgins; these figures "may indicate problem areas that Filipinos have to deal with" (Villar, 1997, p. 201).

Other two-thirds world countries experience many of the same problems that Filipino society wrestles with. In Ecuador common issues are: family violence, extreme poverty, disintegration of traditional family structures and supports, joblessness, insufficient legal protection for victims, and the double standard in machismo culture (Haug, 2000). These are all issues in the Philippines as well as can be seen in the responses to the survey questions in Table 9.

Following is a sampling of the types of issues which Filipino pastoral counselors will face in their ministries. Many of the issues are common globally. However, in a developing country with a weak and strained social service infrastructure, the pastoral counselor rarely has referral options. The family is often his or her only ally in providing support and healing.

Shame

Like most Asian countries, the Philippines is much more a shame-prone, or shame-based, culture than it is guilt-prone. "Saving face" has both a personal dimension (saving *my* face) and a familial dimension (saving the reputation of my family). Not shaming another person, and not saying or doing anything that would bring shame to one's family, are primary motivations which control relationships.

In contrast, the experience of guilt, of an internalized sense of right and wrong with objective criteria by which to assess my behavior, is not a common experience. In fact, there is no exact equivalent for "guilt" Tagalog ("sala"–fault–is close but not the same). For example, if the traffic light is red, and it is safe to go, the Filipino is likely to go no-one is hurt, no harm is done, no wrong is committed.

One Filipino pastor (Baylon, 1997) commented that the spiritually mature Filipino only experiences an objective sense of guilt. Healthy guilt is likely to be experienced when we transgress our own internal values and it is only after we have matured in faith that our internal values have been formed. In contrast, for the Filipino, sin is primarily

TABLE 9. Survey Responses

Question: *What issues do you deal with most frequently in your counseling practice?* **Responses:** • psychiatric disorders and marital problems were the most frequent responses • extramarital affairs is a common issue, as well as substance abuse and sexual abuse **Question:.** *What counseling issues are the most serious issues you see facing the Filipino church?* **Responses:** • marital infidelity and domestic violence • parenting, abuse (emotional/sexual/physical), neglect and abandonment • sexual problems including homosexuality • providing training on marital and family issues, and conflict resolution for churches • helping young people develop Christian values in an increasingly global and secular society • responding to overwhelming social problems like the prostitution of children, the pitiful conditions of street children, and poverty

something I do that hurts another. Bradshaw (1988, 1996) suggests that shame is the basis of spirituality, a proposition which runs counter to much of western theology, particularly in the evangelical tradition, which emphasizes a personal sense of guilt as the basis of coming to God.

The experience of "hiya" (shame) has both negative and positive meanings. To feel shame is to feel exposed, or abandoned (Bradshaw, 1988, 1996). This is a negative aspect of relationships in which the person feels exposed, abandoned or censured by the group because, according to the group norms, you have done something to hurt relationships. For example, what is really "wrong" about an affair is that someone might get hurt. But if no one knows about it, it is OK. Similarly, is it wrong to take or give a bribe if no one else is affected by it? Is it wrong to plagiarize if no one finds out and the student was getting good grades anyway?

Often shaming is used as a social/relational technique for producing conformity. However, conformity has both positive and negative connotations: conforming to healthy, functional norms of behavior is good, whereas conformity for the sake of conformity, or conformity to dysfunctional norms, is negative.

Bradshaw's definition of positive or healthy shame includes the notion that healthy shame sets limits and boundaries for us; shame lets us know how far we can appropriately go in relationships, it allows us to make mistakes and ask for help, to reach out and ask another to show me a better way. This is the positive side of shame in that it encourages belonging to and concern for the group. The group is where one finds security and acceptance which in turn protects the person against the negative side of shame. "Shame as discretion protects the person from the feared pain of shame as disgrace" (Augsburger, 1986, p. 129).

Counseling in the Philippines must take into consideration the complex dynamics of shame and the role it plays in determining people's relational, behavioral and affective worlds.

Marital and Family Problems

Family relationships are central to a Filipino's identity: The Filipino views marriage as "a union not only of two individuals but also primarily of their families" (Medina, 1995, p. 34). In sociological terms, Medina (1991, p. 35) describes the Filipino family as consanguine and the descent system as bilateral, though naming is patronymic. The newlywed's residence can be close to, or with, either set of parents or in a new location.

In Filipino families the "lola" (the grandmother) often holds a special role in the family wielding considerable power. The "ate" (older sister) or "kuya" (older brother) are often the "tagasalo" or "mananalo" (caretaker) in the family with additional responsibilities to care for the other children. This creates a tendency for the "tagasalo" to base their self-worth on their ability to make others happy and to serve them. As an adult they may take this pattern into their marriage and family. Being married to a "tagasalo" can result in a tendency to immaturity ("an extra child"), and may be one of the dynamics of the high rate of extra-marital affairs (Carandang, 1987, p. 65-66).

Another factor that influences Filipino families and causes significant family stress are the 900,000 (1996) Overseas Filipino Workers (OFW) who work primarily in the Middle East and other Asian countries. Fifty-six percent are males, and forty-four percent are females (OFWs increase in 1996, 1997). This government-initiated policy was instituted in 1974 to help solve the unemployment and economic conditions of the country (Go, 1993, p. 44-47). Typically, the OFW is able to visit the Philippines for their holidays, once a year. Families in which one parent works overseas function as single-parent families, unless other family members help out. While the financial stability of foreign income helps many families, and increases the family's status in the community, the marriages and families also experience considerable negative impact.

Child Abuse and Family Violence

Substantial work has been done in the Philippines on the issues of child abuse (physical, psychological and sexual maltreatment and neglect) and "children in exceptionally difficult circumstances" (including children in areas of armed conflict, affected by natural disasters, in exploitative work situations, street children, children subject to abuse and neglect, child mothers, children with disabilities, children in institutions, children of AIDS-affected families, youth offenders, disabled children and indigenous children (dela Cruz, 1997, p. 27). Carandang (1987, 1992) has done considerable work on issues related to special populations of children (e.g., stress, dysfunctional families and autism). Legally law and the Department of Social Welfare protect children and Development is mandated to provide care for children. Hotlines exist for reporting, and numerous non-government social service organizations provide residential care.

While this sounds impressive, the reality of child abuse is a common experience for pastors and counselors. Despite considerable local and international funding for child protection, the government and non-government organizations are simply not able to effectively handle the number of children in need of protection and care, nor the variety of ways in which children are at risk for exploitation.

Women and the elderly are also frequently victims of abuse. The State of the Nation report entitled *The Filipino Elderly* (Domingo et al., 1994), and *Breaking the silence: The realities of family violence in the Philippines and recommendations for change* (Guerrero & Sobritchea, 1997), provide excellent summaries of the statistics, issues, services and future directions in responding to these areas of need. Women's crisis centers, shelters and other religious and social service organizations are attempting to meet the needs of women in distress. A particularly significant social problem in the Philippines is prostitution (Santos, 1998), which has become a global issue since large numbers of Filipinas are sent overseas to be domestic helpers, sometimes a euphemism for prostitutes. The irony is, of course, that the Philippines is considered a country in which family values are preeminent, women are relatively liberated (after all, the Philippines has now elected two female presidents–Corazon Aquino and Gloria Macapagal-Arroyo), children are valued, and the elderly are respected and cared for at home.

Parenting

In an extended family structure which emphasizes close family ties, everyone shares the responsibility for parenting. Grandmothers are particularly important. For middle and upper class families, "yayas" (nursemaids) have a primary role in caring for younger children. As a result children typically have many "figures of identification" (DeGuzman & Varias, 1967). A consequence of having so many people around is what in the west would be considered intrusiveness and lack of privacy. The "family bed" is common in lower and middle-income families. Having one's own room, or space to oneself, is neither valued nor possible in many cases. To highlight the significance of this point, in the Tagalog language there is no word for "privacy"!

For younger children, parenting is characterized by protection, gentleness, permissiveness and respectful obedience to authority figures, suppression of hostility, and early emphasis on responsibility for younger siblings. Preschool children are pushed in terms of academic achievement with parents encouraging children to study and prepare for entrance exams for prestigious elementary schools. As children move into school years there is an increasing emphasis on academic achievement and self-reliance, in addition to the earlier emphases on obedience, respect and non-aggressiveness. Older children are more strictly disciplined. For poorer families, parents will teach and model the acceptance of hardships in life, being thrifty, preserving harmonious relationships and working to improve their economic status (DeGuzman & Varias, 1967; Ventura, 1991).

Parental authority is a primary goal and disrespect and disobedience are strictly punished with corporal punishment widely accepted. Religion is an integral part of most families, and is openly promoted in most public and private preschools and elementary schools.

Gender Issues in Counseling

Feminism, as a philosophy of social change, is not as obvious in the Philippines as in the west, but does exist, particularly in the universities and among social service organizations working with women and abuse issues (Estrada-Claudio, 1990). Lapuz (1977), in her book on marriage, explicitly discusses the impediments to psychological growth for Filipino women (Chapter 10). She identifies issues such as a tendency to fantasy and magical thinking regarding marriage and family roles, and the double standards that exist between the freedom experienced by single women and the traditional family roles of married women, all of which cause significant confusion and stress for women.

According to most, the authority structure is considered to be equalitarian, a view supported by the enactment of *The Family Code of the Philippines* (1987), which is explicitly equalitarian in its provisions (Medina, 1991, pp. 155-156). My own observation is that families are often patriarchal in terms of the public image, with wives and mothers often holding considerable power within the family. This may be because women often work and run family businesses which gives them considerable power and some financial autonomy. This perspective is supported by research data (Contado, 1991, p. 158) which indicated that over 70% of both men and women answered that the husband was the authority figure in the family, though when given problems to decide on as a couple, the wives exercised greater authority.

Additional support for the public-private dichotomy in roles, is that the wife's contribution to the family income often exceeds her husband's (Medina, 1995, p. 28). Among low income families in Manila one study in 1993 found that the wife's income contributed to 95% of the households; the husbands' income was the sole income in only 5% of the families but the wife's income was the only source of income for 33% of the families (p. 28). Despite this fact, the reversal of roles, the "house-husband" concept, is unacceptable especially since it runs counter to the traditional "macho" image of the male breadwinner (p. 29).

The "macho" male image, and the patriarchalism brought to the Philippines by the Spanish, is strongly evident. This clashes with the egalitarian thrust of modern society, bolstered by the Family Code of 1987 which eliminated most discriminatory clauses against women. The result is a double standard in which women have legal rights, but society does not affirm those rights within family and business relationships. Clearly, roles are in transition from a traditional patriarchal view and a gender-based division of labor to a greater emphasis on companionship and partnership model of marriage (Medina, 1991, pp. 124-125). However, as Medina, 1995 (p. 30) states: "the two opposing forces of egalitarianism and double standard remain and continue to impinge on husband-wife relations, blurring the issue of who has the real power."

Lapuz (Pe-Pua et al., 1993) claims that the "disgruntled" women in Philippine society are the married women: "They're always in a cage. They are the most likely to have nervous breakdowns. They are over-represented in all mental health clinics. They are the ones that miss out on adult conversations, the ones isolated from the world. Her life keeps shrinking while his world keeps expanding. And any waves that she makes, she feels so responsible" (p. 34). Often with religiously reinforced rationales, women are socialized to accept suffering and their lot in life, including the likelihood of their husbands engaging in extramarital affairs, yet they often have the freedom to pursue careers, and for higher socioeconomic levels, to hire domestic help.

Filipino males are discussed in a fascinating study by Aguiling-Dalisay et al. (2000, p. 15). They point out that Filipino men are exhorted to act like men ("magpakalalaki ka") whenever they act in a way considered unmanly. They are chided "you act like a woman" ("Para kang babae"). Some traits commonly attributed to males: macho, "hunk," sexually experienced, potent, dominating, unfaithful (p. 19). In raising sons "fathers are looked up to and modeled after while mothers are respected for advice" (p. 81). On the other hand, men desire to protect women in ways that dominate them (p. 83), resulting in a conflicted view of women–low opinion, presumption of female weakness while extolling their virtues (p. 84).

The role of "barkada" (peer group–gang) in adolescent development and adult life emphasizes the value of "pakikisama" (the negative aspect is seen as being overly agreeable in the group). This in turn is seen as causing drug use and other social problems since people cannot resist peer pressure (Santa Rita, 1996, p. 329). Aguiling-Dalisay (2000, p. 90) state that "many men are gender-fair as individuals but become gender-insensitive males when in a group."

According to Aguiling-Dalisay (2000, pp. 90-91), the goal for male transformation in both individual and group contexts is to:

- reflect and act on gender individually and subtly introduce such concepts into communities to which they belong
- conduct research on how boys are socialized
- educate fathers
- work towards complementary relationships in marriage
- provide gender-sensitive environments for young people
- reject spousal or partner abuse in any form
- help them become more like the human beings that they are–to "be in control, not of women, but of themselves" (p. 90-91).

Sexuality

Sex education is espoused in the education system, but little is done in actuality. Some resources are available, for example, Andres (1987), and material from the Catholic church particularly on natural family planning. The major problem is that sex is never discussed by parents (Aguiling-Dalisay, 2000, p. 81). So, in describing adults, Lapuz (1977) suggests:

In or out of therapy, they talk little or not at all to each other about sex. Their signals to each other are mostly all non-verbal. In sexual exchange, there is also too much emphasis on "making a home run" and on sex as standard or routine marital activity, tending to by-pass or waste the warmth and spontaneity which are integral to Filipino nature. (pp. 102-103)

Because of the hesitancy to discuss sexual issues, Lapuz (1977) identifies a number of common problems related to sexuality in marriage (pp. 101-103):

- Individual counseling sessions may be required in order to obtain a clear description of the problem.
- The cultural expectation is that the wife will sacrifice her relationship and her sexual desires and wishes, and focus on tolerating her husband's "needs."
- A husband may experience performance anxiety related to premature ejaculation and disappointment that he is not able to quickly re-establish an erection.
- Aggressivity is seen as normal; "The local equivalent of the vulgar term, 'fuck' is 'fight.' 'Let's go and fight women,' he says to his *barkada* (gang) with a twinkle in his eye" (p. 102).
- "His conscience troubles him little" (p. 102). Guilt is not a major deterrent to extramarital affairs; the imagined consequences of being discovered are the only deterrent. The Filipino husband tends to desexualize his wife in his mind. She represents duty and responsibility as part mother and part policeman. He is more likely to experience "good sex" in a relationship where "duty and responsibility do not intrude" (p. 102).
- "The Filipino male will as yet have to discover aspects of the man-woman relationship not directly related to sexual intercourse, but which emotionally enhance and deepen the total experience. His performance anxiety will be considerably assuaged in a situation where he allows the woman to recognize his vulnerability and to participate, in a non-pressured way, in the sharing of their erotic selves." It may be necessary to help them reorient their perspective of their relationship to not think of each other only as husband and wife (with all the traditional cultural connotations) but as man and woman where passion may more freely be expressed apart from cultural definitions of marital roles and patterns (p. 102).

- In a society that is centered on the family and in which one of the primary, if not the most important, purpose of family life is procreation, infertility is a stigmatized condition. If a newly married couple has not had a child within the first two years shame and self-isolation are common responses. Because of the cultural taboo against talking about it, many infertile couples camouflage their pain well.

Sexual values are in transition with urbanization being a major factor. In 1981, over 70% of women at the University of the Philippines, under 25 years of age, have engaged in premarital sex. In the overall population, 38% of those less than 30 have had intercourse prior to marriage (Medina, 1995). With a strong cultural emphasis on having children, it should not be surprising that, despite the predominance of conservative religious values, 15.4% (1987) of first births were premaritally conceived (Medina, 1995). As indicated previously, the increased frequency of co-habitation also suggests a major shift in sexual values.

Marital Separation and Divorce

Being a Catholic country, divorce is not an option in the Philippines, although an annulment is. Apparently divorce was practiced in pre-colonial Philippine communities, but was prohibited with the imposition of Christianity by the Spanish (Bernardo, 1998). During the American period divorce was allowed in cases of adultery by the wife or concubinage by the husband. The Japanese occupation allowed for nine other grounds for divorce which was repealed in 1944 and replaced in 1950 by a law allowing only for legal separation. The Family Code (1988) reaffirmed that divorce is not permitted, but allowed for legal separation, declaration of nullity and annulment. Both the latter options are allowed when the legal conditions (defect or omission) for a marriage are not met, whereas in other countries divorce is typically allowed when problems occur after the celebration of a valid marriage. However, one of the conditions on which a marriage can be nullified is "psychological capacity." "In practice, Article 36 has become a form of divorce, as valid marriages are declared void every day in the guise of 'psychological incapacity'" (Bernardo, 1998, p. 4). This is particularly the case for middle and upper class people who can afford the court costs, which in effect amounts to a discriminatory policy.

In Bautista and Roldan's (1995) study, women were most likely to initiate marital separation and infidelity was the most common cause. Addictions, irresponsibility, lack of character, constant quarrels, problems with in-laws and lack of communication were also cited as causes. Very infrequently did couples discuss the separation and mutually decide on it. The welfare of the children, the need for a father, and the importance of having a complete family were the most frequently cited reasons by the women for not wanting to separate. For the women in the study, their relatively high tolerance for marital conflict, their view of the role of women, and economic powerlessness were significant contributors to staying married. In terms of how the government and society can help separated women, these women suggested that the government needs to take a pro-woman perspective on the problem, and society needs to remove the stigma of separation which only serves to further condemn women who have already experienced considerable pain and injustice in difficult marriages.

In the absence of affordable divorce, a couple will likely stay together and live separate lives. The "querida" (Spanish for "beloved" but more commonly understood as "mistress") system provides a way for unhappily married couples to meet affective and sexual needs, especially for husbands (Go, 1993, p. 54). Extramarital relationships are generally disapproved of in the society but are quietly tolerated. The frequency and passive tolerance of affairs both in society and in religious contexts, has led to the comment that in the west the marital pattern is serial monogamy while in the Philippines it is a modified polygamy. One pastoral counselor stated that 70% of his marital counseling cases are related to sexual abuse, extramarital affairs and sexual dysfunction (Ardina, 2000).

Another option for the unhappy couple is to separate, legally or otherwise, and live in common-law relationships. The frequency of common-law relationships was 6% in 1994. However, this number has been increasing with the largest increase seen among Manila's urban poor. For the age group 20-24 years old, 40.5% (1993) of young married couples experienced a "live-in" arrangement of at least 3 months prior to marriage (Medina, 1995).

Addictions

Of all mental health problems, drug and alcohol addiction appears to have been taken very seriously and has been responded to by government and the society at large. The Dangerous Drug Act of 1972 established the Dangerous Drug Board which is mandated with the regulation, policing, public awareness, education, rehabilitation and research related to drug abuse in the Philippines (Vidal, 1998). It is significant to note that the Dangerous Drug Board was placed under the Department of Health rather than Department of Corrections indicating the intention to view drug abuse as a health issue rather than a criminal one (Cervera, 1999).

The most commonly abused drug is known locally as "shabu" (Methamphetamine Hydrochloride–a synthetic form of cocaine), almost all of which is imported from other Asian countries. The Philippines is also a high quality producer and exporter of marijuana. Inhalants such as acetone, rubber glue, car wax, and gasoline are a serious problem especially among low-income children. Alcoholism is a pervasive condition with inexpensive local beer and alcohol readily available. Sixty percent of the country's drug users reside in Metro Manila and 80% are considered young people; almost 8% are only 12 years old (Quezon City Anti-Drug Abuse Council, 1997). In 1999 the male-female ratio of drug abusers was 12:1 and the average age was 27 (Sualog, 2001).

The government has mandated that every region of the country should have a drug rehabilitation center but only two government centers are operating. There is no fee for an addict to stay in a government center, but a court order must be obtained so that addicts are usually confined in the center for six months. A directory of non-government rehabilitation centers is available (Vidal, 1998), with many of these operated by religious organizations. The addict or the family must pay for the rehabilitation program, resulting in the emergence of a two-tier rehabilitation system. For those who cannot afford a private center, the government centers provide poor facilities, overcrowding, and inadequate staffing and programming, while for those who can pay the fees, the private centers offer better facilities and programs. Whether government operated or not, it is difficult to determine what recovery rates are achieved. Yet, as Cervera (1999) says, the most serious problem in the Philippines is the pervasiveness and reliance on the "moral" model of addictions. This model pervades the treatment philosophy of most rehabilitation centers.

Interestingly, rehabilitation centers are specifically mandated to provide medical, physical and mental rehabilitation, personality development and *spiritual awareness* (Vidal, 1998, p. 108). However, despite the rehabilitation centers being licensed to operate by the government under the Health Department, it is significant that the operating modalities of rehabilitation centers are quite directive and impositional. Often, a highly structured regime is required of "patients" often including punishment and coercion. It seems that society and the government affirms that this is acceptable because the patient is not capable of logical decision-making; they are, after-all, drug addicts (Cervera, 1999). "Kidnapping" people and having them placed in rehabilitation centers is acceptable. One government center I am familiar with has 1500 patients living in large dormitories. Volunteers run minimal programs, the atmosphere is prison-like, there are very limited mental health services available, and little or no follow-up exists. Residents are mandated by law to live in the center for a minimum term of 6 months. In an economically struggling country, the gap between the ideal and the actual is, unfortunately, quite striking.

Alcoholics Anonymous and related drug abuse recovery groups, which are so prevalent in the west, are almost non-existent here. This self-help, self-led, self-disclosing model of recovery and support appears not to thrive in this culture, perhaps due to the cultural dynamics that are shame-based and rely on authority for leadership. Also the predominance in society of the "moral" perspective of addictions runs counter to the AA "disease" model. One counselor, who was frustrated in trying to track down an AA group for a client, quipped: "Here in the Philippines AA takes the 'Anonymous' in their name very seriously." No listings in the phone book or directories exist, and the only way to contact them is by word of mouth.

Suicide and Depression

Depression does not appear to be as widely experienced in the Philippines as it is in the west. With the high degree of relationality in the Philippines, people are rarely alone. Filipinos often travel with a "kasama" (companion) and may even come to counseling with one. Given the tendency toward isolation in depressed patients, and relationships as both an etiological and treatment component of depression, it may be that the frequency of depression is lower. Another factor may be that Filipinos experience depressive symptoms but label the experience as loneliness.

Statistical data on suicide is always understated since suicide is a censurable action, a taboo, which reflects badly on the victim and on the entire family. Thus, the family doctor or the coroner will declare either heart failure or death by accident as the cause of death (Abarzuza, 1966, p. 118).

Family troubles appear to be the most frequent precursor of suicide (Abarzuza, 1966, p. 142). The fact that many people often live together in small homes, with limited financial resources, can strain family relationships and produce dangerous levels of conflict. Another scenario is a spouse who attempts to gain their partner's affection, or to punish the spouse for an affair, by attempting a romantic "suicide pact" so that "not even death will separate us" (p. 132).

THE TRAINING OF PASTORAL COUNSELORS

Education is highly valued in the Philippines. Colleges, universities, Bible colleges and seminaries are plentiful, even in the rural areas. Many are church related: The Catholic universities are among the very best in the country. Apart from CPE programs which operate in churches and hospitals, most pastoral counseling training occurs in the church-related colleges and seminaries. Most clergy will have taken a course or two in their degree programs on counseling.

A significant need is for printed training materials. A few items, specifically addressing pastoral counseling in the Philippines, have been published (e.g., Parisi, n.d.), but since western printed resources are often too expensive to import, seminars and short-term training programs are quite popular. In addition, all the professional associations in psychology and guidance counseling have annual conferences with some even organizing regional conferences.

Degree programs are also becoming very popular. The Center for Family Ministry at Ateneo University is a well-established Catholic training program with a Diploma and MA degree. This center is directed by Fr. Ruben Tanseco (see the interview in Table 10). At least three of the ten major evangelical seminaries in the country have MA degrees with majors in counseling. At Alliance Biblical Seminary, 31% of the students are enrolled in a counseling program with others taking counseling courses as electives. In November 2001, the Asia Graduate School of Theology, a consortium of eight evangelical seminaries, began an EdD counseling program with a specific focus on counseling and education within the church context. Interest in counseling programs is high, whether it is for personal/spiritual growth, professional ministry, or lay ministry.

In training counselors, some of the obstacles that arise are:

TABLE 10. Interview

Interviewee: Fr. Ruben Tanseco
Position: Director of the Center for Family Minsitry, Loyola School of Theology, Ateneo de Manila University
Training: Pastoral training (doctorate) in Michigan, US.
Experience: Involved in pastoral care for more than 35 years. He contextualized his knowledge and designed programs/seminars for couples, families and the corporate world (e.g., he started Marriage Encounter in 1969 which was popular in the '70s). He has developed programs for family enrichment.
View of Pastoral Care and Counseling:
• Pastoral care is caring for the whole person; counseling is part of pastoral care.
• There are two levels of pastoral care; curative (counseling), and preventive (training, seminars, retreats) which lead to a multiplication of competence. (He finds himself doing both but prefers the preventive mode.)
• CEFAM is both content and process oriented. The content is composed of psychology, spirituality, theology and practice. Spiritual discernment (rather than "direction") is a part of counseling. Discernment leads the person to do God's will.
• CEFAM's outreach program "Daluyan" exposes students to poverty, counseling the poor, eventually helping the poor; the practical is also part of counseling.
• As a pastoral care person in the Catholic church there has been resistance to change.
• There are many weaknesses in the Filipino culture that need change; even within the Catholic church.
• The Philippines is far less a "Christian" country than what it is known for.
• At the beginning, the programs at CEFAM were not usually welcomed; now they are.
• He had a vision for change in families and individuals which was why he put up the center. It was a slow process but at least he had some friends who believed it could be done. CEFAM now caters to Asia through the many students that come for training every year.
Significant Quotes:
• "The whole of life is integrated. My approach to counseling is psychospiritual. You do not separate the sacred from the secular. A counselee's problems are very much related to spirituality. Even sexual problems are."
• "Authentic love plus authentic justice equals peace."

- adapting approaches to the socio-economic status of the counselee
- doing the cultural translation from the western textbooks to the Filipino context
- communicating ethical issues, such as confidentiality, informed consent and multiple relationships to a culture in which intrusiveness is an expression of concern, not an invasion of privacy
- finding qualified and consistent supervision
- funding educational institutions.

Table 11 suggests further steps in the development of pastoral counseling in the Philippines.

Two other obstacles come to mind. As a marriage and family therapist, helping Filipinos to think systemically, is ironically, a difficult task. It is typical, even for Filipino supervisees living in a family/relationship-based culture, to place the "fault" for the cause of the problem,

TABLE 11. Survey Responses

Question: *What is needed to assist the development of pastoral counseling in the Philippines?*
Responses:
- Contextualization: the need to critique objectively and wisely all the different models of counseling that have been introduced in the Philippines, and at the same time consider the experience and reflection done by some Filipino theologians, psychologists and practitioners in the area of psychology and counseling. There is a great need for thinking, writing, and teaching/passing on of the "filipinization" or contextualization of counseling theory and practice here in the Philippines.
- Prevention: implementing preventive education and growth-oriented programs alongside of the church rather than merely waiting for clients to come for counseling.
- Education: information dissemination among church people on what counseling is.
- Research: conducted in the Philippines with Filipino populations.
- Professional training: counseling courses in seminaries should be taught by professionally trained counselors who are in active practice, not just para-counselors or theology professors who had taken only one or two courses in counseling. Although psychology is taught in the colleges and universities, its emphasis is on theories of personality, human development, abnormal psychology, psychometric tests. Very limited training is actually given on counseling methodologies and skills.
- Establishing networks: mutual referral between psychiatrists and counselors to enhance the therapeutic process; the development of existing professional associations for mutual support & stimulation, continuing education, standardization of fees, sponsoring local seminars, advocacy for certain urgent issues in society; linking with other counseling associations in Asia (e.g., Singapore, Hong Kong, Malaysia) for mutual learning/exchange programs.
- Infiltrating society: graduates of counseling programs need to "penetrate" the churches, NGOs, barangay centers, schools, the corporate world, as well as counseling centers, rehabilitation centers, hospitals.
- Resources: obtaining counseling resources is difficult and expensive; it helps and encourages us to have counselors from abroad visit the Philippines to teach courses or present in conferences.
- Special Populations: developing support groups for people struggling with various problems, e.g., survivors of sexual abuse, single parents, parents of kids with special needs, etc.; establishing a refuge for abuse victims and a residential treatment center for youth and adults with emotional/psychiatric problems where a holistic approach to therapy is provided.
- Depth Approaches: how do we encourage Filipino counselees to make a serious commitment to longer term counseling in order to explore issues more deeply? "Contracting" for this kind of therapy may not be perceived well in this context.

and the solution to family problems within the individuals. In addition, it is difficult for them to conceptualize the broader systemic influences on families of the economic system (poverty, social stratification, under and unemployment), the religious system (Catholicism, "folk beliefs" and western evangelicalism), the gender system (confusion of matriarchal tribal roots and Spanish machismo), and the organizational systems (rigid, passive, under-resourced, and rooted in colonialism).

Secondly, Haug (2000), in his description of family therapy in Ecuador stated:

. . . I was told that a cultural expectation clients bring into therapy is to be told by an authority figure what to do. This desire, my Ecuadorian colleagues explained to me, was rooted in the long history of conquest and subjugation, and educating clients (and trainees) about the nature of therapy was built into each initial interview. (p. 12)

This comment is equally true of the Philippines. Every year I am asked this question, and my response is that while responding as a knowledgeable authority is always an option, empowering clients to make their own choices, is, even within this relational culture, more likely to promote change and facilitate healing.

CHALLENGES FOR PASTORAL COUNSELING IN THE PHILIPPINES

Salazar-Clemeña (2000), President of the Association of Psychological and Educational Counselors of Asia-Pacific (1996-1998), in her inaugural address outlined seven areas that she thought warranted immediate attention as individuals and as a counseling organization in Asia:

(a) the absence of guidance and counseling services in many settings and localities;
(b) the underutilization of guidance and counseling services, where these are present;
(c) the lack of properly trained counselors;
(d) the need for culture- and gender-sensitivity in counseling;
(e) the need to increase awareness of counselors' ethical responsibilities;
(f) the scarcity of published literature and studies in counseling; and
(g) the need to promote the professionalization of counseling. (p. 135)

In Table 12 are listed various survey responses concerning challenges and dangers in the development of pastoral counseling.

Pastoral counseling in the Philippines is indeed fortunate to be as developed as it is. Both the openness to counseling ministry within the Christian community and the options for graduate counselor training point toward an exciting and hopeful future for Christian counseling. The development of the Philippine Association of Christian Counselors

TABLE 12. Survey Responses

Question: *What concerns, if any, do you have about the development of pastoral counseling in the Philippines? What dangers do you see?*

Responses:

- Inadequate Training: The training of Filipino pastoral counselors should not be left in the hands of minimally-trained lay counselors, but to those with a deeper knowledge of and respect for Filipino psychology, Filipino theology, and Filipino culture.
- Competition: Because of the influx of different models, each model tends to compete with the other instead of seeing each model as complementing or supplementing another model. There seems to be fragmentation and lack of integration of reflection and thinking together. As of now, the seminaries offering counseling programs vary in their approaches. People tend to make a big issue as to one being better than the other. Instead of comparing and competing with one another, we need to network together to serve the Body of Christ and society at large.
- Differing Worldviews: In the Filipino culture there are still many superstitions and beliefs in the magical and supernatural. Counseling can be mixed up in this, perceived as a supernatural magical thing, either by the counselor or counselee or both.
- Financial Necessities: It is difficult for counselors to persevere in their ministry due to the lack of financial benefits (especially during these difficult times of the Asia-wide economic crisis). How much must one charge so that it is affordable to the client, but also so the counselor can survive? The extremes for the counselor are to be overly generous to the point of eventually having to close down for lack of finances, or to be too rigid to the point that people cannot afford the needed help.
- Lack of Supervision and Continuing Education: The need for supervision of graduates of counseling programs who are actually doing counseling, to maintain growth and integrity in ministry.
- Imbalance: Losing the balance between excellence and professionalism on the one hand and Christian compassion on the other.
- Limited Ethical Reflection: There is little understanding of issues like confidentiality; it hurts to hear of pastors and other para-professional counselors sharing the problems of their counselees with others in the church or during meetings. The implications of a counselee paying with gifts or "in kind" instead of money (e.g., the provincial person who pays in the form of rice and chickens). Counselors abusing counselees and unhealthy liaisons between counselor and counselee.

will be of great benefit to those who are pioneering in this ministry in relative isolation from each other.

Another significant blessing is the degree of openness within society to Christian perspectives. As a Catholic country there is complete acceptance of the use of spiritual resources in counseling. Christian counselors do not need to prove themselves to find a place in society; they have a place alongside Catholic and secularly trained practitioners.

The challenges are, however, overwhelming for Filipino counselors. The social problems, particularly in the urban centers, are complex and discouraging. The economic infrastructure is so limited and unstable that social service resources, which are taken for granted in the west, are either non-existent or so stretched, that quality and comprehensive care is often compromised. Lack of cooperation, even within the Christian community, weakens the ability to respond to needs in substantial ways. The church and the culture do not fully understand counseling, nor do they enthusiastically support the existence of counseling ministry. At this point it would be next to impossible for Christian counselors to financially support themselves in full-time counseling ministry.

Ethical standards do not exist for Christian counselors, and while that may seem like a blessing to those in the west who attempt to function in an overly litigious society, it is a considerable challenge since no accountability structures are in place. Eighty percent of pastors who "fall" in ministry, fall in the context of counseling (Castillo, 1999). My own experience in supervising counseling trainees is that the basic concepts that form the foundation of western professional ethics (confidentiality, dual relationships, informed consent) are not readily understood in this relational context.

Nonetheless, the task is an exciting one, the opportunities are endless, and the people so receptive. Filipinos are adaptable, hard working and resilient, and as such, are eager students and compassionate caregivers. It is a privilege to be a part of the development of Christian counseling in the Philippines.

ACKNOWLEDGMENTS

Thank you to Linda Bubod, MA, for her assistance in interviewing Fr. Fernando Boyagan, Dr. Alfredo Cabrera, Dr. Simplicio Dangawan, and Fr. Ruben Tanseco.

Thank you to the following people for their responses to surveys: Naome Basilio and Pat Benzenhafer (private practice and faculty at Koininia Theological Seminary, Davoa), Dr. Vicentita Cervera (Professorial Lecturer, Assumption Graduate School and St. Anthony Mary Claret College), Dr. Randy Dellosa (Psychiatrist, faculty at Asian Theological Seminary, and Director of Life Change Recovery Center), Thelma Nambu (Samaritana Transformation Ministries), Dr. Margaret Querijero (psychiatrist), and the staff of Door of Hope Counseling Resource Center.

REFERENCES

Abarzuza, J. (1966). *Philippine social values and suicide.* Quezon City, Philippines: Asian Social Institute.
Abesamis, C. H. (1999). *A third look at Jesus*, 3rd ed. Quezon City, Philippines: Claretian Publications.

Aguiling-Dalisay, G., Mendoza, R.M., Mirafelix, E.J.L., Yacat, J.A., Sto. Domingo, M. R., and Bambico, F.R. (2000). Pagkalake: Men in control? Filipino male views on Love, Sex & Women. Quezon City, Philippines: Pambansang Samahan sa Sikolohiyang Pilipino (National Association of Filipino Psychology).

Andres, T.Q.D. (1995, April-June). Values among Pinoys. *Reachout*, p. 12.

Andres, T.Q.D. (1987). *Understanding Filipino values on sex, love and marriage.* Manila: Our Lady of Manaoag Publishers.

Aragon, J.G. (1993). *The theology of conquest.* Quezon City, Philippines: Carlen Press.

Ardina, M. (2000, Sept. 5). Personal communication. Manila, Philippines.

Augsburger, D.W. (1986). *Pastoral counseling across cultures.* Philadelphia, PA: The Westminster Press.

Bautista, V. (n.d.). Christian counseling in the Philippine setting. *Patmos*, vol. II (3).

Bautista, V. (1988). The socio-psychological make-up of the Filipino. In Miranda-Feliciano, E. (Ed.), *All things to all men: An introduction to missions in Filipino culture* (pp. 1-18). Quezon City, Philippines: New Day.

Bautista, V. (1997). Personal Communication. Manila, Philippines.

Bautista, V. & Roldan, A. (1995). Dissolution of marriage: The Filipino woman's perspective. In Perez, A.E. (Ed.), *The Filipino family: A spectrum of views and issues* (pp. 40-56). Quezon City, Philippines: University of the Philippines.

Baylon, B. (1997). Making disciples in the Philippine context. Seminar at Alliance Biblical Seminary.

Beltran, B.P. (1987). *The Christology of the inarticulate: An inquiry into the Filipino understanding of Jesus Christ.* Manila: Divine Word Publications.

Bernardo, J.M. (1998). *The relevance of divorce in the Philippines.* Quezon City, Philippines: Women's Legal Bureau.

Bond, M.H. (Ed.) (1996). *The handbook of Chinese psychology.* Oxford: Oxford University Press.

Boyd, D. (1993). Thailand. In Wicks, R.J. & Estadt, B. K. (Eds.), *Pastoral counseling in a global church: Voices from the field.* Maryknoll, NY: Orbis Books, pp. 107-112.

Bradshaw, J. (1988). *Healing the shame that binds you.* Deerfield Beach, FL: Health Communications.

Bradshaw, J. (1996). *Bradshaw on: The family*, revised edition. Deerfield Beach, FL: Health Communications.

Bulatao, J. (1979). Oh, that terrible task of teachers to teach psychology in the Philippines. *Philippine Journal of Psychology*, 12(1), 33-37.

Calpotura, V.S. (2000). Counseling and the Christian spiritual tradition of Spiritual Direction. In Salazar-Clemeña, R.M. (Ed.)., *Counseling in Asia: Integrating cultural perspectives.* Cebu City, Philippines: Association of Psychological and Educational Counselors of Asia (APECA), pp. 85-90.

Carandang, M.L.A. (1987). *Filipino children under stress: Family dynamics and therapy.* Manila: Ateneo de Manila Press.

Carandang, M.L.A. (1992). *Making connections: A group therapy program for Filipino autistic children and their families.* Manila: Ateneo de Manila Press.

Carino, F. (1992). Some recent developments in Asian theology. In *Currents in Philippine theology*. Quezon City, Philippines: Institute of Religion and Culture, pp. 127-140.

Castillo, C. (1999, Oct. 21). Pastoral counseling in the Philippines. Lecture at Alliance Biblical Seminary.

Cervera, V. (1999, Feb. 27). Addiction counseling. Workshop at the 1999 Regional Conference in Counseling, Bacolod City.

Church, A.T. (1986). *Filipino personality: A review of research and writing*. Manila: De La Salle University Press.

Church, A.T. & Katigbak, M.S. (2000). *Filipino personality: Indigenous and cross-cultural studies*. Manila: De La Salle University Press.

Cimmarusti, R.A. (1996). Exploring aspects of Filipino-American families. *Journal of Marital and Family Therapy, 22* (2), 205-217.

Contado, M.E. (1991). Power dynamics of rural families. In Medina, B. T., *The Filipino family* (pp. 157-161). Quezon City, Philippines: University of the Philippines.

Couples for Christ (1999). First seeds. Mandaluyong City, Philippines: Couples for Christ Global Mission Foundation, Inc. Retrieved Jan. 9, 2001 from the World Wide Web: <http://www.cfcglobal.com/faq.htm>.

Dalton, A. (1983). Clinical Pastoral Care in the Philippines 1964-1969. In Dumalagan, N.C., Becher, W. & Taniguchi, T. (Eds.), *Pastoral care and counseling in Asia: Its needs and concerns* (pp. 43-50). Manila: Clinical Pastoral Care Association of the Philippines.

Decenteceo, E.T. (1999). The "Pagdadala" model in counseling and therapy. *Philippine Journal of Psychology, 32* (2), 89-104.

DeGuzman, J.V. & Varias, R.R. (1967). *Psychology of Filipinos: Studies and essays*. Manila, No publisher.

dela Cruz, M.T. (1997). *Child abuse in the Philippines: An integrated literature review and annotated bibliography*. Manila: University of the Philippines.

dela Torre, E. (1992). A theology of suffering. In *Currents in Philippine theology*. Quezon City, Philippines: Institute of Religion and Culture, pp. 61-68.

Domingo, L.J., Medina, B.T. & Domingo, M.F.A. (1994). *The Filipino elderly*. Quezon City, Philippines: University of the Philippines Press.

Dumalagan, N.C. (1983). Clinical Pastoral Care in the Philippines 1969-1982. In Dumalagan, N.C., Becher, W. & Taniguchi, T. (Eds.), *Pastoral care and counseling in Asia: Its needs and concerns* (pp. 51-60). Manila: Clinical Pastoral Care Association of the Philippines.

Dumalagan, N.C., Becher, W. & Taniguchi, T. (Eds.) (1983). *Pastoral care and counseling in Asia: Its needs and concerns*. Manila: Clinical Pastoral Care Association of the Philippines.

Enriquez, V. (1989, 1994). *Indigenous psychology and national consciousness: the Philippine experience*. Tokyo, Japan: Institute for the Study of Languages and Cultures of Asia and Africa.

Estrada-Claudio, S. (1990, Sept.). Psychology of Filipino Women. Workshop on Feminist Counseling sponsored by the University Center for Women's Studies, University of the Philippines.

Falicov, C.J. (1988). Learning to think culturally. In H.A. Liddle, D.C. Breunlin, & R.C. Schwartz (Eds.), *Handbook of Family Therapy Training and Supervision* (pp. 335-357). New York: Guilford.

Fernandez, E.S. (1994). *Toward a theology of suffering*. Maryknoll, NY: Orbis Books.

Gingrich, F. (2000). Christian counseling in the Philippines. *Christian Counseling Connection*, Issue 1, pp. 4-5.

Gnanakan, K. (Ed.) (1992). *Salvation: Some Asian perspectives*. Bangalore, India: Asia Theological Association.

Gnanakan, K. (Ed.) (1995). *Biblical theology in Asia*. Bangalore, India: Theological Book Trust.

Go, S.P. (1993). *The Filipino family in the eighties*. Manila: Social Development Research Center, De La Salle University.

Guerrero, S.H. & Sobritchea, C.I. (1997). *Breaking the silence: The realities of family violence in the Philippines and recommendations for change*. Quezon City, Philippines: UP Center for Women's Studies Foundation and United Nations Children's Fund.

Hardy, K. (1997). *Race, class and culture*. Videocassette (#V545) from the 55th AAMFT Annual Conference. Washington, DC: American Association for Marriage and Family Therapy.

Harper, G.W. (2000). Philippine tongues of fire? Latin American pentecostalism and the future of Filipino Christianity. *Journal of Asian Mission*, 2(2), 225-259.

Haug, I.E. (2000, Aug./Sept.). A glimpse at family therapy in Ecuador. *Family Therapy News*, pp. 12-13.

Hechanova, L. (1983). Situationer: Socio-economic-political situation in Asia and the church response. In Dumalagan, N.C., Becher, W. & Taniguchi, T. (Eds.) (1983). *Pastoral care and counseling in Asia: Its needs and concerns*, Manila: Clinical Pastoral Care Association of the Philippines, pp. 11-27.

Institute of Religion and Culture (1992). *Currents in Philippine theology*. Quezon City, Philippines: Institute of Religion and Culture.

Jocano, F.L. (1997). *Filipino value system: A cultural definition*. Manila: Punlad Research House.

Johnstone, P. (1993). *Operation world: The day-by-day guide to praying for the world*, 5th ed. Grand Rapids, MI: Zondervan.

Kim, T.C. (1993). Korea. In Wicks, R.J. & Estadt, B.K. (Eds.), *Pastoral counseling in a global church: Voices from the field*. Maryknoll, NY: Orbis Books, pp. 113-120.

Koyama, K. (1974). *Waterbuffalo theology*. Maryknoll, NY: Orbis Books.

Lapuz, L.V. (1977). *Filipino marriages in crisis*. Quezon City, Philippines: New Day Publishers.

Larmer, B. & Meyer, M. (2001, Jan. 29). The return of People Power. *Newsweek* (Asia edition), pp. 8-14.

McGoldrick, M. (1988). Ethnicity and the family life cycle. In B. Carter, & M. McGoldrick (Eds.) *The changing family life cycle: A framework for family therapy*, 2nd ed. (pp. 70-90). New York: Gardner Press.

McGoldrick, M. & Giordano, J. (1996). Overview: Ethnicity and family therapy. In M. McGoldrick, J. Giordano & J.K. Pearce, *Ethnicity and family therapy* (pp. 1-27). New York: Guilford.

Medina, B.T. (1991). *The Filipino family*. Quezon City, Philippines, University of the Philippines.

Medina, B.T. (1995). Issues relating to Filipino marriage and family. In Perez, A.E. (Ed.), *The Filipino family: A spectrum of views and issues* (pp. 27-39). Quezon City, Philippines: University of the Philippines.

Mercado, L.N. (1975). *Elements of Filipino theology*. Tacloban City, Philippines: Divine Word University.

Mercado, L.N. (Ed.) (1977). *Filipino religious psychology*. Tacloban City, Philippines: Divine Word University.

Mercado, L.N. (1982). *Christ in the Philippines*. Tacloban City, Philippines: Divine Word University.

Mercado, L.N. (1992). *Inculturation of Filipino theology*. Manila, Philippines: Divine Word Publications.

Morais, R.J. (1979). Some notes on the historical roots of contemporary interpersonal relationships in the Christian Philippines. *Philippine Journal of Psychology*, 12 (2), pp. 45-49.

NSCD (National Statistical Coordination Board-Philippines) (2000, Aug. 14). Retrieved Jan. 17, 2000 from the World Wide Web: <http://www.nscb.gov.ph/view/people.htm>.

OFW's increase in 1996 (1997, Oct. 29). Press release on the 1996 Overseas Filipino Workers (OFWs). Retrieved Jan. 17, 2000 from the World Wide Web: <http://www.census.gov.ph/data/pressrelease/of9600tx.html>.

Ortigas, C.D. & Carandang, M.L.A. (1993). *Essence of wellness: Essays in Philippine clinical and counseling psychology*. Manila: Ateneo de Manila University Press.

Parisi, F. (n.d.). *Pastoral psychology*. Manila: East Asia Pastoral Institute.

Pe-Pua, R., Lapuz, L. & Escobar, F. (1993). Marriage and responsible parenthood (panel presentation). In Florencio, C.A. & Cabusira, T.L.A., *The Filipino family and the nation: A collection of readings on family life issues and concerns* (pp. 33-42). Quezon City, Philippines: College of Home Economics, University of the Philippines.

Pederson, P.B. (1997). *Culture-centered counseling interventions: Striving for accuracy*. Thousand Oaks, CA: Sage.

Quezon City Anti-Drug Abuse Council (1997, July, 27). Seminar at Good News Assembly, Quezon City, Philippines.

Rieschick, J. (1993). Kenya. In Wicks, R.J. & Estadt, B. K. (Eds.), *Pastoral counseling in a global church: Voices from the field*. Maryknoll, NY: Orbis Books, pp. 31-45.

Ro, B.R. (1992). Salvation in Asian contexts. In Gnanakan, K. (Ed.), *Salvation: Some Asian perspectives* (pp. 17-30). Bangalore, India: Asia Theological Association.

Ruiz, N.R. (2000). Moving toward a culture-specific counseling model for Asia. In Salazar-Clemeña, R.M. (Ed.)., *Counseling in Asia: Integrating cultural perspectives*. Cebu City, Philippines: Association of Psychological and Educational Counselors of Asia (APECA), pp. 1-5.

Salazar-Clemeña, R.M. (1993). *Counseling psychology in the Philippines: Research and practice,* 2nd ed. Manila: De La Salle University Press.

Salazar-Clemeña, R.M. (2000). Epilogue: The APECA Story. In Salazar-Clemeña, R.M. (Ed.), *Counseling in Asia: Integrating cultural perspectives.* Cebu City, Philippines: Association of Psychological and Educational Counselors of Asia (APECA), pp. 135-140.

Santa Rita, E.S. (1996). Pilipino families. In M. McGoldrick, J. Giordano & J.K. Pearce, *Ethnicity and family therapy* (pp. 324-330). New York: Guilford.

Santos, A.F. (1998). *Halfway through the circle: The lives of eight Filipino women survivors of prostitution and trafficking.* Quezon City, Philippines: Women's Education, Development, Productivity and Research Organization.

Siu, P.Y. (2000). Constructing contextual theology in a postmodern Asian society. *Alliance Academic Review 2000,* pp. 87-99.

Song, C.S. (1979). *Third-eye theology.* Maryknoll, NY: Orbis Books.

Sualog, R. (2001, Feb. 10). What is addiction? Seminar at Alliance Biblical Seminary. Quezon City, Philippines.

Tan, S.Y. (1989). Psychopathology and culture: The Asian American context. *Journal of Psychology and Christianity,* 8(1), 61-75.

Tano, R.D. (1981). *Theology in the Philippine setting: A case study in the contextualization of theology.* Quezon City, Philippines: New Day Publishers.

USDS (U.S. Department of State) (2000, Oct.). Bureau of East Asian and Pacific Affairs. Background Notes: Philippines. Retrieved Jan. 17, 2000 from the World Wide Web: <http://www.state.gov/www/background_notes/philippines_0010_bgn.html>.

Ventura, E.R. (1991). Child-rearing in the Philippines. In Medina, B.T.G., *The Filipino family* (pp. 207-209). Quezon City, Philippines, University of the Philippines.

Vidal, P.F. (1998). *War against drug abuse.* Manila: Mary Jo Publishing House.

Villar, I.V.G. (1997). *Western approaches to counseling in the Philippines.* Manila: De La Salle University Press.

Wat, B. (1998, Nov. 12). Personal communication. Hong Kong.

Whelchel, J.R. (1995). *The path to liberation: Theology of struggle in the Philippines.* Quezon City, Philippines: New Day Publishers.

Wong, P.T.P. (1998, July). Assessing multicultural supervision competencies. Paper presented at the XIVth Congress of the International Association for Cross-Cultural Psychology. Retrieved Sept. 16, 1999 from the World Wide Web: <http://www. twu. ca/cpsy/faculty/wong/wong.htm>.

Global Issues of Pastoral Counseling: With Particular Attention to the Issues of Pastoral Counseling in the Philippines

Louise M. Meeks, BA

SUMMARY. This article reflects on pastoral care in the context of the Philippines, integrating the writer's personal experience as it has affected her perspectives on pastoral counseling and her work in the Philippines. It provides an overview of Pastoral Counseling from the perspective of a woman, particularly as it relates to Pastoral Counseling with women in the Philippines. Particular attention is paid to the crucial issue of violence against women. This is done from a very personal approach. The article includes a section on "Issues of Pastoral Counseling in the Philippines" with examples, descriptions and their implications for Pastoral Counseling. Two illustrative case studies are included. *[Article copies available for a fee from The Haworth Document Delivery Service: 1-800-HAWORTH. E-mail address: <getinfo@haworthpressinc.com> Website: <http://www.HaworthPress.com> © 2002 by The Haworth Press, Inc. All rights reserved.]*

KEYWORDS. Philippines, pastoral counseling, cross-cultural, women

[Haworth co-indexing entry note]: "Global Issues of Pastoral Counseling: With Particular Attention to the Issues of Pastoral Counseling in the Philippines." Meeks, Louise M. Co-published simultaneously in *American Journal of Pastoral Counseling* (The Haworth Pastoral Press, an imprint of The Haworth Press, Inc.) Vol. 5, No. (1/2), 2002, pp. 57-75; and: *International Perspectives on Pastoral Counseling* (ed: James Reaves Farris) The Haworth Pastoral Press, an imprint of The Haworth Press, Inc., 2002, pp. 57-75. Single or multiple copies of this article are available for a fee from The Haworth Document Delivery Service [1-800-HAWORTH, 9:00 a.m. - 5:00 p.m. (EST). E-mail address: getinfo@haworthpressinc.com].

INTRODUCTION

The intent of this article is to share my understanding of pastoral counseling and to address global issues of pastoral counseling, with particular attention to the topic of pastoral counseling in the Philippines. Even more specifically, I hope to address contextualization of pastoral care for women in crisis in the Philippines. Having spent many years in the role of client to pastoral counselors, my own observations and insights will be incorporated herein. My husband and I have just completed a four-year assignment as missionaries in the Philippines. During those years there were indeed opportunities to observe and learn directly from conversations and encounters with abused women in the Philippines. Other information for this article comes from the pastoral care classroom experience, as well as additional independent research and reading. Since this is being written during our year in the United States, there have been few opportunities to develop how Filipino pastoral counselors might expand on my observations. However, I do want to note that one such person, Rev. Joniel Howard H. Gico, did visit us in the United States and we had a lengthy dialog on the contents of this article. His comments and suggestions have been included throughout the article in numerous places, which I will not attempt to identify specifically.

To begin with, I am reminded of the charge Jesus gave His disciples and the promise He made to them in Matthew 28:19-20:

> Therefore, go and make disciples of all the nations, baptizing them in the name of the Father and the Son and the Holy Spirit. Teach these new disciples to obey all the commands I have given you. And be sure of this: I am with you always, even to the end of the age. NLT

The promise of His presence–"always, even to the end"–was a key element in my own recovery. In the nearly ten years of my own psychotherapy, many of the issues faced became a part of my own personal experience. The numbers of women who survived abuse in their childhood and are realizing the impact of that abuse in their adult years continues to grow. Some of the most easily identifiable effects are:

- Hurt
- Anger
- Shame or disgrace

- Depression
- Suicidal tendencies
- AND having to cope for the rest of one's life with the residual scar

My story was of a childhood marked by traumatizing abuse. The pain was frequently overwhelming. Addressing these issues for myself has given me insights that I never expected, and at times didn't even want. One of the things that I came to realize was that my pain was truly important to God and He was faithful to protect me, even when others made choices to do things that were outside of His will. He protected me from those who inflicted the abuse–but could not change the reality that those persons had chosen to do things that God did not wish for them to do. This has been a most difficult thing to come to terms with, but the important thing was that God gave me the strength and tools to survive and cope with the injustice that had played such a major role in my life. Graciously, He has also allowed a rather impressive amount of support from people who became a part of my life as I moved through the process of healing and recovery. I was fortunate to have had two wonderful therapists who were members of the American Association of Pastoral Counselors. They served as my guides in the process of the work that had to be done. The result was a re-alignment of my entire being through my own spirituality in combination with some masterful psychotherapy. Dr. David E. Roy, who was my therapist for many years, believed in the "need for a systematic, unifying theory that has the power to show the centrality of spirituality to all psychologically driven growth and healing, as well as to clarify the relationship among these existing perspectives on spirituality and therapy" (Roy, 2000, pp.185-6). In the process I realized that everyone experiences pain in their lives–and God is there for each one in precisely the context of their own pain. When a person experiences pain, it is not really tolerable and what becomes important is how to relieve oneself of that pain. This has been the thrust of my discoveries over the years. Over a period of many years my experiences and pain combined with a new awareness of God's presence in my life as a Protector. What emerged was a relationship with God on a personal level that provided a kind of recovery that only God could have masterminded. It is now my intent to move beyond those past experiences in such a way that others may benefit from what I have observed and learned. It is my hope that others will discover a new relationship with God and see life in a new and more vibrant way. Perhaps they too can replace their pain with a fullness and joy that surpasses understanding. When moving forward is threatened by past events, hopefully they will find the encouragement to discover new capacities to cope. What could be more wonderful than to find a new appreciation for life and be able to grab hold of the perspective that those events in their past are only a piece of who they are. Ideally there will be a discovery and implementation of the gifts that God has given them. In doing so they will find ways to transform their lives into something of great worth. This vision, in combination with our missionary work in the Philippines, is the impetus to contextualize the entire experience in such a way that it can be effective in the Filipino culture.

MY UNDERSTANDING OF THE MEANING OF PASTORAL COUNSELING

Many of the textbooks used in teaching pastoral counseling reflect theories and concepts that seem particularly relevant to my own sense of what pastoral counseling should look like. This section will highlight those resources that have contributed to my shift of focus from being the care recipient to an understanding of what is important in being able to be an effective pastoral counselor. Let me begin with a quote that seems particularly poignant:

> Do you have the patience to wait
> Till your mud settles and your water becomes clear?
> Can you remain unmoving
> Till the right action arises by itself?

> Tao Te Ching 15 (Kornfeld, 1998, p. 27)

Pastoral counseling requires a caring community, which consists of both laity and clergy. This concept is not something new. It has evolved from the early days of Christianity, through the Reformation and into what we currently see reflected in the modern dynamics of psychology and its impact on ministry.

Pastoral counseling, in terms of the care given by clergy professionals, is influenced by the way pastoral counselors care for themselves. Effective pastoral counselors will be true to themselves, while at the same time acting and meeting the needs of others, given their own knowledge and understanding of themselves. By caring for others, pastoral counselors also experience a reflective relationship in which more is learned about who they are themselves at a personal level. That in combination with care given through laity, creates a ministry of the faith community which reminds its members of how God's people are present all over the world and in those relationships that are developed, people remember one another.

The focal points of pastoral counseling should be:

1. First and foremost, developing a concept of hearing and remembering and
2. Relating that concept of hearing and remembering to the arena of pastoral counseling within the Christian community (Patton, 1993, p. 6)

All of us need to learn to love ourselves better. None of us has been loved unconditionally in our families, although some families love and see their children in "good enough" ways. It is God who loves us unconditionally. This is the basis for understanding oneself. Being a guide in someone's journey to discover that reality is the epitome of pastoral counseling.

An essential principle of healing is that people change after they are first accepted as they are. People do not change when others try to change them. Our primary role in the healing of others is to be with them as they discover their own wholeness for themselves. They will learn from our example to practice the art of being accepting. It is a process of discovering–and, in some cases, uncovering and recovering–the healing gifts at a core level within themselves. As this discovery unfolds, balance is achieved by letting go of activities and concerns that are no longer useful and taking hold of new activities that are helpful and needed. It constitutes a sort of internal housecleaning. Pastoral counselors might be compared to gardeners, so to speak, and the clients are the plants being tended.

Wholeness is achieved when openness and responsiveness have been discovered. Conflict loses it potential for being dangerous and individuals learn to love themselves so that they in turn can love others. The pastoral counselor helps others learn to see themselves for exactly who they are and to resolve the conflicts within themselves and with others in such a way that they can accept themselves and through that acceptance truly love themselves and others.

A key skill that pastoral counselors must develop is to being completely available when in the presence of their clients. Kornfeld calls this "static free listening." She says, "It is necessary to identify your own anxiety and to acknowledge it to yourself." Not all anxiety is bad.

Useful anxiety is a signal from yourself that there is imminent danger to yourself or another. In listening to a counselee's distressful story, you might send yourself an anxiety signal that allows you to go into emergency mode. In this mode you are then able to make a necessary intervention. (Kornfeld, 1998, p. 47)

One way to achieve "static free listening" is to concentrate on one's breathing and center oneself in such a way that the mind is clear and full attention is with the client. It is the pastoral counselor's responsibility to truly be with those who are finding their path. To be with them does not require being a genius, but rather being as authentically oneself as is possible at the time. When pastoral counselors are truly connected with themselves, they can make full use of their experiences and gifts. Thus as pastoral counselors become more whole, their experience becomes all the more useful. They will discover that they have within themselves what is needed and they can relax into this truth and listen to others without creating "static." So being able to listen to others carries with it a prerequisite of being able and knowing how to listen to ourselves. "Contrary to what we often believe, spending time with ourselves is not a luxury. It is a necessity" (Kornfeld, 1998, p. 49).

GLOBAL ISSUES OF PASTORAL COUNSELING

One of the first points I want to make is that when talking about pastoral care from a global perspective it is important to recognize that wisdom comes from all cultures and we, each and everyone, have a contribution to make. This section will be an attempt to point out the generalities of pastoral counseling from a global perspective. Then in the subsequent section, the more specific aspects of pastoral counseling, which contextualize those generalities to the Philippines, will be addressed. The reader should remember that the contextualizations are done from my own observations and reflections. Since the Philippines is a country that functions primarily through verbal communications, as opposed to written publications, my resources were limited. It may also be true that I was seeing things through Western eyes and interpreted them from that perspective. Ideally, these observations and reflections could be greatly enhanced through further dialog with Filipino pastors and educators.

If we are to continue to live life on this planet, we cannot exist within isolated cultural, national, or racial boundaries. We are indispensable to one another across all boundaries. Ethnic, cultural, religious, and racial backgrounds can become heritages to be prized, protected, nourished, and cherished, as guides for life-style, but not as boundaries, barriers, or blocks to communication and cooperation between peoples (Augsburger, 1986, p. 18).

I was told by a Filipino pastor of a legend that seems to illustrate this concept of respect for one another without regard or judgment of their cultural backgrounds. It is called the legend of the Peace Child and gets its name from a tradition in Papua New Guinea. When warring tribes of headhunters made peace, they each exchanged a child. The children would grow up with the others' tribe and if in the future, conflict threatened between the tribes again, those children would be the ones sent to negotiate. Such a child was called a "Peace Child."

Theories of pastoral counseling necessarily have universally valid commonalities, but at the same time reflect major ecological, economic and sociocultural variations. Pastoral counseling is a communication process intended to assist the recipient, but that process is impeded when both parties send and receive messages with different meanings which come out of differing world views. There may be different forms of greeting behaviors. The meanings of non-verbal communications such as eye contact, expressive gesture, and body movements may differ. Differences may be evident in perspectives on distance, space, and intimacy. Differing understandings may be present of the surroundings and possibility of control and responsibility in social discourse and expectations of obligation in relation to biological and ethnic family. Valuations may vary radically concerning self-disclosure, the desired outcome of counseling and the nature of time and style of client investment in the process. Ethnic factors may also affect the authority that is accorded to the counselor, including counselor credibility, and there may be overt or covert power dynamics, especially when the counselor is viewed as a representative of the dominant or oppressive culture. Such factors lead toward the sending and receiving of messages which are misinterpreted, substantively affecting matters of goal, process and outcome (Way, 1990, p. 253).

Pastoral counselors who make an effort to understand the history, language, cultural patterns and traditions of other cultures facilitate pastoral counseling in a global environment. All of these are factors that have a profound impact on being able to encourage and bring wholeness in a variety of situations. Both the counselor and the counselee will necessarily need to contribute energy to finding ways of bridging cultural differences in order to work effectively. In our attempt to find people like ourselves, we often do not see others as they really are. We screen out the ways in which they are different. In the words of Rabbi Yechiel Michal of Zloczov,

> It is the duty of every man in Israel to know and consider that in his nature he is unique in the world and that there has never been another like him. For had there been another like him, he would not need to be in the world. Each individual is a new thing in the world and must perfect his own nature in this world. (Kornfeld, 1998, p. 32)

We owe to our neighbors, wherever they may be in the world, the same selfless love that we undeservedly receive from God and gratefully return in worship, in prayer, and in love to our neighbor. This means listening empathically and becoming highly tuned receivers who pay attention to all the communicating signals the client is sending. Pastoral counselors must listen to words, associations, and feelings. They must sense what the clients are experiencing within themselves. There must be an awareness of silence, too–an awareness of what is not being said. When pastoral counselors are in a country that is not their own native land, there must be a clear awareness that empathic relationships always occur in a context that is "the total environment in which we are and which is in us." (Kornfeld, 1998, p. 55). The context of a person's life involves their relationships, work, class, gender, race, and sexuality. It involves their history, culture, and language. It involves the environment of workplace and nature and their communal and spiritual experience. It involves the impact of the world upon them.

Often pastoral counselors mistakenly do not take into consideration their client's total environment.

> Dr. van den Blink says that when he wishes to be listened to with empathy: 'What I want and need is for someone to take the time and trouble to discern the shape of my experience, the gestalt of what I have gone through or what I am struggling with, and to help me understand it better. For in participating in that kind of respectful and caring exploration of my life or my issue or my problem, no matter how difficult or painful, I feel affirmed in my humanity. I feel empowered and begin to understand myself better and am able to see and grasp things about myself.' (Kornfeld, 1998, p. 56)

This awareness comes from a realization that all care for others flows out from God's love for us.

Pastoral counselors must address both universal humanness and particular human aspects. When read through third-world eyes, familiar concepts become disturbing and unsettling. "We must be in dialogue . . . with Christians in other parts of the world who read the Bible in a very different way. . . . When third world Christians listen to the Bible, they hear different things than we hear, to the extent that it even seems as if each of us were reading different books" (Augsburger, 1993, p. 129). These differences can, in reality, offer a greatly enhanced and more accurate understanding of humanity. We live in a global neighborhood–which is greatly expanded over the neighborhood that was known and understood in previous decades. To view individual problems as separate from their context those problems will most certainly be misunderstood. The integration the client experiences must be the result of interpersonal reconciliation within that person's cultural-contextual experience. To miss that concept is to substitute one dysfunction for another in the mistaken hope that any particular pastoral counselor has the unique understanding that will bring about healing (Augsburger, 1993, p. 130). In many ways this idea is applicable to providing care in all circumstances, whether intercultural or not. It is vitally important then to recognize that each person's reality constitutes a unique perspective on life that is, in many ways, synonymous with the differences seen between different cultures at a global level. The intercultural pastoral counselor is necessarily present in an authentic way while dialoguing with persons of other cultures, other values and other faiths. They must be willing to fearlessly cross over and return from an alternate world and religious views. There must be sensitivity to what is universal, cultural or individual. Individuals must be seen as having value in a comparative way with respect to culture and in an equal way with respect to individuality. In working with various cultures, there needs to be sensitivity to the variations, which at times are very wide, in the perception and experience of anxiety, shame and guilt. At the same time, the negative and positive functions of those emotions and moral aspects need to be recognized.

> Sensitivity to God, who calls us to love the world; to the world, which calls us to embrace diversity; and to the uniqueness of persons, which calls us to discover the particularities of God at work

> in each human experience can free us to discard old models and join in the creation of new–as many new models as there are cultures, groups and visions of life's meaning. (Augsburger, 1993, p. 142)

In working with persons of different ethnic and cultural backgrounds, it is critical that pastoral counselors be aware of the tendency to believe at some level that their experience and culture are the norm for all human beings. This tendency has the potential of blinding them to significant differences in the ways the client perceives, feels, solves problems and experiences their worldview. The pastoral counselor's world perception and their need to protect the sanity they feel within that perception also inhibit their capacity to perceive an alternate world (Augsburger, 1986, p. 24).

Issues of power and powerlessness are seen at the core of cultures where oppression has been a part of their history. Third world countries are particularly demonstrative of the effects of a sense of powerlessness that comes from having been oppressed for generations in which they have been under the control of others–whether through political means or through economic means or as a result of a lack of resources of other kinds.

I want to emphasize that providing pastoral counseling across the lines of different cultures at a global level does not mean that those pastoral counselors must adopt other cultural perspectives and values for themselves. It is important that these pastoral counselors acknowledge their own cultural orientation, while at the same time helping the client to understand their situations from a cultural orientation that is different. Some of those differences will be deemed positive and some will be deemed negative. But allowing them is the ultimate objective. By allowing them, they are validated and affirmed. If changes are to occur, those changes need to come at the initiative of the client upon their determination to do so.

> The things which are impossible with men are possible with God. Luke 18:27

ISSUES OF PASTORAL COUNSELING IN THE PHILIPPINES

The Philippines has a long and rich cultural heritage, but suffers from socioeconomic problems, intercultural conflicts, and religious superstitions. Modern pastoral care movements were only begun in the 1960s and were influenced by Western models of pastoral care and counseling. North American models of pastoral counseling were basically imported to the Philippines–as they were also imported into other cultures. Attempts to contextualize approaches have led to adoption of indigenous models of care and endeavors have been made to incorporate them in the development of the theory and practice of pastoral care and counseling. The Philippines was the first country in Southeast Asia to develop a modern pastoral care movement. The Rev. J. Albert Dalton of the U.S. formed the Philippines Association for Pastoral Care in 1965. The first fully accredited CPE training program was conducted in 1966 at St. Luke's Hospital, Manila. There are now nine CPE centers. Students work in hospitals, parishes, and with trade unions. Pastoral care and counseling has become a part of theological curriculum in all major theological colleges. The headquarters of the Philippines Association for CPE is at St. Luke's Hospital, Manila (Pitamber, 1990, p. 1204). Over the years, Filipinos are becoming more aware of the need to address pastoral care within their own cultural context. There are many ways in which the Filipino culture mandates that pastoral care take into consideration the cultural aspects that are specifically unique in the Philippines.

The most important aspects of pastoral care are being able to affirm, validate, listen to, and remember the accounts shared by the client. The primary differences occur in doing so in light of those things which are vitally important in the cultural existence of the Filipinos. Personal experience of the pastoral counselor can have a powerful impact for the clients because of the realization that the pastoral counselor has been through what they they are experiencing. They have a strong sense of being able to relate to the reality that God has allowed the pastoral counselors to resolve what has happened in their lives, so they can trust that God will also do so for them in their own unique context. The incarnational approach to faith is very, very important to Filipinos. For them it is vitally significant to know that Jesus came down to their level and experienced life as they do.

INTERPERSONAL RELATIONSHIPS

Filipinos gain their sense of acceptance and caring from persons other than their biological parents. This occurs more keenly because multiple generations are so much more interconnected and families do not become separated by distance as noticeably as is common in the United States. This intergenerational caring and accepting create an environment that influences children by example more than through verbal teaching.

This concept of a greatly extended family expands the influence of community members. The value of friendship carries with it the understanding that a friend of one is the friend of all. This more corporate way of seeing friendship has a resultant impact of teamwork or group work and has a dynamic bearing on pastoral care with Filipinos. This is reflected in a way that is a bit more subtle–by the fact that effective counseling is best done between persons of the same sex and that the counseling session should be done within view of others. This doesn't mean within hearing, however. The community sense of the Filipinos carries through to so many aspects of life–and when things are done behind closed doors there is a very uncomfortable sense of doing something covertly. This brings to bear the distinct possibility that persons outside of the counseling session might imagine things to be happening that are not if the session is not done in such a way that the appropriateness of the situation can actually be seen.

Even body language affects how pastoral counselors relate to the client. Filipinos avoid looking a person in the eye. Eye contact is highly unusual–and most often a Filipino will look down or avert their eyes when talking to another. The issues of professional boundaries and pastoral misconduct issues will prevail even in the Philippines; however, the specifics of those issues will be somewhat different. Pastoral counselors will need to give heed to respecting the boundaries of others–in a similar fashion to ethical and moral limitations that have been documented and made more legally binding in the United States. The legalities do not yet exist in the Philippines, but the issues, nonetheless, need to be taken into consideration and appropriately respected and honored.

FAMILY SYSTEMS

In a Filipino family, it is most typical that the women control the finances. This is in direct contrast to the way finances are handled in more patriarchal cultures. Other areas of making family decisions and discipline within the family structure also reflect a more matriarchal influence. An elderly woman is highly esteemed within the Filipino culture and regardless of whether or not she is logical, her requests and wishes are given unquestioning compliance. In fact, a woman with gray hair is automatically shown great respect and given utmost consideration without qualification. This can impact decisions to pursue education, selection of marriage partners, career choices, etc. In terms of pastoral counseling, this affects ways in which situations are perceived and solutions devised. The clients may very well have a felt need to receive the approval of the matriarch within their family system to engage in counseling from the outset. Resolution of issues will likely hinge on what is or is not allowed and whether or not they can anticipate the approval of the mother or grandmother or great grandmother who has the final say.

Within many traditional Filipino homes, there is one large room that serves for all living needs–eating, socializing, and sleeping. Homes are frequently occupied by three or more generations. This multipurpose use of the home creates a strong physical closeness and emotional bonding. In spite of this closeness, affection is typically not publicly displayed in the Philippines and discussion of family matters outside of the communal family is rarely done and even frowned upon in most cases. Family members are responsible for one another in every conceivable way–across even the most distant generational connections. If there is a need–whether it is due to health or education or marriage or travel–even distant cousins are contacted and expected to contribute to fulfill the need.

The reality of abuse in the Philippines is only beginning to be recognized–and one of the major reasons is the strong family tie, which does not allow for discussion of those issues outside of the family unit. However, it is becoming apparent that abuse is very present and the close proximity of so many family members within the home and even within a single space is a contributing factor. This communal contextual paradigm is a prime factor to be considered by pastoral counselors in the Philippines.

The marriage relationship is considered with high regard and it is illegal to get a divorce in the Philippines. Couples can separate from one another, but they cannot get a divorce. This cultural and legal reality will have noticeable effects on the resolution of many problems faced by Filipinos.

CONFLICT RESOLUTION

It is interesting to observe that when a group of Filipinos meet to do business and a conflict ensues, the conversation can become very heated. Each party expresses their position and shares their argument. This can go on for a significant amount of time–until such time as everyone feels they have adequately expressed themselves. Then–and this seems very sudden from a Western perspective–the conversation ceases and business moves on to the next subject. There is not the kind of resolution or compromise to which we, as Americans, are accustomed. But rather what seems to happen is that the Filipinos listen to each other and accept each other at face value and once they fully understand each other they are content. No clear decision occurs, but rather an understanding of everyone's opinion and perspective. It seems they are content to move on without making a decision, which would judge one person right and the others wrong. Everyone's input is allowed and differences and conflicts between individuals is simply accepted as a given.

Conflict resolution in the Philippines takes an indirect approach. Commonly a "go between" is used. They will look for someone who is respected, experienced, trusted and unbiased to go to the respective sides and effect the resolution. Frequently this is an older person.

SPIRITUALITY

Another influence that impacts pastoral counseling in the Philippines is their continuing belief that healers have the ability to summon powers beyond themselves. The Filipino name for these individuals is "hilot," or sometimes they call them quack doctors. In a world filled with spirits, the hilot who is most skilled at evoking healing is not seen as deceitful at all. They are simply giving rise to the spirit realities of the worldview of the Filipinos. To an American this seems fraudulent and false. However, in the Filipino mind it is simply a matter of using the spirit realities that have powers of health and illness, sanity and insanity. While it is true that not all "manughilots" are quack doctors and vice versa, early American missionaries made the judgment that these beliefs were evil–thus pushing the practices beneath the surface. However, the result was that Filipinos who became Christians simply didn't share these beliefs with the American missionaries. The practices continue–but are done outside of the awareness of the missionaries. Filipinos continue to rely on these other spiritual resources for much of their daily needs and even the most faithful and devoted Christians are a part of these practices. Understanding these issues is an important part of being able to relate and assist clients and allow them to integrate all of the influences in their experience, including their worldview with respect to spirits.

The pastoral counselor's role should be to present their theology and share their faith in such a way that the client is encouraged to look to the scriptures for answers that will in turn allow them to discover God's direction for themselves. Inasmuch as possible the client is guided by the Holy Spirit. However, where the client has not yet formulated a strong faith, the pastoral counselor really should take the lead in helping to solidify the direction that is most appropriate in any given situation. The more the clients are able to come to those determinations for themselves, the more the changes can take place at a "soul" level within the client, without mandating rules of what is good and evil and without passing judgment. The interpretation and application of scriptural truths must necessarily be fulfilled through guidance of the Holy Spirit within the client's life. The pastoral counselor is the coach to building a relationship within the client that will nurture an awareness of that guidance of the Holy Spirit.

LOSS AND GRIEF

Loss and grief and their accompanying rituals have a very different context from what is known in the United States. Typically a person who dies is embalmed, placed in a casket which is sealed with a glass so that it can remain open for viewing and brought back to the home for "vigil services" which are held practically daily for a period of time that lasts a week or two. The "vigil services" are conducted by any and all groups who were involved in the person's life–including a variety of church groups, workplace colleagues, neighbors, fraternal organizations, political groups, etc. Following this period of vigil services, a necrological service (the formal funeral) is conducted and burial takes place, frequently in above ground vaults, at nearby cemeteries. The attendees accompany the casket to the cemetery and a committal service is conducted there. Due to the length of the grieving time prior to burial and also to the involvement of so many of the colleagues of the one who has died, there seems to be a very healthy sense of the reality of the person's death. The acceptance of this reality seems to reduce some of the need for extensive pastoral care over the long term for family members of the deceased.

REFERRALS

The common practice of referring clients to other agencies when significant needs arise, is less applicable in the Philippines, because those resources have not yet been developed and established. This means that pastoral care encompasses a greater sphere of issues. The resources are being developed and in time the options will increase. However, at this point in time, they are rather limited.

CASE STUDIES

Case #1

While we were in the Philippines, several women sought me out privately and wanted me to help them understand their own experiences of abuse. One such woman told me her story of having been abused at the hands of her father, her uncle and later, even at the hands of an outstanding leader in the Christian community. As is normal, she blamed herself for the abuse and expressed the sense that is common among those who have been abused–that she was worthless. She and I visited regularly for a number of months and we had lengthy conversations about her relationship with God. I encouraged her to share her story and be heard. She had never told her story before and this was a primary need for her. My role was to listen as she shared the things that had happened. As she shared her story, she expressed feelings of anger and a sense of hopelessness that I had seen in myself as I had come to terms with my own abuse story. She was often distraught to the degree that her behavior was uncontrollable and one of the things I felt would be helpful to her would be referring her for more professional help from a psychiatrist. However, due to the stigma attached to psychiatric treatment in the Philippines, she refused to do that. As she shared her story, the two of us spent time formulating her questions, which she then articulated to God as we shared together in a time of prayer. She had many questions and being able to put those questions into words and hence into prayer seemed be a useful process for her.

One of my major objectives in my conversations with her was to impress on her the reality of the fact that God had created her and that she was indeed a precious child of God. We also discussed at length the fact that all of us–including her–are created equally and she is just as valuable in God's eyes as any other human being.

She drew strength from her observance of the healing that I had experienced from the effects of abuse that had occurred throughout childhood and which had continued even beyond childhood. She was encouraged to recognize her own potential for recovering from the hurt and pain that she had in her life. My role with her was that of being an encourager as she worked through the struggles and grew stronger in her own relationship with God.

I did verify with other pastors and professionals that any contact with a psychiatrist in the Philippines would effectively preclude any and all future employment opportunities. Here in the United States, this stigma is not so intense, although we do see some evidence of the impact of having sought psychiatric treatment in political races and perhaps more subtly in other job arenas.

Case #2

Another woman, who came to me upon the referral of another older woman in one of the churches near her home, had a story of having been abused by her husband. This woman was a total stranger to me–but because of her friend's referral she felt confident in asking for help. Her working through a third party for an introduction to me was demonstrative of a very common practice in the Philippines. Direct or self-introductions are not culturally commonplace and to do so is a very uncomfortable practice and therefore it is highly unlikely that those kinds of connections will occur. Again–this woman felt that she could trust me, based on the trust and recommendation evidenced from an older woman in her life.

When she arrived with her letter of introduction, she had physical evidence of the beatings that had occurred. So, my first response was to determine whether or not she needed medical attention. After determining that her physical condition did not require the assistance of a medical doctor, I proceeded to listen to her. She told me of her husband's history with drugs and how he "boxed" her severely while he was under the influence. The bruises that she had on her back were huge and it was clear that she had been very badly beaten.

As her story unfolded, she also told of how her husband had also abused their young daughter sexually. She also needed answers to questions surrounding what she could and should do with regards to her daughter's well being.

For this young woman, I was able to accompany her to the government social services and explore the help they had to offer. As it turned out, their services did not meet her needs and the next step I took with her was to look for other sources of protection and help for her. Although the resources were not yet highly developed, we were able to connect her with a crisis center that had been started specifically as a shelter and resource for women and children who had been abused.

They were able to assist her with some of the more concrete needs she had in getting help for her husband's drug problem.

This was a very difficult time for this young woman and my being able to listen and understand her plight proved to be very helpful. Again, I listened to her and encouraged her to articulate her questions in a time of prayer together and to strengthen her own faith and awareness of the guidance of the Holy Spirit in her life and in her own situation. Her needs were for someone who could listen to her, affirm her for seeking help and give her guidance and direction. A part of the affirmation for her was a need for me to share my own experience and thus substantiate the validity of my own sense of being able to understand her situation. This also reinforced her trust in me and gave credibility to my being able to give wise suggestions.

CONCLUSION

The goal of pastoral counseling should be to bring about spiritual, emotional, physical and intellectual wholeness. In my experience, this is most effectively accomplished through the client's discovery of their solutions and understanding of their specific situations in such a way that the wholeness is accomplished at a truly internal level. The wholeness accomplished in this manner gives an overall sense of well being that cannot be produced through the imposition of the pastoral counselor's belief system and worldview upon the client.

A clear understanding of what pastoral counseling has meant for me gives substance to the conclusion that the key components of a good pastoral counselor are the ability to listen, remember, affirm, and validate the stories of the client. By so doing the client will be encouraged to come to a growing understanding of their own spirituality and to integrate all aspects of their life. Ideally the end result will be to achieve a satisfying sense of wholeness. In the cases documented here–the key to working effectively was being able to relate to the many things that were different in their worldview and in their life experience as influenced by their Filipino heritage.

The implications of working in a culture different from one's own must be learned through study of the cultural differences. Some of this knowledge can be gained through study of the cultural differences that are documented in writing. However, conversations with members of the culture and astute observations of the culture are also very important resources.

Many of the differences will be significant enough that a failure to observe and respect those differences will have a negative impact on the effectiveness of the relationship between the pastoral counselor and the client. Pastoral counselors working outside of their own native culture must be able to adjust their own thinking. Accordingly, they must understand and affirm their clients within the context of the client's worldview.

REFERENCES

Augsburger, David W. 1993. "Cross-Cultural Pastoral Psychotherapy." *Clinical Handbook of Pastoral Counseling, Volume 2*. New York: Paulist Press. 129-143.

Augsburger, David W. 1986. *Pastoral Counseling Across Cultures*. Philadelphia, PA: The Westminster Press.

Kornfeld, Margaret Zipse. 1998. *Cultivating Wholeness: A Guide to Care and Counseling in Faith Communities*. New York: Continuum.

Patton. 1993.

Pitamber, Dayanand David. 1990. "South Asian Pastoral Care Movement." *Dictionary of Pastoral Care and Counseling*. p. 1204.

Roy, David E. 2000. *Toward a Process Psychology*. Fresno, CA & Cedar Grove, NM: Adobe Creations Press.

Way, Peggy. 1990. "Cultural and Ethnic Factors in Pastoral Care." *Dictionary of Pastoral Care and Counseling*. 253-255.

Cultural Landscapes
of Pastoral Counseling in Asia:
The Case of Korea
with a Supervisory Perspective

Steve Sangkwon Shim, PhD

SUMMARY. Is the American (AAPC) model of pastoral counseling possible and feasible in Asian countries? This article describes and analyzes the developmental stages of the AAPC model pastoral counseling in modern Korean society and depicts seven dimensions of contextualization including historical, societal, educational, theological, cultural, clinical, and supervisory contexts. It is suggested that transplanting pastoral counseling to Asian cultural soils requires culturally creative integration. It is specifically noted that Asian notions and meanings of self, familism, veneration for the aged, harmony and interdependence are critically important for integration. The article concludes with the ideas that pastoral counseling, as an emerging and blossoming discipline in the coming years, needs to be developed and nurtured via highly competent trained clinical supervisors in the field. *[Article copies available for a fee from The Haworth Document Delivery Service: 1-800-HAWORTH. E-mail address: <getinfo@haworthpressinc.com> Website: <http://www.HaworthPress.com> © 2002 by The Haworth Press, Inc. All rights reserved.]*

[Haworth co-indexing entry note]: "Cultural Landscapes of Pastoral Counseling in Asia: The Case of Korea with a Supervisory Perspective." Shim, Steve Sangkwon. Co-published simultaneously in *American Journal of Pastoral Counseling* (The Haworth Pastoral Press, an imprint of The Haworth Press, Inc.) Vol. 5, No. (1/2), 2002, pp. 77-97; and: *International Perspectives on Pastoral Counseling* (ed: James Reaves Farris) The Haworth Pastoral Press, an imprint of The Haworth Press, Inc., 2002, pp. 77-97. Single or multiple copies of this article are available for a fee from The Haworth Document Delivery Service [1-800-HAWORTH, 9:00 a.m. - 5:00 p.m. (EST). E-mail address: getinfo@haworthpressinc.com].

KEYWORDS. Pastoral counseling, individualism, integration, culture, ego/self, familism, interdependence, supervision

CULTURAL LANDSCAPES
OF PASTORAL COUNSELING IN ASIA:
AN OVERVIEW

Despite an extremely limited personal exposure to the vastness and diversities of cultures, races, and nations in the continent of Asia, evidence indicates that the growing influence of the North American version of the contemporary movement of pastoral theology/care/counseling has been strongly felt throughout every corner of developing countries in Asia at the threshold of the new millennium.

The contemporary movement of pastoral theology/care/counseling has become a relatively new and emerging discipline in the fields of Christian academics especially in countries like the Philippines, India, Hong Kong, Singapore, Indonesia, Malaysia, Korea, Japan, Taiwan and China and other neighboring countries.

Because of the public use of the English language, the Philippines was one of the first countries in Asia to import the American version of Clinical Pastoral Education (CPE) and the American Association of Pastoral Counseling (AAPC) model of pastoral counseling. This took place long before other developing countries in Asia were exposed to the influences of American versions of pastoral theology/care/counseling. For example, the Philippines had the first certified supervisors in its CPE centers long before other countries in Asia began to have such supervisors.

As pastoral care and counseling was seen to be an invention of American Christian academics, the status and development of pastoral care and counseling in Asia is still relatively young and unfamiliar to the general public and Christian churches in general. In contrast to the advancement of contemporary pastoral care and counseling movements in North America, the main causes for the lower status and underdevelopment of pastoral care and counseling movement in Asia seems to lie in the fact that American mainline seminaries and schools have been historically reluctant to admit and train Asian students and trainees for a variety of reasons. This is primarily due to language and cultural barriers on the part of students and trainees from Asia.

It was in the early part of the 1980s when mainline seminaries and schools in the U.S. began to be more open to admit and train students/trainees from Asia, on a token basis, in the field of pastoral care and counseling. Even these students/trainees were not totally prepared for exposure to the core experiences of clinical supervision and training due to their perceived limitations of language and other cultural barriers.

Most of these selectively admitted students and trainees were educated in the area of pastoral theology rather than in clinical and supervisory contexts. Due to cultural and language barriers, these Asian students felt more at ease with didactic courses/subjects than with clinical training. At best, trainees from Asia were selectively admitted and trained by CPE centers in the U.S.

Consequently, the current field of pastoral care and counseling in Asia seems to have largely been influenced and dominated by the clinical perspectives of the American CPE and pastoral theology discipline. For instance, evidence of the perceived dominant perspectives of pastoral theology and CPE oriented pastoral care in Asia is much evident as reflected by the programs of the 7th Asia/Pacific Congress on pastoral care and counseling held in the summer of 2001 in Australia. Like all other Asian/Pacific Congresses previously held, AAPC perspectives on pastoral counseling were rarely included by keynote and workshop presenters in the programs of the 7th Asian/Pacific Congress.

While the predominant perspective of pastoral care in Asia is that of CPE, signs of the presence of the AAPC model of pastoral counseling are beginning to emerge in Asia. This is evidenced by the fact that, for example, the 2001 AAPC Directory shows a list of several Asian names among AAPC certified membership in Asia.

It is interesting to observe that according to the same 2001 Directory, a comparative survey of certified membership in categories shows memberships from five continents and 30 countries outside of North America. This includes 13 countries with 11 certified members (Diplomate-1, Fellow-8, Member Affiliate-2) from Europe; 8 countries with 9 certified members (D-2, F-3, MA-4) from Asia/Pacific; 3 countries with 3 certified members (F-1, MA-2) from Africa; and 6 countries with 2 certified members (F-1, MA-1) from South America. All in all, outside of North America, the Asia/Pacific continent shows the second highest number, nine, of certified members next to eleven certified members from Europe.

Specifically, there are AAPC members in several countries in Asia and the Pacific including two members certified (MA) from Japan; one Fellow (F) from Singapore; one Diplomate (D) from the Philippines; one member certified (MC) from Hong Kong; and one Diplomate (D) and one Fellow (F) from Korea. In addition, the 2001 AAPC Directory lists the Korean Christian Institute of Counseling & Psychotherapy (KCICP), founded and based in Seoul, Korea, as the first and only service and training center outside North America which is accredited by the AAPC. It is reasonable to expect that these numbers will grow rapidly in the future. As such, Korea offers the strongest base for the AAPC model of pastoral counseling on the continent of Asia at this point in history. In view of these developments, the pastoral counseling movement in Korea requires a detailed review and analysis. This article will focus on the pastoral counseling movement in Korea and further reflect on similar developments on the Asian continent, and do so from a supervisory perspective. The structure of the article will be based on the seven dimensions of contextualization which include historical, societal, educational, theological, cultural, clinical, and supervisory contexts in order to understand and analyze the contemporary development of pastoral counseling in Korea.

The Historical Contexts of Pastoral Counseling

Prior to the WWII, Korea, with its history of over four thousand years, was under the colonial rule of Imperial Japan during nearly four decades. Over the course of this period Korea was forcefully subjugated to Japanese colonial systems of government and education. After WWII, Korea also suffered the ideological and geographical division between North and South. This division, by the two Cold-War superpowers, continues until today, and has left approximately one million families with no chance of contact.

While a Communist government has dominated North Korea, South Korea has been ruled by Western Democratic political systems, having been exposed to Western values and lifestyles. South Korea, under Western democratic systems, has been further reinforced by the influx of strong Christian influences brought by Western missionaries and Korea-based U.S. servicemen, especially after the Korean War in the early 1950s.

Christian churches in Korea, under the strong influence of Western Christianity, have played a key role in the propagation of Western values and lifestyles in Korean society. From this historical perspective it is no surprise that Christian churches in Korea have been highly receptive to the introduction of Western modes of contemporary pastoral care and counseling, particularly in academic contexts. Historically, this influence may be traced back to as early as the late 1960s when a visiting lecturer at the Presbyterian Seminary in Seoul first taught an AAPC model of pastoral counseling. After this initial presentation of the Western mode of pastoral counseling was introduced to Christian academics in Korea sporadic efforts to continue such courses were not successful due to an absence of professors trained in the field. For instance, it was only in the mid-1980s when two or three mainline seminaries in Korea began to hire professors in the specific field of pastoral care and counseling.

The American CPE training program was also introduced to a medical center in the early 1970s in Korea. Since then, there have been only a few medical centers which have started CPE programs, and these continue to be without certified supervisors. There are less than a dozen Korean CPE trainees who have received four or more CPE units from the U.S.

Greater impetus in the field of pastoral counseling in Korea actually began in the early 1990s when a host of PhD holders in the field of pastoral theology and care trained in North America began to appear in Christian seminaries in Korea. In total, there are currently no less than thirty (30) PhD holders in Korea who have been trained, for the most part, in pastoral theology and pastoral care in North America. Among them there are two or three Koreans with PhDs who have been trained in the AAPC model of pastoral counseling in the U.S. It would appear that this sudden increase in PhDs will continue to grow in the years to come. It is also no surprise that this unprecedented increase in scholars is and will continue to play an important role in the development of the contemporary pastoral care and counseling movement in Korea.

It is further worth noting that the predominant perspectives on pastoral care and counseling movement in Korea may readily be predicted due to the fact that these scholars come predominantly from North American academic institutions, and have training in the areas of pastoral theology and pastoral care. As such, the development of the pastoral counseling/psychotherapy movement in Korean Christian academic circles may be quite limited in its perspective, until professors become more clinically oriented.

Thus far an attempt has been made to provide a description of the historical landscape of pastoral care and counseling in Korea. Now, let us take a closer look at the societal contexts in which contemporary models of pastoral counseling are emerging.

The Societal Contexts of Pastoral Counseling

Like many other developing countries in Asia, since the 1970s South Korea has experienced rapid changes in light of urbanization and suburbianization due to the impacts of industrialization and technology. Because of the impacts of modern industrialization and high technology in Korea, the needs for human care services and mental health care increasingly become urgent and of fundamental importance to contemporary citizens in modern Korea. The adoption of Western democratic political and educational systems in Korea have also contributed to the quest for the rights of women and children, and to a wide variety of challenges to traditional family life.

In general, these various cultural and economic influences have contributed to the gradual weakening of the traditional extended family systems and the nuclear family systems, specifically in terms of the increase of fatherless families in Korea. The breakdown or dysfunction of the traditional family has been identified as one of core issues and concerns in contemporary Korea.

Industrial and technological development in Korea has also created a highly competitive society in which highly educational competition has contributed greatly to mental distress among the teenagers of Korea. According to clinical observations, the onset of mental illness in terms of the emotional growth of teenagers appears during the freshmen or sophomore years of college. This delayed onset is partially explained by the fact that youth, especially during the high school years, is systematically suppressed, ignored or neglected due to academic demands related to preparation for college entrance examinations. This extreme pressure victimizes countless numbers of youth, and many must extend this process for two to three years until they succeed in passing the entrance examination for the college/university they wish to enter. Because of this socially imposed moratorium on emotional growth and development (the so called "tunnel of entrance examination hell"), teenagers are exhibiting increased symptoms of depression and other associated symptoms. In a clinical setting, it is personally observed that the most common mental disorders suffered by the young generation in modern Korea are mood disorders (depression), anxiety disorders (obsessive-compulsive disorder and panic disorders), sexual and gender identity disorders, and personality disorders.

Another significant societal factor in the need for human care services has to do with the division of Korea into North and South. In point, this national division has caused the separation of nearly one million families during a period of, thus far, fifty years. The chronic pain and suffering among separated families has been intense and has become a point of national grief and "unfinished business."

In light of these societal factors, the need for the discipline of pastoral counseling began to emerge in recent years in the life of both Christian churches and universities in modern Korea. It is equally true that the fields of human services and mental health care are increasingly recognizing the importance and urgency of psychological services. There is clearly a growing public need and demand for human care services, which includes pastoral care and counseling.

The Educational Contexts of Pastoral Counseling

It is a truism that people in all walks of life in today's Korea are generally motivated by a high sense of educational zeal and commitment to university education and academic achievement for themselves and their children. In the midst of this educational fever, universities and seminaries of all types are experiencing an unprecedented number of students seeking entrance. It would not be an exaggeration to say that there is an overpopulation of students in university and seminary classrooms in Korea. It was roughly in the mid-1990s when academic campuses, both Christian and secular alike, began to respond to the needs and demands for social and behavioral science training and services. In light of this demand, universities in Korea began to open professional graduate schools in counseling psychology or pastoral counseling. This would appear to mark a trend that is not likely to end soon. These newly opened programs in these fields are already overcrowded, and severely lack adequately trained professors in various fields. In spite of the unprecedented number of counseling psychology majors in schools, both Christian and secular offer only limited education and training in counseling psychology or pastoral counseling.

For instance, academic curriculums in pastoral counseling and similar secular fields alike are predominantly theory-oriented with little effort to integrate supervised practice. In the final analysis, students conclude their academic degree in pastoral counseling with little understanding of the importance of clinical training. It is self-evident that theory-oriented education without practical integration jeopardizes students in pastoral counseling in terms of their professional development. In summary, it is a current reality that academic education lacks a systematic and coherent development of the integration of theory and practice.

A second point is that since it is in a relatively early stage, the field of pastoral counseling in Korea tends to copy American theories and methodologies without criticism or cultural adaptation. What is lacking is the integration of Western-oriented theories and methodologies into Korean cultures and the Korean personality. This raises a serious question about the effectiveness of counselors/therapists when they ignore or neglect issues of culture in the practice of counseling/therapy. As expected, it is a serious concern and need that the time is ripe for Korean authors to write Korean textbooks borne out of Korean culture and personality in order to replace the predominant usage of Western/North American textbooks and literature in the field of pastoral theology/care/counseling in modern Korea.

Third, in Christian universities in Korea there exists a profound lack of emphasis on pastoral theology and pastoral care. Academic instructors in the field of pastoral care and counseling have largely ignored or neglected the distinctiveness and contribution of pastoral theology and pastoral care.

From a personal perspective, a serious mistake lies in the fact that all professors/instructors currently teaching in the field of pastoral care and counseling unanimously claim the academic title "professor of pastoral counseling" as their professional identity and specialty in Christian academic contexts in Korea, without exception. Consequently, these "professors of pastoral counseling," without revealing their actual professional training and identity, mislead students in terms of the academic subject of pastoral counseling without teaching the academic subjects of pastoral theology and pastoral care.

In terms of analysis, a major reason for this confusion or distortion in the field may be that the pastoral counseling nomenclature is so popular and so appealing to students and the public at large that most instructors may not want such unappealing nomenclature as "professor of pastoral theology or pastoral care" as their professional and academic identity for the sake of appealing to students in their professional discipline in Korea. In point, it raises an issue of professional identity and integrity in question in one's own professional specialty and expertise in the field.

Fourth, another indication of academic confusion in the field is that the nature of CPE training, for example, is openly advocated as a part of pastoral counseling training by many instructors/professors in Korea. In practice, CPE experiences are considered as key criteria for clinical supervisor qualification in pastoral counseling. One implication of this is a lack of distinction in terms of identity and training between pastoral care/CPE and pastoral counseling. This confusion may be ultimately resolved by the presence of certified CPE supervisors in Korea, but this has yet to take place.

Fifth, in a similar vein, another serious academic confusion that is taking place in Christian academics (and for that matter among the general public) are arbitrary divisions made in practice between the fields of pastoral counseling, Christian counseling, and family counseling/ministry. For example, a recently opened professional graduate school of pastoral counseling in a seminary in Seoul has three academic departments: pastoral counseling, Christian counseling, and family counseling/ministry. In this school, the division between fields is based on the idea of pastors for pastoral counseling and lay people for Christian and family counseling.

This type of academic confusion occurred after the Korea Association of Pastoral Counseling instituted two arbitrary and confused categories in 1997: pastoral counseling and Christian counseling. According to these two categories, local congregation-based ordained ministers are defined as "certified pastoral counselors" in contrast to laypersons who are certified as "Christian counselors." This confusion appears to lie in the fact that "pastoral," "Christian" and "family counseling/ministry" departments in Christian academic contexts use similar textbooks and resources. Those studying in these academic divisions find themselves in the midst of general havoc in terms of professional identity and methodology. Clarifying this academic and professional confusion will require time and increased professionalism on the part of the current Korean Christian academics.

The Theological Contexts of Pastoral Counseling

Like Christian academics in the U.S., Christian academics in Korea tend to define and shape the nature of pastoral care and counseling depending based upon theological orientation. Korea is historically a religiously oriented land whose people are rooted in the religious traditions of Buddhism, Confucianism, Shamanism, and contemporary Christianity. In general, Christians in Korea are greatly influenced by these three traditional religions. Because of these influences, Korean Christians often tend to embrace various traits of other religions in their belief and practices.

In general, Christians in Korea are devout adherents to biblicism/literalism, and devote themselves to prayer and biblical studies. From the perspectives of Western Christianity, or mainline churches in the Western world, Christians in Korea are generally considered to be conservative and evangelical. While Korean Christians are generally conservative in nature, there are four subgroups that can be identified: fundamentalists, conservatives, evangelicals, and progressives, much like the West and other parts of the world.

Fundamentalist and conservative Christians tend to exclusively prefer the notion of Biblical counseling as advocated by Jay Adams. For an example, Adam's well-known book, *Competent to Counsel* (1970), Korean translation in 1982, has been very popular among a relatively large group of Christian fundamentalists and conservatives in Korea who regard psychology as an "enemy" of religious belief.

Evangelical Christians tend to prefer the idea of Christian counseling as advocated by Gary Collins, who regards "psychology" as a "friend" of theology. Collins' *Christian Counseling* (1980), Korean translation in 1984, has become the textbook for evangelical Christians. Collins' books and approaches are also very popular among evangelical-oriented psychologists and psychiatrists in Korea.

In the midst of conservatives and evangelicals in Korea there is a relatively small group of progressive Christians who have been exposed to the influences of Howard Clinebell both through his texts and in person. Clinebell's *Basic Types of Pastoral Counseling* (1966) was translated in 1979, and his revised edition, *Basic Types of Pastoral Care & Counseling* (1984), was first translated in 1987, as well as numerous other books which have been translated into Korean in later years. Clinebell has also visited Korea approximately eight times between 1980 to 1997, with his last visit being on the golden anniversary of his marriage and the 50th anniversary of his ordination. In a sense, Clinebell is the figure who has planted the seed of the AAPC model of pastoral counseling in modern Korea.

In a similar vein, Hiltner's *Pastoral Counseling* (1949, translation 1976) and *Preface to Pastoral Theology* (1958, translation 1968) plus Wise's *Pastoral Counseling* (1951, translation 1965) have been translated into Korean. However, these books have rarely been introduced to and read by students in pastoral care and counseling in Korea.

Those Christians who are in tune with progressive American authors like Clinebell and others are predominantly members of the Methodist and Presbyterians churches.

In sum, in terms of theological orientation and pastoral counseling there are three general subgroups among Christians in Korea: adherents to biblical counseling, Christian counseling, and pastoral care and counseling currently.

In the analysis of the subgroup of pastoral care and counseling here in Korea, one finds a general confusion in terms of the relationship between pastoral care and pastoral counseling. In general the term "pastoral counseling" is used in such ways that include pastoral care and pastoral theology. The result of using the term "pastoral counseling" in such broad ways is a general confusion regarding the distinct identity of pastoral counseling. Consequently, the identity and nature of the AAPC model of pastoral counseling have become particularly obscure. Recently, however, the first Korean AAPC Diplomate has begun to advocate the identity and distinctiveness of the AAPC model of pastoral counseling/psychotherapy. This has resulted in discussions regarding the identity and nature of pastoral theology, pastoral care and pastoral counseling, specifically in terms of concepts presented by CPE in Korea.

The current existence and practice of the AAPC model of pastoral counseling/psychotherapy began to appear with the founding and growth of The Korean Christian Institute of Counseling and Psychotherapy (KCICP). The KCICP happens to be the first AAPC-accredited service and training center outside of North America, and has become the spearhead for a newly emerging pastoral counseling/psychotherapy movement not only in Korea but also in other Asian countries. This would indicate that the AAPC model of pastoral counseling/psychotherapy is well suited to and needed in Asian cultures.

In a sense, not only Korea but also other developing countries in Asia are reaching a developmental stage where it is possible to move from general understandings of pastoral care toward more specific understandings and applications of pastoral counseling/psychotherapy.

The Cultural Contexts of Pastoral Counseling

Contemporary understandings of pastoral care and counseling are expressions of Western culture and personality. The AAPC mode of pastoral counseling is undoubtedly rooted in images that have to do with North American rugged individualism, democratic values and lifestyles. In this sense the AAPC mode of pastoral counseling addresses the needs of American individualism and personality. In view of its cultural roots, the AAPC mode of pastoral counseling encounters cross-cultural conflicts when it is transplanted to another culture. Thus, transplanting the AAPC mode of pastoral counseling into Asian cultures inevitably and naturally faces cross-cultural encounters and conflicts. For example, there are fundamental differences between Korean and North American cultures and values. There are differences between understandings of ego vs. self, individualism vs. familism, affection vs. filial piety, egalitarianism vs. veneration for the aged (hierarchical relationship), justice vs. harmony, functional vs. relational, and independence vs. interdependence. The AAPC mode of pastoral counseling values and stresses the importance of individualism, egalitarianism, justice, function, and independence in all human affairs and relationships. On the other hand, Korean culture and personality emphasizes the importance of familism, veneration for the aged, filial piety, harmony, relationship-centered, and interdependence.

One other critical culture-bound conflict in training or doing therapy is the dependency needs of trainees and clients on supervisors or therapists. It is culturally normal for a trainee or client to be submissive to and dependent on the supervisor or therapist in Korean culture or in other Asian cultures. For instance, an attitude of self-reliance or self-assertion on the part of the trainee in relation to the supervisor in Korea is normally perceived as aggressive, disrespectful or culturally deviant. These points are only a few examples of how Western theories and practices of pastoral counseling/psychotherapy need to be culturally adapted and integrated in light of Asian cultures and personality in terms of training or in therapy.

In terms of dealing with cross-cultural dimensions and dynamics, we have been richly blessed by a variety of cross-cultural counseling theorists and researchers. Of particular help in work with Asian American or Asians in counseling/therapy or cross-cultural supervision are D.W. Sue's two books *A Theory of Multicultural Counseling and Therapy* (1996) and *Counseling the Culturally Different: Theory and Practice* (1999). In the field of pastoral care and counseling Leslie (1979), Augsburger (1986,1992) and Van Beek (1996) are the forerunners in dealing with cross-cultural counseling and awareness.

The Clinical Contexts of Pastoral Counseling

As previously described and implied in our discussions above, Christian churches and seminaries in Korea are being challenged to face the need for services and training in pastoral counseling. Similarly, Christian churches and seminaries are increasingly becoming aware of the necessity and importance of pastoral counseling/psychotherapy within and beyond the Christian community. The beginning of the 1990s was a landmark in the blossoming of many different types of counseling and training centers on university campuses and in the general community.

In the secular counseling domain, a recent survey indicates that there are basically four categories of clinics and training centers that have been established in recent years. These include: (1) clinics/centers related to colleges/universities, (2) government related and supported clinics/centers, (3) public clinics/centers, and (4) private practice clinics/centers. There are approximately two hundred college/university-related clinics and training centers and clinics/centers opened by faculty members. This reflects a government mandate to establish a counseling clinic on every college/university campus in Korea. In addition, many of these colleges/universities also offer graduate courses for professional counselors. Additionally, there are government-sponsored and trained counselors in every junior and senior high school in Korea.

Government-sponsored clinics and training centers are predominantly focused on counseling with teenagers. Among such clinics and centers there are: (1) regional teenage welfare centers, (2) regional social welfare centers focusing on youth and family counseling, and (3) youth counseling and training centers. Additionally, related to the public-sponsored centers/clinics, there are a wide variety of telephone counseling centers which have become quite popular. The Family Legal Service Center is the oldest family-counseling group in Korea. It has several hundred regional branches in various cities in Korea that offer both counseling and training.

Private practice clinics and training centers are very visible and active in Korea. However, they are predominantly training and program oriented, and seldom offer counseling/therapy. Guest lecturers and trainers generally conduct the training courses in these centers. This type of training in counseling is also done in colleges and universities.

There are a small number of private practitioners in counseling/psychotherapy, as well as a number of psychiatrists in private practice. It is estimated that roughly eight or nine out of ten psychiatrists in Korea use a psychopharmacological approach without psychotherapy for mental health patients.

In the Christian domain, the same survey quoted shows that there are five different clinics and centers related to Christian churches in Korea. For instance, there are: (1) local congregation-based clinics and training centers; (2) denomination-based clinics/centers; (3) Christian school and seminary-based clinics and centers; (4) public Christian sponsored clinics and centers, and (5) Christian private practice clinics and centers.

Local congregation-based pastoral counseling and training centers are generally housed and operated by large churches. They normally provide short-term counseling as well as peer-counseling training programs for laypersons. The number of the congregation-based counseling centers does not exceed two dozen, as of present. Without a doubt this number will grow in light of the reality that local churches are increasingly aware of the needs and challenges of their members and of the community.

Denomination-based centers are generally operated as training centers which deal with both clergy and laypeople. Although there are not many of these training centers the impact of their training programs is considerable. They draw large numbers of both clergy and lay leaders for counseling training.

At present, seminary-based clinics and training centers are very scarce, unlike the near universal presence of such centers on secular college and university campuses. The pioneering seminary based center was founded and continues to be operated by a Methodist seminary in Seoul. Following this example, the largest Presbyterian seminary in Seoul has recently opened a student-counseling center. It seems likely that other major seminaries will copy this model in the near future.

Public Christian sponsored clinics and training centers are another popular form of counseling and training. This type of clinic and center is generally sponsored by a group of Christian leaders, both clergy and lay, and generally offers telephone-counseling services, and on rare occasions face-to-face counseling. These centers also provide short-term training programs for amateur counselors. While there are not many of these centers, in comparison to college/university-based counseling centers, they are quite popular and influential within the Christian community.

Private practice clinics and centers belong to the last category of this analysis. Nationally, there are less than a dozen privately operated clinics and training centers in operation. These private centers rarely provide face-to-face counseling/therapy. Instead they generally offer short-term training programs. The leaders of these private centers, based on personal popularity and reputation, draw students/trainees from all parts of Korea and help fill up the gap left by theory-oriented academic training.

These five categories of counseling clinics and training centers in the Christian domain may be divided in six categories in terms of the nature of their services: (1) family ministry/counseling; (2) inner healing ministry; (3) telephone counseling; (4) brief pastoral counseling; (5) pastoral counseling/psychotherapy; and (6) training programs.

What all of this points to is the phenomena of the growth of counseling clinics and centers, in both Christian and secular sectors of contemporary Korea. The unprecedented numerical growth of counseling clinics and training centers in Korea has occurred within the last decade, and will without a doubt continue.

This phenomenon of newly established counseling and training centers beyond academic campuses in Korea may be interpreted as an effort to overcome limitations in academic degree-oriented education and training in both secular counseling and pastoral counseling. To mention just a few, there are clinics that specialize in youth, battered wives, sexual victims, mother only or father only families, family life, mental health care, etc. Interestingly, telephone counseling has become unusually popular in Korea since the early 1970s. This would also seem to reflect the need for absolute privacy, in terms of losing face, as well as practical and accessible counseling.

In view of increasing popularity of counseling we have observed that face-to-face counseling in clinics is still less popular or receptive than anonymous telephone counseling, at least among the general public. When face-to-face counseling is provided, it is mostly offered for no or very low fee, with few exceptions. In summary, these clinics and training centers are attempting to fill the gap left by theory oriented academic university training programs, and to integrate theory and practice in the field of counseling and therapy. In the midst of all of these innovative efforts, face-to-face psychotherapy is still very scarce even though the potential number of clients for in-depth psychotherapy is already beyond the capacity of the supply of professional therapists.

In the similar vein, the practice of pastoral counseling/psychotherapy is rare. The AAPC accredited Korea Christian Institute of Counseling and Psychotherapy (KCICP), located in Seoul, the capitol of Korea, is an exception. The KCICP, which was founded in 1993 in the heart of Seoul, provides pastoral psychotherapy and training for interns and residents in psychotherapy and pastoral psychotherapy regardless of the trainee's religious backgrounds. It is interesting to note that the rigorous and long term clinical training based on AAPC standards offered by the KCICP is not overly popular among Korean trainees. This must be seen in terms of competing centers that generally offer short-term training programs. Normally, Korean trainees tend to prefer short-term training, and do not appear to understand the need for in-depth personal and professional formation.

The Supervisory Contexts of Pastoral Counseling

The core of training students in pastoral counseling, as generally conceived, is clinical supervision and the process of gaining professional credentials. Other than psychiatrists there are no licensing processes for professional counselors/therapists in modern day Korea. Instead, there are several professional organizations or associations, organized only in recent years, which serve to standardize training and issue certificates for their respective constituents.

To mention a few important bodies related to counseling and psychotherapy, both Christian and secular in Korea, there are: (1) Korean Counseling Psychology and Psychotherapy Association (1946); (2) The Korean Counseling Association (2000); (3) The Korean Association of Christian Counseling and Psychotherapy (1999); (4) The Korean Association of Spirituality and Psychotherapy (2000); (5) The Korean Association of Family Therapy (1998); (6) The Korean Association of Pastoral Counseling (1997), and; (7) The Korean Association of Clinical Pastoral Education (CPE) (2001).

It is interesting to note that it is no coincidence that the majority of these professional organizations were established within the last five years. All of these bodies issue certificates of professional competency and seek to standardize clinical supervision. Their requirements and levels of standardizations vary according to their own purposes and goals. The Korean government does not yet recognize the certificates issued by these bodies.

The Korean Counseling Psychology and Psychotherapy Association is one of the oldest organizations yet its standardization of credentials and supervision is limited to college level guidance counseling. The Korean Association of Spirituality and Psychotherapy, on the other hand, has professional standards almost equivalent to The American Association of Pastoral Counselors (AAPC). This organization, then, may be understood as the Korean version of the AAPC model in Korea. For both of these organizations the greatest challenge is the lack or absence of competently trained supervisors.

With the exception of The Korean Association of Spirituality and Psychotherapy (KASP) each of these organizations awards their certificate of clinical supervisor based on the attainment of academic degrees, generally PhD, with no or little experience in clinical training. This serves to continue the problem of a lack of trained supervisors in the field. Because of this phenomenon, most clinical and training centers in

Korea provide therapy and training with no adequate supervision of trainees.

Fortunately, within the last decade clinicians/researchers have begun to publish articles on supervision and training in counseling and psychotherapy in the field (C. T. Kim,1993; H. R. Choi, 1995, 1998; H. S. Shim, 1996, 1998, 1999; K. Y. Kim, 1997; J. C. Lee, 1996). Developing supervisory training and research on clinical supervision appear to be fundamental challenges facing the field of counseling and psychotherapy in the coming years.

One important observation regarding supervision made at the KCICP is the fact that trainees in Korea appear to be more responsive to group rather than individual supervision. This preference may be due to the fact that Korean trainees tend to feel more anxious when they are face to face individually with a supervisor. Trainees tend to be more responsive and to feel less restricted when they are in a group setting surrounded by peers. Korean trainees are not accustomed to being face to face with authority figures, such as a supervisor, alone and frequently hesitate to reveal their inner thoughts and feelings. Their usual manner of being in relationship with an authority figure such as a teacher or supervisor is dependence and compliance. Because of this cultural tendency supervising Asian trainees, such as Koreans, presents certain problems and barriers to Western styles of supervision. In such cases, cross-cultural sensitivities become essential to effectiveness in encounters between Asian trainees and Western trained supervisors.

CONCLUSION

Thus far we have tried to describe and examine the state of affairs of pastoral counseling in Asia, with a particular focus on South Korea. We have overviewed the developmental stages of the pastoral counseling movement in contemporary Korea in view of historical, societal, educational, cultural, theological, clinical and supervisory contexts. We have noted that the AAPC model of pastoral counseling is a newly emerging discipline on the horizons of Christian academics and churches as a way to better respond to human brokenness and dysfunction.

It is also reasonable to believe that the current movement of pastoral counseling in Korea may be seen as a spearhead for such developments in other parts of Asia. The newly emerging energy and vision of the pastoral counseling movement in Korea needs to integrate theory oriented education with clinical training and practice, and further must be culturally sensitive to the needs and identities of trainees and clients. It is of fundamental importance to avoid simply transplanting and applying Western modes of pastoral counseling without taking into consideration deep cultural differences between East and West.

In order to provide and enhance the quality of effective pastoral counseling/psychotherapy, it is self-evident that competent clinical supervision is a critically important element that needs to be safeguarded through creditable professional standardization and supervision. In this regard, it has also been noted that supervising Asian trainees requires supervisors to be keenly sensitive to cultural values, specifically familism and styles of interpersonal relationship.

All in all, AAPC models of pastoral counseling have a new place and function in Christian academics and churches in Asia, but still must be developed and nurtured in terms of cultural, theoretical and methodological integration. It is only through cultural sensitivity and adaptation that pastoral counselors may become effective healing agents in the rapidly changing societies of Asia.

Perhaps a story or a metaphor best illustrates these dynamics. An Asian piano player once brought an American made piano from the U.S. to her hometown in Asia. While in the United States she had learned to play American music. However, she intuitively sensed the inner unplayed Asian tunes within her. She also discovered that the people around her did not necessarily appreciate her long years of training in Western music. The older people in the community were particularly unappreciative of Western music. What she discovered was that Asian melodies and lyrics can be played on an American made Western piano. She discovered that it is not easy to play Asian tunes on a piano, but it is possible and important.

She thus tried to readjust herself to her world. It was not easy. It was hard to adjust her style and consciousness, so deeply influenced by Western music, but with time, practice and creativity she learned. The older generation was particularly appreciative of how she played Asian music on an American piano. On the other hand, she discovered that many younger Asian were very responsive to and appreciative of American music, sometimes more than Asian music.

At last, this Asian piano player discovered ways of reaching out to Asian audiences of all generations. Playing both Western and Asian music on an American made piano required great cultural sensitivity and creativity, but it was possible and deeply fulfilling. Moreover, playing both types of music helped her communicate the joy of music to both young and old.

In conclusion, as time goes by we discover that people in the global villages are more similar than different. An American made piano can be quite useful for the benefit and well being of people in the global village as long as the piano player is sensitive to variations in culture and lifestyle. This article is an attempt to depict what is happening to the Asian piano player with the American made piano in one corner of Asia.

REFERENCES

1. Albott, William L. "Supervisory Characteristics and Other Sources of Supervision Variance." Journal of the Clinical Supervisor (Clinical Training in Psychotherapy). 2, No. 4 (Winter 1984): 27-41.
2. Alonso, Anne, and Shapiro, Elizabeth L. (1992) "Supervising Psychotherapy in the 1990s" in J. Scott Rutan, ed. Psychotherapy For The 1990s. New York: Guilford. 315-337.
3. Archer, Robert P., and Peake, Tom H. (1984) "Learning & Teaching Psychotherapy: Signposts and Growth Stages" The Clinical Supervisor: Clinical Training in Psychotherapy. Journal of Supervision in Psychotherapy and Mental Health 2, No.4 (winter 1984): 61-74.
4. Bell, Carlos R. (2000). "Pastoral Supervision & Cultural Issues" JSTM, 20-2000: 124-131.
5. Bernard, Janine M., & Goodyear, Rodney K.(1992) Fundamentals of Clinical Supervision. Boston: Allyn & Bacon.
6. Blackmore, Gershon T. (1996) "AAPC Theory Paper: Shepherding Moses and Aaron: A View of Pastoral Counseling Supervision" Journal of Supervision and Training in Ministry 17(1996): 185-223.
7. Borders, L. D., and Leddick, G. R. (1987) Handbook of Counseling Supervision. Alexandria, VA: Association for Counselors Education & Supervision.
8. Boyer, P.A., & Jeffrey, R. J. (1984) A Guide for the Family Therapist. New York: Jason Aronson.
9. Cardwell, Sue Webb. (1996) "A Struggle to Achieve Intellectual & Affective Congruence" Journal of Supervision & Training in Ministry 17, (1996): 39-47.
10. Choi, H. R. (1995) "A Model of Individual Supervision and Processes" Journal of Human Understanding (Student Guidance Counseling Institute, Seogang University, Seoul, Korea)16: 21-42 (in Korean).
11. Choi, H. R. (1998) "Educating Counselors and Cooperative Systems of Supervision." Journal of Student Guidance Research (Student Guidance Counseling Institute, Hanyang University, Seoul, Korea) 16: 63-87 (in Korean).
12. Draper, R., Gower, M. & Huffington (1990) Teaching Family Therapy. London: Karnac Books.
13. Ekstein, R. (1972) "Supervision of Psychology: Is it learning? Is it Administration? Or is it Therapy?" in D. E. Hendrickson & F. H. Krause. (Eds.) Counseling and Psychotherapy: Training and Supervision. Columbus, OH: Charles E. Merrill Pub. Co. pp. 153-156.
14. Ekstein, R., and Wallerstein, R. (1963) The Teaching and Learning of Psychotherapy. (2nd ed.) New York: International Universities Press.

15. Estadt, Barry et al. (Eds.) (1987) The Art of Clinical Supervision: A Pastoral Counseling Perspective. Mahwah, NJ: Paulist.

16. Estadt, Barry. (1987) "The Core Process of Supervision." in Barry Estadt et al. (Eds) The Art of Clinical Supervision. New York: Integration Books. 13-37.

17. Ewing, James W. (1987) "Supervision in Long Term Psychotherapy" in Barry Estadt et al. (Eds.) The Art of Clinical Supervision. New York: Integration Books. 122-134.

18. Fraleigh, Patrick W., and Buchheimer, Arnold. (1972) The Use of Peer Groups in Practicum Supervision in Donald E. Hendrickson & Frank H. Krause, (Eds.) Counseling and Psychotherapy: Training & Supervision Columbus, OH: Charles E. Merrill Pub. Co., pp. 246-250.

19. Greben, Stanley E., & Ruskin, Ronald, (Eds.) (1994). Clinical Perspectives on Psychotherapy Supervision. Washington, DC: American Psychiatric Press, Inc.

20. Hendrickson, Donald E. & Krause, Frank H. (Eds.) (1972). Counseling & Psychotherapy: Training & Supervision. Columbus, OH: Charles E. Merrill Publishing Co.

21. Hess, Allen K. (Ed.) (1980). Psychotherapy Supervision: Theory, Research and Practice. NY: John Wily & Sons.

22. Hess, Allen K. (1980). "Training Models and The Nature of Psychotherapy Supervision" in A. K. Hess (Ed.), Psychotherapy Supervision: Theory, Research and Practice. NY: Wiley and Sons. pp. 15-28.

23. Journal of Supervision in Psychotherapy and Mental Health) (Special Issue: Clinical Training in Psychotherapy) Vol. 2, No. 4 Winter 1984.

24. Jernigan, Homer L. (2000). "Clinical Pastoral Education With Students From Other Cultures: the Role of the Supervision" Journal of Pastoral Care, Summer 2000, Vol. 54, No. 2: 135-145.

25. Keeney, B. P. (Ed.). (1983), Diagnosis of Assessment in Family Therapy. Rockville, MD: Aspen.

26. Kim, C. T. & Doh, S. K. (1993) "A Study on Educating Counselors." Journal of Counseling and Psychotherapy (Korea Psychological Association). 5: 13-29 (in Korean).

27. Kim, G. Y. (1995) "A Multiple Baseline Design For an Individual Supervision Model in Counseling Educational methods." in Kim, G.Y., Practices Of Counseling. (Rev.) Seoul: Hakji-sa. pp. 303-361 (in Korean).

28. Lee, J.C. (1998). "Role-Models of New Counselors" Journal of Student Guidance Research (Student Guidance Counseling Institute, Hanyang University, Seoul, Korea). Vol. 16: 89-107 (in Korean).

29. Lee, K. Samuel. (2000). "A Multicultural Vision for the Practice of Pastoral Supervision & Training" Journal of Supervision & Training in Ministry, 20: 111-123.

30. Liddle, H. A., Breunlin, D. C., & Schwartz, R. C. (1988). Handbook of Family Therapy Training & Supervision. New York: Guilford.

31. Mead, D. Eugene. (1990) Effective Supervision: A Task-Oriented Model for the Mental Health Professions. NewYork: Brunner/Mazel.

32. Palmer, Stephen., & Varma, Ved. (Eds.) (1997). The Future of Counseling and Psychotherapy. London: Sage Publications.

33. Paniagua, F.A. (1994). Assessing and Treating Culturally Diverse Clients: A Practical Guide. Thousand Oaks, CA: Sage.

34. Peake, Tom H., & Archer, Robert P. (Ed.) (1984) Clinical Training in Psychotherapy. New York: The Haworth Press, Inc.

35. Rutan, J. Scott. (Ed.) (1992). Psychotherapy for the 1990s. New York: Guilford.

36. Shim, H. S. (1996). "A Study on Supervision in Counseling." Journal of Human Understanding (Student Guidance Counseling Institute, Seogang University, Seoul, Korea). 17: 1-14 (in Korean).

37. Shim, H. S. (1998). "A Study on Evaluative Criteria For Counselors." Unpublished PhD Diss., Sook Myung Women's University (in Korean).

38. Shim, H. S. (1999). "Supervision for Education of Counselors." Journal of Student Guidance Research (Student Guidance Counseling Institute, Hanyang University, Seoul, Korea). Vol. 17: 87-117 (in Korean).

39. Shim, Steve S. (2001). "Counseling Asian Americans" (in publication).

40. Steere, David A. (ed.) (1989) The Supervision of Pastoral Care. Louisville, KY: Westminister/John Knox.

41. Stoltenberg, C. D., & Delworth, U. (1987). Supervising Counselors & Therapists: A Developmental Approach. San Francisco: Jossey-Bass.

42. Tiller, Darryl J. (1989) "The Self as Instrument" in David A Steere (Ed.) The Supervision of Pastoral Care. Louisville, KY: Westminster/John Knox. 146-160.

43. Williams, Antony. (1995). Visual & Active Supervision: Roles, Focus, Technique. NY: W. W. Norton & Co.

The Future Landscape
of Pastoral Care and Counseling
in the Asia Pacific Region

Robert Solomon, MD, PhD

SUMMARY. In recent decades, pastoral care and counseling practitioners in the Asia Pacific region have identified various issues and concerns such as poverty, religion, and culture. While these issues continue to be important as the region enters into the new century, they are further exacerbated, and new issues are created, by the rapid and disorienting change that the region is going through. The dominant process of globalization has made persons, families and communities feel helpless against powerful global forces at work. While some good has been noted in this process, there is also cause for deep concern as traditional modes of pastoral care and social cohesion are eroded, and life is made increasingly stressful. This article argues for a community approach to pastoral care and counseling that would be relevant in these circumstances, and explores two examples of how the pastoral care of the community can be practiced: helping communities to cope with stressful change and to experience reconciliation and the healing of deep social fractures. *[Article copies available for a fee from The Haworth Document Delivery Service: 1-800-HAWORTH. E-mail address: <getinfo@haworthpressinc.com> Website: <http://www.HaworthPress.com> © 2002 by The Haworth Press, Inc. All rights reserved.]*

KEYWORDS. Pastoral counseling, Asia Pacific Region, cross cultural

[Haworth co-indexing entry note]: "The Future Landscape of Pastoral Care and Counseling in the Asia Pacific Region." Solomon, Robert. Co-published simultaneously in *American Journal of Pastoral Counseling* (The Haworth Pastoral Press, an imprint of The Haworth Press, Inc.) Vol. 5, No. (1/2), 2002, pp. 99-118; and: *International Perspectives on Pastoral Counseling* (ed: James Reaves Farris) The Haworth Pastoral Press, an imprint of The Haworth Press, Inc., 2002, pp. 99-118. Single or multiple copies of this article are available for a fee from The Haworth Document Delivery Service [1-800-HAWORTH, 9:00 a.m. - 5:00 p.m. (EST). E-mail address: getinfo@haworthpressinc.com].

99

INTRODUCTION

The topic I have chosen is "The Future Landscape of Pastoral Care and Counseling in the Asia Pacific Region." I would like to approach this topic from a "personal perspective." Let me first say something about my "personal perspective." Each of us develops views and opinions based on our own unique experiences. Naturally, my views are colored by my own limited experiences. Much of that has to do with where I live and work–in Southeast Asia. The Asia Pacific is a large geographical entity though no one can confidently say where its boundaries lie. It is quite impossible to develop a global view that seriously takes into consideration all local contexts in this region. Nevertheless, we can see broad patterns, thanks to globalization and improved communications.

I do travel a fair bit in this region and have the privilege of seeing different widely divergent contexts. In this respect, let me mention a few cameos from my recent travels in the region.

1. In the park in central Phnom Penh in Cambodia, you will find many children huddled along the perimeter, taking shelter under the old trees. These are the street children of Phnom Penh who gather at a number of places, trying to survive in a harsh world. They are the victims of a tragic history of war, violence, neglect and corruption. These children are malnourished, illiterate, and suffer from illnesses and sores. Some Christians operate a bus that visits several of these places where street children gather in Phnom Penh. They have converted the bus to allow them to welcome the children in, give them a bath, dress up their wounds and sores, feed them with eggs and bread, and teach them songs and games. Some of these children end up in orphanages run by various NGOs in Cambodia. These children need to be cared for, given education, and be given an opportunity to find a future with hope. They also need protection from those who would use them for the growing flesh trade.

2. The road from China's old capital Nanjing and its commercial centre Shanghai is about 300km. Last year when I had to travel on this road, I expected a long journey on old trunk roads going through ancient villages and old farms. The ancient villages and farms are still there along the way, but in between they are being replaced with new townships. The road, to my surprise, was a modern highway most of the way. It was a smooth and quick journey. Along the way were modern pit stops with shops and amenities you would find anywhere in a developed or rapidly developing country. Shanghai is a web of frenzied activity. Construction work can be found everywhere. The people are busy logging on to

the new economies of the 21st century world. China is changing fast. With this rapid change come social and psychological tensions as people struggle with a constantly changing social order and the loss of old anchors for personal and social well-being.

3. A group of medical students and doctors gathered in the small university town of Salatiga in east Java at a conference where I spoke. I could sense much anxiety among them for their country was going through a very difficult time. In the Maluku islands, terrible violence marked the relationship between Muslims and Christians. Elsewhere, churches were being burned. I met a young medical student from Ambon in the Maluku islands where many had died as a result of inter-ethnic fighting. He had seen things which had changed him. How was he going to deal with his own anger and fears? His homeland had become a living hell. I also met those who had firsthand experience of seeing a church being burned by extremists. I was told that one of the topics in training sessions for leaders and on pastoral care was what to do when your church is burned, or when your church is attacked by a mob. I met someone who described in graphic detail what happened when a mob attacked Sunday morning worshippers in his church. Later I read in the papers about the Christmas bombing in Jakarta in December 2000. Christians were urged by their pastors and leaders not to retaliate against Muslims because it was believed that the perpetrators were motivated politically rather than religiously. During this conference in Salatiga we received news of the bombing of the Philippines Ambassador's house in Jakarta. The students were disturbed by the news, for their country seemed to be falling apart.

My personal view is shaped by my own experiences and observations and understanding of the various contexts which comprise the Asia Pacific region. Due to my own limited experiences, I shall confine my observations to the Asian part of the region. I do recognize that there will be other personal views and that we need a collage of views to see a more whole and accurate picture.

LANDSCAPES:
PAST, PRESENT AND FUTURE

The topic also deals with the "future landscape." It calls for the skills of a futurist. Some futurists use primarily the processes of cognition and analysis; and others intuition and gut feelings. I do not pretend to be a futurist and therefore hesitate to paint pictures of future landscapes, lest they turn out to be wishful thinking rather than accurate predictions. Nevertheless I will try to look at a few trends and processes that I see which might influence the way pastoral care and counseling develops and is practiced in the Asia Pacific region.

To look at possible future landscapes, one should wisely look at where we have been and where we are. This is the 7th Congress of Pastoral Care and Counseling in Asia and the Asia Pacific region. A look at the themes of the previous congresses may be a useful exercise to gauge the concerns of the past two decades in our field:

1. 1982–1st Congress (Manila): Pastoral Care and Counseling in Asia: Its Needs and Concerns
2. 1984–2nd Congress (Tokyo): No declared theme
3. 1986–3rd Congress (New Delhi): Theme unknown
4. 1989–4th Congress (Manila): Ministry to the Aging in Changing Asian Values
5. 1993–5th Congress (Bali): Pastoral Care and Counseling in Pluralistic Society
6. 1997–6th Congress (Seoul): Pastoral Care and Counseling in the Context of Asia-Pacific Religions
7. 2001–7th Congress (Australia): Pastoral Care and Counseling in Changed Societies

Here we note a concern to grapple with pastoral care and counseling issues in relation to the complexities of Asian contexts, especially in relation to multi-ethnic and multi-religious societies that are going through significant changes.

A book entitled *Counseling in the Asia Pacific Region* was published in 1993, containing articles by eleven authors from Korea, Malaysia, Indonesia, Hong Kong, Singapore, Japan, Australia, and New Zealand.[1] One could say that the book contains a snapshot picture of the landscape in counseling in the Asia Pacific region as it was ten years ago. If that is true, then looking at the contents of the book would be an interesting and useful exercise for us.

The book looks at eight countries and cultures and explores the counseling movements within these contexts. In Malaysia, counseling emerged in the educational contexts of schools and the need to provide guidance for students. The problem of drugs in the midst of rapid social change provided the motivation for counselor training and counseling programmes in schools. In Singapore counseling developed in the context of a church outreach programme whose aim was to help troubled individuals. Over the years, counseling has developed to embrace a larger and more diverse vision and has grown by adaptation of western models to fit an urban Asian context. In Indonesia, counseling developed as an attempt to help youth in the midst of socio-political change. In China, counseling has to deal with the axis between traditional values about familial and social structures associated with such things as power, authority and shame, and the forces of modernity and change that have become part of the landscape. In Japan, counseling developed in the context of medical and clinical sciences, and had to seriously face the issues of culture and modernization, and the appropriateness of western methods. In Korea, counseling moved from a therapeutic to a developmental focus as a response to social change and progress. In New Zealand, counseling had to deal with both the individual and social spheres as well as the social and economic relationships between the immigrant white settlers and the native Maori population. In Australia, counseling developed in the contexts of schools and universities, with the need to provide vocational and career guidance.

In summing up the discussion, editors Othman and Awang highlight 5 key issues for counselors and counseling in the Asia Pacific region: identity, drugs, ethics, stress, and family. They argue that the counselor identity crisis needs to be addressed in the region by defining the profession of counselors. Further they point out that the growing problems of drug addiction and other social problems have to be seriously tackled by counseling. They also lament the degeneration of moral and ethical values and urge counselors to reinstate lost Asian values so as to bring about social harmony amidst rapid social change. Othman and Awang also address the growing stress levels produced by modern life in the region and the need for counseling to meet this challenge. Finally, they ask the question, "How can we as counselors help fill the vacuum created by the breakdown of the extended family system?"[2] They also rightly point out the need to develop indigenous forms of counseling which would be more culturally appropriate and therapeutically more effective.

Almost ten years later, we ask whether these key concerns continue to be felt among counselors working in Asia. Certainly stress continues to be expressed in many areas of life, in greater measure many would add. The family is also undergoing changes in structure, function, attitudes, and rituals. Social values and norms are also caught in swirling changes. Some would see it positively; others would see it as giddying social vertigo. The problem of drugs comes up with many avatars–a changing array of designer drugs for new generations. The counselor continues to face some kind of identity crisis, though counseling is increasingly accepted in Asian societies, especially as a last resort in urban environments where traditional forms of care and support have fast disappeared.

While the concerns identified ten years ago remain today, major changes have also taken place during the last decade in Asia that will significantly affect the practice of pastoral counseling. I will highlight a few of these for our discussion.

Globalization

In today's world the fact of globalization is keenly observed. Economics now is not a local thing, for what happens in the USA affects the bus driver in Davao, or the farmer in Karnataka, or the factory worker in Guangdong. Recessions and economic downturns can hit a region like a tornado, like the Asian crisis in 1997. Randolph David has argued that the process of globalization has both positive and negative effects. Some of the negative results of globalization include the dislocation of indigenous peoples, cultural erosion, and the loss of community life.[3]

Whatever the effects of globalization may be, the fact remains–we are living in an increasingly interconnected and networked world. Which brings me to my next observation.

The Growth of Technology

Asia is in the throes of a technological revolution, in particular in the booming field of communication technologies. Cellular phones or mobile phones are appearing in many parts of Asia, even in rural areas. Telecommunication companies have to decide whether to push development in many parts of Asia by skipping various stages, normally seen as a logical sequence of development. For instance, with the explosion of cell phone technologies, the question arises whether governments are spending wisely laying out telephone lines and building public telephones in the old fashioned way.

Knowledge Explosion

With the Internet sweeping across Asia, the social experience in Asia is changing quite rapidly. Governments are increasingly finding it difficult to control the flow of information, which in the past could be tightly controlled in the traditional media of the press, radio, and television.

People can be in touch with one another and communities can be formed through the Internet against the wishes of the powers that be. It also means that people are better informed today. Patients can check up on the their diseases and question the medical opinions of their doctors. People can also find out more about personal well-being. One wonders how all this will affect counseling and people helping. Whatever the case might be, policy makers and others are talking about knowl-edge-based economies (KBE) as the wave of the future. For a genera-tion being brought up in virtual reality, an economy based not on the tangible but on its opposite should not be surprising or shocking. But for the rest in the community, these radical ideas are quite mind boggling. And before people can think about KBEs, we now have what is called the "new economy."

The New Economy

The new economy represents the new order of things that have al-ready appeared in many of our societies. Older fabrics of society are be-ing discarded for newer arrangements, which are focused on economic competitiveness. Global market economics demands that the social or-der be re-arranged to sharpen the economic edges of nations and re-gions. Based on efficiency, profitability, and short-term commitments, the new economy would certainly redefine what we understand com-munity to be.

Violence

In spite of these brave new changes in the emerging Asia, there are also disturbing signs of violence in several areas, most notably in recent times. One has only to remember the pictures of beheaded Madurese in Indonesia in early 2001 to register this observation. What lies behind this violence? Often it has to do with ethnic conflicts and with experi-ences of injustice or marginalization.[4] Racial tensions are as rife today as at any time. Economic progress, educational development, and at-tempts to forge multi-racial societies in many parts of Asia do not seem to have made significant inroads into producing racial harmony. Where communities seemed to have achieved some measure of racial har-mony, it turns out often to be only a thin veneer that hides unresolved tensions, stubborn prejudices, and deep wounds. Seemingly minor inci-dents can trigger a violent conflict between ethnic groups, like the recent clash between Malays and Indians in an urban squatter settlement in Kuala Lumpur.

Poverty

While urban Asia is going through many spectacular changes, with high rise landscapes dominating many cities, modern technological gadgets flooding eager markets, and a rising middle class, the fact still remains that Asia's poor remain today in the billions. With the relentless urbanization of Asia, and the transformation of most local economies to fit in with the globalized market economy, the plight of Asia's poor is made more desperate. Many Asian countries have seen many years of impressive economic growth. But this has also produced new groups of the poor. Many who move from rural areas to urban centres in search of a better life find their dreams shattered as they struggle with life in squalid urban ghettos, and without any significant resources or voice.

Irresponsible governments and societies suffering from the plague of corruption exacerbate this problem further with very little being done for those who need help the most. As a result, the plight of the poor takes on many pathetic shapes. We know of how the poor are exploited as cheap labour in many parts of Asia, of how young children are forced into prostitution, and of how they live in terrible conditions caught in an endless cycle of poverty and misery.

AIDS

AIDS came to the world's attention in the 1980s. Once it was seen to be a western, if not an American problem. Then AIDS came to be associated with Africa. Many countries in sub-Saharan Africa suffer from the AIDS plague with significant sections of their populations being wiped out by the deadly disease. What is not so readily noticed is that AIDS is becoming a major problem in Asia, and that if unchecked, the problems of AIDS in the next few years will most sharply be felt in Asia. Already the disease is reaching crisis proportions in Indo-China and South Asia. There are an estimated 7 million people living with HIV infection in Asia and the Pacific. In India alone, there are as many as 5 million sufferers. Remembering that 60% of the world's population lives in Asia, and that the sharpest HIV infection rate is in Asia, short of a cure being discovered in the near future, this problem will influence the shape of pastoral care in the Asian contexts.

Asia is in many ways at a crossroad, caught in a rapidly changing situation. The winds of significant change are sweeping across the many faces of Asia. Asia is in flux. Pastoral care and counseling in this context must take on a few significant stances to help Asian communities find their footing and fulfill their potential. It is in this light that I now offer what I deem to be some key aspects of the shape and approach of pastoral care in the Asia of the early part of the 21st century. I realize that I struggle here between choosing to predict or prescribe. I think it is a mixture of both elements that you will find in what follows. At times it is more of a prescription, only because of the need I feel for a pastoral counseling and care approach that would meet the needs and challenges of the future.

COUNSELING IN COMMUNITY

In the networked and globalized world, medieval English poet John Donne's observation that "no man is an island" is particularly true. In the interconnected world, where the world has shrunk into a "global village" as media philosopher Marshall McLuhan has put it,[5] it is quite impossible to think of any one individual without some form of reference to his social and natural environment which impinge on him more and more significantly. McLuhan's global village is shrinking still further, aided by rapid and dizzying developments in Internet and communication technologies.

The field of modern psychology and psychotherapy initially paid great emphasis to the therapy of the individual through the approaches taken by Sigmund Freud and Carl Jung and many others who followed them. This was followed by the person-centered approach taken by Carl Rogers, which became a definitive model of pastoral counseling for some time. However, many found these approaches wanting in that they did not take sufficient notice of larger forces at work in society and culture that affect the individual in his or her functioning.[6] The fact that individuals are in relationship is something that is increasingly recognized as having important implications for the practice of pastoral care.

Hence, for example, in the field of systems theory and therapies associated with this group of schools, a greater emphasis is given to interactions between individuals in a grouping. However, the approach is still largely confined, for all intents and purposes, to the context of the nuclear family. This context needs to be broadened to take into serious consideration the larger social and cultural forces that affect us, increasingly more so than the relationships in the nuclear family. It is good to take heed of what the well-known sociologist Peter Berger wrote in his primer, *Invitation to Sociology* many years ago.[7] He describes persons as actors standing on stage and the feeling is that the actors are acting on their own accord. However, he invites the actors to look up first of all to notice that there are strings attached to them to make them move on stage, and secondly to notice who the puppet masters are. According to him, this act of awareness frees one. The point here is that the larger socio-cultural and political forces do affect individuals in more ways than one. In this light it is possible to identify the need to see the larger systems at work and to understand the counseling process from that perspective.

Theorists such as Michael Rustin, Barry Richards, Karl Giglio, and Robert Young are well known for their work on bringing a psychoanalytic understanding of the larger social realities, trends and phenomena.[8] They attempt to understand and explain social and personal realities. In a rather simplistic way, we can say that their perspective tends to see society as the creation of the individual psyche. The social (outer) world is a creation of the private (inner) world. In his well-known books,[9] *Escape from Evil* and *The Denial of Death,* Ernest Becker has argued that the psychic denial of death in the inner world creates much of culture and social life, these being nothing more than the denial of our own mortality (through our focus on possessions, power, and so on). According to this perspective, self creates society. That notion is understandable in a western world that has experienced what has been called the Enlightenment, as a result of which the individual is seen as, in many ways, "above society." It is therefore not very surprising that we have psychologists like Erich Fromm writing about the basic human condition as a conflict between the desires of the human individual and the suppressing and stifling demands of society,[10] or the theologian Reinhold Niebuhr writing of *Moral Man and Immoral Society.*[11]

Asian cultural and intellectual development has taken on a different path than that which has been described. In Asia, the emphasis traditionally has been that of seeing society as coming before the individual.[12] In Singapore, the government came up with a set of national values in the early 1990s. One of the values was "society above self." There was some opposition to that from a small group of intellectuals and some adjustments were made, though the original "society above self" value has been retained.[13]

There seems to be suspicion about discussions on social well-being among groups of intellectuals in Asia. In a society where social conformity has been enforced to maintain a measure of "social harmony," one can understand how an emerging consciousness of the value of the individual can help see enforced social conformity as a stifling prison for individuals who want to exercise their freedoms.[14] I presented a paper entitled, "The Cult, The Crowd, and The Community"[15] at the 3rd Theory Building Conference of the International Pastoral Care Network for Social Responsibility at Seoul in 1997. In the paper I tried to discuss processes which produce all three types of social relationships in contemporary Asia, and gave examples. I found some of my Korean brothers and sisters not too keen about the word "community." I realized that to them there was not too much difference between the cult and the community. Community was a bad word. I wondered whether their experience of community was in a more homogenous society than that in which I have to live in Singapore, and whether that coloured the way we each understood and felt about the word "community."

My point here is not to discuss which is more important, philosophically, politically, and therapeutically: the self or society. Rather, it is to show that there is a close undeniable relationship between the private and social worlds, and between individual and collective identities.[16] Also, it is to show that while some psychoanalytical theorists have tried to demonstrate the connection from the "self creating society" point of view, there may be a need, especially in the Asian contexts, of showing the connection in the other direction. Does society create the self?

It is true that in the earlier schools in 20th century psychology and therapy, for example, the objects relations school, the role of the mother in shaping the psyche of the child, was emphasized. Our primary relationships with significant others (largely understood to be family members, especially one's parents), were understood to be psychogenetic. In other words, they were seen to determine the shapes and climates of our inner worlds. However the social determinants were confined to the narrow world of the infant's home. One, however, needs a larger view of the social world, which affects our private worlds. There is not much, to my knowledge, in counseling literature in this direction. The behavioral therapy people pay close attention to the social world but they ignore the private world and therefore the significant connection between the two worlds. The social world affects us more deeply than merely modifying our behavior. It helps to shape our inner worlds, and how we construct and comprehend our realities.

Interestingly one group of writers may help in this venture. In early and mid-twentieth century, some social anthropologists such as Ruth Benedict attempted to show how culture shapes personality.[17] They were basically taking a "society shapes self" approach. Though I have difficulty accepting several of their conclusions, I believe that their methodology is worth a revisit especially as we think of pastoral care and counseling in 21st century Asia. In a similar vein, though taking a different approach, the more contemporary writings of sociologist Robert Bellah point our how "habits of the heart" are shaped by social and cultural patterns and forces and why it is necessary to help create the "good society" to produce and nurture good and healthy individuals.[18]

In understanding pastoral care in Asia, one has to understand how our cultures have shaped us in our inner worlds, before we can effectively care for individuals. In an interesting study of how the elderly in Singapore cope with terminal illness and old age, sociologist Kalyani Mehta has shown how the various ethnic groups cope differently because of their cultural and religious perspectives.[19] In counseling individuals, one must take seriously his or her social and cultural grounding. I have spoken to a number of people from mainland China and many have begun to see how growing up in an environment where atheism was enforced as the official philosophy has affected them deeply, and how they find it difficult to reverse what is deeply embedded.

Today, vast changes are taking place. While people have been shaped in their experiences by the traditional cultural patterns and shapes, they are also being influenced by globalised culture being promoted by globalised media and a globalised economy. Japanese social philosopher Kenichi Ohmae has observed what he calls the "californiazation of taste" and argues that Japanese youth today are closer culturally to American youth than to their own elders in Japanese society.[20] In other words, people in Asia, and for that matter elsewhere, are being shaped more and more, not so much by intrapsychic or intrafamilial dynamics, but by powerful social forces, either enforced, or carried by popular winds of influences. If we ignore these forces, and still turn all our attention to the intrapsychic or familial worlds, then we may miss the boat in trying to provide effective pastoral care to people. Wendy Griswold has shown the negative impact of post modernity on community–depthlessness, the rejection of metanarratives, and the fragmentation and breakdown of connections, leading to a denial of depth, history, and meaning. She asks the question whether the new media and communication technologies can help to reverse this by producing a new globally conscious community.[21] We wonder whether the answer lies in such technological solutions. Whatever the case may be, the analysis is correct in looking at the larger social forces at play.

My point here is that in counseling people and helping them, we need to take serious consideration of the part played by socio-cultural forces in shaping the values and personalities of people. This has at least two implications for pastoral care.

Firstly, in providing pastoral care, we would come across social trends and realities that bring harm to people. They may benefit a few but bring harm to many. I am here talking about social injustices, which bring untold suffering to individuals. For instance, if there is a problem with drug addiction in a society, pastoral care givers can help these victims by counseling them, and helping them to break their addictive habits and remain free from them. However, there is no point doing this endlessly without addressing the social forces that contribute to this problem. In this case it could be an ungodly combination of crime syndicates, corrupt officials, social frustration due to a lack of opportunities, and so on. Pastoral care therefore has to become prophetic. Counseling cannot be confined to the counseling room in Asia or be organized simply along a clinical professional approach. Helping people cannot be relegated to the privatized sphere. It must be a personal act in a public world.[22]

This brings me to the second implication. Pastoral care is an act involving not only individuals but also communities. We need to develop new paradigms where we think of the pastoral care and well-being of communities. How can we care for communities in such a way that they thrive with health and in which can thrive individuals? For us in the Christian community, we do have models for the pastoral care of congregations or parishes.[23] This would involve taking care of community identities, rituals, stories, and relationships which nurture individuals and families. It involves providing hope and vision, direction and sustenance to these communities. We will have to rediscover some of these old patterns and incorporate them to our pastoral care approaches.

This, of course, does not mean that we simply learn how to manage social groups. Even in church, congregations are increasingly managed as corporations out to produce results. They are being managed by CEOs rather than ministered to by pastors. What we need is the shepherding model for communities, which can incorporate both the care of individuals as well as the care of the community. Both go hand in hand.

I will summarize here by saying that my first major point in talking about the future shape of pastoral care in Asia is that pastoral care and counseling must be done in community. We have to modify hitherto dominant models in counseling, rediscover some old but helpful ways of understanding the pastoral care of communities, and see that pastoral care and counseling has to have both prophetic and therapeutic functions in community.

This also brings me to my second major point, that is, the pastoral care of communities in fast changing Asia, may have to focus on helping these communities cope with the giddying changes that are taking place all over Asia.

HELPING COMMUNITIES TO COPE WITH CHANGE

We have already seen how rapid change is taking place in Asia. Much of this is riding on massive waves of technological innovation. As James Burke and Robert Ornstein have argued in their book *The Axemaker's Gift,* technology promises to change our environment, but in doing so, it also inevitably changes our minds.[24] And then it goes on to change us. Such is the power of technology. Today, our tools determine our agenda, our values, and our lifestyles. They affect our relationships too. Think of a car with four people, each talking on a mobile telephone, but not to one another. How life has changed!

If the pastoral care of communities is to be an important aspect of pastoral care and counseling, then we must also think of how to help whole communities, not just individuals and families cope with the rapid changes taking place today.

There is increasing evidence of social pathology related to the sense of disorientation produced by the flux of change that seems to be a characteristic aspect of modern life. The rising tide of suicides among young people, the increasing incidence of domestic violence and abuse, the collapse of community life, and the increasing sense of alienation and loneliness are all symptoms of a society that is facing tremendous stress because of the high speed of change. This is not to deny that change itself produces many benefits in society such as healthy innovations in social activities. Here, I am focusing on the speed of change rather than change itself.

An excessive dose of change can lead to the loss of roots that sustain communities. Today, this is happening in many places. The displacement of people, the loss of communal stories, the dismantling of traditional forms of pastoral care are all valid concerns in this light. In today's globalized world, the local is threatened by the global. If the fuel for the globalizing machine is efficiency, profit, and competition, then it spells disaster for a world that has been nurtured by more human concerns developed locally in many parts of the world. The dismantling of villages to give way to urban sprawls has also resulted in the loss of many useful and healthy social interactions that have traditionally formed an essential part of pastoral care. Colin Mackerras, Richard Maidment and David Schak have argued that in the Asia Pacific region, tradition and modernization exist side by side and do influence each other. However, in this interaction, modernization seems to have the greater impact, and they predict that in time to come many traditional lifestyles will give way to the modern.[25] The evidence all around seems to support their argument.

What can we do, then, as pastoral care givers? I think we have to think in terms of community, and help communities cope with the negative aspects of rapid change. Part of the solution would be to help communities remember their stories and identity. Let me illustrate with an example. The Iban are an indigenous people in East Malaysia. Traditionally they have lived in communal long houses and their lives and economies have been organized in terms of these long houses. Because of the rapid urbanization taking place, young Iban people are moving out to the towns and cities. The long houses, in time to come, may disappear. Meanwhile in the towns, the young Iban suffer disorientation, miss the traditional forms of help, and often fall into personal problems. Attempts are being made by the church to build communal housing for these Iban in the towns. In a sense, this is like shifting the long houses to the towns, so that the social and communal disruption among the Iban is minimized. The Christian Iban leadership is also re-examining Iban customs and rituals to recover some of the pastoral aspects of these practices so that the community can be helped to cope with modern pressures.[26]

All this is to say that for the future, we may have to rethink our approaches in pastoral care and counseling. The community itself may need to be seen as the client or patient. Theory-building activities must take place and we will have to help communities in the way we have been helping individuals and families. We may have to think of how communities experience stress, anxiety, grief, loss, identity crisis, and depression, and of how they develop, and suffer dysfunction. We will have to study the secret of resilient communities, communal myths, scripts, coping styles and so on. We will also have to deal with issues of justice and compassion for these are important markers of the health and well being of a community. The field of counseling has had a long relationship with psychology. It is now important to widen the relationship with significant new partners such as sociology, anthropology, economics, politics, education, and health care, so that the care of communities, especially to help them cope with rapid change, can be achieved.

HELPING COMMUNITIES
TO EXPERIENCE RECONCILIATION

Another implication for the pastoral care of communities in Asia, besides helping them to cope with change, has to do with the many fractures that exist in Asian contexts. The ongoing tensions between China and Taiwan, Japan and China, North and South Korea, India and Pakistan, are a few examples. Moreover there are many tensions between ethnic and other groups in many places; the Sinhalese and Tamils in Sri Lanka, Tibetans and Han Chinese, Burmese and Karen, Chinese and Malay Indonesians, and so on. Needless to say, the gender divide[27] and inequalities and oppression, and the divide between the haves and the have nots[28] are other important areas where justice and reconciliation are required at the larger community levels.

Many of these divisions have resulted in violence over the years, gathering for all concerned painful memories. Some of these wounds are very difficult to heal. The task of pastoral care is to help bring healing and to stop vicious cycles of violence and revenge. This calls for true reconciliation.

Such reconciliation is not easily achieved for it calls for taking responsibility, repentance, the asking of forgiveness, and the forgiving of others. Pastoral care would include at least two levels. The first level would be in the area of mediation. We are already seeing conflict mediation ministries emerging in several Asian cities, helping people at the level of small groups and families. I suspect that this will become more common in the days to come. In some places we are seeing the emergence of family courts which attempt to bring healing and reconciliation in families while avoiding the unhelpful process often encountered in the regular courts.

While providing mediation at the domestic level is one thing, dealing with fierce hostilities existing between ethnic groups is quite another. At the present moment, I do not know of any real impact made in this area by our field of pastoral care and counseling. I know for instance that several years ago an Anglican archbishop acted as a mediator between the Myanmar government and the Karen fighters. However, we have very little experience and expertise in this area. This calls for special pastoral, negotiation and mediation skills. These skills would not be entirely new to us for we do practice similar skills in pastoral care and counseling as practiced presently. However, it is a whole new ballgame in many ways, and requires a new paradigm of seeing pastoral care as that which is provided also to whole communities.

While conflict mediation is one aspect of this ministry of pastoral care helping communities to experience reconciliation, at another level, reconciliation calls for more than skills. There is a spirituality involved when we talk about reconciliation. It is the ability to forgive even as justice is sought. In his book *No Future Without Forgiveness,* Archbishop Desmond Tutu recounts his experience in South Africa which saw so many years of apartheid.[29] Memories were filled with the pain, injustices, beatings, killings, discrimination, and sufferings of the black South African communities. When apartheid was removed as a socio-political structure in the country and a new day was born under the leadership of Nelson Mandela, there were suggestions to bring the cruel perpetrators of apartheid to trial and subsequent just punishment. Others felt that there should be general amnesty. The country found another way by forming the Truth and Reconciliation Council, headed by Tutu. The idea behind this Council was to encourage guilty parties to come forward to tell the truth. Those who do so would be pardoned and granted amnesty. In this model, emphasis is paid both to truth as well as forgiveness.

This form of spirituality is well expressed in the Christian theology of the cross. In his epistle to the Ephesians the apostle Paul writes, "For he himself is our peace, who has made the two one and has destroyed the barrier, the dividing wall of hostility, by abolishing in his flesh the law with its commandments and regulations. His purpose was to create in himself one new man out of the two, thus making peace, and in this one body to reconcile both of them to God through the cross" (Eph. 2:14-16). Here Paul refers to the enmity between the Jews and Gentiles and how this is resolved by finding a transcending reality and identity and relationship that enables them to be reconciled in Christ. This spirituality of finding larger transcending identities that can bring healing by bringing people together in peace is something that is central to a pastoral care approach to communities that are divided or estranged from other communities.[30]

IN CLOSING

In closing I want to summarize what we have seen together. We have noted that while the endemic pastoral care issues in the Asia Pacific contexts such as poverty and culture remain, at the beginning of the 21st century these problems are further exacerbated by rapid, dizzying and disorienting change. These changes have been brought by the strong winds of globalization against which individuals, families, and local communities feel helpless. An increasingly global economy and culture threaten local economies and cultures that have existed over long periods of time. In some cases, this process may be seen as good, such as when knowledge becomes more readily available and empowers the ordinary man and woman. In other cases, we see the negative results such as the breakdown of traditional modes of pastoral care and social cohesion, and the increasing stress of life.

As we face these global trends related to the economy, culture and other realities of life, we cannot but consider pastoral care and counseling done not only at the level of the individual, but also at the level of the community, for what is happening in societies has profound (and often disturbing) effects on individuals and families. Pastoral care and counseling must therefore be seen as going beyond the counseling room to the communal spaces and structures. Pastoral counseling in community can focus on several issues. We looked at two of these: helping communities to cope with rapid and disorienting change, and enabling them to experience reconciliation, as they suffer from deep fractures, painful memories, and deep animosities. This calls for some radical changes in our usual approaches to pastoral care and counseling, our paradigms, and our partners in inter-disciplinary dialogue and collaboration.

NOTES

1. Abdul Halim Othman and Amir Awang (Eds.), *Counseling in the Asia-Pacific Region* (Westwood, Connecticut; London: Greenwood Press, 1993).
2. Ibid., p. 134.
3. Randolph S. David, "Asian Societies in the Age of Globalization," in *Faith and Life in Contemporary Asian Realities* (Hong Kong: Christian Conference of Asia, 2000).
4. See Nicholas Kristof's observation in Nicholas D. Kristof and Sheryl Wu Dunn, *Thunder from the East: A Portrait of A Rising Asia* (New York: Alfred A. Knopf, 2000), ch. 1 (Search for Sorcerers in Indonesia) where he describes the witch-hunt and violence (including beheading) that occurred in various parts of Indonesia following the economic crisis that began in 1997.
5. Marshall McLuhan and Quentin Fiore, *The Medium is the Message* (New York: Random House, 1967), and Marshall McLuhan and Bruce R. Powers, *The Global Village: Transformation in World Life and Media in the 21st Century* (New York: Oxford University Press, 1989).

6. Though Carl Jung did speak about the collective unconscious.

7. Peter Berger, *Invitation to Sociology* (Harmondsworth: Penguin, 1966).

8. See, e.g., Michael Rustin, *The Good Society and the Inner World: Psychoanalysis, Politics, and Culture* (London, New York: Verso, 1991).

9. Ernest Becker, *Escape from Evil* (New York: Free Press, 1975), pp. 28-29; *The Denial of Death* (New York: Free Press, 1973).

10. Erich Fromm, *Psychoanalysis and Religion* (London: Victor Gollancz Ltd., 1951); *The Sane Society* (New York: Holt, Rinehart and Winston, 1955).

11. Reinhold Niebuhr, *Moral Man and Immoral Society: A Study in Ethics and Politics* (New York, London: C. Scribner's Sons, 1932).

12. Donald G. McCloud, *Southeast Asia: Tradition and Modernity in the Contemporary World* (Boulder, Colorado: Westview Press, 1995), pp. 270ff. This idea of society above self has been criticised by several western writers. Greg Sheridan, *Asian Values, Western Dreams: Understanding the New Asia* (St. Leonards, NSW, Australia: Allen and Unwin, 1993) has argued, on the other hand, that there is much misunderstanding in this case because of the wide cultural divide.

13. Jon S. T. Quah (Ed.), *In Search of Singapore's National Values* (Singapore: Times Academic Press, 1990), pg. 1. After considering the feedback from various organisations and individuals, the government came up with a final version of the "Shared Values" which were adopted on 15 January 1993: nation before community and society above self, family as the basic unit of society, community support and respect for the individual, consensus, not conflict, and racial and religious harmony.

14. See P. W. Preston, *Pacific Asia in the Global System: An Introduction* (Oxford: Blackwell, 1998), p. 218, where he observes that Asia may be "lucky to have escaped the trials of Western individualism or unfortunate to be mired in an anti-individualist traditional culture."

15. Robert Solomon, "The Cult, The Crowd, and the Community: Tensions in Unity and Diversity in Asian Contexts," *Trinity Theological Journal* (Singapore: TTC), vol. 9 (2000), pp. 79-96.

16. See Rodney Bruce Hall, "Collective Identity and Epochal Change in the International System," in Yoshinobu Yamamoto, *Globalism, Regionalism and Nationalism: Asia in Search of Its Role in the 21st Century* (Oxford: Blackwell, 1999).

17. Ruth Benedict, *Patterns of Culture* (New York: Mentor/New American Library, 1934). See also Robert A. Levine, *Culture Behavior and Personality* (London: Hutchinson and Co. Ltd., 1973).

18. Robert Bellah et al., *Habits of the Heart: Individualism and Commitment in American Life* (New York: Harper and Row, 1986); and *The Good Society* (New York: Knopf, 1991).

19. Kalyani Mehta, *The Dynamics of the Very Old in Singapore*, PhD Thesis, National University of Singapore, 1995.

20. Kenichi Ohmae, *The End of the Nation State: The Rise of Regional Economies* (New York: Free Press, 1995), pp. 29-30.

21. Wendy Griswold, *Cultures and Societies in a Changing World* (London: Thousand Oaks; New Delhi: Pine Forge Press, 1994), pp. 148ff.

22. See Tetsunao Yamamori, Bryant L. Myers, and David Conner (Eds.), *Serving With the Poor in Asia: Cases in Holistic Ministry* (Monrovia, California: MARC, 1995), an interesting collection of examples in this direction.

23. See Edwin Friedman, *Generation to Generation: Family Process in Church and Synagogue* (New York, London: Guilford Press, 1985), where he builds on a model of the congregation as a family.

24. James Burke and Robert Ornstein, *The Axemaker's Gift: Technology's Capture and Control of our Minds and Culture* (New York: Jeremy P. Tarcher/Putnam, 1997), p. xii.

25. Colin Mackerras, Richard Maidment and David Schak, "Diversity and Convergence in Asia-Pacific Society and Culture," in Richard Maidment and Colin Mackerras (eds.), *Culture and Society in the Asia-Pacific* (London, New York: Routledge, 1998), pp. 11-12.

26. Stewart Damat Mambang, *A Case Study on the Use of Ritual in Pastoral Ministry in the Iban Context,* MTh Thesis, Trinity Theological College, Singapore, 1998.

27. For an interesting Asian view different from the western feminist perspectives, see Louise Edwards and Mina Roces (Eds.), *Women in Asia: Tradition, Modernity and Globalization* (St. Leonards, NSW, Australia: Allen and Unwin, 2000).

28. See Jonathan Rigg, *Southeast Asia: The Human Landscape of Modernization and Development* (London, New York: Routledge, 1997), pp. 69-151 where he shows how the marginalised cope in the midst of modernization and development.

29. Desmond Tutu, *No Future Without Forgiveness* (New York: Doubleday, 1999).

30. See Tadashi Yamamoto (Ed.), *Emerging Civil Society in the Asia Pacific Community* (Singapore: Institute of Southeast Asian Studies; Tokyo: Japan Center for International Exchange, 1995) for a secular approach to seeking such transcendence through the creation of civil societies.

Pastoral Counseling in Chinese Cultural Contexts: Philosophical, Historical, Sociological, Spiritual and Psychological Considerations

Simon Yiu Chuen Lee, DMin

SUMMARY. This paper is an introduction to a Chinese perspective on pastoral counseling and how pastoral counseling is different and distinctive when practiced and applied in a Chinese Christian community. "Chinese" culture is presented from philosophical, historical, sociological and psychological perspectives and refers in this text specifically to Chinese communities in Hong Kong and Canada. The basic intention of this paper is to note how these various cultural considerations inform us in terms of how pastoral counseling can be done within Chinese Christian communities. *[Article copies available for a fee from The Haworth Document Delivery Service: 1-800-HAWORTH. E-mail address: <getinfo@haworthpressinc.com> Website: <http://www.HaworthPress.com> © 2002 by The Haworth Press, Inc. All rights reserved.]*

KEYWORDS. Pastoral counseling, cross cultural, Chinese

INTRODUCTION

This paper is an introduction to a Chinese perspective on pastoral counseling. Our purpose is to explore how pastoral counseling is differ-

[Haworth co-indexing entry note]: "Pastoral Counseling in Chinese Cultural Contexts: Philosophical, Historical, Sociological, Spiritual and Psychological Considerations." Lee, Simon Yiu Chuen. Co-published simultaneously in *American Journal of Pastoral Counseling* (The Haworth Pastoral Press, an imprint of The Haworth Press, Inc.) Vol. 5, No. (1/2), 2002, pp. 119-149; and: *International Perspectives on Pastoral Counseling* (ed: James Reaves Farris) The Haworth Pastoral Press, an imprint of The Haworth Press, Inc., 2002, pp. 119-149. Single or multiple copies of this article are available for a fee from The Haworth Document Delivery Service [1-800-HAWORTH, 9:00 a.m. - 5:00 p.m. (EST). E-mail address: getinfo@haworthpressinc.com].

ent and distinctive when practiced and applied in a Chinese Christian community. To do so we need to first understand what "Chinese" culture means from philosophical, historical, sociological and psychological perspectives. Throughout the paper, we will note how these various cultural considerations inform us in the way our pastoral counseling should be done within the Chinese Christian community.

Depending on one's knowledge of and encounters with Chinese people, one's response to the mention of the word "Chinese" would differ from another's. While some may think of the 1.3 billion people populating Mainland China, others may have images of their local Chinatown or Chinese restaurant. Still others may associate the word with residents of Taiwan, Hong Kong, or with people of Chinese descent living in other parts of the world. Each of these impressions, however accurate or informed, presents a different picture of who the Chinese people are and demonstrates on the whole that they are far from a homogenous ethnic group.

Beyond individual notions, a brief look at factual information about Mainland China will further convince one of the many faces of the Chinese people. While the majority of the population is made up of Han Chinese, there are also 55 official minorities in China. Spoken amongst the Han and the minorities are 205 living languages, meaning that Chinese from different areas of the country may not be able to have a comprehensive conversation. The written form of Chinese language has also evolved so that on the Mainland, simplified characters are used whereas Taiwan and Hong Kong continue to use traditional characters.

The diversity extends beyond those places with the most Chinese to international locations where Chinese have migrated. Singapore, Malaysia, North and South America, Europe, Australia and so on, are all home to many generations of Chinese. Furthermore, Chinese culture is unique in each locality as the Chinese vary in their adherence to the "traditional" ways of their ethnic background and in the influence of the local culture. From experience, the author has found that some Chinese cultural customs are better observed in parts of Malaysia than in Hong Kong as immigrants make the effort to maintain their ethnic identity in the foreign environment. In contrast, the offspring of Chinese immigrants and the generations thereafter may know very little about their cultural heritage and identify almost solely with their country of birth and residence.

As the task of comprehensively defining what "Chinese" means and looks like in every context is nearly impossible, we shall focus on Chinese communities in Hong Kong and Canada. The Hong Kong Chinese community represents what is considered more typically traditional Chinese whereas the Canadian Chinese community represents a deviation from this. Hopefully, the contrasts between these two Chinese groups will help to define what is the essence of being "Chinese." Then, based on this understanding, we will continue to look at how pastoral counseling can be conducted in a more sensitive and relevant manner.

The choice of Hong Kong and Canada is first of all due to the author's familiarity with these two places, having lived and worked there for long periods of time. But a more important reason is that counseling in general and pastoral counseling in particular are more developed in these two places. While counseling itself is a relatively young science in China, and pastoral counseling, as we know it in the West, is still quite foreign to the Christian Church in China, there are at present at least four seminaries in Hong Kong that offer pastoral counseling as a major in their graduate programs and the author is presently serving as a professor in one of them. The author is involved also in developing a Doctor of Ministry program in Pastoral Counseling and Family Ministries jointly between the Alliance Bible Seminary and Tyndale Theological Seminary in Ontario, Canada, for those serving in the Chinese churches in North America.

Therefore, throughout this paper, we will explore how, given the uniqueness of the cultural context of the Chinese Christian community, especially in Hong Kong and in Canada, pastoral counseling takes on a distinctive shape. As a seminary professor and church pastor in the Chinese church community, as well as a professional counselor in Hong Kong, the author is most interested in working towards a counseling model that is "Chinese," that is, takes seriously the Chinese cultural context, but also that is "pastoral," that is, applicable and effective in the Chinese Christian community. This paper could be considered as a primer towards that goal. We will first briefly review a philosophical perspective of the Chinese culture.

PHILOSOPHICAL PERSPECTIVE
OF CHINESE CULTURE AND COUNSELING

Most Chinese today are not familiar with Chinese philosophy academically as fewer and fewer people have formal studies in the Chinese classics. However because traditional Chinese culture is passed on from generation to generation, through family practice and oral tradition, and through social customs and cultural norms, it is deeply embedded in their minds, yielding the typical Chinese mindset. It is possible that many Chinese themselves are unaware of the influence these cultural views have on them. Their thinking, emotions and actions may be unconsciously governed by certain traditional Chinese cultural ways, or they may be reacting to these traditions. Counselors that deal with Chinese clients must understand these cultural factors in order to counsel sensitively and effectively. Within the church, this type of cultural mindset also influences the way the members behave and relate to one another. Sometimes what is presented as "biblical" ways may in fact be "Chinese" ways of doing things, or simply traditions they have been accepted from the past. Whether it is pastoral care or counseling, it is necessary to distinguish between what is "Christian" and what is simply "cultural." Because Chinese culture is by and large humanistic in nature, there are some similarities in ethical standards and moral behavior, an obvious example being the Chinese notion of filial piety and the Christian teaching of honoring one's parents. However the philosophical or theological basis may be very different. A pastoral counselor must differentiate between what is "Christian" and "cultural" also because of their mutual influences, and therefore he or she may be able to use some of the cultural similarities as bridges to pastoral counsels.

In Chinese culture, the self can attain its completeness only through integration with others and the surrounding context, especially the family context (Gao & Ting-Toomey, 1998). When we talk about counseling with respect to personal and interpersonal needs in the Chinese context, to the Chinese mind we are in fact referring to giving counsel as to what is appropriate behaviors in the areas of personal conduct and interpersonal relationships. The former refers to what it means to be human, and how personal psychological health and well-being can be achieved. The latter refers to what it means to be human in the context of society, and how social harmony and prosperity can be maintained. We shall examine these briefly.

In terms of personal psychological health, Confucius (551-497 B.C.) often referred to his model of an ideal man or perfect gentleman. For example, Confucius taught, "The ideal man or gentleman is satisfied and composed, while the mediocre man is full of distress" (*Analects,* Book VII, Chapter XXXVI). In other words, a psychologically healthy person is one who is fulfilled and emotionally balanced. On the other hand, a psychologically unhealthy person is one who is constantly worried and full of anxieties. Thus for traditional Chinese, a sign of maturity is the ability to appear calm, cool and collected, and being able to contain one's emotions. A cultured person is one who is able to hide both his joy and anger. This explains the "reserved" character that many Chinese have, and in counseling this reserved nature should not be misinterpreted as the person lacking in feelings or emotions. Furthermore, to have to admit that one is anxious and is unable to handle a situation is a tremendous blow to one's self-image. At the risk of being overly simplistic, this illustrates how this type of philosophy of equating maturity with being reserved with one's feeling and emotions can be the root cause of many mood disorders such as anxiety, stress and depression among many Chinese who lack the ability to express their feelings, particularly anger and pain. Fundamental to cognitive-behavioral therapy that can be used in pastoral counseling is the correcting of such faulty thinking that can paralyze a person. The goal of the pastoral counselor should be the building of healthy self-concept based on a biblical understanding of the doctrine of man.

In regards to interpersonal relationships, Confucian philosophies again dominate the cultural values of Chinese down through the centuries. We shall focus on two basic concepts, *jen* (humanity), and *li* (ritual). *Jen* is a Confucian concept that has been variously translated as benevolence, perfect virtue, goodness, and love. It is the basis of all goodness. It is interesting to note that etymologically, the Chinese character for *jen* is made up of the word for man, and the word for two (signifying a community), meaning "man in society." This reflects the thinking that a person finds his identity in society–a corporate identity. A virtuous man is one who lives in harmony with others. Confucius said: "Do not do unto others what you would not like others to do unto you" (*Analects,* Book XII, Chapter II). One can readily see how this is similar to the "golden rule" in Christian love. This Confucian teaching has become a pillar in the philosophical basis for personal and corporate conducts for the Chinese. While this thinking that is akin to the Christian concept of brotherly love is highly desirable for the individual, this type of mentality has also developed into a corporate personality in Chinese society. Because collectivism, consideration for others, is given such high priority, many Chinese must lose their personal identity to the corporate identity that they put on. Pedersen (1994) points out that "individual counseling has even been described as destructive of collectivistic societies in promoting the individualistic benefits of individuals at the expense of the social fabric" (p. 47). Duan (2000), after comparing Western cultural roots for counseling with the cultural context of China and reviewing the psychological implications of individualism and collectivism, concludes that effective counseling in China needs to accommodate both individualistic and collectivistic values.

Pastoral counseling must help each person restore a unique identity as an image-bearer of God, while at the same time empower one to live authentically and harmoniously within one's community. This is possible because of our Trinitarian theology that emphasizes harmonious relationship as well as our redeemed and restored personal identity in Christ. This is perhaps also a good corrective for the overly individualistic thinking that we find in the West. Psychological counseling started at the beginning of the 20th century in the West with a psychodynamic and intrapsychic approach, now regarded as the first force of psychotherapy. It viewed psychological problems from the perspective of the internal psychological dynamics within a person. The second force, the cognitive-behavioral approach, as well as the third force, the existential-humanistic approach, are both focused on the individual as well. It is only in the final quarter of the last century that counseling has turned to a family focus in the form of family therapy. It appears to the author that a Christian perspective of the individual and the family brings a balanced approach to family counseling. Pastoral counseling that emphasizes the importance of the family is well suited to the Chinese cultural context. In other words, the strong emphasis on the family in Chinese culture and Chinese pastoral counseling brings another important corrective for western-styled counseling which has in the past focused on the individual exclusively.

This leads to the second important concept, *li,* which means ritual, rules of propriety and good form, etc. *Li* is the code of propriety in the five dyadic relationships: between father and son, there should be affection; between ruler and minister, there should be righteousness; between husband and wife, there should be attention to their separate functions; between old and young, there should be a proper order; and between friends, there should be faithfulness (*The Works of Mencius,* Book III, Part I, Chapter VIII).

The relationship of the self to others is not merely an other-directed relational orientation, but a cultural perspective that Ho (1991) describes as "methodological relationalism" which implies reciprocity, interdependence and interrelatedness between individuals. This is the basis of all interpersonal relationships in a nutshell for the traditional Chinese society. From this we see the root of filial piety, the deference of authority, the proper place and man and woman in society, the respect for elders, and the loyalty among friends. Herein lie both the strength and weakness of human relationships within traditional Chinese community. The obvious strength is the intended result of an ordered and structured society. Everyone knows where he or she belongs and how they should behave.

The weakness lies in the difficulty in developing deep and genuine relationships. Authoritarianism in parenting occurs quite "naturally." Positional power in a patriarchal society is easily misused or abused. Chauvinism and spousal abuse can develop routinely. Many formal and superficial relationships (social rituals) exist. In the terms of social exchange theory, favors exchanged in various ways, such as giving, buying or owing favors, govern the dynamics of human interactions in complex overlapping and interlocking relationships. To be right involves gaining the proper "favor" as well as being "reasonable." Often times, "favors" become more important than "reason." Understanding these complex rituals is critical to the counseling process when dealing with Chinese. The "respect" in the West for the individual and its ego-centric approach in counseling must be balanced with the premium placed in Chinese culture on social protocols and its community-based perspectives in counseling. These social rituals must be respected and accepted as part of a cultural norm, and pastoral care and counseling should have as its goal to help Chinese people to go beyond the rituals and develop genuine interpersonal relationships based on mutual respect and Christ-centeredness. Teaching from the Proverbs and other teachings in the Bible shed further light on godly conduct and interpersonal relationship and should be taught as the underlying principles in family and social relationships.

Case Illustration Number 1

Ming Wah was a young teenager on probation for shoplifting and I was asked by the court to counsel the boy. This was because, as his pastor, I was acting as his character reference when he appeared before the judge, and the boy was not charged provided I agreed to provide counseling for him. I discovered very quickly in the first session that Ming Wah was unhappy at home, and his shoplifting incident was committed for amusement and to see whether he could get away with it. Ming Wah came from a middle class family and his father was always busy. I decided that it would be beneficial to bring his parents in for the second session.

The parents agreed reluctantly to come but throughout the session appeared calm and agreeable. Ming Wah however was unusually quiet and restless. Before the end of the second session I realized that the parents thought all along that counseling was just for the boy who was delinquent. The father thought his only role was to enforce the rules, especially now that the boy was caught red-handed. That he might have contributed to the kid's behavioral problem never entered his mind. The mother was more understanding, but stood on the husband's side because she did not want to upset him. She agreed with her husband that the boy was ungrateful for what the parents were trying to do for him. The session ended only with the agreement to meet again.

Subsequently I met with the boy separately several times and found out what his main grievances were. They were practical things like letting him have his own phone in his room and letting him stay out later at night. In essence, he was trying to find his own identity and wanted his parents to treat him as an adult. I then met with the parents who thought the boy was not responsible enough to have those things. I played the role of a mediator trying to negotiate a deal with the parents for promise of good behavior. In the end I succeeded and had a final session together to seal a verbal contract.

Lessons to be learned: The parents were traditional Chinese who simply demanded obedience from the child, while the child was trying to assert himself in the process of forming his own identity. Individual counseling was combined with family counseling. The parents felt pressured when they were confronted with having to face parenting responsibility. A better way was the "shuttle diplomacy" technique that was used subsequently. In fact, the parents eventually came to church because they felt respected in the end and were grateful for what I had done for the boy in helping him change his behavior.

CHINESE CULTURAL PERSPECTIVE AND COUNSELING

In general, Ho (1992) has been able to identify seven common characteristics of Asian culture. They include,

1. *Filial piety.* Often children are expected to sacrifice their own personal desires and ambitions to comply with family wishes.
2. *Shame,* used as a method of reinforcing expectations and proper behavior.
3. *Self-control.* In Chinese, *yin-nor,* is to show stoicism, patience, uncomplaining attitude and tolerance.
4. *Assumption of a middle position,* reinforcing the social norm, looking for consensus, in order to foster an individual's sense of belonging and togetherness.

5. *Awareness of social milieu,* so as to maintain social solidarity.
6. *Fatalism,* believing that one is powerless over one's own destiny.
7. *Inconspicuousness,* based on the fear of attracting attention.

The above Asian cultural characteristics apply to Chinese culture in general. The more traditional a Chinese family is, the more the above points apply. These are values passed on from generation to generation, especially through the early socialization process. Sue and Sue (1991) also identified similar Chinese cultural values among Chinese Americans, and suggest the need for assertiveness training. Pastoral counselors do well to remember these general cultural characteristics especially when dealing with people from a strong Chinese background. Let us now take a closer look at a traditional Chinese family.

In a traditional Chinese family, age, sex and generational status are very important because they determine the role behavior of each member (Sue & Sue, 1999). The father, the patriarchal head of the family, has unquestionable authority over the rest of the family. The son's first allegiance is to his family of origin. Females are subservient to the males, and committed to the home. Wives are to be obedient to their husbands as well as their mother-in-laws, and expected to bear children, especially sons. Today this type of pattern is still true, but to a much lesser degree due to the influence of the West. However, an understanding of this traditional family structure is critical for the counselor to enable him or her to uncover the hidden family dynamics. Often family cohesiveness and conformity may create problems in terms of adaptability and independence for the individual family members.

From the above discussion, we can see that filial piety is centrally related to many psychological conflicts within the Chinese family, and this has been recently studied in the counseling context (Kwan, 2000). Kwan concludes that counselors need to be sensitive to the persistent influence of filial piety on Chinese people's self-construal and intergeneration relationships (p. 34). He suggests the need to identify filial conflicts, articulate conflictual emotions, manage guilt feelings, and facilitate interpersonal and intrapersonal compromises (pp. 34-38). Pastoral counseling can bring effective healing in these areas by providing sound biblical principles of parent-child relationship and facilitate the process of offering and receiving forgiveness where there have been hurts, and in restoring wholesome family relationships.

Apart from the fact that roles and role behaviors are carefully and rigidly defined, personal and family problems are also to be dealt with subtly and indirectly rather than openly. Restraint of possibly disruptive emotions and behaviors are emphasized as virtues in the development of the Chinese character. Co-dependent relationships and conformity (compliance) to family norms are often prolonged within the family because of the expectation on the family member to submerge one's aggressive tendencies, including the inclinations to act independently. Pastoral counselors must be sensitive to these realities and be patient when trying to bring changes to these situations.

The family and its reputation must come first ahead of personal rights. The behavior of each individual member of a family will reflect favorable or unfavorably on the entire family, bringing credit or shame and disgrace ("losing face"). Thus there is a well-known saying among Chinese that says family shames must never be exposed to outsiders. This explains why problems are handled as much as possible within the family, and public admission of these problems is frowned upon. Therefore, counselors must assure their clients of their adherence to the standards of confidentiality and privacy. This, however, becomes an issue in the case of pastoral counseling, especially within the Chinese Christian community, when the principle of confidentiality conflicts with the need for church discipline. Therefore it is best that pastoral counseling and church discipline are kept separate, and when the need for church discipline arises, that the goal is still for reconciliation and restoration, and the process done very sensitively. In most cases, the senior pastor and some key leaders can adequately handle church discipline. There should be a balance between openness and clarity in public teaching and privacy and sensitivity in personal counseling.

Guilt and shame are also inculcated to enforce conformity to family norms. Parents constantly appeal to children's obligations to the family. Sue rightly points out that when Chinese children attempt to act independently, they are told that they are selfish and inconsiderate and not showing gratitude for all their parents have done for them (Sue & Sue, 1999). This pattern of motivation by inflicting guilt obviously creates many conflicts between the parents of an older generation and their children brought up in the North American society where they are encouraged to think independently and express their feelings freely. Chinese parents believe it is within their rights to expect certain things from their children and cannot understand or accept any resistance from them. Children may comply with their parents' wishes but yet remain defiant and thus harbor anger and resentment in their hearts. Francis Hsu, a past president of the American Anthropological Association, in the book, *The Mental Health of Asian Americans,* points out that for many Asian Americans, compared to other Americans, social restraints are often internalized according to family values, therefore, arousing feelings of guilt or shame can act as powerful means of social control (Sue & Morishima, 1982, p. 71). However often what is gained in terms of social control is lost in terms of individual psychological well-being. The pastoral counselor must be able to differentiate between true earned guilt and false unearned guilt. The pastoral counselor must help family members involved in conflicts to learn to speak the truth in love and bring about Christian reconciliation and forgiveness.

The counselor must also help individuals to develop personalities of their own as well as maintain harmonious family relationships. Psychological studies have shown that Asian Americans possess a more practical and applied approach to life and problems than their Caucasian counterparts. Such studies indicate that the typical Chinese character is: less autonomous, more dependent, conforming, submissive to authority, inhibited, less impulsive, law abiding, less assertive and more reserved. There is clear submergence of individuality to the welfare of the family (Sue & Sue, 1999). Part of the task of pastoral counseling is to help a person develop mature Christian character within the Christian community. Pastoral counseling should be tied to the ministry of spiritual formation. Because of the nature of Chinese culture this combination is easily accepted because pastoral counseling will be viewed as a growth process rather than simply problem solving.

Case Illustration Number 2

Mr. and Mrs. Lee asked for help from me when their eighteen-year-old daughter, Sandy, decided to stay with a man twice her age whom she had come to know in her summer job in a town outside Toronto. They were filled with bewilderment, shame and guilt for what had happened and wondered where they had failed as parents.

Their daughter has been the model child in the family, and she did well in school and attended our Chinese church with her parents regularly. Mr. and Mrs. Lee were very strict with her and did not allow her to do many things, but Sandy appeared always to be content with what she had and never turned against her parents. Therefore, the parents were totally taken aback when Sandy shocked them with her decision. What happened was that this man whom she had met taught her many things and allowed her to do all the exciting things that she had never had the chance to do. She was deeply hooked. She told her parents that she loved them, but that she had never been happier in her life staying with this man. Obviously the parents were devastated.

My counseling with the parents had two goals: the first was to help the parents sort out the guilt and shame that they were experiencing, and the second was to help the parents remain hopeful and always ready to accept the daughter when she wants to return. The parents came to understand the cultural factors that caused their daughter's "sudden" change of behavior, and realized that it was really not their "fault." Eventually the daughter came back having learned her lesson and became wiser as a result.

Lessons to be learned: Guilt and shame can either be earned or unearned. People suffering from guilt and shame must be given full and unconditional acceptance and empathy, before being confronted. This case is also a good example of how cultural factors can influence our behaviors.

SOCIOLOGICAL PERSPECTIVE
OF CHINESE CULTURE AND COUNSELING

Closely related to cultural perspectives are sociological factors in the Chinese context. As mentioned in the introduction, Chinese culture (or "Chineseness") takes on a different character depending on the social milieu in which it is being cultivated. The historical and social backgrounds of a place influence the nature of Chinese culture. We shall examine two typical "Chinese" cultural contexts, one that is closer to its native soil, Hong Kong, and the other, transplanted in a foreign land, Canada. If Chinese culture were to be put on a continuum between Eastern and Western characteristics, then Hong Kong Chinese culture will be closer to the Eastern end of the continuum and Canadian Chinese culture will be around the center but tilting towards the Western end. Sensitivity to how much a Chinese person is affected by his or her culture will be critical to effectiveness in counseling. Furthermore to counsel Chinese immigrants in Canada and the rest of North America, there is the added challenge for the counselor to deal with problems that result from the client being uprooted from their native soil. The children of these Chinese immigrants who are more acculturated yet still under the authority of their more traditional parents represent a further dimension of cultural identity. We shall examine the historical backgrounds that lead to the differences in the situation in the East as well as the West.

THE SPECIAL SOCIO-HISTORICAL BACKGROUND
OF HONG KONG AND COUNSELING

The former British colony of Hong Kong is actually quite different from Mainland China. China's cultural heritage is over 4,000 years old. The present People's Republic of China was established in 1949 and has been under Communist rule since then. Meanwhile the Nationalist Chinese from the Mainland also set up their own (Nationalist) Republic in Taiwan. Since the death of Chairman Mao in 1976, and the subsequent reopening of Mainland China, China has gone through many changes, including rapid economic and social changes. Politically, China re-gained sovereignty over Hong Kong in July, 1997 and Macao in December, 1999, and insisting on Taiwan's unification with China under a one-China policy. Chinese who have lived in Hong Kong, Macao or Taiwan in the last 50 years have to come to terms with these new political realities and many have chosen to migrate to the West.

Going back further historically, the Island of Hong Kong was seized from the Chinese by England in 1841 after the Opium War, and in 1898 further concessions were made when Hong Kong was ceded to the British by the Chinese imperial government for 99 years. The expanded area included Hong Kong and the islands nearby, Kowloon, and the New Territories. After the Sino-Japanese war and after the People's Republic of China was established in 1949, many Chinese, especially from Guangzhou (Canton), but also from Shanghai, moved and settled in Hong Kong. This explains why the Chinese dialect spoken in Hong Kong is Cantonese, even though the formal spoken language in China is Putonghua (Mandarin). Many of these people established flourishing businesses and as a result of the economic boom, new prosperity was brought to Hong Kong, making it a major financial center in Asia. Because of the British colonial rule and the exposure to the West, Chinese in Hong Kong have adopted a lifestyle that had a modern western flavor, which inevitably alters the nature of their Chinese culture. To counsel Chinese from Hong Kong we must be aware of their historical roots and its western influence. This also explains why counseling in general and pastoral counseling in particular, being patterned after the West, are better accepted in Hong Kong than in Mainland China.

The population of Hong Kong has been growing rapidly, and the latest census in 2001 shows that the population has reached 7 million. As the total area of Hong Kong, including land reclaimed from the sea, is only 422 square miles, Hong Kong is one of the most densely populated cities in the world. Because of the high cost of land, living expenses are very high. Most families live in small high-rise apartments of less than 500 square feet. So even though the average household earning is very high compared to other Asian countries, a large portion of that goes into the cost of housing. Because of these reasons and the rapid pace of life in Hong Kong, people in Hong Kong are living under constant pressure. Not only are adults under tremendous pressure because they are busy working from 9 to 9 each day, children too experience much stress because of an education system that puts a great premium on academics and emphasizes rote-memory. Self-destructive and even suicidal behaviors are common not only in the adult population, but also in the youth sector due to the constant daily pressure they experience. Families and marriages become strained resulting in poor family relationships and many unhappy and broken marriages. Also because of the need for many husbands to constantly travel north into China on business, additional strains are put on the marriages, and men often become involved in extra-marital affairs or have mistresses in China. One can see that there are many needs for care and counseling among these people. Pastoral counselors should be sensitive to the heavy pressure people in Hong Kong are experiencing. Pastoral care includes providing spiritual and psychological resources to ease the tension from their daily lives. Pastors should be involved in giving support and helping people who must travel away from their spouses in order to guard against sexual and other temptations.

Politically, when Hong Kong was returned to the sovereign rule of China on July 1, 1997, it became a Special Administrative Region (SAR), and the Chinese government put in place the Basic Law. The guiding principle of the Basic Law is the concept of "one country, two systems," under which Hong Kong is allowed to maintain its capitalist economy and to retain a large degree of political autonomy for a period of 50 years. Even though not much has changed on the surface, people are skeptical and uncertain about the future. However, the main challenge for Hong Kong since 1997 has been largely economical as it faces the Asian financial crisis, the threat of a global economic recession, and the re-structuring of Hong Kong's economy, especially when Mainland China is becoming a member of the World Trade Organization. At the dawn of the new millennium, unemployment in Hong Kong is at an all time high. The housing market has dropped 50% from its peak in 1997, making many homes with big mortgages financial liabilities instead of assets. Chinese people in Hong Kong undergoing these political uncertainties and economic pressure are made more susceptible to all sort of mental, psychological, emotional, relational and spiritual problems.

Some become involved in gambling and fall deeper into debts from high interest loans. Others develop problems with substance abuse. Often times, Christians in the church who are experiencing problems try to put on a brave front so as to maintain fellowship in the church, leaving the problems unresolved until it becomes too late. Pastors should be caring and constantly on the watch for the psychological and spiritual well-being of the members. Pastors should be careful not to add pressure to the members of the church by over-burdening them with too many activities. Regular times of fellowship, sharing, and retreats should be planned to help relieve the pressure the members of the church experience.

Case Illustration Number 3

Mrs. Chan (from Hong Kong) was referred to my wife and I for counseling because her husband had just admitted to having an extramarital relationship with a female staff member, prompted by his frequent business trips to China. She was totally devastated and was in a state of shock and denial. She was afraid to ask her husband for more details because she wanted to believe that it was just an isolated incident of indiscretion. We encouraged her to stay strong and arranged for a second session that would include her husband.

We asked to see the husband, Mr. Chan, alone half an hour before the second session where I confronted him about the extent of the affair. Mr. Chan admitted that the affair had gone on for more than a year, but he did not have a heart to tell his wife. When he claimed that he still loved his wife I challenged him to be honest with his wife and to work out the relationship. This he did. Naturally the wife was deeply hurt.

In the third session two weeks later, the wife came alone and announced that she had already made up with the husband. I was surprised but remained supportive. Later on we discovered that the husband did not keep his promise to leave the third party. The only thing we could do was to appeal to them both to work out their relationship for the sake of their son. The husband also underwent church discipline, while the wife was given support by another female pastor on staff.

Lessons to be learned: In this case, the victim wanted to save face despite the hurts that her husband had brought her from the affair. The husband and wife had been drifting apart for a while, but the wife was in constant denial of the failure in their marriage, resulting in perpetuating the affair even after the husband's admission of guilt. This marriage would have a better chance to survive had the couple been more willing to admit their inadequacies earlier.

THE HISTORICAL BACKGROUND OF CHINESE IN CANADA AND COUNSELING

There have been many waves of immigrants of Chinese from China, Hong Kong, Taiwan, and other parts of Asia to the West, especially North America, creating different sub-groups of Chinese in these foreign lands. Each Chinese immigrant family also has to deal with issues of adjustment, which include family and cultural dislocation, change of work or unemployment, language difficulties and so on. We shall focus on Chinese immigrants in Canada.

Briefly speaking, historically, we can say that there have been three main waves of Chinese immigrants to Canada (Jim & Suen, 1990, p. 8). Starting in 1858 with the gold rush, and during the years from 1866 to 1880 when the Canadian Pacific Railways were built, many thousands of Chinese workers (mostly single males) went. They suffered much hardship and discrimination. When the Head Tax was introduced in 1885 and the Chinese Exclusion Act was in place from 1923 to 1947, immigration slowed to a trickle. Today there are third-generation Canadian-born Chinese that came from that era. Needless to say, they are much more acculturated than the recent Chinese immigrants. They should be less resistant to counseling and their values would be more Canadian than Chinese.

When the Chinese Exclusion Act was repealed in 1947, Chinese immigrants slowly started to come to Canada again. But the second wave of Chinese immigrants really started with the Immigration Amendment introduced in 1967 based on the "Merit System." Many educated professionals arrived and those who were students stayed. Most of them came from Hong Kong, but some also came from other parts of South East Asia. Today this is the main group of Chinese Canadian. They are bi-cultural and mostly middle-class, with parents who are more traditionally Chinese and the children more typically Canadian. Still maintaining a strong Confucian work ethic, these Chinese parents often apply a great deal of pressure on their children to excel. Over and above their regular schoolwork, these children often have to perform well in their piano lessons, Chinese classes and so on. They find themselves in a double bind, and either rebel and inevitably make the parents unhappy or succumb to pressure to comply and remain miserable. They also feel inadequate if they cannot meet their parents' expectations. Counseling such families requires understanding of the generational gap as well as of the differences in values held by the parents and the children. Furthermore, general pastoral care should include facilitating more communication between parents and children in the family as well as in the church. Too often the church instead of facilitating family togetherness, separates the family members into their own peer groups in most church activities, creating even more gaps between each other.

The third wave of Chinese immigrants arrived during the eighties and the nineties. They are mainly from Hong Kong and Taiwan. Because of the fear of political instability in Hong Kong, as 1997, the year the British colony returned to the sovereign rule of China, drew near, more and more Chinese immigrants arrived in Canada and the United States from Hong Kong. Similarly, Taiwanese also came because of the political uncertainties between China and the Island State. These groups have come with the "Made in Hong Kong" or "Made in Taiwan" brands of Chinese culture, which are highly pragmatic and materialistic. These new Chinese immigrants are often stereotyped as being very wealthy and unfriendly. In fact, the very wealthy are only the minority, as many are from the middle or lower-middle class. Many are perceived as unfriendly because they either lack the language ability or lack the social skill and the sense of security to reach out.

In the last decade of the 20th century, another group of Chinese immigrants arrived from Mainland China. Even though we cannot describe this as a "wave" as the number is not as large as the earlier groups, this is definitely quite a distinctive group. Some of them are scholars who have stayed and sought asylum as a result of the June 4th incidence of 1989 in China. The rest are new immigrants who have applied successfully to join their relatives here or come on their own merit since the reopening of China in the last ten years. Because of their experience under Communist rule on the Mainland, their background again is very different from the other Chinese who came before them. They tend to stay with their own group and often find it hard to trust others. Almost all of them speak only Putonghua (apart from their own dialects) and therefore may have difficulties in communicating with other Canadian Chinese who are predominantly Cantonese speaking. They also have varying degrees of command of English. Because of their background, many are unable or unwilling to verbalize their feelings and thinking, often appearing to give acceptance and consent when they hold the opposite. In order to work with this group of people, one needs to win their trust first in order to gain access to what they are thinking and feeling. Because they value their self-dignity, it is also very important to give them due respect and not look down on them because they are different. Pastoral counseling must be conducted with the full knowledge of the differences of these various groups of Chinese immigrants, so that the appropriate counsel and advice can be given.

Meanwhile, there are some Chinese immigrants who, having obtained their Canadian citizenship, have returned to where they came from, leaving their children in Canada to fare for themselves. If the children are juveniles, they may be prone to join up with poor company, and therefore exhibit delinquent behaviors. It is important to adopt a life-span perspective in understanding and counseling Chinese living in multicultural Canada, because each life stage has its own challenge and set of problems (Baruth & Nanning, 1999). This is where the Canadian Chinese church community can play a major role in reaching out to these people. Many churches provide help to these immigrants when they first arrive, but fail to continue to provide on-going pastoral care and counseling for these people.

Case Illustration Number 4

John and Mary came to me recently for premarital counseling. They were both born and raised in Canada. The issue that came up in the session was whether or not John would invite his father to the wedding. I discovered that John had a love-hate relationship with his father who divorced his mother when he was still a boy. The boy grew up under the loving care of his mother.

Counseling brought out the high cultural value of filial piety. John had to wrestle with this cultural norm and his intense dislike of his father. Psychologically and socially he always had a need for a father figure in his life because his father had failed to be one. I helped him come to terms with his cultural value and belief, and helped him sort out his mixed emotions. He was encouraged with the knowledge that God is the loving father who is always there for us.

Lessons to be learned: Many cultural values that we hold are good and much needed. However, if and when realities do not match our ideals, counseling may be needed to help us face the situation. We can see from this case how cultural values can have a strong, lasting and controlling influence in our lives.

CULTURAL ADJUSTMENTS OF NEW CANADIAN
CHINESE IMMIGRANTS AND COUNSELING

New immigrants go through a great deal of cultural adjustments. Uprooting themselves from their well-established careers and fast-moving lifestyle, these Chinese immigrants often find themselves totally lost in Canada, having to learn or re-learn everything from driving to conversational English. Because there are now so many Chinese in the major cities of Canada, these Chinese immigrants tend to flock to their own people, and retreat to the comfort zone of their own kind, thereby slowing the process of integration into Canadian society.

After years of being independent and autonomous, the parents suddenly discover that they have lost their identity and their security, often becoming dependent even on their young children. They can become depressed from feelings of uselessness and boredom. Many equate the three years wait for Canadian citizenship as imprisonment. In many cases the fathers often keep a job or business going in the East, leaving the wives and children to struggle for themselves in Canada. They are the so-called "astronauts" because they fly back and forth so much and seemingly spend more time in space than on earth.

Very often, the long separations cause couples to move further and further apart from each other emotionally, or extra-marital affairs develop, resulting in many broken marriages and homes. At the same time, indulgence or neglect of these immigrant children lead to their poor academic performance or delinquent behaviors. Some of these kids, in order to gain social acceptance, fall prey to peer pressure, engaging in antisocial behaviors and making poor choices in relationships.

New Chinese immigrants, because of the adherence to traditional methods of problem solving, such as reliance on hierarchical authority and male domination, frequently cannot make the necessary changes in their transition. Effective counseling of new immigrant families require an appreciation of the tremendous adjustments and heavy pressure these people experience. Pastoral counselors can begin to help those families that are Christian to view their immigrant experience as part of their sojourn on earth, looking to the Lord as their shepherd and guide.

The adjustment process of each immigrant family can be conceptualized in four stages characterized variously as: traditional, dual cultural, assimilated or integrated (Jim & Suen, 1990, p. 10). Very often the various members of a multi-generational Chinese Canadian family find themselves at different stages of acculturation, and therefore dual cultural dilemmas exist in areas ranging from the concept of family to the views on rights and privileges (Jim & Suen, 1990, pp. 11-12). Inter-generational conflicts often develop between new immigrant parents who hold on to traditional child-rearing methods, and their children who quickly adopt the values and ways of their peers in the Canadian society (Jim & Suen, 1990, pp. 13-16). Both the parents and their children have to be taught coping skills to deal with the many changes and to overcome the conflicts as a result of the adjustment. The pastoral counselor plays an important role in facilitating this process.

Another simple model of conceptualizing the degree of acculturation and ethnic identity of new immigrants has been devised using the two variables of *assimilation* and *ethnic identity* (Kitano & Maki, 1996). Four types can be identified using this model: Type A, high in assimilation and low in ethnic identity; Type B, high in assimilation and high in ethnic identity; Type C, high in ethnic identity and low in assimilation; and Type D, low in ethnicity and low in assimilation. If we apply this to the Canadian Chinese situation, Type A describes those who are quite Canadianized, while Type B describes those that are bicultural (Chinese and Canadian). Those in Type C include new immigrants who have yet to assimilate to the Canadian society while those in Type D feel alienated from both the dominant Canadian culture and their own ethnic group.

The above model is useful in identifying the various types of Chinese immigrant groups (as well as other groups) in Canada (and elsewhere). The Chinese churches in Canada need to develop specialized ministries for these diverse groups of Chinese immigrants. Despite the ideal of the Canadian mosaic, the acculturation of these diverse groups of Chinese immigrants takes different routes and integration into the mainstream of Canadian society takes time and effort. A major part of pastoral care and counseling will be to help the various groups adjust to the Canadian contexts. In the past, some Chinese churches in Canada have tried to hang on to Type C Chinese ethnic identity because new immigrants are more comfortable with a Chinese context, or maintain a Type B bicultural situation because that is what they started with when they were first established. This is understandable and appropriate, and the needs of its members are better served by making the cultural context similar to what they are comfortable with. However, the author's experience is that one cannot turn against the natural process of acculturation and it is important to shift the ministry to match the changing social profile and cultural makeup of the members. The nature of pastoral care and counseling should adapt to the ever-changing cultural characteristics within the Canadian Chinese church.

Case Illustration Number 5

Mr. and Mrs. Fu were new Chinese immigrants in a small city in Canada. They owned a small Chinese restaurant and worked hard everyday till the early hours of the morning. Before their daughter, Karen, went into Senior High School, she used to help out at the restaurant. The parents have stopped asking her to help so as to encourage her to study hard to prepare for entrance into university in a few years time. When they found that Karen wanted to leave home, they were devastated and furious.

Because Karen was not of age and could not live by herself, it was arranged through the school and social services for her to live in a foster home. I did separate counseling for the daughter and the parents and again acted as a mediator. Often I would meet her after school in a nearby donut shop and later meet with the parents at home. I discovered that there were many cultural differences between the parents who were very traditional Chinese and the daughter who was very westernized. The parents were encouraged to learn more about culture in Canada and be more accepting of their daughter. Gradually Karen was encouraged to visit the parents at home, and then come back for the weekends. Eventually when Karen was ready for university, she moved back home. The whole family came to church as a result of this experience and has remained ever since.

Lessons to be learned: Generational and cultural gaps result in many breakdowns in parent-child relationships, especially, in my experience, among many new Chinese immigrant families. The church can play a role in bridging that gap. Counseling in these types of cases is very time-consuming, but the investment is definitely worthwhile.

GENERAL COUNSELING CONSIDERATIONS IN MULTICULTURAL PERSPECTIVES

Before going further in looking specifically at pastoral counseling in a Chinese church context, it is important to note that in the last 20 years, professional counselors and psychologists working in the secular sector in the West have already started to pay great attention to cultural factors in counseling. This is very encouraging and makes it all the more urgent that we should do the same in pastoral counseling. However it is important to note that much of their work, as is expected, predominantly still starts from a North American base and viewpoint, and so it is done naturally from cross-cultural and multi-cultural perspectives. That is not to say that their work is not valuable or that counseling in different cultures has to be entirely different and original. On the contrary, because many of these scholars are themselves bi-cultural, they have provided many valuable insights in contextualizing counseling in different cultures. Nevertheless, there is still a need for further reflections on counseling from an indigenous and national perspective.

Here we shall take a look at the contribution of some of these scholars. One prominent group of writers has called attention to the importance of "cultural intentionality," and has identified their approach as "multicultural counseling and therapy" (MCT), now referred to it as the fourth force of counseling theory (Ivey, Ivey, & Simek-Morgan, 1997, pp. 131-205). As we have mentioned, the first force is psychodynamic counseling and therapy, the second is cognitive-behavioral counseling and therapy, and the third force is existential-humanistic traditions such as person-centered theory, logotherapy and Gestalt Therapy. This fourth force is not in opposition to the first three historical forces of counseling and psychotherapy, as it seeks rather to enrich the others. MCT recognizes that although we are all unique human beings, we are also influenced by different multicultural factors. Therefore, awareness of issues such as race/ethnicity, culture, and gender that affect how each of us construct meaning in the world, is important in the practice of counseling. In this theoretical orientation, the counselor would seek to bring a balance between the individual, family, and multicultural issues within the context of the client. MCT also draws from the research done by Sue (1995) on multi-cultural counseling and is continuously being refined and developed (Sue, Ivey, & Pedersen, 1996).

The MCT frame of reference has been heavily influenced by its desire to view counseling and psychotherapy as liberation of the self from personal, social, and economic oppression. Cheatham (1990) warns against the danger of culturally insensitive counseling especially with African-American clients and feels that counseling has been used as an instrument of oppression as it has been used to transmit a certain set of individualistic cultural values. While this postmodern judgment that counseling is probably misused this way in many incidences, the present author believes that this does not mean that pastoral counseling should be or can be non-foundational and value-free (Lee, 1999). Nevertheless, this reminds us that culturally insensitive counseling can be oppressive. The above proponents of MCT encourage the adoption of the Afrocentric (versus the Eurocentric) worldview that takes seriously the background and history of the African-Americans, a view first popularized by Molefi Kete Asante in his book, *The Afrocentric Idea* (1987). The Afrocentric worldview has been described as "holistic, emotionally vital, interdependent, and oriented to collective survival," in contrast to the North American Eurocentric worldview which is analytical, egocentric, independent and so on (Ivey, Ivey, & Simek-Morgan, 1997, p. 139). The Afrocentric view is further contrasted against the Eurocentric view in that it: emphasizes oral tradition versus clear written tradition, uses a "being" time orientation versus a linear "doing" time orientation, focuses on harmony versus individuation, and points at respect for elderly versus orientation towards youth. The authors also suggest that children of Chinese origin (among others) often have a life orientation closer to that of the Afrocentric worldview than to the European-North American worldview. While this is probably true regarding many aspects of Chinese culture, there are also understandably, major points of departure. Therefore, for the purpose of this paper, we will look at Chinese culture mainly in contrast to the dominant North American culture. Nevertheless, this textbook is a valuable contribution to the understanding of counseling and psychotherapy from a multicultural perspective. The authors have included a practical exercise on generating culturally relevant theories of helping, based on the Afrocentric theory. Multicultural perspectives are also added to the first three forces of counseling and psychotherapy.

It is interesting to note that the latest edition of the above-mentioned text includes for the first time, discussions on spirituality as an important part of the counseling and therapy process. This is evidence that many psychologists are now taking spirituality seriously in the practice of counseling and psychotherapy. We have already seen evidence of that in some major publications by the American Psychological Association (APA) such as *Handbook of Psychotherapy and Religious Diversity* (Richards & Bergin, 2000), *Integrating Spirituality into Treatment* (Miller, 1999), *A Spiritual Strategy for Counseling and Psychotherapy* (Richards & Bergin, 1997), and *Religion and the Clinical Practice of Psychology* (Shafranske, 1996), just to name a few. The spiritual stance taken by these authors are understandably pluralistic and open-minded. It is time that scholars in the field of pastoral counseling take themselves seriously as having an important role to play in pointing out pastoral counseling's uniqueness and effectiveness based on Christian spirituality. One way to do that is to view each person holistically as a spiritual, cultural and social being, integrating our spiritual faith and the understanding of our cultural makeup.

In the counseling of Chinese clients, it is important to remember that often the process of early socialization in the Chinese family has taught them to be relatively inhibited and therefore less aggressive, more reserved, conservative, or quiet. Social reserve should not be misinterpreted as the absence of emotions, and the acquired restraints of emotions should be respected (Axelson, 1999, pp. 150-151). In other words, though it is still important in the process of counseling to focus on the feelings and emotions of the Chinese client and to encourage him or her to externalize them, there should be great sensitivity and respect for the client if he or she is very reserved, especially in front of others. In a pastoral setting, the pastoral counselor should work hard to gain the trust of the counselees and not pressure the counselees to disclose all their feelings before they are ready.

Cultural variables that may affect the assessment and treatment of Asian clients include stereotyping, familism (individual-family relationship), roles of children and wives, public suppression of problems, and indirect versus direct forms of communication (Paniagua, 1998, pp. 58-61). Issues such as the importance of the extended family, the central role of the father and the proper place of children and wives, the effect of shame and guilt on personal behavior and family dynamics must all be considered in the process of counseling. Paniagua (1998) continues to point out various keys that are important at different stages of counseling. In the first session, because the client desires to have a therapist that he or she can look up to, the therapist should demonstrate the two qualities of expertise and authority (p. 61). Other points to note include, maintaining formalism and conversational distance, expecting expression of mental problems in somatic terms, providing concrete and tangible advice, and so on (pp. 61-67).

These are all valid points to consider in counseling involving Chinese clients in general. In the case of the pastoral counselor, pastoral integrity and godly authority are very critical to effective counseling. A pastoral counselor should surpass the level of advice giving, and engage in providing spiritual direction. Pastoral counseling should be linked to the ministry of spiritual direction because it is often through the time of prayer and quiet meditation with the church member that the client can go beyond trying to solve problems to discern the heart of God. Often we find that the problems that the member is experiencing may not have a quick solution, but pastoral counseling combined with spiritual direction can give comfort and new vision for the person involved. The author believes that this type of pastoral and spiritual counseling, the counseling of the soul, is well suited to the Chinese cultural context because of the respect given to people in authority and because of the central place of prayer in Chinese Christian spirituality.

There are several points worth noting in the summary guidelines suggested by Paniagua (1998) regarding the recommended modalities of therapies that would be best suited for Asian clients (pp. 69-73). Paniagua believes that behavioral approaches are recommended because "they are concrete and directive and do not emphasize the exploration of internal conflicts leading to enhancement of the 'shame' that the client experiences by reporting his or her problems" (p. 70). Personally the present author believes that behavioral approaches appear effective simply because they are tangible and measurable methods, but if we do not deal with the inner conflicts, then the counseling can be just symptomatic relief. Therefore pastoral counseling should start with a cognitive-behavioral approach, but should not stop at that. Further and deeper spiritual direction should also follow.

Family therapy is also recommended simply because as a unit, family is more important than the individual. However, there are some additional factors to note in using family therapy with Asians (Berg & Jaya, 1993). Some of the factors are:

1. Problem-solving techniques emphasizing negotiation rather than confrontation should be used, with the therapist acting as the authoritative mediator.
2. To enhance a peaceful negotiation, clients should be seen separately before the family members are seen together in the family session.
3. Give due respect first to the head of the family.
4. Family therapy must be (a) problem focused, (b) goal oriented, and (c) symptom relieving on a short-term basis.
5. Determine the parental authoritative role as perceived by the children. This is because the vertical, hierarchical structure of the Asian family is different from the horizontal and democratic style of the typical North American family.
6. Approach the different issues from a family relationship perspective.
7. Avoid embarrassing the family members in front of each other.

The above suggestions are all very useful in counseling Chinese clients and are valid in varying degrees depending on how traditional the

Chinese family is or how acculturated it is to the local culture. Biblical teaching concerning the respect due to parents support the use of family therapy techniques in pastoral counseling. However one must differentiate between the proper place of authority versus the negative impact of authoritarianism.

Case Illustration Number 6

Mei Ling was from China and came on a student visa to Canada. She came to me with her fiancé, Karl, a Canadian ten years her senior, asking me to help them in their wedding. I told them that they must go through premarital counseling to which they promptly agreed. The counseling that took place revealed that there were many differences between them, especially culturally. I encouraged them to postpone their wedding plans. They were reluctant at the beginning, but eventually agreed. The subsequent counseling was useful in helping them establish more firmly their reasons for getting married.

Lessons to be learned: In this case, I suspected correctly that the desire to obtain permanent residence in Canada was also a factor in Mei Ling wanting to get married to Karl. Counseling helped to sort out not only the cultural differences between Mei Ling and Karl, but also the motivation for marriage. Counselors need to be discerning in their helping relationships.

SPECIFIC PASTORAL COUNSELING CONSIDERATIONS IN THE CHINESE CHURCH

This paper is intended to be descriptive rather than prescriptive. Throughout the paper we have commented on different aspects of pastoral counseling in light of the special nature and situation of Chinese people in the Chinese community in general, and in the Chinese church in particular. Understanding these backgrounds and the theoretical foundation of Chinese culture is critical and pre-requisite to the effective practice of pastoral counseling. In this section we shall go further and consider some more specific and crucial principles in pastoral counseling in the Chinese Church setting.

Traditionally in the Chinese church, "counseling," offered by some pastoral workers could best be characterized as "advice-giving" or "admonition." The "counselor" is an authority figure that makes a judgment, which is then given to the "counselee." There is much use of

Scripture. Forgiveness, repentance and prayers are emphasized as the solutions to most problems. This is akin to what is commonly associated with Jay Adam's model of "nouthetic counseling." When problems have arisen as a direct result of sins being committed, this straightforward confrontive approach definitely has its rightful place. However, psychological and emotional problems often are complex and may require the use of other supplementary methods to enhance the counseling process.

The other approach, used by pastoral caregivers who have some counseling training, is the person-centered (Rogerian) counseling method. With the use of unconditional positive regard and empathy, the counselee is encouraged to reflect on his or her own feelings to gain insight into his or her problems. As with clients of other populations, this non-directive, non-confrontative approach is helpful to many Chinese suffering from stress, anxiety, depression, and other similar mood disorders. However, somewhat paradoxically, the expectation of many Chinese counselees is to gain some insights into his or her problems from "the expert" or "the teacher," and therefore may be disappointed if the counselor merely redirects the questions back to them.

Like many things in life, there should be a happy medium. The pastoral counselor in a Chinese context must know when to play the priestly role, and when to be just a "good listener." Pastoral counselors should expand their repertoire of skills in order to counsel more effectively. Traditional "tools" can be used more creatively. For example, the pastoral counselor can use the lament psalms to help a counselee deal with anger and resentment. Parables and stories are especially effective among Chinese, as one picture is worth a thousand words. Nathan's use of a parable in his denunciation of David's sin with Bathsheba (II Samuel 12) is a classic example. Metaphors have also been found to be useful in effective counseling (Lee, 1983). The use of Chinese idiomatic sayings, metaphoric speech and anecdotes would be most effective with traditional Chinese clients that have a good grasp of Chinese culture. Such usage would be non-threatening, respectful, and less directive to the counselee who would appreciate it as "subtle" wisdom. In all instances, the pastoral counselor should try to integrate biblical principles with psychological perspective, and be sensitive to the nature of the Chinese context (Lee, 1992).

Apart from the above considerations in individual and personal counseling, we must also treat the Chinese family as a social system, as we have alluded to above. Working with Chinese families requires taking a holistic view of health. In other words, social, psychological, physical, and cultural factors have limited meaning when viewed in isolation. Young (1995) in her research of marriages in Hong Kong concludes that as 'affective individualism' is used to characterize modern marriages in the West, 'affective familism' could be adopted to characterize contemporary marriages among Chinese in Hong Kong. The Chinese church should put more effort in building up its marriage and family ministries, including a strong emphasis on family life education, premarital counseling, and marriage enrichment program. The author has found the Prepare-Enrich Inventories produced by Life Innovations, now available in Chinese, very useful as an assessment tool for couple relationships. Based on the 15-page computer report from the responses of a couple to the questionnaire, the pastoral counselor can help a couple deal specifically with the different issues they face in the relationship, instead of going over teaching already familiar to the couple or merely touching the surface of the issues. Besides this, marriage enrichment retreats where couples put aside everything to work on their relationship for several days have been found to be very effective in enriching marital relationships.

The tendencies among Chinese to try to be self-reliant, and Chinese families to try not to expose "family shames" that we have already discussed mean that there will be resistance to counseling in the Chinese community. Often problems are left unresolved for too long and allowed to "snowball" to such an extent that counselors can do very little to remedy the situation. Preventive counseling or education is therefore very important. As mentioned above, the Chinese Church in Canada needs to develop specialized educational and service ministries for the different groups of Chinese immigrants. Also, to encourage Chinese people to accept counseling and to make it less threatening, to begin with, pastoral counseling may be presented as "sharing and discussion times," and problems to be viewed as "growth issues." However, pastoral counseling should be more structured than general pastoral care. Chinese people like to know how long it would take to "cure the problem" and therefore it would be good to structure counseling in a certain setting and definite time frame with obvious goals and objectives so that there is clear expectation and commitment to the process. Too often pastoral counseling within the Chinese church becomes abortive because of the lack of this sort of structure.

Furthermore, because confiding in a lay counselor or someone who is your peer is much less threatening to a counselee, every church should develop a strong lay counseling program to provide pastoral care to its members. The pastors can conduct regular training for the lay-leaders to equip them for lay counseling and care of other members. The pastor or pastoral counselor should also be equipped to deal with more serious cases within his or her area of expertise, and know when to make referrals to trained and experienced professionals, the psychotherapists and family therapists. The pastoral counselor must learn to work hand in hand with the trained professionals and give the proper communal support the client needs. But no matter what level of counseling ministry we are involved in, to practice counseling successfully in the Chinese context, we must become familiar with the multi-facet historical, sociological, cultural and psychological dimensions of the people we serve, begin with some of the concepts presented in this paper, and continue to develop them more fully.

Case Illustration Number 7

Stephen and Tracy both grew up in Hong Kong, but met while they were studying in England. They were working in Hong Kong and had been married for three years. Their marriage was under a great deal of stress because of problems stemming from the in-laws' lack of acceptance of the wife. Even though Tracy had tried very hard in the past to please her mother-in-law, she always responded with disappointment. Stephen continually seemed to be caught in between trying to please his mom and also his wife.

My counseling had focused on helping Tracy build stronger self-esteem and helping Stephen to be more understanding and supportive of Tracy, especially in front of his mother. Counseling also focused on helping Tracy to be herself, doing her best and not hoping for a return, learning to be more relaxed. They were urged to attend a marriage enrichment weekend and that proved to be helpful for them. Because Stephen and Tracy are now communicating better with each other, they have been able to achieve greater intimacy in their relationship. Tracy's relationship with the mother-in-law has also improved.

Lessons to be learned: With Chinese, in-law problems usually exist between the wife and the mother-in-law, and much less between the husband and his mother-in-law as is the case in the West. Nevertheless, the same principle of sensitivity on the part of the spouse and respect goes a long way in paving the path for better in-law relationship. Marriage enrichment retreats have been found to be useful in the Chinese church, but gentler approaches should be adopted so that the spouses become more open with each other and do not become defensive.

We have tried in this paper to point out the different elements in Chinese culture, paying special attention to the philosophical, historical, sociological, psychological and spiritual perspectives. What we have found is that Chinese culture can mean different things to different people. Furthermore, individuals may be relatively unaware of the influence their heritage and current environment has on their attitudes, behaviors, choices, and feelings. Therefore, it is necessary to discern how an individual has been affected by traditional and non-traditional ideas with regards to relationships, roles, individualism, etc., as this will have a bearing on their well-being and their receptiveness to pastoral counsel. Sensitivity to the cultural background of the specific Chinese community that we are dealing with will help us engage in more relevant and effective counseling.

REFERENCES

Asante, M. (1987). *The Afrocentric idea.* Philadelphia: Temple University Press.

Axelson, John A. (1999). *Counseling and development in a multicultural society.* Pacific Grove, California: Brookes/Cole Publishing Co.

Baruth, Leroy G. & Manning, M. Lee (1999). *Multicultural Counseling and Psychotherapy: A Lifespan Perspective.* 2nd ed. Upper Saddle River, New Jersey: Prentice-Hall.

Berg I.K. & Jaya, A. (1993). Different and same: Family therapy with Asian-American families. *Journal of Marital and Family Therapy, 19,* 31-38.

Cheatham, H. (1990). Empowering Black families. In H. Cheatham & J. Stewart (Eds.), *Black families* (pp. 373-93). New Brunswick, NJ: Transaction Press.

Duan, Changming (2000). Counseling in the Chinese Cultural context: Accommodating both individualistic and collectivistic values. *Asian Journal of Counseling,* Vol. 7, No. 1, 1-21.

Gao, G. & Ting-Toomey, S. (1998). *Communicating effectively with the Chinese.* Thousand Oaks, California: Sage Publications, Inc.

Ho, D.Y.F. (1991). Relational Orientation and methodological individualism. *Bulletin of the Hong Kong Psychological Society, 26-27,* 81-95.

Ho, M.K. (1992). *Minority children and adolescents in therapy.* Newbury Park, California: Sage Publications, Inc.

Ivey, A.E., Ivey, M.B., & Simek-Morgan, L. (1997). *Counseling and psychotherapy: A multicultural perspective* (4th ed.). Boston: Allyn & Bacon.

Jim, Eva & Suen, Peggy. (1990). *Chinese parents and teenagers–Transitions and cultural conflicts.* Vancouver, British Columbia: Council for the family.

Kitano, Harry H.L. & Maki, Mitchell T. (1996). Continuity, change, and diversity: Counseling Asian Americans. In Pedersen, Paul B., Draguns, Juris G., Lonner, Walter J. & Trimble, Joseph E. (Eds.) *Counseling Across Cultures,* 4th ed. Thousand Oaks, California: Sage Publications, Inc.

Kwan, Kwong-Liem Karl (2000). Counseling Chinese Peoples: Perspectives of Filial Piety, *Asian Journal of Counseling*. Vol. 7, No. 1, 23-41.

Lee, Simon Yiu Chuen (1999). Postmodernism and narrative therapy. *Jian Dao* Issue 13/*Pastoral Journal* Issue 8, Hong Kong: Alliance Bible Seminary, 275-296.

Lee, Simon Yiu Chuen (1992). *Equipped to counsel: A Training Manual for Christian Counseling in the Chinese Church*. Unpublished Doctoral Dissertation. Portland, Oregon: Western Conservative Baptist Seminary.

Lee, Simon Yiu Chuen. (1983). *An exploration in the use of metaphors in effective counseling*. Unpublished MA Thesis. Vancouver, British Columbia: University of British Columbia.

Miller, William R. (ed.) (1999). *Integrating spirituality into treatment*. Washington, DC: American Psychological Association.

Paniagua, Freddy A. (1998). *Assessing and treating Culturally diverse clients*. 2nd ed. Thousand Oaks, California: Sage Publications, Inc.

Pedersen, Paul (1994). *A handbook for developing multicultural awareness*. 2nd ed. Alexandria, VA: American Counseling Association.

Richards, P.S. & Bergin, A.E. (2000). *Handbook of psychotherapy and religious diversity*. Washington, DC: American Psychological Association.

Richards, P.S. & Bergin, A.E. (1997). *A spiritual strategy for counseling and psychotherapy*. Washington, DC: American Psychological Association.

Shafranske, Edward P. (ed.) (1996). *Religion and the clinical Practice of Psychology*. Washington, DC: American Psychological Association.

Sue, David & Sue, Derald Wing (1991). Counseling Strategies for Chinese Americans. In Courtland C. Lee & Bernard L. Richardson (eds.) *Multicultural Issues in Counseling: New Approaches to Diversity*. Alexandra, VA: American Association for Counseling and Development.

Sue, Derald Wing & Sue, David (1999). *Counseling the culturally different* (2nd ed.). New York: John Wiley.

Sue, Derald Wing (1995). Toward a theory of multicultural counseling and therapy. In J. Banks & C. Banks (Eds.) *Handbook of research on multicultural education*. New York: Macmillan.

Sue, D.W., Ivey, A., & Pedersen, P. (1996). *A theory of multicultural counseling and therapy*. Pacific Grove, CA: Brooks/Cole.

Sue, Stanley & Morishima, James K. (1982). *The Mental Health of Asian Americans*. San Francisco, California: Jossey-Bass Inc.

Young, Katherine P.H. (1995). *Understanding Marriages: A Hong Kong Case Study*. Hong Kong: Hong Kong University Press.

Pastoral Counseling in Indonesia

Aart Martin van Beek, DMin, DTh

SUMMARY. This article discusses the development and current identity and functioning of Pastoral Counseling in Indonesia. Cultural contexts in Indonesia are presented, and particular attention is paid to relations between Holland, the United States and Indonesia in terms of the implantation of models of Pastoral Care and Counseling. A central issue addressed is how these models have been adapted to Indonesian cultural contexts. Case studies are provided as means of illustrating and exploring challenges, issues and trends in Pastoral Counseling. A Holistic approach is suggested as the most adequate model for Pastoral Counseling in modern Indonesia. *[Article copies available for a fee from The Haworth Document Delivery Service: 1-800-HAWORTH. E-mail address: <getinfo@haworthpressinc.com> Website: <http://www.HaworthPress.com> © 2002 by The Haworth Press, Inc. All rights reserved.]*

KEYWORDS. Pastoral counseling, cross cultural counseling, Indonesia

INTRODUCING INDONESIA

Indonesia is the fourth largest country in the world in population as well as the largest Muslim nation. It stretches from the Indian Ocean to the Pacific over three time zones and straddles the equator. It is an archipelago made up of between 13.0000 and 14.000 islands,

[Haworth co-indexing entry note]: "Pastoral Counseling in Indonesia." van Beek, Aart Martin. Co-published simultaneously in *American Journal of Pastoral Counseling* (The Haworth Pastoral Press, an imprint of The Haworth Press, Inc.) Vol. 5, No. (1/2), 2002, pp. 151-173; and: *International Perspectives on Pastoral Counseling* (ed: James Reaves Farris) The Haworth Pastoral Press, an imprint of The Haworth Press, Inc., 2002, pp. 151-173. Single or multiple copies of this article are available for a fee from The Haworth Document Delivery Service [1-800-HAWORTH, 9:00 a.m. - 5:00 p.m. (EST). E-mail address: getinfo@haworthpressinc.com].

151

including major ones such as Java, Bali, Sumatra, Sulawesi, most of Borneo and half of New Guinea. The island of Java (one-third the size of California) is home to about half the population of two hundred million). The capital Jakarta, a sprawling metropolis of approximately ten million people is located there. About ten percent of the population is Christian, but there are also Buddhist and Hindu minorities.

HOLLAND-AMERICA LINE: A BRIEF HISTORY

One might ask why a non-Indonesian writes about Pastoral Counseling in Indonesia. There are several reasons. First, I have been fortunate enough to be a participant in and observer of the building of a Pastoral Counseling movement in Indonesia. Second, my own cultural experience largely mirrors the cultural influence on Pastoral Counseling in Indonesia.

To underline the second point, it is necessary to emphasize that Pastoral Counseling as a movement is a culture. Culture in my definition consists of "meaning providing processes." Therefore culture is always in process. The objective of this article is to impact this process so that the Pastoral Counseling culture will become broader, wider and deeper. Nevertheless Pastoral Counseling as a discipline is largely a post-World War II phenomenon that grew out of the positivism of that age, particularly in the potential of the individual lying dormant in each of us. It could not have developed the way it has without the parallel development of therapy entering into the mainstream of American culture. There are of course different ways Pastoral Counseling contributes in, e.g., the United States, but it is clear that it depends on and is conditioned on a positive view toward the sharing of one's inner life with a trained professional. In many countries, Indonesia included, this positive view is by no means a given. This is a major issue impinging on the growth of Pastoral Counseling in Indonesia as well as the indigenization of the movement.

Pastoral theology and a basic understanding of pastoral care came to Indonesia across the Indian Ocean, from The Netherlands, for centuries the colonial power ruling the Indonesian archipelago. Pastoral Counseling came across the Pacific from the United States much later. Thus there is a Holland Line and an America Line. It is important to distinguish between the two, not in the least because they are marked by a different point of departure. Pastoral theology and pastoral care as presented by Europeans to Indonesians is deductive by nature. Their origins lie in dogmatic and ecclesiastical concepts that were translated to the context of pastoral ministry. For instance, one takes the dogmatic and ecclesiastical concept of "shepherd" and extrapolates from there how the pastor should operate in a parish setting.

Pastoral Counseling, on the other hand, is more inductive in nature. It begins with the experience the counselee presents to the counselor, which is then analyzed and interpreted with the hope of positively impacting the life of the counselee. These approaches seem incompatible with each other. Nevertheless, if the counselor is to be pastoral, she or he will have to find a way to reconcile them.

At the time I started working on the island of Java (1982), there were four loci for pastoral theology in Indonesia, all of which were on Java. The Jakarta Theological Seminary in the West of the island (where I taught from '91 to '96) was the home of the pastoral theologian Dr. J. Ch. Abineno. An Indonesian from the region of West Timor and married to a Dutch woman. He had been trained in the traditional pastoral/practical theology which I encountered in The Netherlands in 1975. It entailed bringing theological concepts to bear on the pastoral situation, but was largely a theoretical exercise. Professor Abineno defined pastoral thinking in Indonesia for approximately three decades by the early eighties. The Jakarta Seminary is a home to many students across the archipelago, with the most prominent traditions being Reformed and Lutheran. In Indonesia Protestant denominations are mostly defined by region and ethnicity. Although the nation uses the Malay language of Bahasa Indonesia as the Lingua Franca, churches often operate in one of roughly one hundred and fifty indigenous tongues. Thus one will find several Protestant denominations in North Sumatra for example, mostly along ethnic lines. The theology of these churches can be traced back to the theology of the missionaries that introduced the Christian faith to various regions.

In Central Java, there was the theological School in Yogyakarta, which although increasingly multi-denominational, was established to train pastors for the Chinese and Javanese Reformed churches of Central Java. In the early eighties, Tjaard Hommes, a Dutch born Congregationalist pastor who had taught pastoral theology for many years at Notre Dame, was establishing an academic graduate program in inductive theology. His goal was to train Indonesians to reflect theologically on their pastoral activity, Pastoral Counseling being part of that activity. At that time he ran a program in several regions in Indonesia known as the Doctor of Pastoral Studies Program of the South East Asia Graduate School of Theology. This School is a regional school designed to train

professors for South Asian seminaries allowing students to write disser-
tations in their native languages. Dr. Hommes approach in a sense
brought the European tradition of theoretical reflection together with a
keen American focus on praxis and problem solving.

In Salatiga, about three hours to the north the Satya Wacana Christian
university (where I taught from '84-'87) had adopted an American approach. The School of Education had established a counseling and guidance center very much modeled after the educational counseling services
in the United States. In the Department of Theology a Mennonite Pastor
and Church Leader, Mesach Krisetya, had been trained in Clinical Pastoral Education in Indiana and at a seminary in Bangalore by Dr.
Prasantham, an American trained Indian supervisor. His dream was to
start CPE in Indonesia. We were able make this dream come true in
Salatiga in the eighties and Jakarta in the nineties by establishing two Indonesian CPE programs. This was achieved by engaging in a partnership
with the Indonesian Association for Health Services (Indonesian Hospital Association). Mesach was also instrumental in restructuring the curriculum at the multi-denominational Faculty of Theology (with its many
students from the Eastern islands of Indonesia) with the help of the education and guidance department. Students took courses in Pastoral Counseling and group dynamics and personality theory, which was unheard of
at that time in Indonesia. An interesting discussion emerged at the university about the definition of Pastoral Counseling at the university. Referring to the function of Pastoral Counseling as defined by Howard
Clinebell in *Basic Types of Pastoral Counseling* (Rev. Ed. Nashville:
Abingdon, 1984) which includes "guiding" and "guidance" and "counseling" this became part of Pastoral Counseling in the eyes of the university's theologians. The counselors at the education department (the
largest and oldest departments of the university) disagreed, believing that
Pastoral Counseling should be subordinate to what they were doing.

At the same time in East Java, in the town of Malang, at the Evangelical
SAAT seminary, Pastoral Counseling training was introduced by Yakob
Susabda, a Rosemead, CA trained Chinese pastor. His method tried to introduce spiritual concepts prevalent in the American evangelical and fundamentalist churches in combination with counseling techniques.

THE HOLISTIC HEALTH CARE MOVEMENT

In Yogyakarta, at Bethesda hospital (where I worked from '82-'84),
another movement was taking shape. How this movement related and

relates to the developments in Salatiga jump-started by Mesach and his cohorts in the education department of the university would and will determine the shape of Pastoral Counseling in Indonesia. It was a movement for Holistic Health Care that sought to bring the physical, mental, spiritual and social treatments together in one approach. The Indonesian Association for Health Services was formed in 1983 at Bethesda hospital. It committed itself to promoting the principles of holistic health care as outlined, not by the Holistic Health proponents in North America, but by the World Health Association and the Christian Medical Commission of the World Council of Churches. These organizations put a strong emphasis on socio-economic problems as a cause of physical diseases. The causal effect between such problems and diseases was understood as more than evident at the hospital. At one end of the hospital heart disease and strokes would be prevalent, among the more well to do patients, while on the other end the poor would suffer from typhoid and tuberculosis (cancer, injuries from traffic accidents and mosquito-borne diseases would cut across the board).

Bethesda had established a community development unit as a part of its operations, led by Dr. Paulus Santosa, a dentist who had become a community development specialist. Relationships were established with some of the poorest villages in the region around Yogyakarta, particularly in the infertile limestone region of Gunung Kidul near the Indian Ocean coast. The hospital provided livestock credit aid, helped villagers dig wells connecting to underground rivers and assisted in the engineering of simple construction projects. They oversaw a weighing and nutrition program for newborns and a pregnancy-monitoring program. Meanwhile the hospital, with aid from outside the region, established a mobile vasectomy and tubectomy program to help curb the population growth on the densely packed island. Entire village populations followed the example of either the village head or his wife in receiving voluntary sterilization, all in one day.

At Bethesda hospital we developed an analytical tool for overall health evaluation. This holistic tool established contextual indicators for the physical, mental, spiritual and socio-economic health of individuals, families and communities. It helped us draw connections between, e.g., physical problems and social causes or mental and spiritual conflicts. The Indonesian Christian Association for Health Services often discussed these questions in its journal. However, because there were so many different connections to be drawn, health care personnel tended to develop their own 'pet connections.' There were those who were preoccupied with the connection between economics and physical health, but often personnel with a charismatic theological background would prefer to focus on the relationship between spiritual and physical health.

The work on wholeness by Howard Clinebell, who was my intellectual mentor at Claremont, seemed a natural fit with the emphasis on wholeness. Over the years a consensus began to develop that Pastoral Counseling was to be a "whole making" exercise.

TERMINOLOGY AND THE HELPING CULTURE

What is a pastoral counselor? Mostly, "pastoral" was explained in reference to its Latin and Greek roots, although we felt discomfort at the lack of intelligence of sheep being shepherded. The pastor of the congregational "flock" tended to have a rather authoritarian relationship with the people. He (or more recently she) was in the business of providing information about the meaning of the Bible and giving advice about personal matters he or she had no understanding of. The "pastoral" term would only underline that role, rather than challenge it. And the main challenge in care giving, whether it was by pastors, doctors, nurses or social workers was to teach them to listen and make the care seeker stronger rather than more dependent. The idea of mutuality in the helping relationship was not common. At Bethesda we spent several years training every nurse and social worker and general practitioner to take on a new perspective. Specialists would not attend, for they were at the top of the hierarchical pyramid. Because they would not follow suit, the motivation of other staff over time eroded. Thus we were largely unsuccessful in changing the helping culture of the hospital. Theological students would be more open, simply because they shared the same professional background as the trainers. It is understandable, naturally, that it is hard to change a helping culture without changing the larger culture within which it operates. For example, Indonesian families and physicians routinely withhold information about their physical health or the status of their loved ones. The helper's authority more often than not goes unquestioned. For second tier health care staff, such as nurses, changing the culture is very difficult. They are generally overworked and grossly underpaid.

There are those who question whether the helping culture should even be changed. Would not more harm be done than good by challenging the way things are done? One might contest that viewpoint by referring to my definition of Culture: cultures are always in process. Why has the culture not changed based on inductively acquired information

concerning the patient's well being? That is why most of the professionals I know in the field of Pastoral Counseling in Indonesia strongly
stress the analysis of the care seekers' context.

The word "counseling" did not exist. It took several years to distinguish between pastoral 'care' and pastoral 'counseling.' I believe a consensus has grown in this area also. Pastoral care is considered the more
general work of caring from a background of Christian motivation,
while Pastoral Counseling requires more skills, is more focused and often contractual in nature. No term for 'counseling' has been coined;
rather the term 'konseling,' is used. However, a pastoral counselor by
the name of Totok Wiryasaputra, a Protestant who has spent many years
doing workshops on pastoral care for Catholic religious and health care
workers, suggested the word "pendampingan pastoral" for "pastoral
care." Mendampingi means to sit next, accompany, or sit at the same
level as another person. This term has gained popularity and has been
used for titles of books on the subject.

WHO IS A PASTORAL COUNSELOR?

This question is as complicated as the previous one. I know of very
few people who call themselves pastoral counselors. There is an awareness of the long road to that identity in the United States. There are no
adequate supervisory procedures, even between peers, in existence in
Indonesia. There are those who have studied more Pastoral Counseling
than others, specifically those who have received training in clinical
pastoral education abroad, or even in Indonesia itself.

Overall, one would expect a pastoral counselor to be theologically
trained. But this is not necessary. In the basic unit of clinical training we
provided, about half of the participants have been nurses or doctors. A
fair number of them have been Roman Catholic sisters. Priests are so
overwhelmed by their sacramental duties that much of the pastoral
work falls to the sisters. The move from theologically trained to other
personnel is a groundbreaking development in the field of Pastoral
Counseling internationally. Its potential impact therefore becomes
much wider, albeit also more diffused. For Indonesia itself the growth
of the Pastoral Counseling movement has been a boost for ecumenical
relations. The country had inherited the rigid split of the Reformation
that existed in The Netherlands for many centuries, each tradition having its own schools, newspapers, radio and television broadcast services. When after the (supposedly Communist-led) coup of 1965, all

Indonesians were supposed be official adherents of a recognized religion, Catholicism and Protestantism were classified as separate religions.

THE BASES OF PASTORAL CARE AND COUNSELING

We can think of Pastoral Counseling as being based in four loci. The first of these is the Church. The second of these is the clinical or hospital setting, the third is the academic setting and the fourth is the office. What happens in each of these settings all has bearing on the development of pastoral care and counseling. This is true in the United States, in Europe, as well as in Indonesia or any other country. Conversely, what happens is the overall cultural setting affects what happens in each of these settings.

Church based pastoral care and counseling is what I am mostly engaged in myself now and now more than ever I realize its importance. It has become more important to me largely because of my Indonesian experiences with holistic approaches. Serving an ethnic church in an urban setting in California, every day I see around me the needs of a community that at times looks like a community with third-world struggles not unlike those faced by Indonesians. The difficulty with church based pastoral care and counseling is that has a passive approach. The pastor expects persons in need of care to come to her or him. It does not work well if the pastor is not actively involved in the life of the community. Indonesia has taught me that while our perspective must be holistic and our goal must be to make persons, families and communities whole through the church, the spine as well as the heart of this pastoral ministry is pastoral care and counseling. From there pastoral care and counseling must reach everything in ministry.

Although many younger pastors in Indonesia today have received basic pastoral care and counseling training, it is hard to imagine how they can hold on to the rudimentary skills they were taught while facing the challenges of parish life. Their skill and understanding is not deep enough to challenge traditional ways of care giving. This situation is exacerbated because most denominational leaders have not been trained in Pastoral Counseling. There is no continuing education program in place that I know of which focuses on the strengthening and the upgrading of pastoral care and counseling skills.

Hospital-based pastoral care and counseling have been the most explored approach to the discipline. Hospitals have often been very enthusiastic about the development of these skills. There have been some practical concerns encouraging this development in the past decade or so. Hospital administrators were beginning to consider nurses and other hospital staff with inferior bed-side-manner skills as liabilities in the competitive world of increasingly privatized health care services in the large cities. 'Pastoral' nurses would provide good marketing. Nurse managers were beginning to take courses in 'therapeutic communication.' The interest in 'pastoral' counseling was fueled by the minority position of the Protestant and Catholic churches. It became clear that more and more of the Roman Catholic hospitals (who were very well organized) were providing the students while they had no staff to do the training. This cooperation became very fruitful.

In the mid-eighties the first three-month long full-time Clinical Pastoral Education program were developed in Salatiga. Students would be placed in hospitals throughout Central Java and came to Salatiga for supervision and training. In the early nineties a program was opened at the Protestant Cikini hospital in Jakarta, with that hospital and the nearby Roman-Catholic Carolus hospital functioning as clinical laboratories.

Pastoral Counseling could not take root in the culture of the Church without a change in academic curriculums. Satya Wacana University took the lead in this. In the following decades other theological schools did the same. In 1998 an Indonesian woman pastor and lecturer at the UKIT University in Tomohon received her doctorate in Pastoral Counseling through the South East Asian Graduate School of Theology. She wrote her dissertation in Indonesian on the relationship of trauma, communication and power in two Clinical Pastoral Education units at Cikini Hospital in Jakarta.

A few years earlier one of the first Pastoral Counseling centers opened at that hospital, thereby opening the door to office-based Pastoral Counseling. The name of the center used the word "Pendampingan" and shared a building with the social work department of the hospital. There is a future for office-based Pastoral Counseling in Indonesia, but standardization and quality of supervision will be significant problems. At present anyone can hang out his or her shingle. My hope is that standards will be based on some of the holistic principles that were so painstakingly developed over the years.

BASES AND CASES

To provide a picture of the unique problems of Pastoral Counseling in Indonesia, I have chosen four case descriptions, each corresponding to a different base, beginning with church-based counseling, followed by hospital, academia and office-based Pastoral Counseling.

Church-Based Pastoral Counseling

The pastor of a church at the outskirts of the capital is called to visit the house of a church member. This church member is quite frantic because his aunt who is visiting from the city of Ambon in Eastern Indonesia is acting quite strangely. When the pastor arrives at the modest house on the main street out of the city, she is led into a dark stuffy room where the aunt is sitting in a chair. She is heavy-set and appears disheveled. She seems to have difficulty breathing. "Shouldn't she go see a doctor?" the pastor asks. The lady in the chair replies, while pressing down on her chest with her hand: "It's no use. I am going to die. They have done black magic on me. They have put pins in a doll back in Ambon." "Why would they do that" the minister asks. "Because they want my land. If I die, my family can claim the land." The nephew explains that the aunt has cancer and is suffering from much anxiety. The pastor, who is quite young, has received basic Pastoral Counseling training, but she has not been trained to handle this kind of psychological problem. The minister is scared. Her own parents were migrants to Java from Eastern Indonesia and her mother was a firm believer in black magic. Her mother also insisted she had witnessed a number of apparitions of ghosts of various shapes and sizes over her lifetime. The minister feels unskilled to handle these powers. At the same time she is not fully convinced the woman is not a hypochondriac or suffering from paranoia of some kind. But she doesn't know much about mental illness and she does not know where to go. Most people in Indonesia have no health insurance, and treatment by a psychiatrist carries a cultural stigma. She takes the woman's hands and begins to pray for healing from evil and suffering.

I am trying to approach this case from the perspective of the pastoral care giver. She has her own cultural baggage she carries around with her. This is the world from which she must try to tackle this problem. It is not an uncommon problem in Indonesia. People hear incredible stories about the supernatural regularly. For most Indonesians mental illness and the world of magic blur together. A pastoral counselor must approach these problems first from inside the reality of those seeking help. It is of course tragic that there are many incidences of mental illness which are treated as a type of possession. This is where Pastoral Counseling skills could be of great benefit.

Hospital Based Pastoral Counseling

A chaplain visits the tuberculosis ward of a major hospital. The floors have just been swept, so he is told to wear a mask to protect himself from the bacilli. He walks between the steel beds with thin mattresses. Each patient has a metal cup with a lid on his or her nightstand, used as a spittoon. He approaches the bed of a woman of about fifty-five. She is a double amputee and she has been in the hospital for five years. He knows her well. He has been visiting her every week for about a year now. She rarely receives visitors, and he knows she looks forward to seeing him. She does not care that she is a Muslim and he is a Christian caregiver. They are both Javanese. And even if he were not Javanese, it would not really matter.

But this time the visit is different. He has come to bring her good news, but he knows it will not necessarily be good news to her. "You are going home," he says. "Home? Where is home? This is home for me." He explains that she is leaving the hospital. There is a long silence. Then she speaks again: "Look, I have a little radio and I've got some knitting I can do and my food comes three times a day. It isn't bad." She smiles. Tears appear in her eyes. The chaplain swallows. "You are going to live with your son. He wants to take you in." "But he has no room." "Don't worry, we have helped add a room to his house." He explains how the hospital community development unit has provided the bamboo material to expand her son's simple woven bamboo house. "You will be happy there, otherwise you may never get out of here." It has taken many case meeting of the community developers, social worker, chaplain, nurses, financial administrators and attending physicians to come up with this plan. She could not be in on them for fear she would sabotage the process. Now the chaplain has to deal with the patient's feelings over the end of an era. He feels guilty about not consulting her on this question, but the hospital could not do anything for her and she had been a patient free of charge for more than four years. It raises deep questions about how the pastoral counselor can network with all agencies for the benefit of persons in need of assistance.

Academy Based Pastoral Counseling

A young man comes into the office of his professor at the university. He is in love and his girlfriend is pregnant. He is a theological student and the girlfriend is a Muslim. He has received a scholarship from a rather traditional Protestant denomination. Once the leaders of that denomination find out that his girlfriend is pregnant, he will have to come before an assembly and confess his sin, then marry her. He may be asked to leave the church. But this is not the extent of the problem.

"My girlfriend is in the hospital," he sighs, his head hanging down. "What's wrong?" his teacher asks. "Are there complications with the pregnancy?" "No, she drank insecticide, she tried to kill herself." He starts sobbing. "Why have I made such a mess for everybody!"

Inter-religious (and inter-ethnic) relationships pose an enormous problem in Indonesia, as do unwanted pregnancies and suicide attempts. These attempts often express a mixture of manipulation and desperation.

The professor will try to work with his student and then try to meet with the two of them when she leaves the hospital. Any decision they make is bound to be very painful.

Office-Based Pastoral Counseling

A Muslim man comes to the newly opened Pastoral Counseling center in the heart of the city. The center is separate from, but located next to and financed by the Catholic hospital. The man is an engineer and a devout Muslim. He has studied in Singapore and knew about counseling centers there. Aside from his years in Singapore, the man has never lived anywhere but this small city. He is very concerned about confidentiality.

"I have come here because no one knows me here. If I go to a Muslim, someone will know someone I know and eventually everybody will find out about my problem." "Why did you come to see us?" asked the counselor, a social worker with one unit of Clinical Pastoral Education as her training. "Well, there is this other woman, nothing has happened, but we love each other. My wife doesn't know about it." "Tell me about it," said the counselor. "How do I know I can trust you?" asks the man.

The challenge is for the counselor to help this man in a brief period of time (one or two visits), He is well educated and will expect a certain level of expertise. Most of the persons coming into office-based counseling will be college-graduates at least. The counselor has very little expertise and faces an up-hill struggle to help this client.

SKILLS AND EMPATHY

How does a pastoral counselor approach these cases? How can he or she apply a basic knowledge of counseling techniques–some Rogerian, cognitive, behavior-modification, problem-solving or family-counseling, crisis-counseling–in order to make some difference that will lead to growth, to increased strength, to enhanced skills or to a lessening of suffering? I have asked myself these questions many times. In the first years in Indonesia I struggled deeply with my own relevance and the relevance of the discipline called Pastoral Counseling that seems so vital in specific contexts in the West. I remember vividly sitting in my first office at Bethesda hospital, next to an open walkway. My office windows were made of chain link fence material. All I had in that space was a desk. During visiting hours the village people in their sarongs, shuffling on their plastic sandals over the tile floor would pass this office on their way to the low-cost wards where patients stood in line with up to thirty others in a room. The villagers gawked at me, as if I was a rare primate that has just been donated to the hospital for the entertainment of the suffering. I had studied Indonesian for five months, but had trouble uttering more than a few dozen words. Several times a day my Indonesian counterpart, Totok Wiryasaputra would come to see me. He had studied English for many years, but was not able to utter more than a few dozen words. The hospital director, Dr. Guno Samekto, had put us together, but we had no clue how we would manage to work together. We were like the blind and the lame trying to lead each other. He had almost no knowledge of Pastoral Counseling and I had very little knowledge of the pastoral context. It was a starting point and a state of mind. In a sense that state of mind and that starting point always stayed with me. Even giving class at theological schools I was always keenly aware that someone could present a pastoral case and I would not know what to do with all my American counseling theories.

   Within the Pastoral Counseling in Indonesia there quickly developed a consensus that skill training should be the priority. Trainees in pastoral care and counseling should know the basics of entering into a therapeutic conversation, reviewing the presenting problem, possess the knowledge on how to keep that conversation going, how to boil down the issues in such a way that both counselor and counselee could grasp them. They should also know how to formulate a simple action plan and make an inventory of the factors conducive to realizing the plan as well as the obstacles. During the first years at the hospital in Yogyakarta and at the Satya Wacana University skill training was the priority. Since knowledge of Pastoral Counseling was so rudimentary, much of the CPE program was structured around the teaching of skills. How well the trainee grasped these skills was evaluated in verbatims. Over the years the verbatim has become a widely accepted teaching tool for pastoral care and counseling in seminaries all over the country. It gives entry into the ever-changing culture, especially in the cities.

There was one book that provided us with invaluable techniques we could teach in Pastoral Counseling and this was Gerard Egan's *The Skilled Helper*, (Monterey: Brooks/Cole, 1982). If there ever was a book that could help novices become counselors in a variety of socio-economic and cultural settings, this would be the book. Most books on Pastoral Counseling speak about what should be happening or what it is, rather on how to make it work. Much time was spent on translating concepts as "primary-level and advanced empathy," "genuineness," "self-disclosure," etc., into Indonesian understandings. Students of Pastoral Counseling were able to gauge their progress by reference to these concepts. Egan's book allowed us to lay a sound practical foundation that was relatively unbiased culturally. In any of the four cases presented above, any of the caregivers could have been able to use these skills in approaching the care seeker. We discovered, however, that not just the level of skill determined the success of the pastoral encounter. Of course there were differences between caregiver and person in need of care, social status, education, cultural experiences, language, religion and theology. I will discuss these below. While we found that some verbatim records of pastoral encounters would expose the adequate use of empathy, in others the students would fall into a pursuit of information, much of which was either intrusive or irrelevant to the helping objective the counselor might have. This has to do with the fact that some trainees were very nervous about silences of any kind. There were also a number of persons in need of care who were not forthcoming with information. There are a number of reasons for this, not the least being the possibility of breaches of confidentiality. When a student uncomfortable with silences approaches a person uncomfortable with sharing personal information freely, often an interview would ensue that sometimes looked like an interrogation. This interview would lead the student into a direction of his or her own making, and ultimately into a therapeutic cul-de-sac. After that the only alternative left to the student would be to break the encounter off with prayer or some sentences of advice, usually pointing in the directions of actions the person in need of care had already attempted in the past.

The students therefore were urged to find a balance between the exploration of feelings and the hunt for factual information. But it was often difficult to prevent the student from succumbing to the temptation of feeling the, albeit illusive, power of information. Here we confront the prevalent helping culture head-on: The helper is in a position of cultural, economic or physical power. The persons in need of help resist this power. They wait for the commitment of true "pendampingan," sitting next to, as an equal. When Dr. Adriana Lala, a DTh graduate in Pastoral Counseling, identified the issues of authority, communication and trauma in her dissertation, she put her finger on this prevailing helping culture. Why should a patient, lying vulnerable in a hospital bed expose his or her traumas to a person trying to exert power over her or him? Indonesia had always been run by authoritarian rulers and when someone, from a village official to police man to a general, see the opportunity to use their power, the temptation is great, because chances are they have known the experience of powerlessness before.

There are also situations where the person who was presumed to need help exerted his or her authority over the student. At times these people are highly proficient in the use of Bible passages, at times they are high-ranking military personnel, or perhaps advanced age or social status of some kind makes them feel superior.

To nudge students in the direction of increased empathy, it became important to practice genuineness, openness and self-sharing. We found it helped break down barriers to effective intervention. Whenever the verbatim and discussion of the verbatim focused on information rather than empathy, it was more difficult to get to a discussion of the pastoral-counselor in training as a person. Whenever there was an attempt at empathy, the door was open to that discussion. Because Indonesians are taught to keep feelings below the surface, in Clinical Pastoral Education students as much as possible often kept feelings under wraps. But if the supervisor or one of the other students gained access to this world of feelings, emotional dam breaks could be quite powerful.

The discussion of empathy as a practice in pastoral care and counseling was deepened with the introduction of the "interpathy" which put simply means empathy across cultures (see David Augsburger, *Pastoral Counseling Across Cultures*, Philadelphia: Westminster, 1986). In conclusion the expression of empathy and interpathy became central to Pastoral Counseling skills, although both counselor and counselee often resisted them.

TOWARD A HOLISTIC MODEL FOR PASTORAL COUNSELING

How do we move from Pastoral Counseling skills, most importantly empathy to a model that takes into account most if not all of the questions I have touched on? The answer lies in the reality of life in Indonesia. In countries where most care seekers are not overwhelmed by socio-economic problems and social injustice as their primary concern, the skills of counseling, specifically the expression of empathy, are often applied as if the pastoral encounter were taking place–as I have said earlier–within a vacuum. The primary focus is on the inner world of the counselee. Of course the relationships that impact this inner world become part of the areas to be explored, but the care seeker has enough resources at her or his disposal to have power to make major decisions about her or his life. In economically developing or poor countries people who seek help are much more determined by their own powerlessness. Any model for Pastoral Counseling in Indonesia therefore must take into account the social context in which the counselee seeks to find her or his way. In addition the complexity of ethnic and religious life in the country forces the pastoral counselor to gain cross-cultural understanding and to formulate certain theological principles.

While the expression of empathy and additional skills in counseling open the door to the inductive knowledge of the counselee's world, basic analytical concepts from various disciplines bring in some deductive elements also. Consequently knowledge of the counselee's world has led us to certain theological principles discussed below that provide a deductive component to the model. The most important of these principles underlies the objective of the Pastoral Counseling exercise, namely "seeking to make people whole" or borrowing the more nurturing title of Margaret Kornfeld's new book *Cultivating Wholeness* (New York: Continuum, 2000). With regard to the cases presented above, the whole making effort would focus, specifically in the first case, on exploring trauma in family relationships, the quality of religious and spiritual life and the maturity level of personal theology and the economic aspects of the crisis in their interrelationship. In the second case the main focus would be the emotional well being of the tuberculosis patient who may not cope with change well, the relationship with her son and the economic implications of her move. With regard to the third case, the task of whole making cannot ignore the theological and spiritual ramifications of the girlfriend's pregnancy and the social fragmentation that might result as well as the mental integrity of the theological student and his girlfriend. In the last case, we have a situation of inter-religious counseling. How can a trust level be established that will help the man confront his issues in a way that does not jeopardize the integrity of his entire frame of reference?

With the whole making objective as a principle, a multi-disciplinary approach to Pastoral Counseling in Indonesia follows logically. In so doing, we bring together the academic base of Pastoral Counseling and the hospital/health care base, for the holistic approach in the health care context, expressed through the attention of physical, mental, socio-economic approach finds a parallel in the academic approach through an inter-disciplinary emphasis. One could include many different areas in this interdisciplinary approach, but we have chosen disciplines that most inform the practice of Pastoral Counseling, namely theology, hermeneutics, cultural anthropology, sociology and psychology. I would like to examine these briefly below.

Theology for a Pastoral Counseling Model

The role of Pastoral Counseling in Indonesian society has been subject to sharp debate. Those within the evangelical movement have often claimed that Pastoral Counseling should be subordinated to evangelism. Pastoral Counseling thus would become a tool for conversion used by Christians in a predominantly Muslim society. Convictions such as these forced the Pastoral Counseling movement, however small it may be, to come to terms with the theological foundation for its activity in Indonesia. It was not enough for them to affirm that the objective of making whole persons, families and communities is based on faith in God who seeks to make human beings and their total environments whole. It needed theological principles for all that it did. In the context of this discussion, Poling and Miller's book (*Foundations for a Practical Theology for Ministry*, Nashville: Abingdon, 1985) has provided a helpful framework. They give six models for practical theology. The first model states that practical theology uses theology to enrich service within the church. The second model states that practical theology uses social/human sciences to enrich the service within the Church. The third model states that practical theology uses theology in the service toward society as a whole. The fourth model advocates that the social/human sciences are used for service to society as a whole. The fifth model claims that practical theology connects social/human sciences and theology in service to society as a whole. The sixth model states that practical theology connects theology and the social/human sciences in service within the Church.

When we consider these six models in light of our discussion thus far and in light of the four cases, we could draw the following conclusions: in the church-based encounter where the pastor visits the woman who feels black magic has caused her cancer, the pastor should use a combination of psychology and theology for use within the Church (model 6). In the second, hospital-based setting, the appropriate model seems to be model 4, where a person from society at large is assisted with the help of social/human sciences. In the academia-based pastoral setting, theology and psychology would be used for the Church setting in dealing with the theology students (model 6), but model 4 (society as a whole) in dealing with the girlfriend in the hospital. Again, with regard to office-based case 4, the appropriate model would be number 4, because social/human sciences are used to help someone from the society at large. The evangelicals who wish to use Pastoral Counseling as a tool for conversion would prefer model three, while traditional European pastoral theology might gravitate toward model one. In summary, flexibility is called for. Of course the application of these models represents only one example of how theology can be used to form a holistic methodology.

Hermeneutics and Cultural Anthropology

Hermeneutics as a human science and as a theological sub-discipline is still undervalued in Pastoral Counseling. It deals with the question of understanding the experience and intention of another person. Yet pastoral counselors are all familiar with the term "The Living Human Document," one that perfectly bridges the old textual understanding of hermeneutics with its new psychological understanding. In the Indonesian context an understanding of the Living Human Document cannot be divorced from cultural anthropology. In my own book (*Cross-Cultural Counseling*, Minneapolis: Fortress Press, 1996), I presented categories for doing hermeneutics in a cross-culturally sensitive way through the systematic exploration of identity, the sense of belonging in inter-relationships. I made the claim that if these areas are examined carefully with regard to the problems the counselee presents, the dangers of acting in a cross-culturally insensitive manner will be greatly diminished. With respect to the first case, this would mean that the pastor should explore how this woman sees herself, within which groups she experiences a sense of belonging and what her worldview is. Then the pastor needs to ask questions about inner tensions in her self-concept, conflicts for this parishioner between allegiance to one group over another and tensions caused by conflicting worldviews. Next the pastor needs to explore whether there is a conflict between her worldview and her sense of belonging or between her identity and her worldview, etc. For instance, if her sense of belonging is strong among the people whom she accuses of haunting her through black magic, this will have great consequences. In the resolution of the matter of course the pastor, from a theological point of view, might choose to challenge this woman's worldview concerning black magic as the cause of her cancer.

In the second case, there seems to be no problems with worldview, but identity ("I am a perennial patient") and sense of belonging ("this is my home now") are prominent. In the third case, the student's sense of belonging (in the Church and with his girlfriend) shows an inner conflict while there is also a conflict between his worldview and his identity (he is a lover, but also a prospective leader of the Church). In the fourth case the examination of worldview will be precarious, since the pastoral counselor is not likely to have full comprehension of the values of a secularized Muslim. This will have to be explored cautiously. In addition the counselor will have to touch on the client's self-concept over against his belonging with his wife, the other woman or both (polygamy is not altogether illegal in Indonesia).

Using these categories in Pastoral Counseling in a culturally diverse situation is crucial because each situation is different. The culture of each individual is constantly in process and dynamic. The simple model I just suggested gives insight into the cultural context of each counselee, no matter what his or her cultural background is. Again the discussion of hermeneutics and cultural anthropology in constructing a holistic method for Pastoral Counseling is much broader than just this one model.

Sociology and a Method for Pastoral Counseling

As I made clear earlier, the socio-economic condition of a counselee or counselees is very important. Undoubtedly it plays a role in each of the cases, although most clearly in case one (the battle over land) and two (the hospital's cost and the price of a new home for the tuberculosis patient). Money is always a problem in Indonesia as it is in all developing nations. Sooner or later it forces itself into the counseling relationship. The first reality pastoral counselors will have to accept is that unless they work for one of the few institutions with ample resources or their Pastoral Counseling duties are secondary to their primary occupation, they will never be paid for their services. Making a living as an office-based counselor does not seem viable at this point in time.

A second reality the pastoral counselor must face, as I explained earlier, is that the pastoral counselor cannot operate in a vacuum. There must be a good referral system in place, especially in the city where creative ways of helping people are more needed than in the traditional countryside. I struggled with this problem and finally wrote a small book in Indonesian on the "strategy of integrative care." It deals with strategies for health care organization, social workers, rehabilitative institutions, social welfare organizations, churches and mental health professionals to work together in a network with a shared formalized referral procedure. I do not know if it made an impact, because the book is not as widely used as the others (on pastoral care, Pastoral Counseling and on addiction), perhaps because such a system would have to be imposed from outside, rather than grow from the ground up. In the holistic analysis model that Bethesda hospital used for determining social health, the following aspects were included: physical environment, relationships, economic situation, cultural expression, education and community involvement.

In exploring the socio-economic condition of the counselee, "empowerment" is a crucial concept. In the face of poverty and injustice, whole making involves empowering persons to make their voice known, to address injustice. Depending on the social environment of the counselee we can speak of different levels of empowerment. For example the degree to which a pastoral counselor could empower a counselee in a more predictable, established rural environment is different from the degree to which a counselor could empower a middle class citizen in the city where legal aid and other resources might be available.

Psychology and a Model for Pastoral Counseling

Naturally, psychology is important in developing a model for Pastoral Counseling. The fact that I discuss it last is to make a point. Psychology is almost the only discipline informing Pastoral Counseling in most developed nations. Theology, sociology, hermeneutics and anthropology all appear to be dispensable. But a holistic model requires attention to all these aspects.

Much of what Indonesian students of Pastoral Counseling are taught in the area of psychology is similar to what students of the field would be taught in economically developed nations: the emotional stages of dying, the stages of grief, the characteristics of addiction and the ways to treat it, the nature of interaction and group dynamics, the stages of conflict, the dynamics of families and of course the three steps in crisis counseling. But within the psychological component to a Pastoral Counseling method in Indonesia, it is important to keep the holistic perspective going. If we take the three functions of the psyche, emotion, cognition and motivation, we can examine them in their interrelationship. For instance, in the first case the cognitive abilities of the parishioner are impaired by an emotional life that is out of control. In the second case the motivation for stability is propelled by fear of loss of the familiar surroundings and an inability to reflect (cognitive) about a new living situation. In the third case, the theological student has become entangled because of lack of control of his impulses, so that his emotions are now overwhelming him. The counselor must nurture the cognitive side. In the final case, the counselee is confused about what he wants (motivation), but is not overwhelmed by emotion.

Some therapies have a specific preference in choosing the functions of the psyche. Rogerians choose emotions, Harperians choose cognitive/rational abilities and Glasserians emphasize motivation and behavior. Yet most pastoral counselors these days choose to work eclectically, often with more than one counselee or entire families. For pastoral counselors in Indonesia it will be increasingly necessary to have a grasp of each of these therapies. In Indonesia I have found that certain ethnic groups respond better to cognitive approaches in counseling rather than emotion-focused approaches. Behavioral approaches seemed to work better with young people. The challenge however is to instill a basic understanding of pastoral care and counseling.

PASTORAL COUNSELING EVALUATION AND THE HOLISTIC MODEL

In a book on Pastoral Counseling in Indonesian, I included a checklist of skills (largely based on Egan's book) to use in evaluation. For the holistic analysis of the context I adapted the holistic model developed at Bethesda hospital, completed by categories for theological analysis of the case. In a small book I wrote in Indonesian recently on basic pastoral care I devoted a chapter on evaluative questions in pastoral care/simple Pastoral Counseling. I begin by referring to the functions of pastoral care and counseling (borrowed from Clinebell, *Basic Types of Pastoral Care and Counseling*, Nashville; Abingdon, 1984). These are "sustaining," "guiding," "reconciling," "nurturing" and "healing." A "whole making" function was then added. The counselee or supervisor is then asked to evaluate to what degree the counselor has exhibited these functions in pastoral care. In case one the "healing," "sustaining" and "reconciling" functions appear most needed. In the second case, the "guiding" function is strong, because the patient must be made to see that a way out is possible. But also "sustaining" in a time of anxiety is important. In the third case, "sustaining" is important because the student is in a state of crisis, but "guiding" is going to become significant as will "reconciling" as the student has to face the Church leaders who sent him to the theological school. In the fourth case, "guiding" will be a function that will be sought by the counselee. Whole making underlies the effort in all three cases. It is an overarching function.

Next on the evaluation list are theological questions. Some of these are: To what extent does the counselor use the Bible or prayer appropriately in the pastoral encounter? Is the counselor able to put the needs of the counselee above the urge to proclaim? To what degree is the counselor able to discover the emotional wounds underneath the religious conversation on the surface? These questions of course can vary as the holistic model can vary from context to context.

Next are some anthropological/hermeneutical questions. These include: To what extent is the counselor aware of his or her own opinions concerning the counselee's situation? To what degree is the counselor aware of the expectations of the counselor by the counselee? To what degree does the counselor satisfy those expectations? To what degree is the counselor aware of the dynamic of identity, sense of belonging and worldview in the counselee's experience?

Next is the sociological component. This includes a question such as the following: To what extent is the counselor aware of a socio-economic crisis? To what degree is the counselor aware of the influence of social groups on the presenting and underlying problems? To what degree is the counselor aware of the empowerment level at which the counselee can be addressed?

The psychological skills follow. Questions featured are: To what extent does the counselor employ cognitive skills, emotional skills or motivational skills? To what degree is the counselor aware of the most pressing needs of the counselee? Is the caregiver aware of the intensity of the crisis the counselor is facing?

Finally, since this is a holistic approach, we look at integration. Evaluation questions include: To what degree can the caregiver crystallize a clear and simple diagnosis from the information he or she has obtained? To what degree is the caregiver able to help the care seeker to formulate a simple plan of action based on that analysis?

THE ROAD AHEAD

I hope that through the information provided above readers will feel challenged to see beyond psychological models for Pastoral Counseling to holistic models. The one outlined above is particular to Indonesia and may not even be valid there for much longer. I believe that Pastoral Counseling, if it lets itself be led–inductively–by the true needs of people needing help and not by its own need to maintain itself, can play a crucial role in society. It cannot do so by merely being office-based or even being hospital/institution-based. I believe pastoral counselors should be concerned not so much with carving out a little niche in the mental health care economy, helping to maintain a system as a theologically schooled alternative to other mental health professionals, but with fulfilling its own holistic mission as true servants in a society filled with people in pain. I believe this will be much more fulfilling in the end, albeit unsettling.

Pastoral Care and Counselling:
An Asian Perspective

Anthony Yeo, MA

SUMMARY. This article discusses current issues in Pastoral Care and Counselling from an Asian perspective, with specific attention paid to Singapore. Relationships between psychological theory and practice and pastoral ministry in terms of the role of therapeutic conversations in Pastoral Care are explored. Specific therapeutic attitudes and approaches are discussed as they relate to pastoral ministry. The affect of various global trends in pastoral ministry on churches in Asia is also discussed. *[Article copies available for a fee from The Haworth Document Delivery Service: 1-800-HAWORTH. E-mail address: <getinfo@haworthpressinc.com> Website: <http://www.HaworthPress.com> © 2002 by The Haworth Press, Inc. All rights reserved.]*

KEYWORDS. Pastoral care, pastoral ministry, pastoral counselling, Singapore, Asian context

A PERSONAL JOURNEY

My foray into pastoral care and counselling came about when I was introduced to the Churches' Counselling Centre back in 1971. This Centre was the first known Christian counselling service not only in Singapore, but also in the South East Asian region.

[Haworth co-indexing entry note]: "Pastoral Care and Counseling: An Asian Perspective." Yeo, Anthony. Co-published simultaneously in *American Journal of Pastoral Counseling* (The Haworth Pastoral Press, an imprint of The Haworth Press, Inc.) Vol. 5, No. (3/4), 2002, pp. 175-189; and: *International Perspectives on Pastoral Counseling* (ed: James Reaves Farris) The Haworth Pastoral Press, an imprint of The Haworth Press, Inc., 2002, pp. 175-189. Single or multiple copies of this article are available for a fee from The Haworth Document Delivery Service [1-800-HAWORTH, 9:00 a.m. - 5:00 p.m. (EST). E-mail address: getinfo@haworthpressinc.com].

The service was initiated by a group of laity and pastoral folks from the Methodist Church, in particular, the Wesley Methodist Church. There was also some collaboration from the Anglican Church as well (Annual Report, 1967).

When the project was launched in 1966, it was managed by an American missionary pastor, the late Rev. Dr. Gunnar Teilmann. Other missionaries with some form of counselling training assisted him. Occasional professional staff included professors on sabbatical leave from theological seminaries in the United States.

Since those early days, I have been inducted into this field through exposure to Clinical Pastoral Education and my further graduate work in pastoral psychology and counselling. I had since also been associated with this Centre which became the Counselling and Care Centre, diminishing its pastoral image to reflect its outreach to a population that has been largely non-Christian.

My role expanded when I became a regular part-time faculty member of Trinity Theological College from 1983, as well as being a visiting lecturer to various theological institutions in Singapore and Asia including India, Malaysia, Indonesia, Philippines and Thailand.

It has also been my privilege to observe the development of pastoral care and counselling the 1960s. During the '60s and '70s, the influence came primarily from the Clinical Pastoral Education movement, with strong emphasis on pastoral care from a hospital based orientation. Much of what was taught tended to focus on pastoral care rather than counselling.

This could probably be affected by the beginning development of counselling and psychotherapy as a profession in Asia as well. At that time, this was just beginning to be introduced to Asia, with a stronger emphasis on guidance and educational counselling rather than psychotherapy. Psychology as a discipline was also relatively new to the region as most universities were focused on developing disciplines related to the socio-political and economic milieu following the Second World War.

The subsequent decades witnessed a significant growth in the counselling profession. All kinds of therapeutic approaches were making inroads into Asia. Counselling and psychotherapy started to gain acceptance as a form of intervention for life's problems.

The Church in Asia was no less affected by what was happening in society at large. Those who attended church were becoming open to seeking counsel from pastors and other Christian workers. Missionaries found themselves needing to attend to social-psychological issues besides the work of evangelism and Christian nurture.

From the '70s and '80s onwards, pastoral care and counselling became a required course in most seminaries. In Singapore, this was first introduced in Trinity Theological College. The other seminaries or Bible colleges were cautious in their reception of psychology and counselling, dismissing that to the secular and to some extent, the demonic (Yeo, 1981). In a sense, counselling was more acceptable to the so-called liberal wing of the Christian community. This seemed to be the trend in the Western world and was the way counselling was introduced to the Christian community in Asia.

For instance, pastoral counselling in India came via the more liberal schools, including one significant contribution by the late Dr. Frank Lake (1986) from Britain, whose work in Clinical Theology took roots in the '60s in Vellore, India. His work also influenced the Churches' Counselling Centre in Singapore as well, when his work was introduced by one of his associates. He subsequently made a visit to Singapore.

The more conservative, evangelical community was more familiar with Bible teaching with emphasis on the work of the Holy Spirit in transforming people and society. Counselling with its psychological framework was regarded as tending to the natural, without much attention given to building a strong Biblical foundation for living, nor obvious intervention of the Holy Spirit in daily affairs.

However, with the increasing economic development of most Asia countries, social conditions took on a more materially developed state. Although most Asian countries would be considered third world in economic terms, many urban centres were fast becoming first world environments.

The Church, especially the more conservative wing, became more sensitive to social changes. With it came its openness to incorporating counselling as an integral aspect of Church life, in particular, pastoral ministry.

Since the '90s Singapore churches, along with other Asian Christian communities saw an increasing number of Christians entering the counselling profession. In fact, for some time, Christians tended to dominate the helping professions in Singapore. Churches were also offering counselling services as a distinct programme to the community. In addition, many churches and Christian organizations started to form counselling services for specific target groups, such as families in crisis, drug abuse, the older folks and those afflicted with mental illness.

Within the context of theological education, seminaries started to introduce master's programmes in counselling. These programmes are identified as Christian Counselling or Pastoral Counselling degree programmes, with some being offered as majors in Master of Divinity or Theology programmes.

It would seem that the trend towards giving prominence to counselling in the Church and theological education would continue. Asian theological institutions will follow the development of its Western counterparts with more seminaries including counselling as a degree programme.

PERSPECTIVE ON PASTORAL CARE AND COUNSELLING

As I see it, there may be a need to observe the trend in pastoral ministry and the training of pastors. Pastoral care and counselling have been highlighted by many sectors of the Christian community in Asia as a needed service for people. It is not uncommon to hear Christians and pastoral personnel alike lamenting that the world is getting more complex, problems are becoming overwhelming and the stress of life seems to be taking its toll on people.

Hence, the obvious need for more psychological help. Likewise, it has almost become imperative that pastors in particular be better equipped to minister to people. And counselling skills would form a major component within the repertoire of pastoral skills.

In light of such development, it may be useful to reflect on the role of pastors and reaffirm their ministry in the nurture of Christian life and community. It would also help to observe the needs of Asian churches and the demands of pastors in meetings needs of members.

My contacts with churches and pastors in various parts of Asia have impressed me with a constant need for pastors and related ministry workers to provide Christian nurture for life in society. The Christian population has been growing in Asia. Much of it has been connected to the fall of the communist system and the openness of many Asian countries to the outside world.

The impact of globalization and cyber age has also contributed to a fairly borderless world. This seems to have benefited the spread of Christianity. With this spread comes the growth of Christian communities, with a greater demand for pastoral leadership.

The need of most Asian churches would be for trained pastoral personnel to provide an urgent need for pastoral care.

This in its Biblical context would obviously refer to nurture of Christian character, equipping for service, provision of care and empowering for struggles of life (Jn. 21:15-17; Eph. 4:11-12; I Pe. 5:2; Eph. 6:10-11).

Given the demands of the Church and the primary role of pastoral personnel, it would seem reasonable to expect that pastoral care be a major role and activity of pastoral personnel. This is also the primary need of Christians, as it has been for centuries since the early days of the Church.

It may be useful to concentrate on care rather than counselling as there is a substantive difference between the two. Care has a wider focus with clearer Biblical injunctions given to care and build one another up. It also has a stronger pastoral emphasis.

Counselling can be differentiated in that it tends to be focused on dealing with problems of living, including disruptions to personal and family life. It is also closely related to treatment of problems, often associated with some acquired skills in psychological counselling.

Pastoral ministry incorporates pastoral care, with counselling comprising only one aspect of such care. As such it could be postulated that generally, people need care, not necessarily counselling. Pastoral care embraces the various dimensions of attention given to members of the congregation regardless of need and problems. It does not presuppose problems.

Pastoral care is about giving attention to nurture and empowerment for living. It is also premised on the belief that if people are accorded appropriate care as a part of Christian community (I Cor. 12:14-26), then it could be possible that they would have sufficient resources for dealing with life's problems.

The pastor would be the teacher/pastor who would teach Biblical truths relevant to life situations. This would be done within the context of Christian community where support would be given for managing all kinds of human experiences.

In performing such pastoral care, it would be useful to access knowledge and skills from the field of counselling and psychology. This would shift attention from counselling to pastoral care and the application of counselling skills for pastoral ministry.

PROPOSAL FOR PASTORAL CARE

If there is a generalization that can be made of Asians, it is their rather communal orientation to relationship. People tend to connect at the personal level, with a tendency for conversations as a form of social interactions. Although urban folks tend to relate at a more formal level, especially in business and professional relationships, church members still prefer a casual relationship with pastoral personnel.

In some situations, it may even be considered offensive to take a clinical approach to talking about problems in a pastoral context. Hence a structured, formal counselling situation would probably be associated with a clinical setting rather than a church setting.

It is also possible that church members would rather consult with pastoral personnel outside the church context. Homes, hospitals and other non-church settings are more likely places for conversations about life's dilemmas. In such settings, counselling may take place. Should any follow-up be deemed necessary, it may not be as structured and formalized as in a clinical setting (Ho, 1987; Hsu in Tseng & Wu, 1987).

Church members may tend to disregard boundaries and expect access to pastoral personnel whenever any need arises. They would also expect visits and initiative for contacts to be made by the pastor. Such expectation could be attributed to a village mind-set where elders of the village inquire into welfare of households in the community. They are also readily accessible for conversations and consultations whenever the need arises. Appointments and scheduling of visitation times are almost foreign to them.

In a sense, such an approach is reminiscent of Richard Baxter's (1974) pastoral concerns in taking care of the flock and inquiring about matters of the soul. In *The Reformed Pastor,* he advocated that pastors should seek to be counselors of souls and inquire into well-being of families as well as seeking to strengthen those who are strong. Pastoral care would then be extended to all members of the flock.

Generally, formal counselling tends to be an exception rather than the norm. Hence, it may be expedient to enter into pastoral conversations rather than counselling. It will connote a less formal situation, with pastoral personnel taking time to meet with members for pastoral conversations, as discussed by Faber and Schoot (1962) and developed further by Noyce (1981). Hopefully, conversations in everyday situations could be shifted to being pastoral where problems could be discussed, guidance given, encouragement offered and healing experienced.

If such an orientation were to be adopted for pastoral care, the emphasis will be less on counselling, more on a personal, casual, informal setting for counselling to take place within the context of pastoral conversations.

This would fit well with the evolution of the professional practice of counselling and psychotherapy, especially within the past decade. With the influence of postmodernist thinking, the trend has been towards therapeutic conversations and communication (Gilligan & Price, 1993; Wachetl, 1993; Yeo, 2000a). This has provided an expanded perspective for counselling, as the emphasis is on resilience, strengths and resources in a conversational style that seeks to induce healing in the process of counselling.

Pastoral personnel would be oriented to engage members in healing conversations in their routine dealings with members. The emphasis would be less on techniques or strategies for counselling intervention. Instead, the greater concern is to utilize opportunities for influencing the process of conversation towards some therapeutic effects.

Unfortunately, most pastoral personnel tended to express difficulty in offering time to members for such conversations. This is often attributed to pressure of time. Many of them tended to be inundated with administrative work and demands of meetings with minimal available time for pastoral visits and informal encounters with members. Many pastors have been moulded to function as CEOs (Chief Executive Officers), with the church as a large corporation.

Perhaps it would be more expedient for Asian churches to restrain themselves from expecting pastoral personnel to function as administrative leaders in order to release them for pastoral care. Pastoral care would then be a major function of pastors. However, this need not be their sole responsibility due to the demands of growing numbers in the churches. The larger membership of the church could be recruited to participate in this shared responsibility of pastoral care.

This would obviously require that pastors give attention to equipping members for ministry. The role and function of pastoral care would then be shared by a larger group of ministry personnel, with church members being equipped to reach out to one another in care and concern. Burden bearing (Gal. 6:2) and demonstration of care through the ministry of encouragement (I Thes. 5:11) could then be a shared experience.

THERAPEUTIC CONVERSATIONS IN PASTORAL CARE

In offering a pastoral care paradigm for counselling, it is proposed that therapeutic conversations form a significant activity in pastoral ministry. Such conversations derive from counselling and psychotherapy from a postmodernist perspective that adopts a view of therapy of uncertainty and empowerment (Amundson, Stewart & Valentine, 1993). It espouses an approach that seeks to focus on the interview as conversation with healing intent, despite the lack of some clear intervention strategies.

It has been proposed that the interview or conversation would be intervention itself (Tomm, 1987). The intention is for the therapist to engage a person in conversation through the use of questions and comments that solicit responses of a healing nature. Through such process of therapeutic conversation, healing can be experienced, resources for solutions identified and change initiated. No formal, structured problem solving may be necessitated.

Therapeutic intent would then be predicated on the premise that change comes about when difference is experienced in facilitating people to "expand their view of life, enlarge their repertoire of coping resources and enable them to make choices for change in themselves, their situation or environment without destroying life itself" (Yeo, 1993, p. 5).

This view of change provides a basis for engaging people in conversation without imposing a particular strategy or technique. Instead, it opens space for exploration of alternatives and possibilities in enhancing human functioning. Problems may not be solved, yet a different view can be adopted, coping resources can be accessed and changes can be made in the way a person responds to a problem situation.

In order for this to be incorporated into counselling for pastoral care, Anderson's (1997) ideas on conversation in a therapeutic context could be helpful (p. 111). The following characteristics basic to all conversations are:

1. All participants enter a conversation with a framework that includes what they bring from their everyday lives.
2. Each conversation occurs within a context.
3. Each conversation is embedded within and will become a part of myriad other past and future conversations, i.e., no conversation is a single event.
4. Each conversation has a purpose, expectations, and intentions that all participants contribute.
5. Each outer, spoken conversation between participants involves inner, silent conversations within the participants.

Therapy can be considered as conversation since it also bears the above features. There is dialogical interaction between persons in the therapeutic relationship made possible through talking. It is in this context that therapy has been identified as the talking cure (Wachtel, 1993).

These characteristics of conversations when applied to a therapeutic context, brings to focus a sort of shared inquiry between the persons in conversation. It involves recognition of dialogical space, collaborative exploration, shared intention to learn about and attempt in understanding the other, without any assumption that one knows what the other is trying to say or mean.

It may require that the therapist, in this case the pastor, adopt an open mind, seeking to listen, understand and empathize. It is a way of offering a beneficial presence to people that leads them to feel acknowledged, appreciated, affirmed and accepted. In a pastoral sense, grace is administered, healing can be experienced, and strength restored.

It is therefore preferred that therapeutic conversation avoids being problem-saturated which tends to focus on problems, pathology and in a pastoral context, morality. This would influence the conversation towards being investigative, interrogative, evaluative and interpretative. The possible effect is that the person would tend towards a negative view of self, depreciation of self-worth and concentration on problems. Judgment is experienced with a sense of being diagnosed and pathologized.

In place of such a stance in pastoral conversation, it is proposed that pastoral personnel adopt the following ideas derived from therapeutic conversation for pastoral conversation:

1. Adopting an exploratory approach.
2. Keeping an open mind, and adopting a not-knowing position
3. Being respectful.
4. Being health-oriented and strength-based rather than deficit-based.
5. Adopting a systemic and multi-perspectival orientation.

Adopting an Exploratory Approach

It has been suggested that therapists could learn to adopt a stance of being a tourist rather than a tour guide in working with clients (Caesar & Roberts, 1991). This posture orients the therapist towards curiosity, like a tourist who would normally be curious in exploring and learning about new places on a tour.

In therapy, the client is the tour guide, the one who knows what to disclose, where to proceed in exploring issues and the kind of information to share. Effectively, the therapist would need to be guided on a tour of terrains of the client's inner world of self and relationship. S/he has the information and would normally be in a good position to lead the process of disclosure.

The job of the therapist is to facilitate and stimulate conditions for this process to happen. In this sense, an exploratory approach for pastoral conversation offers the pastor an opportunity to know more about his members. S/he is to discard the usual posture of a preacher and teacher who is supposed to dispense Biblical knowledge and information. This position insists on a listening role.

Keeping an Open Mind and Adopting a Not-Knowing Position

This is related to the exploratory approach advocated. It involves coming to a person without any fixed agenda, pre-determined goals and foreknowledge as to what should be the subject matter for dialogue. Whilst one may believe in the miracle of dialogue (Howe, 1963), this miracle can best be realized by coming to a person with the idea that a pastor does not yet know the person.

The pastor, like the therapist operating from this framework, cannot fully understand another person and will need to be informed by the other. There is no privileged information on his part, which would lead to an attitude of wanting to learn about the other and hear what is being said.

The expert in this conversational encounter is not the pastor, but the person. S/he is the one who knows and can offer information about issues, problems and dilemmas.

There is also an attitude of humility, which would restrain the pastor from telling, teaching, instructing, or imposing his knowledge and interpretations. It means acknowledging that the person has the information, interpretation and opinions about what is of concern to her/his situation.

In recommending a not-knowing posture, it does not mean that the pastor does not know anything. It does mean that we do acknowledge what we know from our learning, training and study. What helps is to suspend our knowledge and be open enough for the other to let us know.

Being Respectful

This suggests respecting a person's views and information in an accepting manner. To accord a person such respect requires being attentive to him/her and acknowledging that we hear what is said. It conveys that we value what is said and affirms that the person is made in God's image and therefore worthy of our respect.

Being respectful would also mean we would be quick to listen and slow to speak (Prov. 17:27-28, 18:13; Jas. 1:19). There will be no urgency to probe and comment. Opinions will be withheld and any response from the pastor would be to facilitate disclosure.

Such expression of respect will also take into consideration family roles and hierarchy. In Asia, many families are still fairly structured and respect for senior members of families in pastoral conversation should be expressed. For instance, one would avoid asking younger members, especially children, to be expressive of their feelings and opinions of their parents or elders. It might be more appropriate to ensure that family hierarchy is not disrupted.

Another aspect of respect would mean being respectful of those who may choose not to enter into conversation of a personal nature. There will be no attempt to coerce someone into conversation. Exercising sensitivity means being aware of those who may wish to speak and those who may not, either for now or for a long time.

Being Health-Oriented and Strength-Based Rather Than Deficit-Based

The medical model of diagnosis and treatment has influenced the tradition of psychotherapy and counselling. This had been characterized by a tendency to focus on illness with the view to seeking a cure.

However, there has been a movement since the days of influence from humanistic psychology and the work of Carl Rogers (1951) to focus on the goodness of people. This has gained momentum with the orientation towards resilience and resourcefulness (Walsh, 1998).

Being strength-based includes adopting an orientation towards appreciating people's inner and outer resourcefulness in the midst of struggles and dilemmas of life. It is an orientation that views people and problems in the context of their strengths, without ignoring the reality of problems.

This will lead the therapist to engage in conversation that will explore resources in their lives, identifying attempts at resolving problems and focusing on helping people utilize available resources to enhance strengths.

The pastor can learn to engage in such conversations instead of the tendency to inquire into problems, sin and judgment. In attempting to minister grace, the pastor would focus on helping people appreciate God-given grace and strength which often come in the midst of weakness or "thorn in the flesh" (I Cor. 12: 7-10).

Health-oriented conversations would also minimize or eliminate accusatory elements, which may lead to greater guilt and shame. Instead, the pastor seeks to engage in "exculpatory" conversations (Wachtel, pp. 68-86). As we understand Christ's sacrificial work of redemption is to exculpate us from sin, likewise, pastoral conversation can give attention to alternative language that provides positive connotations to behaviour and problems. In the process, he feels exculpated, empowered and exonerated.

This can be illustrated in the way we tend to attribute negative or "problem" meanings to behaviour. A person who has a problem is often deemed weak or ill. Perhaps it is a natural response to a difficult situation, as in a person who is depressed and grieves deeply at the sudden loss of a loved one who has died in a serious accident. Talking with the person about the pain and seeking to view the depression as a natural response in such a situation minimizes guilt and shame. Taking a different, neutral or preferably positive view can open up possibilities for living with life's problems.

In a sense, the wisdom of Philippians 4:8 could be applied in conversation that would hopefully be gracious and healing (Col. 4: 6). Thinking of whatever is excellent and praiseworthy can be a healing experience for people. Wounded people can benefit to hear themselves talk about affirmative aspects of life's experiences.

Adopting a Systemic and Multi-Perspectival Orientation

Those who advocate therapeutic conversations tended to be influenced by systemic thinking, which generally views human phenomena from a multi-perspectival orientation. It builds on the individualized, intra-psychic view of people and problems to include viewing a person in relation to the larger context of life (Barnes, 1998; Bertalanffy, 1968; Minuchin, 1974).

Problems in people do not arise from within alone, but from a myriad network of connections with family of origin, interaction with other systems of life and in relation to feedback from information outside of the self.

Hence, whatever affects a person can be viewed from more than one viewpoint. Problems are not the outcome of one single cause, and may not necessarily be located in the person. Although this may challenge the traditional Christian position of personal sin, it does offer the possibility that personal sin is not always the cause or major contributing factor to dilemmas of life.

When a pastor engages a person in such conversations, there can be openness to explore alternative views of problems, which can also lead to exploring options for resolution. There is less need for rigidity and being confined to one cause and one solution.

A systemic perspective also invites the pastor to consider himself as part of the therapeutic system. He could also be part of the problem system and by his participation in the conversation, could be contributing to problems that people present to him.

Adopting this view offers the possibility of avoiding being part of the problem system. Instead, the pastor would seek to be part of the healing system and in the process, facilitate conversation in an exploratory manner. Different views of problems could be explored, which could lead to opening psychological space towards a healing experience. When this is facilitated, space can be opened for exploration of varied solutions or ways of living with dilemmas of life.

In I Corinthians 13:12 the apostle Paul teaches that whatever we know on earth, we know only in part. This is indicative that whatever we know of people and problems is necessarily partial, suggesting that there is always another point of view. Hence there is always another way to view people and problems, another way to deal with them as well.

In a sense, there is hope. And pastoral conversation would do well to offer and instill hope.

A Personal Response

It is inevitable that churches in Asia will continue to be exposed to global trends in pastoral ministry. What has taken roots in North American churches and seminaries is affecting the Asian scene as well. This is true of the prominence that counselling is having in pastoral ministry.

In view of current and future trends in pastoral ministry, there is a need to think about the role of counselling and counselling training in the Church. Reference has already been made of the need for pastoral personnel to provide shepherding functions to the Christian community. This is a primary role of pastoral personnel, but not the sole responsibility and prerogative of the pastor. It is a shared ministry that espouses the view of care being administered by members of this community (Yeo, 2000b).

If this were to be facilitated, counselling should be practiced in the context of pastoral care offered by pastoral personnel but realized through participation by the members of the community.

This will not be a formalized structure of lay counselling as normally advocated (Tan, 1991) by Christian mental health professionals. It is instead a contextual, informal and interactive approach of counselling facilitated through relationships and experienced via conversations.

Members will be equipped to appreciate counselling or therapy as conversation, with the intent to offer healing experiences. This equipping process involves pastoral personnel in teaching Biblical precepts on Christian community in their care for one another, nurturing of members as shepherds of the flock (Ecclesiastes 34) and experiencing therapeutic conversations in lived experiences of interaction.

It requires that pastoral personnel be trained in counselling skills for pastoral ministry. This involves rethinking for Asian theological education. The traditional model adopted from the West would need modification. The focus and goal of theological education is equipping for pastoral ministry, with strong emphasis on practical theology. Counselling will not be given prominence but instead form an integral component of pastoral care.

Since there are still scarce resources for educators in counselling for pastoral ministry, it is also recommended that Asian theological institutions avoid channeling limited resources for degree programmes in counselling. This will hopefully minimize the possibility of graduating counsellors with insufficient expertise, which universities and other professional training institutions can offer.

Counselling skills, especially in therapeutic conversation can then be incorporated as a comprehensive approach to theological education for ministry. It may also involve renaming of counselling courses, usually identified as Pastoral Care and Counselling, Pastoral Counselling, Biblical Counselling or Christian Counselling.

If it is constituted within the context of pastoral ministry, perhaps such courses could be identified as Counselling Skills for Pastoral Ministry. This places focus on the context, which is pastoral and the activity, ministry-related. Counselling skills become integrated within the larger framework of pastoral care, an aspect of pastoral ministry. Counselling does not take on greater prominence. In fact, it may not need to feature, but be incorporated as pastoral care. Pastoral conversation can then be the means of care in pastoral encounters.

Perhaps this is the way ahead for Asian Christian communities. A way for people to be brought into the fold of Christian community and provided Christian nurturing, mediated through conversations facilitated by pastoral personnel.

REFERENCES

Amundson, L., Stewart, K., Valentine, L.N. (1993). Temptations of Power and Certainty. *Journal of Marital and Family Therapy*, 19, 111-123.
Anderson, H. (1997). *Conversation, Language, and Possibilities, A Postmodern Approach to Therapy*. New York: Basic Books.
Barnes, Gill Gorell (1998). *Family Therapy in Changing Times*. London: Macmillan.
Baxter, Richard (1974). *The Reformed Pastor*. Edinburgh: Banner of Truth Trust.
Bertalanffy, L.V. (1968). *General Systems Theory*. New York: Brazillier.
Caesar, P. Lynn, Roberts, Marjorie Friday (1991). A Conversational Journey with Clients and Helpers: Therapist as Tourist, Not Tour Guides. *Journal of Strategic and Systemic Therapies*. 10: #3 & 4, 38-51.
Churches Counselling Centre (1967). *First Annual Report*. Singapore.
Faber, Heije, Schoot, Eber van der (1962). *The Art of Pastoral Conversation: Effective Counseling Through Personal Encounter*. Nashiville: Abingdon.
Gilligan, Stephen, Price, Reese (1993). *Therapeutic Conversations*. New York: W.W. Norton.
Ho, M.K. (1987). *Family Therapy with Ethnic Minorities*. California: Sage.
Howe, Reuel L. (1963). *The Miracle of Dialogue*. New York: Seabury Press.
Hsu, Jing (1985). The Chinese Family: Relations, Problems and Therapy. In Tseng, Wen-Ching and Wu, Y.H. (eds.), *Chinese Culture and Mental Health*. Florida: Academic Press.
Lake, Frank (1986). *Clinical Theology (abridged version)*. London: Darton, Longman & Todd.
Minuchin, S. (1974). *Families and Family Therapy*. Cambridge: Harvard University Press.
Noyce, Gaylord (1981). *The Art of Pastoral Conversation*. Atlanta: John Know Press.
Rogers, C.R. (1951). *Client-Centered Therapy*. Boston: Houghton Mifflin.
Tan, Siang-Yang (1991). *Lay Counseling*. Michigan: Zondervan Publishing House.
Tomm, Karl (1987). Interventive Interviewing: Part II. Reflexive Questioning as a Means to Enable Self-Healing. *Family Process*. 26; June.
Wachtel, Paul L. (1993). *Therapeutic Communication*. New York: Guilford Press.
Walsh, F. *Strengthening Family Resilience*. New York: Guilford Press.
Yeo, Anthony (1980). Psychotherapy And The Christian. *Impetus*. Singapore: Graduates Christian Fellowship.
Yeo, Anthony (1993). *Counselling: A Problem-Solving Approach*. Singapore Armour Publisher.
Yeo, Anthony (2000a). Counselling in Postmodernist Thinking. In Salazar-Clemena, Rose-Marie (ed.), *Counselling In Asia: Integrating Cultural Perspective*. Philippines: Association of Psychological and Educational Counselors of Asia-Pacific.
Yeo, Anthony (2000b). Counselling in the Twenty-First Century–A Personal Perspective. In Lim, Isaac (ed.), *The Christian Church in 21st Century Singapore*. Singapore: National Council of Churches.

Pastoral Care in Latin America

Sara Baltodano, MPhil

SUMMARY. The article introduces an approach called "Liberating Pastoral Care to the Poor"; it has a biblical background, which maintains that oppression, exploitation, marginalization and discrimination are considered scandalous in the perspective of the Gospel. "Liberating Pastoral Care" takes into account the ecology of the poor, and considers them as active subjects who can change their own situation. Pastoral care among the poor is a vision, a struggle that is full of hope. There is no time for passive expectation, only active work; sometimes hoping against hope. Poor families, the principal object of this research, have complex problems and therefore need complex analysis and solutions. *[Article copies available for a fee from The Haworth Document Delivery Service: 1-800-HAWORTH. E-mail address: <getinfo@haworthpressinc.com> Website: <http://www.HaworthPress.com> © 2002 by The Haworth Press, Inc. All rights reserved.]*

KEYWORDS. Pastoral care, patoral counseling, Latin America, poverty

[Haworth co-indexing entry note]: "Pastoral Care in Latin America." Baltodano, Sara. Co-published simultaneously in *American Journal of Pastoral Counseling* (The Haworth Pastoral Press, an imprint of The Haworth Press, Inc.) Vol. 5, No. (3/4), 2002, pp. 191-224; and: *International Perspectives on Pastoral Counseling* (ed: James Reaves Farris) The Haworth Pastoral Press, an imprint of The Haworth Press, Inc., 2002, pp. 191-224. Single or multiple copies of this article are available for a fee from The Haworth Document Delivery Service [1-800-HAWORTH, 9:00 a.m. - 5:00 p.m. (EST). E-mail address: getinfo@ haworthpressinc.com].

INTRODUCTION

At present, our continent has many needs. One of these is reconciliation, especially in places where there have been wars, such as Central America or Chile. A variety of pastoral counselors are emphasizing this aspect of pastoral care. Nonetheless, in this article we will concentrate on poverty.

Pastoral Care and Counseling always occur within social, political, economic and religious contexts. As such, this article will begin with a discussion of poverty in Central and South America in order to understand at least one of the powerful forces that influence life in these regions. Only then will it be possible to discuss the current state of Pastoral Care and Counseling, and offer concrete suggestions, or models, which better respond to the needs of this cultural context.

My interest in this topic developed 25 years ago when I began to live and work as a counselor and teacher among poor people in Colombia. In 1982 I was appointed as a professor in the Presbyterian Seminary in Bogotá. Since that time two suspicions have arisen within me. First, Latin American theological institutions, with few exceptions, have taught pastoral care from an individualistic rather than communal perspective. Second, the Protestant pastoral perspective has been dualistic, in the sense of addressing the "spiritual realm" and not taking sufficiently into account the "secular realm." Accordingly, the desperation, hopelessness and powerlessness of the poor have seldom been important matters for pastoral care, perhaps with the exception of Basic Christian Communities.

This article, therefore, has as its principal aim to present a proposal for pastoral care to the poor called "Liberating Pastoral Care" that is rooted in the contemporary situation of poverty in Latin America, in insights of Liberation Theology, and in the work of Basic Christian Communities.

To accomplish this objective, I will adopt the methodology of Liberation Theology, as described by Leonardo and Clodovis Boff: "seeing," "judging" and "acting."[i] There is, however, a preliminary stage for those who use this methodology which can be understood as "a living commitment." I believe that I, and everyone who commit themselves to work in solidarity with the poor, must begin with this "living commitment," or run the risk of simply expressing an academic or abstract interest which is highly vulnerable to the difficulties of such work. In reading of the present work it will become clear that I am not writing from a neutral position. Those who have lived and worked among the poor in Latin America cannot take a detached position on such an important matter in their pastoral practice. Therefore, it will not be a surprise to discover that what follows is a sympathetic study of Liberation Theology and its work among the poor.

As far as method is concerned, the first stage in liberating methodology is "seeing." This means studying the reality or actual situation of a problem, which, in this case, is poverty. Accordingly, I will start with a description of the context of poverty. The second stage is "judging." This involves studying what the scriptures say about poverty. Liberation Theology has been chosen because it was born in Latin America, where the majority of the people are poor, because of its preference for the poor and denunciation of poverty as caused by sin, oppression and injustice, and because it works with the poor through Basic Christian Communities which provide hope in the face of poverty. The third stage is "acting." It is here that a proposal for Liberating Pastoral Care will be offered.

Description of the Context

In the '70s, in Girardot, Colombia, I knew a poor family that lived in a slum neighborhood called "Las Brisas del Bogotá." It is a very hot city where the temperature in the shade can be more than 95° F. The poor neighborhood where this family lived was located on the riverbank of the Río Bogotá, which is considered one of the most polluted in the world. The river is the "sewer" of the city of Bogotá, which has more than five million inhabitants. The river, until now, has received no treatment and barely supports animal life.

The González family lived in a shack with a single room that served as bedroom, kitchen, and living room. They built a barrack from used wood that had an earth floor, where they slept on wooden boards covered with hay mats. The village had no services, such as electricity or running water. Since the population could not drink the water from the river and because of a high percentage of cases of gastroenteritis, the government installed a communal tap of drinkable water which served the entire neighborhood. However, due to the lack of water, some took baths in the polluted river.

Pedro worked loading and unloading trucks in a coffee warehouse and María was a housewife. María did not work outside the house because she had small children, and because Pedro told her that men have to maintain their family and women should assist their husband and children. Both were illiterate and 22 years old. They were not married, had lived together for five years, and had three children. María was pregnant again. They once lived in the countryside, but immigrated to the city a year earlier looking for a better life. But when asked what was a better life for them, they were not sure what it meant exactly, how they could obtain it or what they would do if they had it. This and other "González families" can teach a great deal about poverty and the meaning of pastoral care which changes lives.

Facing the pain of poverty and its consequences there is frequently a feeling of impotence, and it is difficult to write about poverty without feeling that it is superficial. Facing complex problems requires deep analysis and assertive proposals. Here, however, I can only offer a few reflections, conscious that there is much more to say.

The question arises: How can poverty be defined? Some encyclopedias define it as, "the lack or inadequacy of material resources to satisfy the basic necessities of life."[ii] The difficulty arises in defining what are considered "basic necessities," because something that is a luxury in one society, may be without importance in another, or totally unknown in others. Basic necessities, then, have different connotations from one country to other, and in different historical moments. For this reason, "basic necessities" is a relative, not absolute, concept. Another dictionary takes into account a different dimension: Voluntary poverty means to take religious vows in an ordination ceremony.[iii]

It is not an easy task to define the causes of poverty in Latin America, and there are many perspectives regarding the problem. Our continent suffers the phenomena of collective poverty, which is more than an individual issue. This reflects a permanent inadequacy in the majority of the population. Impoverishment becomes even worse when there are natural disasters, for example: Hurricanes (Honduras and Nicaragua, 1998; Caracas, 1999), wars (Central America in the decade of the '80s), migration either due to violence (Colombia, since the '50s) or poverty (from Nicaragua to Costa Rica), and earthquakes (different dates in Managua, Mexico City, Colombia, San Salvador in 2001). It is the poor who suffer most after natural disasters. Houses in the slums are the first to collapse because of their fragility, and it is the poor who remain during wars, while the rich often escape to the United States or Europe.

In this work we will address only three points of view about poverty: socioeconomic, gender and ethnical, and anthropological perspectives.

Socioeconomic Point of View

This perspective affirms that one of the causes of poverty is neocolonialism, which is defined as the means by which large parts of Latin

America, Africa, and Asia are incorporated into the international capitalist economy.[iv] During the 1960s there was a large paradigm shift in the field of economics in terms of Latin America. In 1965 the Theory of Dependence was born via the signing of a declaration by approximately one hundred Latin American economists from seventeen countries. This process marked a methodological and political rupture from positivist North American economic theories.

However, there remain at least two main ideas regarding developed and underdeveloped countries. The first is that both participate in the same lineal process. Consequently, underdeveloped countries should develop following a natural course of events. The second idea is that all economies are interrelated, but move in contrary directions to others.

Rostow believes that all underdeveloped countries need to go through similar phases in order to develop, and thus defends the idea of a linear process.[v] On the other hand, Frank points out that these phases and the thesis of Rostow are incorrect because they do not correspond to the reality of the past or the present of the countries considered underdeveloped.[vi] At the present time, underdeveloped countries cannot develop due to the lack of the basic conditions that Rostow mentions. For example, they do not have the necessary surplus capital to begin the process and, when a country does generate such capital, its leaders often divert these funds for personal use.

The antithetical idea proposes that development produces underdevelopment. It considers that underdevelopment is caused by the nature of the relationship between countries of the center and those of the periphery. According to Hinkelammert:

> Although it can be said that developed countries exist next to underdeveloped countries, it is always necessary to insist that the last ones developed form a part or are appendixes of the first ones. The theory of underdevelopment should explain why they exist and why underdeveloped areas arise in a world impregnated by the dynamics of development of their centers.[vii]

The so-called "center countries" have the economic power to govern the development of other countries through the manipulation of class, technology, power of decision and trade. The theory of development has taught that it is necessary to diffuse capital, technology and institutions, but expanding capital creates a significant debt in underdeveloped countries.[viii] Technology is only diffused partly and creates dependence on center economies, those that decide both the prices of the raw materials that they buy and the manufactured products they sell and that promote or impede exports through definition of quotas. Also, peripheral countries and institutions bound to economic liberalism are interested in duplicating the high level of lifestyle of the centers.

Added to these factors, other social situations, such as violence and natural catastrophes, have generated poverty in large sectors of population. For several decades, military governments, that invested a high percentage of the national budget in armaments, ruled various Latin American countries. Currently, political ruling classes that are frequently concerned with serving their own interests govern many countries in Latin America.

Gender and Ethnical Point of View

Another factor that produces poverty, that is often forgotten, is gender. Discrimination against women has made them poor. The IV Women's Conference, Beijing, 1995, declared that poverty has "the face of a woman." Women are the poorest among the poor.

From the ten main areas of concern outlined in Beijing we will highlight only two: poverty and economic inequality. There has been a considerable increase in the number of people that live in misery, mainly due to the long-term world economic crisis, structural adjustments, the failure of initiatives to fight against poverty, and civil conflicts in many regions of the world. The burden of poverty in Latin America falls in a disproportionate form on the more than 219 million Latin American women.[ix] Women's access to economic resources, or any other opportunities, is considerably smaller than that of men. Women frequently must provide for home expenses in situations of increasing shortage, and as such are forced to make adjustments that are rarely taken into consideration. Furthermore, there is a significant increase in the number of women serving as the "head of the household."

Here are some simple facts:

- Women compose more than 60% of the rural poor population of the world which surpasses a thousand million.
- In 1988 564 million women lived in situations of poverty in rural areas, which represented an increase of 47% from the period between 1965 and 1970. In Latin America many poor women work as domestic servants. The majority, who work in cities, have emigrated from rural areas.[x] Frequently these girls, generally younger than 20 years of age, identify with the family they work for, and in-

stead of realizing their oppressive situation idealize the *modus vivendi* of the family. As such, they adopt the value system of the family and, consequently, have difficulty relating to people in their own socioeconomic group.[xi]

• Women are in charge of a third of the families in the world. In Costa Rica, for example, 51% of children do not have legal recognition from their father.

Other significant information:

• If the domestic work of women were properly remunerated and included in national income, gross national product would increase between 20 and 30%. In Latin America many women work in invisible and unpaid ways, providing for the material needs of their working husband by cooking meals, cleaning and raising children. Therefore, the "invisible work" of women alleviates the husband of this responsibility and thus generates higher corporate profits.[xii] According to this idea, despite the fact that work in domestic life is not considered as part of the economy, their invisible service restores the energy of the workers and thus maintains the economy.

• At present women represent 41% of the total labor force in developed countries and 34% worldwide. Nonetheless, their salaries are from 30% to 40% lower than those of men in similar positions.

Besides gender, there is another factor that must be considered in any study regarding poverty in Latin America: the *ethnical* one. There are two groups that, besides being poor, face constant discrimination: blacks and natives. Natives prefer to be called *"originally people"* and in this work this term will be used. According to Leopoldo Zea "blackness" and "nativism" are ideological concepts that are used like banners by groups seeking freedom from stereotypes attributed to originally people from Africa and Latin America by dominant groups.[xiii] It is a fight against the so-called right of domain of those who conquer and colonize. The word "indigenous," with its accompanying stereotypes, is seen as an invention of powerful groups trying to justify the exploitation of originally people.

There are four Latin American countries that have a large percentage of *originally* population: Guatemala, Ecuador, Peru and Bolivia. According to statistical studies, 53% of the population in Guatemala is composed of originally people. Among this population 40% speaks their native language, divided among the 21 ethnical groups, each with its own language.[xiv] In Peru, for example, Quechua is spoken by 27% of the population and Aymara by 30%. In May of 1975, Quechua was declared as the second official language of Peru because more than the half of the population speaks it. Around half of the Bolivian population is *originally* and speaks Aymara (25.22%) and Quechua (34.4%).

It is important to clarify, however, that *originally people* are neither totally native nor becoming extinct. Almost invariably, they are a mix of races. They may be considered, in general, as economically poor, but with rich and living cultures and traditions.

In terms of the black population, in some Latin American countries they do not feel like part of the culture, mainly because they are a minority and for many years they have lived in isolated areas. This is the case of the Caribbean coast of Costa Rica and Nicaragua, where the main language is not Spanish but English, and the main religion is not Catholic but Protestant.[xv]

The situation of Brazil is different. Brazil has the second largest black population in the world, after Nigeria, and yet was the last to abolish the black slavery (May 13, 1888). It is said that in Brazil there is not marked racial discrimination, but this statement does not agree with daily reality. Brazil is considered a white country, where blacks do not have opportunities unless they adopt white attitudes and behaviors. For this reason, among the black population there exists a *branqueamento* (whitening) attitude or ideology that threatens to destroy the original African culture that still exists. Even so, there are groups that promote the importance of being black and of maintaining black culture and religion. In reality, Brazilian culture is greatly influenced by African cultures.

In general, black people must face the fact that they have the nationality of the countries where they live but, at the same time, are not accepted by their fellow citizens as equal partners, nor are they accepted as Africans. Both conflicts, the desire to be accepted by the dominant culture and yet reject the dominant society indicate that a system of double thinking has been created.

Returning to *originally people,* in modern Latin America there persists an attitude of discrimination and segregation. In urban areas, they generally live in poor shanties and, in rural areas, live far from *ladino* people.[xvi] For this reason, Rigoberta Menchú, a live witness to the struggle of native peoples, points out:

> This does not allow us to forget, but screams at us to see what we refuse to see. We Latin Americans are clever enough to denounce

the unequal relationships that exist in North America, but we forget that we are also oppressors and that we are also wrapped in relationships that can only be described as colonial. Native peoples are considered different in Latin America, and only taken into account when they are needed as a labor force.[xvii]

Although *originally* and black people have been systematically discriminated against, there is no doubt that originally people are a different situation from black people. *Originally people* have a culture, a language and traditions that belong to them and maintain them alive. Even more, they are not known by their ethnic origin or race, as are blacks, but by their own culture (Aztec, Mayan, Inca, Aymara or Chibcha). Today, many are intentionally proud of their *originally people* heritage. It is interesting that Zea's statement points out that the concepts of "blackness" and "nativisms" have different origins. According to Zea, "blackness," as awareness of domination and discrimination based on the philosophy of the supposed superiority of the white race, has its origin in black groups that have refused to continue to suffer due to the color of their skin. In contrast, "nativism" is not an ideological concept created for the *originally people* but for *mestizo* people.[xviii] *Originally people* do not demand recognition of their humanity, since they feel part of a concrete millenarian humanity. But *mestizo* people seem to need affirmation as concrete human beings. These are Latin Americans who seek definition in order to obtain the unity of their being.[xix]

Anthropological Point of View: The Culture of the Poverty

In relation to the anthropological point of view, Oscar Lewis has developed a theory regarding poverty. The theory points out that the "culture of poverty" exists and is present in different contexts.

The culture of poverty is not just a matter of deprivation or disorganization, a term signifying the absence of something. It is a culture in the traditional anthropological sense in that it provides human beings with a design for living, with a ready-made set of solutions for human problems, and so serves a significant adaptive function.[xx]

Lewis affirms that some people have lived in the culture of poverty for generations and thus must survive in it. In spite of the fact that they are from different countries and cultures, "their behavior seems clearly patterned and reasonably predictable."[xxi] For example, in the poor neighborhoods of London, Mexico City, Puerto Rico or New York, there are "similarities in the family structures," in "the nature of kinship ties," in "the quality of husband-wife and parent-child relations," in "time orientation," in "value systems," and in "the sense of community."[xxii]

According to the Lewis observations, families that belong to the culture of poverty generally present the following characteristics: a high rate of mortality; shorter life expectancy; children and women usually work; no affiliation with medical services; one room dwellings lacking privacy; frequent use of violence in child education; wife abuse; active sexual life from an early age; couples in free union common-law marriages; high incidence of abandoned wives and children; families centered around the mother which tends to create close relationships with maternal relatives; predominance of the nuclear family; predisposition to authoritarianism and great insistence on family solidarity, which is an ideal seldom realized; and a widespread belief in male superiority and *machismo,* or definitions of masculinity.[xxiii]

Nevertheless, not all poor people belong to the "culture of poverty." This was the case for Jews in Eastern Europe. Their tradition, culture and religion provided identification with other Jews in the world. Equally, this is the case of persons and families who became poor, for a variety of reasons. These groups seldom have the characteristics of people in the culture of poverty. On the other hand, not all poor people who achieve economic stability abandon the culture of poverty.

For this reason, those who belong to the culture of poverty do not constitute a class but a culture with certain attitudes toward life. They rarely have any awareness of class and history, and frequently ignore that there are millions of people suffering from similar problems around the world. It would appear that they only recognize their own problems and have a strong sense of being alone or of belonging to nothing. Nevertheless, when they discover their history and become aware that there are others in the world in similar situation, they begin to join labor unions or syndicates. From that moment forward they tend to leave the "culture of poverty" even if they continue to be desperately poor.

Lewis goes on to say that the culture of poverty is born in different historical contexts. It usually begins when a stratified social system passes through a process of disintegration or enters a phase of transition. The transition from feudalism to capitalism is a case in point. Another situation are conquests where free people are enslaved in some form during several generations. A third example is the disappearance of the tribal system and emigration from rural to urban areas. In Latin America, the combination of these situations has allowed the emergence of the culture of poverty in the period since the Spanish conquest. In this context, poverty is not a transitional but a permanent situation.[xxiv]

According to Lewis there is a way to eradicate the culture of poverty, although not poverty itself. The way is to offer changes in value systems, self-concept, attitudes and the feeling of exclusion from their own country or context. At the end of the '70s, he found that despite the continuation of poverty after the revolution in Cuba, the poor experience less despair and apathy, and have a new sense of power and importance.[xxv] It is worth noting that the socioeconomic and political situation of Cuba has changed since then.

It is important to note that Lewis' theory of the "culture of poverty" has been criticized and is controversial in the field of anthropology.[xxvi] Without the intention of defending the theory, I would like to point out some ideas that could help in understanding Latin American poverty.

The first point is the transmission of values. The transmission of values from generation to generation among poor families should not be considered a determining factor. The poor can break the chain through awareness of their situation of misery, through joining with other poor people to struggle against poverty, and through changing their attitude toward life. The second point is the importance of historical changes in Latin America that helped in the creation and perpetuation of poverty. Case in point is the disappearance of the tribal system and emigration from rural to urban zones. This second factor deserves particular attention, particularly from a pastoral perspective. This is the case in Colombia, where thousands of displaced families are escaping the violence from guerillas and paramilitary groups. One specifically pastoral response to this cultural reality is the Mennonite Church in Bogotá which created a refuge for families arriving in the city.

Having presented these concepts of poverty let me try to define who the poor in Latin America are. Who are the poor in a continent where the vast majority is poor? The poor who are in need of Pastoral Care are:

- Those who are unemployed or sub-employed and have few hopes of finding employment.
- Those who have no sense of belonging and feel isolated.
- Those who receive little or no social service from the government, frequently in terms of health and education. Those whose children do not attend school, even if it is free, because do not have money

to pay for transportation, uniforms and school supplies. Those whose children sporadically attend school, but drop out during the year due to lack of organization at home, poor nutrition, and lack of motivation from family.

• Those who do not have political, economic and social power and do not belong to social organizations.
• Those who are exploited, oppressed and need justice.

Pastoral Care in Latin America

What is happening in Latin America in the field of Pastoral Care? This question will be discussed in two moments. The first moment will present Protestant, or what is commonly called "Evangelical," Pastoral Care. The second moment will present Catholic Pastoral Care, which is generally called Popular Pastoral. In Latin America the term "pastoral care" does not exist; it is commonly called "pastoral" or "pastoral counseling," but in fact what is being done is pastoral care. This division between Catholic and Protestant is important because, on the one hand, unfortunately both churches work separately, and, on the other hand, because Protestant churches are a minority in Latin America. It is worth noting, however, that there are a few ecumenical organizations that emphasize "working together rather than on coming together."[xxvii] These groups generally rely on the principles and practices of Liberation Theology. Therefore, is not completely valid to consider Liberation Theology as an exclusively Catholic movement. Further, although Liberation Theology was born within the Catholic Church there are many Protestant theologians who contribute to this movement, and this presence bolsters some Protestant participation in ecumenical organizations.

The division also has a practical function. Protestant approaches to pastoral care are generally more influenced by the United States while Catholic approaches are more closely tied to Liberation Theology. However, it is important to take into account that several Protestant theologians, such as Rubem Alves and Julio de Santa Ana, are considered ecumenical because of their work with Catholics theologians. Notwithstanding, both Catholic and Protestant churches are profoundly influenced by the vast majority of conservative members.[xxviii]

Protestant Work in Pastoral Care

Although there are many Protestant theological institutions in Latin America which teach pastoral care and counseling, it is not possible to say that there is a Latin American model in this field because of the repetition of ideas from Europe and the United States.

According to Maldonado, the way to know what is emerging as pastoral care in Latin America[xxix] is by reviewing the literature produced and surveying activities organized around this topic. There are three sources that can be used in such a review: translations, indigenous publications, and publications by Latin American organizations. In the Protestant area, the vast majority of literature in pastoral care in Spanish and Portuguese are translations from English,[xxx] French,[xxxi] and German.[xxxii]

Regarding indigenous publications in pastoral care, some samples are: Jorge A. León,[xxxiii] Daniel Schipani,[xxxiv] Lothar Hoch,[xxxv] Jorge E. Maldonado,[xxxvi] Bernardo Stamateas,[xxxvii] Eleny Vasão de Paula Cavalcante,[xxxviii] various theses,[xxxix] and publications in Spanish and Portuguese by foreigners teaching in Latin America.[xl]

Translations of non-pastoral counseling and therapy texts are amply spread. Examples of these are Fromm, Freud, Skinner, Berne, Rogers, Frankl, Minuchin, and Haley. These authors frequently form the base for teaching and training in pastoral care in theological seminaries.

Maldonado highlights three organizations in Latin America that have published materials on pastoral care.[xli] First, the journal *Psicología Pastoral* founded in Argentina in 1972 by ASIT (Asociación de Seminarios y Institutos Teológicos del Cono Sur–Association of Theological Institutions of the South Cone of South America). This group organized the first Latin American congress of pastoral psychology in Buenos Aires in 1981. Second, the Corpo de Psicólogos e Psiquiatras Cristãos (Body of Christian Psychologists and Psychiatrists), founded in Brazil in 1977. The primary aim of this group is to promote the integration of the Christian faith with psychology, psychiatry and related sciences. This association also has given courses and has published some manuals.[xlii] Third, EIRENE (Latin American Association of Family Pastoral Care) founded in Argentina in 1979. While this group was initially Argentinean, it is now a continental movement with educational institutions in Mexico, Venezuela, Colombia, Brazil, Ecuador and Peru. EIRENE is perhaps the only Latin American organization that is interested in pastoral counseling with the family. It is worth noting that it teaches a systemic approach to the family. Also, this association has publications and organized various congresses.[xliii]

In spite of the fact that pastoral counseling with the family has not historically been taught in Latin American theological institutions, this situation is changing. Examples of this are EIRENE (Ecuador and

Brazil) and Universidad Bíblica Latinoamericana (Costa Rica) which initiated courses with a systemic approach to Pastoral Counseling with the Family in 1988. Also, the Consejo Latinoamericano de Iglesias (CLAI–Latin American Council of Churches), which the majority of the Latin American Evangelical or Protestant churches belong to, decided, in 1988, to enlarge the Secretariat of Women and Children into a Secretariat of Family Pastoral Care. This enlargement took place because a unilateral focus on women or children tends only to emphasize an individualistic view of human beings. Julio de Santa Ana asserts that the Protestant concept of pastoral–to be interested in the individual and to be centered only on the pastor and the preaching of the Word of God–is paradoxically contrary to one of the greatest contributions of the Reformation: the universal priesthood of believers.[xliv]

In summary, it is possible to say that pastoral care in Latin America has followed the individualistic approach of Protestant-American models, with the exceptions of the growing interest in doing pastoral care from systemic perspectives. Also, there are other ecumenical and Evangelical organizations that aim to widen the concept of pastoral to include the collective action of the church. In Brazil CEDI (Centro Ecuménico de Documentação e Informação), a continental organization, CELEP (Centro Evangélico Latinoamericano de Estudios Pastorales) with its seat in Costa Rica, and CEDEPCA (Centro de Estudios Pastorales en Centro America) with headquarters in Guatemala are representative of this tendency.

Catholic Work in Pastoral Care

In the Catholic world the term "pastoral" was influenced, at the beginning of the 1960s, by *Gaudium et Spes,* one of the most famous papal encyclicals, which studied the function of the church in the modern world. In contrast to the Protestant concept of pastoral care, the so-called Pastoral Popular (Popular Pastoral Care), which is a new Catholic approach to pastoral care based on Liberation Theology, is based in a communal perspective. It is defined by its focus on the care of the poor in Latin America, who in fact are the majority of the population, and for this reason is called 'popular.'[xlv] It is important to explain that not all sectors of the Catholic Church work with a focus on the poor, and that a large number of priests remain attached to traditional perspectives within the church. However, in some countries, such as Brazil and Nicaragua, the Popular Pastoral Care field shows considerable development. The existence of the Popular Pastoral Care is in itself a denunciation that the Church has separated itself from the pueblo (the people).[xlvi] Popular Pastoral Care combines common elements of pastoral theology (ecclesiology, Christology, Biblical interpretation, etc.) with a deep knowledge of the situation of the poor in Latin America.[xlvii]

Rubem Alves stresses that pastoral care is in a great degree determined by the social, political, economic environment.

> If a congregation is located high on the social ladder, and its members enjoy wealth, prestige, and power, it will tend to be committed to the dominant order of things, and its pastoral care emphasis will be pressured to respond to demands placed on it by its institutional setting.[xlviii]

In a continent full of the poor, pastoral care must not respond to the demands of the few. In a situation of poverty "no pastoral care can bring consolation to a mother and a father who see their child dying of hunger."[xlix] From a Liberation Theology perspective, suffering is not an individual problem and cannot and must not be "healed" by using interpretative and emotional manipulation of one's inner life. There is another way: "Pain and suffering can and must be transfigured when they are planted as seeds of a new creation."[l] Pastoral Care means both transforming the immediate situation of a family who must watch the death by hunger of their child and the transformation of society such that this tragedy no longer happens to any child: a new creation.

In order to begin the struggle, the poor must have hope. For Sobrino the hope of the poor is as great as the scandal of poverty in Latin America.[li] Accordingly, the future can be created and built based on hope and on identity and solidarity. Their solidarity will lead the poor to act as collectively in order to free themselves of oppression and poverty.[lii]

Liberation Theology would appear to fail to leave room in pastoral care for the personal dimension of life because of its communal viewpoint. However, this is not the case. This viewpoint considers that we are transforming and building a world together for the benefit of all and not for just a few. Therefore,

> ... the "thing" that has healing power is neither the theology used by the pastor as a tool nor his specific training in the field of pastoral psychology. It is rather the personal participation in a community that suffers together and that, because of this very fact, is wholly committed to the creation of a new world.[liii]

For Boff and Boff there are many Latin American pastors who are seeking a theology that better interprets the reality of injustice in which the people they shepherd live.[liv] Therefore, the relationship between popular pastoral care and Liberation Theology has been close, with the former receiving valuable contributions from the latter. The most important contribution to Popular Pastoral Care from Liberation Theology is the concept of the existence of only 'one history.' In this history God is acting through the poor such that the poor are active subjects who participate in the process of their own liberation and not simple passive objects.[lv] Accordingly, Popular Pastoral Care must travel together with the poor as they seek liberation.

Another contribution from Liberation Theology is a Christology that emphasizes both the humanity of Christ and his liberating message to the oppressed.[lvi] Popular Pastoral Care also incorporates the biblical interpretation of Liberation Theology which understands that the poor, the exploited, the marginalized and the discriminated exist in a society with deep social conflicts, which is a scandal in the Gospel's perspective.[lvii] Moreover, Popular Pastoral Care is based on the liberation concept of ecclesiology with its foundation in the preference of the church for the poor.[lviii] The Catholic Church hierarchy has strongly rejected the concept of the popular church or Basic Christian Community because it goes against its historical identity.[lix]

To summarize, Popular Pastoral Care is based on two main principles. The first is a theology of the Kingdom of God, the full realization of the Kingdom in the future, which today is manifest in the liberation of the poor.[lx] This is a 'double-edged' concept. Bonthius shares this concept when he states that the best theological perspective on poverty is the eschatological (Lk. 1:51ff and 6: 20ff).[lxi] The risk of this perspective is that it can easily hinder the urgency of the manifestation of the Kingdom of God: the liberation of the poor now (see Matt. 6:10, 12:28, Mk. 1:15, 9:1).

The second principle of Popular Pastoral Care is the participation of the poor in their own liberation in such a way that any pastoral care from "outside" or from "higher to lower" has failed because the poor have rejected 'assistanceness.'

Pastoral Care with the Poor Through Basic Christian Communities (BCCs)

Having studied the theoretical framework of Latin American Theology what will now be analyzed is the way it is practiced with the poor, especially through the Basic Christian Communities.

Basic Christian Communities (BCCs) are small groups–approximately ten people–who meet in houses, chapels or in the shade of a tree.[lxii] The people who belong to them are believers who are often, but not always, poor and oppressed. They are people who are breaking into the history of Latin America and its church.[lxiii] They often come from the lowest socio-economic strata of society. They are domestic servants, industrial and agricultural workers, bricklayers, peasants occupying the land without title of ownership (sometimes for generations), and rural migrants to the cities.[lxiv] In other words, they are churches of people despoiled by society of their land, jobs, wages, health, housing, schooling and labor unions.[lxv] Notwithstanding, there are some who come from the middle and even upper classes, such as pastoral workers and laity, who have committed themselves to the cause of the poor.[lxvi]

Galdámez provides examples of members of BCCs in El Salvador where he worked.[lxvii] One of these is Berta, Carlitos' mother.

> Carlitos was five years old. He had no toilet in his house, so he had to go to the bathroom a few yards outside his little shack. One night she heard him screaming. His intestine had come out. We took him to the hospital in a taxi. I'd never seen this. What could be the matter? The diagnosis: "Malnutrition, second degree." What can we do for him? "Tell his mamá to give him an egg a day and a piece of meat. And milk, too." Berta didn't have the money for the taxi we took to the hospital, much less for this prescription! She had five more children, and her husband was a garbage collector.

Another member is Pedro, a carpenter.

> Pedro was a good carpenter, but out of work. The community found steady work for him. It was far from home, though, and he had to find lodging in another city. The evening before he was to leave I went to see him. "You know what?" he began, "I'm not going to be able to take that new job. I've started a little piece of work for a friend of mine. I can't back out of my promise." I argued with him. I told him that he had a chance to have a steady job and security. I told him he should think about his wife and kids. "Right, Padre, I'm very grateful to the community. But a pal is a pal, and I promised. You see . . . " I had nothing to say. I couldn't appreciate his line of reasoning. I didn't understand. I began to think Pedro was just a big old softie, and would rather just wander around here with nothing to do. I was judging him rashly. And when I looked

him in the eye, I could see that here was some other reason. And the reason was this. Pedro was a freelance. Every two or three days he would finish a little job and some grocery money would come in. So life was bearable. Nobody starved. But what would happen if he took a new job far from here? He would have to go off and work for a month before getting paid. And how would he and his family eat in the meantime? There he would be, far away, where nobody knew him and nobody would give him credit. Where would he sleep? He didn't even have a hammock to take along. But the worst thing was that his wife and kids only had a three days' supply of groceries. All in all, he'd rather keep looking for small jobs and try to make it one day at a time. When he'd finished, I felt guilty for thinking unkindly of him. I had never realized that for a poor person it's even hard to take a better job!

BCCs sprang up in reaction to heavily hierarchical frameworks that produce inequities. Thus, they have their place in history and represent a new experience of the church in communion.[lxviii] Although BCCs probably began in Brazil, they have spread to other Latin American countries[lxix] such as El Salvador, Honduras, Guatemala, Mexico, Nicaragua,[lxx] Panama, Colombia, Ecuador, Peru,[lxxi] Bolivia, and Chile. According to Leonardo Boff, BCCs are true churches and not merely groups with some "ecclesiastical elements."[lxxii] He considers there to be three obstacles to understanding the BCCs. The first problem is that it is difficult to understand their nature. They are churches that appeared as a response to the question: "How may the communal experience of the apostolic faith be embodied and structured in the experiences of people, who, in Brazil and throughout Latin America, are both religious and oppressed?"[lxxiii] The second obstacle is that it is difficult to understand the concern of BCCs for social justice and, therefore, to recognize their emergence as a factor of protest (taking the prophetic role of denouncing the abuses of the system) and for the growth of liberating ideas. The third and final obstacle is the difficulty in realizing that the poor can decide for themselves. In some circles of the church, there persists the preconception that the poor are still minors and, thus, in need of control, orientation and supervision.

The members of the BCCs do not want to have a dualistic concept of "religious life" and "secular life" which destroys both the life of faith of those who claim to be Christian and the credibility of that faith in the eyes of those who are not.[lxxiv] Unfortunately, for those who have a dualistic concept, "the religious life" has often been an impediment to the people's clear understanding of their oppressive situation. In addition, oppressors frequently encourage resignation or seek individualistic solutions to poverty. Nevertheless, religious belief also signifies the existence of an immense possibility for liberating faith.[lxxv] According to Gutiérrez there is only one history.[lxxvi] This means that there is no division between secular history, which is not interested in theological implications of events, and sacred history, which is only interested in the actions of God. He points out that salvation occurs through historical encounters with God and the poor and oppressed who are earnestly seeking liberation.

Hence, "secular life" unites with "religious life." The members of BCCs reach an acute social awareness not as the fruit of leftist ideological infiltration but of the effort to understand the Bible in the context in which it was written–in communities of poor people. Their faith generates commitment in order to transform society as a way to begin the Kingdom here and now.[lxxvii] The signs of the presence of the Kingdom among the poor are as follow: Those who were silent now speak; those who felt rejected, alienated and self-depreciated now feel liberated and joyful and feel that they have become the "host of the feast"; those who were discredited now participate, and; those who were individualistic and divisive now are cooperative.[lxxviii]

In BCCs, the people do theology at a popular level without a dualism between secular and religious life. They do, general, oral theology, which uses symbols and gestures. For example, some groups use a tree with rotting fruits and poisoned roots to represent Capitalism. Another example occurred during a course about the Book of Revelation when a group organized a meditation by drawing a beast with seven heads facing a wounded Lamb on the pavement. The director asked the group to put names over the heads. The members chose "multinationals," "external debts," "military dictatorship," "national security law," and names of unpopular politicians. Someone wrote under the lamb "Jesus the Liberator." A woman added, "The poorest of the poor."[lxxix]

In this perspective, grass-roots communities form the church within society (with preferential option for the poor) rather than society being within the church. The whole fabric of society receives the influence of this new viewpoint of communal praxis of solidarity which has the potential to create a new form of social coexistence, opposed to bourgeois society.[lxxx]

In Latin America churches are being prodded to move from the side of the powerful to the side of the poor.[lxxxi] The basic communities have rescued the liberating massage of Jesus that had been forgotten. Although there are some similarities, BCCs are not reproducing the early communities of the New Testament, but are creating fresh strategies to resolve present-day problems in the light of the word of God which they read and interpret in terms of their own situation.[lxxxii]

Therefore, the mission of the church, including BCCs, is not to exist in itself, but to evangelize.[lxxxiii] That mission is to ponder and live the faith in a liberating way, to commit oneself to the oppressed, to fight for dignity, and to help build a society more in conformity with the standard of the Gospels. This mission, however, must not be framed in a specific society or culture, but in the service of a universal cause.[lxxxiv]

Barbé explains in great detail how to work with the poor in the creating of a basic community.[lxxxv] The first step is to live together with the poor, winning their confidence and breaking with former class-position. It means embracing the cause of the poor and oppressed. During this period, it is important to pray together with them because it is a common language–even among those who do not know each other–and because prayer is peculiar to Christian groups. The next step is to restore the voice to the poor. They think that their word has no worth, and they are discouraged when they think they know nothing. The poor frequently develop the habit of self-depreciation. For this reason, it is very important that the humble discover that this is not true. To do this they must listen and speak to each other.

For example, (a) they can tell what happened to them today, (b) introduce their family, relatives or friends, and (c) tell something about their past. This process may take time, but it allows people to enlarge their capacity for listening and speaking. Barbé gives an example of a woman who, when asked what had happened to her his day, answered, "Who, me? Nothing interesting. The usual, washing the laundry, cooking . . . " She was asked to give more details, such as what time she woke up, how many times she got up at night to feed her baby, and how much time she spent doing one thing or another. She heard that who she was and what she did had importance.

With time and patience it is possible to listen to a woman tell how she was placed as a domestic servant at the age of thirteen, how her patron took advantage of her, and how she never told her mother anything because she was an important source of income to her family. With time and patience it is possible to listen to a young man tell about his hunger when he was a child during a journey to the big city looking for a "better life," and how his father and he avoided seeing each other because his father knew he was hungry and he knew his father had no money to feed the family.[lxxxvi]

It is also important to relate peoples' past to the history of the nation or the world. Barbé offers an easy method: to write down in a column (or tell a story if the person is illiterate) significant life events and in a parallel column important historical events in the life of the country that happened at the same time. "Thus the very poor learn to find their place in general history; historical memory is amplified."[lxxxvii] Nevertheless, they must also evoke their future. In similar way, in one column persons can write (or tell) what they would like to get, before anything else, for themselves and their families, in a second the obstacles to each "dream," and in a third one, their initial solutions. In these three columns they are using the Latin American Theology methodology of "seeing," "judging" and "acting." Moreover, in a fourth column they could write down an eschatological texts, words of Jesus, words from the prophets or parables that clarify how the Kingdom is to be realized. After that, they can share their expectations with other members of the community.

Another activity is to narrate a typical workday. Such a narrative can be created by drawing a plan of a person's work area and how it relates to the whole factory. They can also explain how they would reorganize the factory if they could. The same activity could be done in terms of their own house or neighborhood. All these exercises have the aim of helping the poor to recover their voice, their power of speech. Consequently, they will be able to speak about themselves, their time (personal history) and their space (home, family, friends, and work place).

The poor also need to restore their power of action. BCCs, therefore, have a specific organizational structure: a coordinating team (elected or chosen),[lxxxviii] a common fund, a yearly or monthly program, regular general assemblics, and several meetings each week.[lxxxix] BCCs are churches led by lay people that seek decentralization of power from one person (a priest) to a communal one.[xc] They do not only have intra-church tasks (i.e., Biblical groups, catechisms, and liturgical celebrations) but extra-church tasks (i.e., people's struggles in the barrio). According to Leonardo Boff, the analysis of problems in a specific situation and the search for solutions is an expression of liturgy.[xci] Even so, in grass-roots communities the political and faith aspects sometimes diverge. Both have to be united and deeply rooted in the Biblical message and the people's situation, but unity " . . . must be pondered, worked out, and systematized. This complex reality conditions our work, but it also points to our task."[xcii] Therefore, it is not possible to ignore the dialectical character of the word-action interrelationship and the dichotomy that certain theologies try to impose.

Members of BCCs consider that the main cause of their poverty, not the only one but the main one, is the capitalist system. Communities denounce as unjust and contrary to God's will the individualistic spirit of accumulation: " . . . this does not mean Marxism, it just means Gospel–the Gospel read in the context of inequitable oppression."[xciii] This leads the BCCs to enter into relationships with popular movements. It is clear that a church community could not turn itself into a party cell. Its members, nevertheless, can maintain critical position in terms of different political parties and support those that defend the rights and interests of the people.[xciv]

Accordingly, the revolution that Latin America needs is more radical than a Marxist one. It must be a thoroughly social revolution, not just economic. This means that such a revolution involves all realms: politics, economics, family, culture, and religion. In other words, everything related to society. It is possible that Latin America will inaugurate a model for a new society, a valid alternative to the models of Capitalism and Marxism which are chained to their patterns of gross materialism and truncated humanism.[xcv]

Nevertheless, BCCs can make up for the lack of popular movements, groups (civil right organizations), cultural affairs (literacy campaigns, legal advice networks) or economic affairs (organization of cooperatives). But where there are enough secular organizations in existence, BCCs are always particularly careful to maintain their separate identity, their specific difference from popular movements.[xcvi] Galdámez gives two examples of this idea.[xcvii] He narrates how Carlitos, who needed an egg and a piece or meat every day if he was to get well, was helped through a secular organization called *Caritas*. This organization provided nutritional assistance not only to Carlitos but also to many undernourished children and pregnant women in El Salvador. On the other hand, individual communities can start cooperatives that can lend money to members, but only with great difficulties.[xcviii] An example of this is Cristina who was left by her husband and did not know how she would survive with three children. With a loan from the cooperative she set up a lunch stand. She made tortillas (a flat round corn cake), filled them with cheese or beans, and sold them. The loan included everything she needed: corn, beans, cheese, crackling, a jug for water, a frying plate, and a bit of kindling. It was not a big loan, but she was immediately able to make a living. She found a good location on the pavement near the bus stop. Also, somebody helped her to learn to give change, because she did not know arithmetic.[xcix]

Popular Pastoral Care in Latin America begins with a structural approach. The poor are agents of their own liberation, and Popular Pastoral Care is not done from outside but from inside. When the poor, as a collective body, struggle for their own liberation it undoubtedly results in conflict and structural change. Floristán calls this approach *pastoral crítico-profética* (critical prophetic approach).[c] This perspective considers pastoral care as public praxis that transforms the existing unjust society by transforming the dominant class and its *modus operandi* through non-violent confrontation. It is based on a biblical recovery of the history of salvation in which God liberates the oppressed.[ci]

Popular Pastoral Care, as in any structural approach, runs the risk of not offering personal and immediate care for those who suffer. BCCs, however, try to fulfill both aspects. Therefore, grass-roots communities have a double function: (1) to take care of individuals, families and small communities, and (2) to serve as agents of social change in the community. This change, however, is not performed by priests but by the pueblo (people) themselves. In this manner the poor take their place in the history of Latin America and seek their own liberation. I believe that this is the strength of Popular Pastoral Care.

As a result, Popular Pastoral Care has two aims: (a) personal care through the work of grass-roots communities, and (b) care of societies. For Segundo, the primary task of any pastoral action in Latin America is evangelization at personal and social levels.[cii] According to Segundo, authentic evangelization consists of communicating only the very essentials of the Christian message (Good News), which is defined within the community. Since there is little time to offer the Good News in a changing continent such as Latin America, Popular Pastoral Care must keep pace with these awesome changes. Popular Pastoral Care has not adequately fulfilled its task of evangelization due to the existence of the false idea that Latin America is an evangelized continent. In reality Christian values are not highly regarded here, and there are many Latin Americans that do not know the message of the Good News.[ciii] For this reason a new approach to pastoral action is necessary.

Twenty years ago, Popular Pastoral Care transformed the traditional concept of what was understood as pastoral in Latin America,[civ] making way for the critical-prophecy tendency. According to Galilea, after Puebla (1979), where Popular Pastoral Care was evaluated and some of its ambiguities discussed, there was increasing awareness of the need to decrease social emphasis and increase spirituality.[cv] Moreover, in the 1980s various revolutions or *coup d'états* deposed dictatorships, for example, in Nicaragua, Paraguay and Argentina. This process of democratization affected grass-root communities in these countries. For example, memberships decreased in areas where BCCs were the only place to encounter and express liberty. This decrease in membership is not a surprising fact. According to Clodovis Boff,[cvi] BCCs can make up for the lack of popular movements, but where there are enough secular organizations in existence they must always be careful to maintain their separate identity from popular movements. In this way, BCCs have been purified, and there are less people who try to manipulate them in accordance with their political ideologies. These events have matured some groups and, without the loss of social consciousness, have put an emphasis on the importance of faith and evangelization. Galilea, however, warns that BCCs are capable of going to spiritual extremes and forgetting the sociopolitical aspect that is their distinctiveness. Hence, he believes that Popular Pastoral Care must be attached to both Medellín and Puebla. They must posses both sociopolitical and spiritual identities.

The changes produced in BCCs, due to political changes, leads us to the concept of the 'context' of pastoral care. In this respect, Thayer states, "Pastoral care does not occur in a vacuum, but within a matrix of social processes."[cvii] Great Britain, the U.S.A. and Latin America have different contexts and, therefore, different approaches to pastoral care, even they have similar interests in political issues and the poor. In an article about ethical framework for pastoral care, Poling states that Liberation Theology criticizes traditional ethics " . . . because it does not attend carefully enough to the question of oppression in human relationships."[cviii] Accordingly, Liberation Theology reinterprets ethics in relation to social critique, as seen from oppressed communities. Undoubtedly, the ethical framework for pastoral care as seen from the ideology of the dominant culture is different. For Poling there is an "ethic of liberation" which understands that injustice and oppression are relevant to ethics.[cix] "There are choices based on a lack of social power and thus the ethics is vastly different from those with privilege."[cx] From the perspective of Dussel, a Christian ethic of liberation involves doing something for the Other as other (the poor, the neighbor) without any interest but serve them.[cxi] This is "praxis of gratuity" or "praxis of liberation." There are two other praxis that are either indifferent or evil. One is the "subjugate praxis" in which the person selfishly (the evil One) looks to his/her own benefit by oppressing others; this is an evil praxis. The other is the "praxis of necessity" in which the person does something because he/she needs to do it; this is an indifferent praxis.

I am convinced that Popular Pastoral Care is pertinent in the Latin American context. Pastoral care to the poor in the first world may be considered as special care to a minority group, but this is not so in Latin America where the vast majority of the population is poor.

To conclude this part, here are some words from Leonardo Boff:

> The grassroots communities are discovering that they can be Christian without being conservative; that they can be human beings of faith and, at the same time, deeply committed to the destiny of the society; they can hope against hope, and hope in eternity, while still keeping their feet on the ground and involving themselves in the struggle for a better tomorrow here within our present history.[cxii]

Towards a Liberating Pastoral Care to the Poor (LPC)

In this part I will propose an approach which will be called "Liberating Pastoral Care to the Poor." It is based on the principles that have been studied and analyzed throughout the present work. While this proposal may be applied specifically to Latin America, it may be utilized in other contexts, with the respective adaptation to a particular historical situation.

At this point I will highlight the major elements of Liberating Pastoral Care (LPC) which must be considered in order to shape them into a unified approach. First, it is important to state that this proposal has a biblical background. Oppression, exploitation, marginalization and discrimination are considered scandalous in the perspective of the Gospel. This is based in the belief that Jesus came to preach the good news of liberation to the poor and sinners. Pastoral action, besides being committed to the poor, must remain attached to the biblical message of liberation. As Gustavo Gutiérrez suggests, pastoral action is "contemplation in action." Accordingly, I present this proposal based on these presuppositions.

Eco-systemic perspective: Liberating Pastoral Care (LPC) must take into account the ecology of the poor. That is, it must take into account the dynamics of poor families in their environment and the structural relationship between poverty and consequent problems. Poor families are part of a society composed of interdependent systems (school, church, job setting, neighborhood, socioeconomic situation, political situation, and so on). Poverty, in one way or another, is a product of social processes.

Poor families are composed of subjects and not objects: LPC, therefore, considers poor families as active subjects who can change their own reality. The poor who are awakening to their condition are ready to struggle against it. Accordingly, LPC does not consider the poor as passive objects.

Commitment to the poor: The LPC approach is not indifferent to poor families. Therefore, those who are committed to the poor will take their side and also work with them in the struggle for the transformation of oppressive and dehumanizing social orders. In this way, it is not possible to accept neutrality, because to be neutral in fact is to place oneself on the side of the oppressor.[cxiii]

Care for the family within a perspective of the whole of society: LPC has a structural approach to society, but without neglecting the needs of individuals. Nonetheless, they must not be seen from an isolated perspective, but from a communal one.

No dualism between spiritual and secular realm: LPC does not divide social life into "spiritual" and "secular." There is only one history in which the secular and the spiritual worlds are equally important. Thus, because the poor are important to God and the church, they must no longer be dispossessed of their place in history as active subjects.

Work in hope: LPC is a committed approach to poor families in their struggle to change the present situation that maintains them oppressed and trapped in poverty. This is a struggle full of hope. It is not passive expectation, but active work. In some places and in some situations it is necessary to hope against hope.

Contextual perspective: LPC understands that societies can change. Accordingly, this approach cannot remain immune to social influences, but must maintain its commitment to the poor as they seek liberation.

Interdisciplinary: Because LPC has a systemic and a non-dualistic approach, it must work with other disciplines, such as economy, sociology, politics, psychology, theology, and anthropology, and other related disciplines. Poor families, principal object of this research, have complex problems and therefore need complex analysis and solutions. To work as a team is the ideal way. However, such teamwork is not always possible, especially in Latin America where poor communities cannot pay for such services. The only way to have teamwork is if team members donate their services. When there is no team, a pastor or layperson, without pretending to be a 'know-it-all,' can inform him/herself about important themes, adapting them and creating others.

Adaptation of techniques: Interdisciplinary leads LPC to look for different techniques in order to co-operate with the poor in their liberation. These techniques have to be adapted to specific and particular historical situations and places. For example, where there is an under organized family, eco-structuralist techniques can be adapted and practiced.[cxiv] Where education is necessary, the educational model of Paulo Freire can be used.[cxv] Where biblical study on poverty is needed, biblical interpretations from Liberation Theology can be employed. Where a study of class struggle is needed, a critical approach to Marxism can help. Where an economic analysis is required, dependency theory can be used. And so on.

Development on three levels: LPC can be studied, analyzed and perfected from within three levels of church structure: professional, pastoral and popular.[cxvi] However, the flow of ideas and changes must come from the popular level, from the poor themselves, in order to be realistic. This is due to the failure and rejection that some approaches have experienced as a consequence of being imposed from "outside" the poor.

Constant updating: LPC is not a finalized approach. It must be constantly updated and closely tied to the social and historical context in which it is developed, as well as taking into consideration differences between generations.

CONCLUSIONS

I believe that Basic Christian Communities in Latin America have helped very much in relating individual with community. They have kept in mind the needs of both within distinctive historical contexts. Pastoral care and counseling to the poor must be done within the awareness of the fundamental need for structural change. Liberating Pastoral Care does not pretend to solve the problems of poverty. It believes that poor individuals and families can transform the present situation by joining with each other in order to present a solid and united front. Families, as groups, must not be neglected, but all family counseling must be kept in perspective in terms of whole society. This is also true of counseling with individuals.

It is difficult to know when the *pueblo* will achieve this aim. For this reason, Liberating Pastoral Care and Counseling has an eschatological perspective, but without neglecting the present where the Kingdom is beginning to be constructed.

I do not seek to provide the last word in this matter by presenting a revolutionary proposal. I do hope, however, that this work will motivate ongoing discussions on major issues related to poverty and pastoral care which are urgent in Latin America. I also hope that this work will help in the ongoing development of pastoral care.

NOTES

i. Boff, L. & Boff, C. (1986). *Cómo hacer Teología de la Liberación*. Madrid: Paulinas, pp. 33-58.

ii. *Enciclopedia Hispánica* (1991-1992).

iii. *Diccionario de la Lengua Española* (1984).

iv. (1975). Commission on the Churches' Participation in Development. *Breaking the Chain of Oppression*. Geneva: World Council of Churches, p. 23.

v. Rostow, W. W. (1960). *The Stages of Economic Growth–A non-communist manifesto*. Cambridge: Cambridge University Press.

vi. Frank, A.G. (1971). *Sociology of Development and Underdevelopment of Sociology*. London: Pluto Press, p. 19.

vii. Hinkelammert, F.J. (1983). *Dialéctica del desarrollo desigual*. San José: Editorial Universitaria Centroamericana, p. 16.

viii. Cf. Hinkelammert, F.J. (1988). *La deuda externa de América Latina: El automatismo de la deuda*. San José: Departamento Ecuménico de Investigaciones.

ix. Note that this statistic is from 1987. Wilkie, J.W. (Ed.) & Lorey, D. (Co-Ed.). (1987). *Statistical Abstract of Latin America*. Vol. 25. Los Angeles: UCLA–Latin American Center Publications, table 655, part I.

x. Cf. the research of Rutté García, A. (1973). *Simplemente explotadas: El mundo de las empleadas domésticas en Lima*. Lima: DESCO–Centro de Estudios y Promoción del Desarrollo. He concludes that 88% of the domestic servants in Lima come from the rural areas. Also, see the research of Jelin, E. (1976). Migración a las ciudades y participación en la fuerza de trabajo de las mujeres latinoamericanas: El caso del servicio doméstico. *Estudios Sociales*, (Buenos Aires: CEDES), No. 4.

xi. Cf. Smith, M.L. (1973). "Domestic Service as a Channel of Upward Mobility for the Lower-Class Woman: The Lima Case," in Pescatello, Ann (Ed.). *Female and Male in Latin America*. Pittsburg: University of Pittsburg, pp. 191-207.

xii. Larguia, I. & Dumoulin, J. (1975). Aspectos de la condición laboral de la mujer, *Casa de las Américas*, 88, p. 18. Cf. (1985). La mujer en el desarrollo: estrategia y experiencias de la Revolución Cubana, *Casa de las Américas*, 24(149), 37-43.

xiii. Zea, L. (1984). Negritud e indigenismo. In *Temas de Antropología Latinoamericana*. Bogotá: El Buho, pp. 89-108.

xiv. Burgos-Debray, E. (Ed.). (1985). *I, Rigoberta Menchú: An Indian Woman in Guatemala*. Trans. from Spanish by Ann Wright. London: Verso, p. 2.

xv. Cf. Stennettee, L. & Chevannes, B. (1983). La situación de la raza negra en América Latina y en el Caribe. In *Teología de la Liberación y comunidades eclesiales de base*. Salamanca: Sígueme, pp. 65-73.

xvi. It is an expression used in Guatemala for those who are neither white nor *originally people*.

xvii. Burgos-Debray (1985), pp. XIIf.

xviii. People of mixed European and Amerindians.

xix. Zea (1984), pp. 91s.

xx. Lewis, O. (1966). "The Culture of Poverty," *Scientific American*, 215, 4, 19-25, p. 19.

xxi. Ibid. Lewis thinks that at the age of six or seven years old, children of shanty-towns have already learned the basics values and attitudes of their subculture. That fact does not allow them to be psychologically ready to take advantages of opportunities and changes that that they will face on life (Ibid., p. 21).

xxii. Lewis, O. (1987). *Antropología de la pobreza. Cinco familias.* México: Fondo de Cultura Económica, p. 17. This is a research of five Mexican families that migrated from Tepoztlán to Mexico City. The author registered the anthropological discovering of the important changes that take place in the process of migration from countryside to urban areas.

xxiii. Lewis, O. (1979). *Los hijos de Sánchez.* México: Joaquín Mortiz, pp. XV-XVIII. Lewis makes calculations that at least the third part of the disadvantage socioeconomic groups in Mexico, belong to the "culture of poverty."

xxiv. Ibid., p. XIX.

xxv. Cf. Lewis, O.; Lewis, R.M. & Ridgon, S.M. *Living the Revolution* [3 volumes: *Four Men* (1977), *Four Women* (1977), *Neighbors* (1978)]. Chicago: University of Illinois.

xxvi. To a better analysis of criticism, cf.: Valentine, Ch. (1968). *Culture and Poverty.* Chicago: University of Chicago; Townsend, P. (1979). *Poverty in the United Kingdom.* A Survey of Household Resources and Standar of Living. Middlesex: Pinguin; Labbens, J. (1966). *Reflections on the Concept of a Culture of Poverty.* Paris: International Committee on Poverty Research, Bureau de Recherches Sociales; Schorr, A.L. (1964). "The Non-Culture of Poverty," *American Journal of Orthopsychiatry,* 34, 5.

xvii. Beeson, T. & Pearce, J. (1984). *Vision of Hope. The churches and change in Latin America.* London: Fount Paperbacks, p. 41.

xviii. To be informed of the conflict from within the Catholic church itself and from the government, see Beeson & Pearce (1984), chapter two Mission in Conflict, pp. 29-52; Eagleson, J. & Sharper, P., (Eds.) (1979). *Puebla and Beyond.* Documentation and commentary. Trans. from the Spanish by John Drury. Maryknoll, N.Y.: Orbis Books; and Pope John Paul II, Sobrino, J., McDonagh, F., & Filochowski, J. (1980). *Reflection on Puebla.* London: Catholic Institute of International Relations.

xxix. Maldonado, J.E. (1983). La psicología pastoral que surge en América Latina, *Boletín Teológico,* 18, 23, p. 162.

xxx. Writings of authors such as H. Clinebell, L. Crabb, Jr., C.G. Osborne, and W. Oates.

xxxi. Writings from P. Tournier.

xxxii. Writings from K. Coch.

xxxiii. (1971), La tendencia al suicidio, *El Evangelista Cubano,* 5, 24-28; (1971), *Teología de la Unidad.* Buenos Aires: Aurora; (1973), *Psicología de la experiencia religiosa*; (1976), *Psicología Pastoral para todos los cristianos.* Miami: Caribe; (1977), *La imagen de Dios y el hombre nuevo*; (1977), *Lo que debemos saber sobre la homosexualidad*; (1978), *Psicología Pastoral de la iglesia.* Miami: Caribe; (1966), *Introdução à Psicologia Pastoral.* São Leopoldo: Sinodal; (1996), *Hacia una Psicología Pastoral para los años 2000.* Miami: Caribe; (1998), *Psicología Pastoral para la familia.* Miami: Caribe. Jorge A. León, Methodist pastor; doctorate in Philosophy from the University of Havana; doctorate in Theology from the Protestant School of Theology, Montpellier, France. He is Cuban resident in Argentina since 1967.

xxxiv. (1969), *La angustia y la dimensión trascendente*; (1982), *El arte de ser familia*; editor with Pablo A. Jiménez of *Psicología y Consejo Pastoral* (Decatur, GA:

Asociación para la Educación Teológica Hispana (AETH). Daniel Schipani is Argentinean resident in USA.

xxxv. (1989), Aconselhamento pastoral e liberação, *Estudos Teológicos*, 29/1, 7-17; (1985), Psicologia e serviço da liberação: posibilidades e limites da psicologia na pastoral de aconselhamento, *Estudos Teológicos*, 25/3, 249-270; (1991), *Perguntando pelo sentido da vida*. São Leopoldo: Sinodal. Lothar Carlos Hoch, was borne in São Pedro do Sul (RS), doctorate in Practical Theology/Pastoral Counseling of Philipps-Universität de Marburgo, Germany. Nowadays, he is professor in postgraduate studies of Escola Superior de Teologia (EST) en São Leopoldo, Brasil.

xxxvi. He prepared some autodidactic material for EIRENE (Latin American Association of Family Pastoral Care). (1998), editor of *Fundamentos bíblico-teológicos del matrimonio y la familia*. Buenos Aires: Nueva Creación. Note: Carlos Tadeu "Catito" Grzybowski, psychologist and family therapist and Executive Secretary of CPPC (Body of Christian Psychologist and Psychiatrics), a Brazilian group, and translated some materials of EIRENE to Portuguese.

xxxvii. (1995), *Aconsejamiento Pastoral: Una respuesta biblioterapéutica a la conflictividad emocional del ser humano*. Barceloa: Clie; (1977), *Endemoniados: El ministerio de sanidad interior frente a la realidad demoníaca*. Barcelona: Clie; (1997), *Técnicas de aconsejamiento pastoral*. Barcelona: Clie. El Dr. Stamateas is a pastor of a Baptist Evangelical Church in Buenos Aires, psychologist and professor of Pastoral Counseling.

xxxviii. (1989), *No leito da enfermidade: Manual de Capelania Hospitalar; Aconselhamento a pacientes terminais*. São Paulo: Casa Editora Presbiteriana.

xxxix. Only some examples: Streck, V.S. As contribuições da terapia estructural de familias y da terapia narrativa para o aconselhamento pastoral com famílias problemáticas de baixos recursos, thesis for doctorate of Instituto Ecuménico de Pós-graduação em Teología, São Leopoldo, Brazil; Researches made in the Seminario Bíblico Latinoamericano, San José, Costa Rica: Rosario, X. (1990), Proyecto Centro Cristiano de Asesoramiento Familiar; Vanegas Guzmán, H. (1992), Conflicto y violencia familiar: Un análisis desde la perspectiva de la Psicología Pastoral; Yucra Castaño, S.D. (1993), Hacia una pastoral comprometida con mujeres peruanas en situaciones de sobrevivencia.

xl. Giles, J. (1979) *La psicología y el ministerio cristiano*. Hoff, P. (1996). *O pastor como conselhero*. São Paulo: Vida; Schneider-Harpprecht, C. (1994). *Como acompanhar doentes*: São Leopoldo: Sinodal; Steck, V.S. & Schneider-Harpprecht, C. (1996). *Imagens da família: dinâmica, conflitos e terapia do proceso familiar*. São Leopoldo: Sinodal; Schneider-Harpprecht, C., org. (1998). *Fundamentos Teológicos do Aconselhamento Pastoral*. São Leopoldo: Sinodal.

xli. Maldonado (1988), pp. 13ff.

xlii. (1982), *Graça de Deus e Saúde Humana*; (1983), *Parapsicologia, Espiritismo e Psicopatologia*; (1984), *O Lugar do Sagrado no Processo de Ajuda*.

xliii. Among its several publications there are: *Fundamentos teológicos del matrimonio y la familia; Una teología para el matrimonio y la familia; La familia en la Biblia*. EIRENE has celebrated congresses in Costa Rica (1982) and Colombia (1984) which have gathered pastors, psychologists, psychiatrists, laypersons and professors of theological institutions.

xliv. Santa Ana, J. (1987). *Por las sendas del mundo caminando hacia el Reino*. San José, Costa Rica: Departamento Ecuménico de Investigaciones (DEI), p. 25.

xlv. Galilea, S. (1989). La Pastoral Popular en América Latina, *Pastoral Popular*, 194, 12-16, p. 12.

xlvi. Castillo, F. (1989). Teología de la liberación: un aporte a la pastoral popular, *Pastoral Popular*, 194, 21-24, p. 21.

xlvii. Galilea (1989), p. 12.

xlviii. Alves, R. (1977). Personal Wholeness and Political Creativity: The Theology of Liberation and Pastoral Care, *Pastoral Psychology*, 26(2), 124-136, p. 133.

xlix. *Ibid.*, p. 134.

l. *Ibid.*

li. Sobrino, J. (1985). *Spirituality of Liberation. Toward Political Holiness.* Trans. from the Spanish by Robert R. Barr. Maryknoll, N.Y.: Orbis Books, p. 161. For more information about the hope of the poor, see his chapter 11: The Hope of the Poor in Latin America, pp. 157-168.

lii. Gutiérrez, G. (1981). The Irruption of the Poor in Latin America and the Christian Communities of the Common People. *The Challenge of Basic Christian Communities*. Papers from the International Ecumenical Congress of Theology. February 20-March 2, 1980, São Paulo, Brazil. Edited by Sergio Torres and John Eagleson. Trans. from the Spanish and Portuguese by John Drury. Maryknoll, N.Y.: Orbis Books, p. 111.

liii. Alves (1977), p. 136.

liv. Boff, L. & Boff, C. (1986). *Cómo hacer Teología de la Liberación*. Trans. from the Portuguese by Eloy Requena Calvo. Madrid: Paulinas, p. 28.

lv. Castillo (1989), p. 21.

lvi. Galilea (1989), p. 14. See Boff, L. (1972). *Jesus Christ Liberator*. Maryknoll, N.Y.: Orbis Books, pp. 43-46. Here he develops a Christology characterised by: (a) the primary of anthropology over ecclesiology–human beings are more important then the institutional church; (b) the primacy of the utopian over the factual–the kingdom is anticipated in history and it is in process; (c) the primacy of the critical over the dogmatic; (d) the primacy of the social over the personal; (e) the primacy of orthopraxis over orthodoxy. The topic of "orthopraxis" in pastoral action is well studied by Segundo Galilea and Vidales, R. (1972), *Cristología y pastoral popular*. Bogotá: Paulinas.

lvii. Castillo (1989), p. 21.

lviii. Galilea (1989), p. 14.

lix. Castillo (1989), p. 24.

lx. Galilea (1989), p. 14.

lxi. Bonthius, R.H. (1969). A Theology of Poverty: Prelude to Pastoral Care of the Poor, *Pastoral Psychology*, 20, 21-29, p. 23.

lxii. Boff, C. (1981). The Nature of Basic Christian Communities. *Concilium*, 144, 53-58, p. 53.

lxiii. Gutiérrez, (1981), p. 89.

lxiv. Barbé, D. (1987). *Grace and Power*. Base Communities and Nonviolence in Brazil. Trans. from the French by John Pairman Brown. Maryknoll, New York: Orbis Books, p. 89.

lxv. Boff, L. (1981). Theological Characteristics of a Grassroots Church. *The Challenge of Basic Christian Communities*. Papers from the International Ecumenical Congress of Theology. February 20-March 2, 1980, São Paulo, Brazil. Edited by Sergio Torres and John Eagleson. Trans. from the Spanish and Portuguese by John Drury. Maryknoll, N.Y.: Orbis Books, p. 135.

lxvi. Boff, C. (1981), p. 54.

lxvii. Galdámez, P. (1986). *Faith of a People*. The Life of a Basic Christian Community in El Salvador. Trans. from the Spanish by Robert R. Barr. Maryknoll, New York: Orbis Books, pp. 22, 24f.

lxviii. Boff, L. (1986). *Ecclesiogenesis*. The Base Communities Reinvent the Church. Trans. from the Portuguese by Robert R. Barr. London: Collins, p. 1. BCCs in Brazil developed mainly due to two historical facts: (a) In the 50s the Catholic Church had a scarcity of ordained ministers. This fact permitted the laity to be entrusted with more responsibility. In 1956 dom Angelo Rossi started an evangelization movement with lay catechists in order to reach regions in the vast Brazil countryside where nobody had evangelized. It was the beginning of a new ecclesiology giving form to a new theology. The catequesis became the center of the community and meeting halls were built which served not only as religious centers, but were used for school, sewing lessons and for general meeting. [Boff, L. (1986), pp. 2f]. (b) Barbé (1987, pp. 92f) adds another factor: the repression resulting from the military *coup d'etat* in Brazil in 1964. At the beginning, the clergy supported it but later conflict of interests arose. The people used the church to express their complaints about acts of repression to them. Then, after the toughening of the military regime in 1968, many religious and priests took the option for the poor and oppressed.

lxix. Cook, G. (1985). *The Expectation of the Poor*. Latin American Base Ecclesial Communities in Protestant Perspective. Maryknoll, New York: Orbis Books, p. 7.

lxx. Cf. D'Escoto, M. (1981). The Church Born of the People in Nicaragua. *The Challenge of Basic Christian Communities*. Papers from the International Ecumenical Congress of Theology. February 20-March 2, 1980, São Paulo, Brazil. Edited by Sergio Torres & John Eagleson. Trans. from the Spanish and Portuguese by John Drury. Maryknoll, N.Y.: Orbis Books, pp. 189-191. Also, in the same book the article "The Experience of Nicaraguan Revolutionary Christians," by Juan Hernández Pico, pp. 62-73.

lxxi. Gutiérrez (1981), pp. 115-119.

lxxii. Boff, L. (1986), p. 13.

lxxiii. *Ibid.*, p. 37.

lxxiv. Barreiro, A. (1982). *Basic Christian Communities*. The Evangelization of the Poor. Trans. from the Portuguese by Barbara Campbell. Maryknoll, New York: Orbis Books, p. 63.

lxxv. Gutiérrez (1981), pp. 113f.

lxxvi. Gutiérrez (1977), chapters 9-10.

lxxvii. Boff, L. (1986), p. 41.

lxxviii. Barreiro (1982), pp. 57, 60.

lxxix. Boff, L. & Boff, C. (1986), p. 27.

lxxx. Boff, L. (1981), p. 137. According to him, in socio-historical terms BCCs "are the first thing that has really occurred in the church outside the old framework of the Christendom system and with roots in the common people." *(Ibid.)*

lxxxi. Muñoz, R. (1981). Ecclesiology in Latin America. *The Challenge of Basic Christian Communities*. Papers from the International Ecumenical Congress of Theology. February 20-March 2, 1980, São Paulo, Brazil. Edited by Sergio Torres and John Eagleson. Trans. from the Spanish and Portuguese by John Drury. Maryknoll, N.Y.: Orbis Books, p. 153.

lxxxii. Boff, L. (1981), p. 140.

lxxxiii. Muñoz (1981), p. 151.

lxxxiv. Boff, L. (1981), p. 140.

lxxxv. Barbé (1987), pp. 95-105.

lxxxvi. *Ibid.*, p. 98.

lxxxvii. *Ibid.*

lxxxviii. See three testimonies of coordinators of BCCs, Carlos Zarco Mera, Leonor Tellería and Carlos Manuel Sánchez, (1984), *Concilium*, 176, 65-70.

lxxxix. Barbé (1987), p. 88.

xc. Boff, L. (1981), p. 136. He does not reject power itself but its use in benefit of an elite.

xci. *Ibid*, p. 138.

xcii. Gutiérrez (1981), p. 114.

xciii. Boff, L. (1986), p. 42.

xciv. *Ibid.*, p. 43.

xcv. Boff, C. (1987), pp. 113f.

xcvi. Boff, C. (1981), p. 56.

xcvii. Galdámez (1987), p. 24.

xcviii. Cooperative can protect from usurers who work among the poor. For example, for a 100 pesos loan, the usurer get 10 pesos of interest the first day plus 10 of the capital, then he/she get the same payment for ten days. In this way, the usurers double the money in only 10 days. Some poor people become trapped in this system and they do not see a way to be out of it.

xcix Galdámez (1987), p. 33.

c. Floristán, C. (1984). The Models of the Church which Underlie Pastoral Action, *Concilium*, 176, 71-78, p. 73.

ci. Based in Floristán's pastoral ideas, R.L. Kinast (1980) writes an article entitled The Pastoral Care of Society as Liberation, *The Journal of Pastoral Care*, 34(2), 125-130. He states that "What is needed [in pastoral care] is a view that is sufficiently pastoral, sufficiently theological, and sufficiently societal to ground the pastoral care of society. The most hopeful development in this regard so far has come from the liberation theologians of South and Latin America." (pp. 125f.)

cii. Segundo, J.L. (1978). *The Hidden Motives of Pastoral Action*. Latin American Reflections. Trans. from the Spanish by John Drury. Maryknoll, N.Y.: Orbis Books, p. 110.

ciii. *Ibid.*, p. 121.

civ. Galilea (1989) considers that Popular pastoral care was born forty years ago in Latin America but received recognition from the CELAM in 1968. Before that time, pastoral care in Latin America could be placed in a new Christendom tendency, one of four tendencies in pastoral ministry presented by Floristán: (a) Old Christendom in which there is a close union between church and state with the result of an oppressive pastoral approach that contributes to the marginalisation of the poor. (b) New Christendom, similar to the first one, but in which education is added and there is some basic work in the church. Oppression is recognised and defended but not at the risk of alienating the established powers due to the church's identification with the dominant class. (c) Missionary-witness tendency with existential-humanistic-personalistic philosophy but without an adequate theological analysis of the human situation. These three are the traditional concept of pastoral work. And (d) Critical-prophecy tendency discussed above. These tendencies were analysed by Kinast (1980) based in Floristán's work entitled "Método teológico de la teología pastoral" in *Liberación y Cautiverio: Debates en torno al método de la teología en América Latina*. Mexico: Comité Organizador, 1975, pp. 235-253.

cv. Galilea (1989), p. 15.

cvi. (1981). The Nature of Basic Christian Communities in *Concilium*, 144, 53-58, p. 56.

cvii. Thayer, N.S.T. (1985). *Spirituality and Pastoral Care*. Philadelphia: Fortress Press, p. 15. Also see chapter one of Browning, D.S. (1976). *The Moral Context of Pastoral Care*. Philadelphia: Westminster, pp. 17-37.

cviii. Poling, J. (1988). An Ethical Framework for Pastoral Care, *Journal of Pastoral Care*, 42, 301-306.

cix. *Ibid.*, pp. 302ff.

cx. *Ibid.*, p. 303.

cxi. Dussel, E. (1978). *Ethics and the Theology of Liberation*. Maryknoll, N.Y.: Orbis Books, pp. 38-41.

cxii. Boff, L. (1981), p. 143.

cxiii. Cf. Selby P. (1988). *Liberating God: Private Care and Public Struggle*. London: SPCK, p. 88.

cxiv. Minuchin, S. & Montalvo, B. (1967). Techniques for working with disorganized low socioeconomic families, *American Journal of Orthopsychiatric*, 37, 880-887; Aponte, H.J. (1974). Psychotherapy to the Poor: An Eco-Structural Approach to Treatment. *Delaware Medical Journal*, 46, 134-144.

cxv. Freire, P. (1970). *Pedagogía del oprimido*. Buenos Aires: Siglo XXI.

cxvi. Boff, L. & Boff, C. (1986), pp. 19-32.

Pastoral Action in the Midst of a Context of Economic Transformation and Cultural Apathy

Ronaldo Sathler-Rosa, PhD

SUMMARY. This article presents and critically analyzes the current process of economic globalization identified from the perspective of the so-called emerging countries. Specifically, the engagement of globalization as an economic, cultural and political process with diverse contemporary religious phenomenon is explored in terms of its implications and applications for Pastoral Counseling and Action both in terms of Brazil, specifically, and South America, in general. The pastoral-theological theory grounding of this paper comes from Practical Theology. Within this frame of reference the metaphors of the reign of God and the theology of God's grace are presented in terms of their relevance for Pastoral Care and Counseling. *[Article copies available for a fee from The Haworth Document Delivery Service: 1-800-HAWORTH. E-mail address: <getinfo@haworthpressinc.com> Website: <http://www.HaworthPress.com> © 2002 by The Haworth Press, Inc. All rights reserved.]*

KEYWORDS. Pastoral, theology, economy, Latin America, pastoral counseling

---

[Haworth co-indexing entry note]: "Pastoral Action in the Midst of a Context of Economic Transformation and Cultural Apathy." Sathler-Rosa, Ronaldo. Co-published simultaneously in *American Journal of Pastoral Counseling* (The Haworth Pastoral Press, an imprint of The Haworth Press, Inc.) Vol. 5, No. (3/4), 2002, pp. 225-237; and: *International Perspectives on Pastoral Counseling* (ed: James Reaves Farris) The Haworth Pastoral Press, an imprint of The Haworth Press, Inc., 2002, pp. 225-237. Single or multiple copies of this article are available for a fee from The Haworth Document Delivery Service [1-800-HAWORTH, 9:00 a.m. - 5:00 p.m. (EST). E-mail address: getinfo@haworthpressinc.com].

"The seven social sins . . . politics without principles, wealth without work, education without character, commerce without morality, pleasure without conscience, science without humanity, and worship without sacrifice." (Mahatma Ghandi, in Oka 1998, 33)

INTRODUCTION

This article will discuss various traits of contemporary economy, its effects on Pastoral Counseling and Theology and its pervasive influence on shaping of cultures. I have chosen this perspective or approach because I believe that in Brazil, as well as in many other so-called "developing countries," economic influences fundamentally influence our notions of personal and cultural identity, the place and function of the church and the meaning and process of Pastoral Counseling. I have chosen to enter this discussion via this perspective, instead of by directly discussing the identity and function of Pastoral Counseling, because of my belief that micro- and macro-economic influences must be understood in order to accurately understand the identity and function of any specific ministry. This does not mean that Pastoral Counseling, or any other ministry of the Church, is totally dependent on or influenced exclusively by economic factors. That is an unacceptable reductionism. However, in order to understand any ministry of the Church, in this case Pastoral Care and Counseling, it is important to understand key aspects of the context in which ministry takes place. In Brazil, and I believe in many other so-called "developing countries," one of the most important contextual influences is that of economy. Pastoral Counseling and Theology exist within specific cultural contexts, and the cultural context of Brazil is profoundly affected by economic systems. Such systems do more than regulate the flow of capital. They impose implicit systems of value and identity that directly affect individual, group and institutional identity and functioning. For this reason I believe it to be of fundamental importance to explore the relations between Pastoral Counseling, Pastoral Theology and economic systems.

In this article the current process of economic globalization is critically identified from the perspective of the so-called emerging countries. Specifically, the engagement of globalization as an economic, cultural and political process with diverse contemporary religious phenomenon is explored in terms of its implications and applications for Pastoral Action and Pastoral Counseling both in terms of Brazil, specifically, and South America, in general.

The pastoral-theological theory grounding this paper comes from Practical Theology. Within this frame of reference two specific theological concepts underlie this essay: the metaphor of the reign of God and the theology of God's grace. Major presuppositions of this analysis are:

1. Pastoral Care and Counseling of individuals and families is not adequate to address the current social and economic conditions of most of the global population.
2. Pastoral caregivers have a special vocational call which implies that their mission goes beyond the limits of a congregation or institution.
3. Pastoral care agents together with the churches can create and develop prophetic-pastoral channels to fulfill the public dimension of the ministry of care.
4. Pastoral Theology should establish a dialogue between the data supplied by social and human sciences, and the demands of the message of the reign of God. In fact, to make pastoral action effective, socio-analytical mediations are necessary to unveil society's mechanisms (cf. C. Boff 1998).

DEFINING THE CONTEXT

There are several metaphors which attempt to depict the present historical context. Among others, "global village," "global factory," "country-earth," "first worldly revolution," "third wave" (Ianni, 1998, 15). The use of multiple metaphors suggests that the current scenario is still open, as an emerging reality, for more and better definitions.

As a way of exploring the economic as well as cultural aspects of our current scenario, let me point out some descriptions by four different scholars.

First of all, it is important to consider some history. A three-day interfaith conference was held in Malaysia in 1997 promoted by the International Movement for a Just World with the cooperation of Australia-based International Christian Peace Movement. In a lecture Chaiwat Satha-Anand (1998, 136), professor in Political Science at Thammasart University, Thailand, states that the so-called modern world system "is said to have originated in Western Europe between 1450 to 1640, and is often called 'the long sixteenth century.' The need for labor, raw materials and markets fuelled the expansion of trade and culminated in European colonization of much of the world, justified by its own religious ideology. However, only in the twentieth century has such a 'world' system become truly global."

Second, Herbert Anderson (1999, 7), a Lutheran pastor and professor of Pastoral Theology at the Catholic Theological Union, Chicago, drawing on Robert Schreiter's work calls our attention to the several definitions of globalization. However, there is a general agreement that globalization has to do with growing interconnections among the fields of politics, economics and sociology. "Globalization is a world-wide social phenomena in which things are fragmenting or splintering and reluctantly coming together simultaneously," Anderson writes. As a consequence there exists a "proliferation of political, economic and cultural centers of power," the world became a multipolar reality lacking a clear map. Living in a *multipolar* world is especially difficult for cultures and persons who have presumed political dominance or cultural superiority.

Third, according to Lester Ruiz (1993, 8), "we are living in a time of world-changing events. Historical conditions are changing at an almost unimaginable rate forcing us to redefine our ways of thinking, feeling, and acting. We are witnessing, indeed, participating in, not only the acceleration of history, but in a profoundly uneven, not to mention deeply contradictory and contested, transformation of that history."

Relying on several studies, Ruiz (8) contends that "there exists a single, integrated global economy, oriented around a capitalist ideology." Global economy is meant to convey the idea of an "extensive and fairly complete global division of labor." Besides, it presupposes an "integrated set of production, distribution and consumption processes" connected to corporations. Corporations become part of a "complex set of interlocking enterprises" that have an enormous amount of capital and power by means of which they play an unbalanced influence on cultures.

Indeed, for David R. Loy (1998, 65), a Zen Buddhist scholar, "from the very beginning corporations have also had an incestuous relationship with the state. In the sixteenth century, nation-states as we know them did not exist."

In a rather long footnote Loy (72) states that "the United States was born of a revolt against corporations, which had been used as instruments of abusive power by British kings. The new republic was deeply suspicious of both government and corporate power." Loy also says that "Lincoln complained shortly before his death: 'Corporations have been enthroned. . . . An era of corruption in high places will follow and the money power will endeavor to prolong its reign by working on the prejudices of the people . . . until wealth is aggregated in a few hands . . . and the republic is destroyed.' Rutherford Hayes, who became president in 1876 due to a tainted election and back-room corporate dominated elections, later declared: 'this is a government of the people, by the people and for the people no longer. It is a government of corporations, by corporations, and for corporations.' "

Even though the current process of economic globalization is subject to change, there exists a common understanding that the major contemporary economies have some common features. Among them are the globalization of the market as well the regionalization of capital. In other words, we are experiencing a globalization of production and territorialization of consumption. Also, it is characterized by "hierarchy and unevenness that links economies as diverse as those of the advanced capitalist stages as well as those more popularly called 'semi-colonial, semi feudal or postcolonial, even postmodern' " (Ruiz 1993, 8-9).

Fourth, M. Douglas Meeks (1998), a theological reader of the present time, asserts that "the global market economy is not only full of promise, it is also full of threat." There is a constant increasing gap between rich and poor as well between impoverished countries and affluent countries. Migration is another factor that can contribute towards economic troubles. The mass migration of "non-skilled" workers to "brain-power" areas of production might become a disturbing factor within the market web.

PASTORAL ANALYSIS

Why is it important to examine the impact of economic transformation upon religions and cultures?

First, because the current globalized economic system is "beginning to influence some of the values and worldviews that lie at the heart of the great religious and cultural traditions." Being more specific, "notions of good and bad, of right and wrong; perceptions of the role of the individual and the community, the character of interpersonal and inter-group relations, conceptions about the purpose of life and the significance of death are being transformed by the seductive power of global capital and global consumerism, the global market and the global media" (Camillery and Muzaffar, 1998, preface).

Second, in spite of differences, broad generalizations and the need for critical reexamination, there are some common perspectives among religious as well as cultural communities. To a certain extent, religions share common grounds "in regard to environmental protection, ethical economic behavior, moderate consumption patterns, principled political conduct, community welfare . . . and the dignity of the human person . . . ." These shared ideals "transcending religious and cultural boundaries . . . can help check the negative consequences of globalization, while strengthening its positive aspects" (Camillery and Muzaffar, preface).

What would be the major issues that have emerged from this context that have to do with pastoral *praxis* and pastoral-theological theory? I submit two issues related to the current process of economic transformation that deserve the attention of religious leaders, both lay and clergy.

The first issue is the 'social apartheid' (Cristovam Buarque) process. Anderson (1999, 7), drawing on Schreiter's work, states that globalization "includes a fundamental redistribution of wealth, making some people and some nations very wealthy while others are driven deeper into poverty and despair. . . . If there is a new bipolarization, it is between the rich and the poor. Our experience of globalization at the end of this century has been escalated by the new communications technology."

Jung Mo Sung (1998), a Brazilian Roman Catholic lay theologian, professor at the Methodist University of Sao Paulo, in an article entitled "Hunger for God, Hunger for Bread, Hunger for Humanity: A Southern Perspective"[1] points out the similarities between the American continents. Sung (35) asserts that "the most obvious is the great concentration of wealth in contrast to extreme poverty: in Latin America, between pockets of wealth in a sea of poverty; in Canada and the United States, between pockets of poverty in a sea of wealth."

A growing number of people have been excluded from the marketplace. However, they are not excluded from society and "from the reach of those means of communication that create in the excluded the same desires for consumer goods that drive the rest of the population." Therefore, we face a tragic situation. Since the disposable are still living among us they are "stimulated to desire sophisticated and superfluous consumer goods at the same time that they are denied the possibility of acquiring the basic necessities for signified survival" (Sung, 36).

The greatest factor that generates social exclusion is "structural unemployment." It is called structural unemployment "because it is not a part of a present constellation of political-economic factors, the fruit of an economic recession that will pass or be eased by economic growth." The structural unemployment mirrors the established model of global economy intertwined with technological revolution. Sung (36) cites Peter Drucker who wrote in 1989: "In the industrial economy production [has] ceased being 'connected' to employment, and the movement of capital, and not of trade (whether goods or services) [has become] the driving force of the world economy."

In the named pre-modern societies people used to work to live. In our modern, or post-modern industrially advanced societies people live to accumulate wealth. Besides, "the financial system–which should be linked to the service system–has increased and become more important, and is, to a large degree, disconnected from production. Wealth is financed and, to a large degree, fictitious–a matter less of tangible goods than of numbers blinking on a computer screen" (Sung, 37).

The process of social exclusion is based on some theoretical assumptions. I will pinpoint a piece of the "logic of exclusion" as mentioned by SUNG in an unpublished paper. There is juxtaposition between the logic of competition, "of the 'survival of the strongest,' that many–the 'weak'–will be excluded from the market, sacrificed along way. But in contrast to those who defend the indelible dignity of all persons and the consequent right to life, they say that these sacrifices are necessary for progress. We cannot understand the force of this affirmation if we do not have in mind the sacrificial, theological tradition that was so much a part of western Christianity. Michael Novak, the prophet-theologian of the market, takes up this tradition to defend the excluding logic of the market: 'If God desired that His beloved Son suffer, why would He spare us?"

The second issue is what Hugo Assmann (1996, 380) termed a "culture of insensitivity." In Assmann's own words, "The primary factor in the present world situation is certainly the terrible power of the logic of exclusion and the growing insensitivity of most persons in relationship to it."

Apathy, indifference and a lack of sensitivity seem to be a major trait of many societies. It is more than a personal attitude. It is part of a cultural pattern that idolizes 'success' [profit] and the 'winners' to the detriment of the victims [of economic exploitation]. The victims become visible in the faces of the unemployed, the two-thirds of the world that is impoverished, children, women, Indigenous persons and others. Apathy is an expression of violence. In Rene Girard's own terms the exploitation of the 'surpluses' is a type of sacrifice derived from insensitivity (Sathler-Rosa, 1998, 20).

Such a culture of insensitivity, particularly in the context of South and Central America, does not develop by chance. It is a consequence of historical, social and anthropological factors. Following my colleague SUNG (1998), I will highlight some of those factors.

First, there exists a widespread "concept of the inevitability of inequality and social exclusion."

Second, there is the notion that the poor are poor not only because it is inevitable but also because it is culturally ingrained. The 'winners' are doing nothing less than profiting from their just rewards. On the contrary, the poor are seen as guilty of their own poverty and that they are receiving their just rewards.

These assumptions are seen as 'incarnations' of a transcendental judge and justice. These market mechanisms are a secularized version of the theology of retribution so criticized by Jesus and by the reformers through the theology of grace. In a more ecclesiastical setting a modern religious version exists as the 'theology of prosperity,' or 'prosperity Gospel.'

A PASTORAL-THEOLOGICAL AGENDA

I attempt to lay down a provisional pastoral-theological agenda in light of the contemporary contour of various cultures and societies. This agenda attempts to respond to the predicament inflicted on the world as a result of the 'idolatry of the marketplace' (Franz Hinklammert).

First, pastoral theology might contribute towards a clear comprehension of the complexities of the economic-social-political forces engaged in globalizing the market and cultures. Thus, we need to enlarge the knowledge of the field through other fields of knowledge, such as the human and social sciences. "The specific nature of pastoral theologizing is to establish a dialogue between the data supplied by social [and human] sciences and the demands of revelation. In fact, to make pastoral action effective, socio-analytical mediations are necessary to unveil society's mechanisms" (Sathler-Rosa, 1993, 32).

Clodovis Boff (1998, 378) says that human sciences such as Psychology, History, Linguistics, and the social sciences, e.g., Economics, Sociology, Political Sciences, and Anthropology take as their object of study the human being. These sciences help us to understand human beings, their interactions, cravings, limitations and the 'order of things' (Michel Foucault) that they establish for themselves. Moreover, they are important auxiliary sciences to help theology and pastoral care agents to bring about faith into history and culture, though the scientific character of the sciences and their academic autonomy does not make them exempt from critique by theologians.

From a Practical Theology view, theology does not concern itself only with God; it scrutinizes the human processes that lead to know God and the events which happen between human beings and God, and among people in their search for meaning (Sathler-Rosa, 1993, 36).

Second, we cannot forget the biblical connections between love and justice. Justice is the implementation of love. To work for justice within primary relationships as well as between communities, churches and nations is a perennial goal of all pastoral practices. As the professor of social communications Clifford Christians (1999, 15) says, "our long-term goal ought to be normative thinking on distributive justice widely shared by churches, media users and producers, teachers and students, government regulations, and engineers. A general understanding of justice is nurtured as we call one another to account within participatory media where we have a voice and a hearing."

The recovering of the "dangerous memories" (J. B. Metz) of our Judeo-Christian heritage may subvert the *status quo* of congregations, institutions and communities of faith. Francis Fiorenza's introduction in the book *Faith and the Future,* in response to J. B. Metz's writings, calls our attention to the fact that "critical analysis of modern society takes particular aim at the crisis of the church posed by bourgeois religion. The bourgeois virtues of autonomy, stability, competitive struggle and performance obscure the messianic virtues of repentance, compassion, an unconditional love for the 'least of the brethren'" (1995, XIV).

Third, we must educate congregations in terms of how to become "communities of resistance and solidarity" (Sharon Welch, 1985). Congregations might be considered political models that invite people and communities to live abundantly.

To resist means to be in opposition to practices, legislations, and policies that would work against the goal of creating a culture of peace and justice. It is a difficult, subversive and dangerous task. It brings back the messianic hope and memories.

The theological principle of critical solidarity means an invitation to find pastoral ways of exerting mutual care among the members of the community. In addition, the community is invited to accomplish several ministries–or a variety of methods of doing enlightened pastoral care with others, nature and at the political-public level (see Fowler, 1991). The idea–and ideal–of solidarity is to support justice-love based relationships, i.e., opportunities and recognition of one's capabilities and fair differentiation.

Many of us in the field are increasingly becoming aware that the role of the clergy needs to be reshaped. Strategies or models of ministry and pedagogical tools must be preceded by an exploration of the fundamental attitudes of clergy towards such a community. What we are will be reflected in our work.

As one fundamental attitude, I would say that pastoral leadership, particularly in a "society of knowledge" (Peter Drucker), is not to be performed in a 'bossy' way. Rather, we are challenged to reexamine the ways Jesus fulfilled His ministry. Jesus was "compassionate, attentive, and respectful." In other words, we need to recognize Jesus' radical and merciful power. Also, we may remember that Mary, Jesus' mother, in the words of Douglas Meeks, sent Him to the kitchen to "do something about the wine." As we revisit the story of the first miracle in John 2, we learn that our pastoral duties are not as "transcendental" as they use to be. We have to deal with "down-to-earth" issues and concerns.

Fourth, we need to search for ecologically anthropocentric-oriented pastoral action anchored in an appreciation and respect for diversity. The traditional theocentrism of many pastoral practices focus on, for instance, preaching about different interpretations of the Scripture, polemics on the history of God, indoctrination or moralist teachings.

Ecologically anthropocentric-oriented pastoral action assumes that Jesus did not incarnate for the sake of the Divinity, but for the sake of women, men, creation and the cosmos. Pastoral care considers human questions and human aspirations, establishes a pastoral dialogue on the issues involved, and correlates them to appropriate pastoral responses. Pastoral work takes on a hermeneutical perspective. It would look like a shared pilgrimage in which pastoral care givers attempt to facilitate the process of self-knowledge, the search for meaning vis-à-vis the anthropological and theological concept of Image of God and the whole Creation. This pastoral approach would seek to integrate the "whole-biosphere well-being perspective" as well as for the "whole-human family well-being perspective" (Clinebell, 1996, 79-81). This approach requires attentive and continuing study of the economic, cultural and political influence on people's lives.

At this point a few words regarding anthropocentrism are in order. I do not mean a certain kind of modern anthropocentrism that, in J. Moltmann's words (1995, 188ff), "has robbed nature of its soul and made human beings unembodied subjects." Ecologically anthropocentric-oriented pastoral care of individuals, systems, world and nature "can be fitted into the conditions for life on earth and into the symbiosis, or community, of all living things in a way that is not a nostalgic and 'alternative' flight from industrial society, but which will reform it until it becomes ecologically endurable for the earth, and is integrated into the earthly fellowship of the living." It means that one of our tasks as pastoral agents is "to decentralize human culture and to incorporate it harmoniously into a single web with nature" (Moltmann, 1995, 193).

Fifth, this submitted pastoral agenda would incorporate into our current care of families and persons the public dimension of pastoral work. A particular goal of this aspect is to look for ways of witnessing prophetic and messianic concerns for the underprivileged. Larry Graham (2000, 10) asserts, in accordance with Bonnie Miller-Mclemore, that "pastoral care and counseling is moving from exclusive focus upon the 'living human document' to attend also to the 'living human web.' "

An image that could illustrate the public dimension of pastoral ministry is to join hands with social and communitarian movements that are struggling for a just distribution of land, equal opportunities for women and men, and against economic exploitation. A model to implement the public dimension of pastoral duties, for example, would be to confront, i.e., to offer another perspective, to policy-makers, politicians, business persons, and entrepreneurs in order to show the reality of those who are the victims of their economic decisions. As Konrad Raiser points out in his address at the Jubilee Consultation 1996, "any perception of reality, in particular of social reality, is shaped and conditioned by a perspective which reflects the social position and the interest of those who speak or act. This was brought home to me very dramatically at an ecumenical hearing about the international debt crisis. A senior representative of the World Bank, fully convinced of the validity and realism of his analysis, was confronted with the testimony of people from countries which had experienced structural adjustment programs. They spoke about a reality which he had never seen or experienced personally. Under the impact of these testimonies, he said somewhat helplessly: 'Could it be that we have become blind and cannot see reality?' "

Sixth, we need to reexamine the past and be hope-oriented. Many of our legitimate critiques of institutional and ecclesiastical bodies would be much more effective if we knew the past factors that have molded us—and our congregations—and tailored us into a "bourgeois religion" rather than into a radical Christian commitment. Hope-oriented pastoral action would be "utopian-oriented," that is, would reject the 'dictatorship' of 'facts,' or of the so-called 'common sense.' 'Common sense' may take the form of expressions such as 'this is the way things are,' 'we cannot change it,' and 'this is the way we do business.'

However, pastoral agents operating with a hope orientation analyze history, grasp the origins and circumstances of facts and are not encapsulated by the facts.

'Hope' is one of the constitutive elements of the theological metaphor of the reign of God. Hope for the coming reign, in Jewish tradition, was more than merely an addition to the pious duties of the law. The hope that comes from Jesus' message is the unique spring of "knowledge and guidance for living. Whatever God demands from [men and women] is comprehended in the message of His imminent kingdom" (Pannenberg, 1977, 54).

The concept of hope is even more significant when it is articulated in concrete and conflictive situations. Gustavo Gutierrez (1973) discusses how Ernst Bloch has used this predominantly theological category. According to Gutierrez (216), Bloch has pointed out that humankind dreams of the future and hopes for it; moreover, Gutierrez says, "it is an active hope which subverts the existing order. . . . Hope is the most important as well as the most positive and liberating [of the expectation affections]. Hope is a daydream projected into the future; it is the 'yet-not-conscious' . . . the psychic representation of that which 'is not yet.' . . . But this hope seeks to be clear and conscious. . . . When that which is 'yet-not-conscious' becomes a conscious act, it is no longer a state of mind; it assumes a concrete utopia function, mobilizing human action in history. Hope thus emerges as the key to human existence oriented towards the future, because it transforms the present."

Hope belongs to "expectation affections" together with anguish and fear (Ernst Bloch). Hope makes us foresee the unseen and move towards its realization.

NOTE

1. There is another article from the same publication entitled "Hunger for God, Hunger for Humanity: A Northern Perspective," by Heidi Hadsell.

REFERENCES

Anderson, H. (1999) "Seeing the other whole: A habitus for globalization." In Ballard, P. & Couture, P. (Eds.). *Globalization and difference. Practical Theology in a world context.* Fairwater, Cardiff.

Assmann, H. (1996). "Por una sociedad onde quepan todos." In Duque, J. (Ed.). *Quarta jornada teologica de Cetela.* San Jose, Dei.

Boff, C. (1998). *Teoria do metodo teologico.* Petropolis, Vozes.

Camilleri, J. & Muzaffar, C. (Eds.). *Globalization: The perspectives and experiences of the religious traditions of Asia Pacific*. Malaysia, IMJW.

Christians, C. G. (1999). "Ethics, economics and innovation: The future of account-ability." In *Journal of the World Association for Christian Communication*, 2.

Clinebell, H. (1996). *Ecotherapy–healing ourselves, healing the world*. Minneapolis, Fortress.Fowler, J. (1991). *Weaving the new creation. Stages of faith and the public church*. New York, Harper.

Graham, L. K. (2000). "Pastoral theology as public theology in relation to the clinic." In *Journal of Pastoral Theology, 2000*.

Gutierrez, G. (1973). *A theology of liberation: History, politics and salvation*. Mary-knoll, NY, Orbis.

Ianni, O. (1998) *Teorias da globalização*. 5th ed. Rio de Janeiro, Civilizacao Brasileira.

Loy, D. (1998). "Can corporations become enlightened? Buddhist reflections on TNCs." In Camilleri, J. & Muzaffar, C. (Eds.). *Globalization: The perspectives and experiences of the religious traditions of Asia Pacific*. Malaysia, IMJW.

Meeks, M. D. (1998). *The global economy and God's economy*. [Unpublished paper].

Metz, J. B. & Moltmann, J. (1995). *Faith and the future*. Maryknoll, NY, Orbis.

Oka, G. B. (1998). "A Hindu perspective." In Camilleri, J. & Muzaffar, C. (Eds.). *Globalization. The perspectives and experiences of religious traditions of Asia Pacific*. Malaysia, IMJW.

Pannenberg, W. (1977). *Theology and the kingdom of God*. Philadelphia, Westminster.

Raiser, K. (1996). *Utopia and responsibility*. [unpublished paper].

Ruiz, L. E. (1993). "Pastoral care and counseling in 21st century Asia: Meditations on the creation of a world made new." In KrisetyA, M. (Ed.). *Pastoral care and counseling in pluralistic society*. Bali, Indonesia, ACPCC.

Satha-Anand, C. (1998). "Spiritualizing real estate, commoditizing pilgrimage: The Muslim minority in Thailand." In Camilleri, J. & Muzaffar, C. (Eds.). *Globalization: The perspectives and experiences of religious traditions of Asia Pacific*. Malaysia, IMJW.

Sathler-Rosa, R. (1998). "Response to the lecture of Hans-Martin Gutmann from a Brazilian perspective." In *Intercultural Pastoral Care and Counseling*, 4.

Sathler-Rosa, R. (1993). "O que e Teologia Pratica. Notas introdutorias." In *Simposio*, 8 (4), XXIII, 36.

Sung, J. M. (1998). "Hunger for God, hunger for bread, hunger for humanity: A south-ern perspective." In Bolioli, O. (Ed.). *Hope and justice for all in the Americas*. New York, Friendship Press.

Sung, J. M. (1999). *Contributions of theology in the struggle against social exclusion*. [Unpublished paper].

Welch, S. (1985). *Communities of resistance and solidarity*. Maryknoll, NY, Orbis.

Planting Pastoral Counseling Seeds in Brazilian Soil: Creating and Recreating Models

James Reaves Farris, PhD

SUMMARY. This article describes Pastoral Counseling in Brazil in terms of its major challenges and possibilities. Particular attention is paid to the influence of Brazilian cultural contexts and their influence on issues of the identity and practice of Pastoral Counseling. Contrasts and relations between Pastoral Counseling in Brazilian and North American contexts are explored. The place and influence of imported theories and practices as well as the development of models that are unique to Brazilian contexts are considered. The fundamental proposal of this article is that Brazilian cultural contexts greatly influence the theory and practice of Pastoral Counseling, and that while distinctly Brazilian models of Pastoral Counseling are slowly developing they are still deeply influenced by imported models and methods. *[Article copies available for a fee from The Haworth Document Delivery Service: 1-800-HAWORTH. E-mail address: <getinfo@haworthpressinc.com> Website: <http://www.HaworthPress.com> © 2002 by The Haworth Press, Inc. All rights reserved.]*

KEYWORDS. Pastoral counseling, pastoral theology, cross cultural counseling, Brazil

[Haworth co-indexing entry note]: "Planting Pastoral Counseling Seeds in Brazilian Soil: Creating and Recreating Models." Farris, James Reaves. Co-published simultaneously in *American Journal of Pastoral Counseling* (The Haworth Pastoral Press, an imprint of The Haworth Press, Inc.) Vol. 5, No. (3/4), 2002, pp. 239-252; and: *International Perspectives on Pastoral Counseling* (ed: James Reaves Farris) The Haworth Pastoral Press, an imprint of The Haworth Press, Inc., 2002, pp. 239-252. Single or multiple copies of this article are available for a fee from The Haworth Document Delivery Service [1-800-HAWORTH, 9:00 a.m. - 5:00 p.m. (EST). E-mail address: getinfo@haworthpressinc.com].

INTRODUCTION

Pastoral Counseling is profoundly influenced by cultural context. Looking at the theory and practice of Pastoral Counseling from a cultural perspective other than one's own reveals how profound such influences can be. Though considerable change is taking place, many of the dominant models for Pastoral Counseling have been and continue to be constructed within North American contexts. The purpose of this article is to describe and analyze Brazilian Pastoral Counseling as it takes place within Protestant traditions. The reasons for limiting the discussion to Protestant traditions will become clearer during the discussion. The goal of this presentation is to reveal the complexity and richness of Pastoral Counseling as they take place in a cultural context outside North American matrixes, and thus enable more serious reflection on questions of identity, diversity, normative models and implicit beliefs.

This is an important task for three reasons. First, cultural, and specifically economic, realities in Brazil have greatly influenced how Pastoral Counseling and Pastoral Action are done and understood. This leads to questions of how cultural context and the practice of Pastoral Counseling are intertwined. Second, concerns with practical matters such as HMOs, insurance billing, center and practice management and other such realities which are often of considerable importance in North American contexts may generate implicit beliefs that such issues are of fundamental importance to all Pastoral Counseling and all Pastoral Counselors. Intercultural dialogue regarding the theory and practice of Pastoral Counseling can help provide needed perspective. Third, there is a tendency to believe that the theoretical models of one group in one cultural context can be readily generalized to other groups and contexts. If, for example, Object Relations Theory, Brief Therapy Models and certain Theological Understandings of Revelation are of particular importance to my group, it is easy to believe that such ideas are of near universal importance. Intercultural dialogue opens the possibility of seeing how groups and individuals in different cultural contexts understand the relationship between the theory and practice of Pastoral Counseling, and thus challenge our notions of universality.

The implicit danger in any such conversation is to speak in generalities. It must be made clear that there is no such thing as "The" North American model of Pastoral Counseling or "The" Brazilian model of Pastoral Counseling. There do exist, however, tendencies that can be identified and discussed. For example, in spite of the presence of Family Systems Theories, and other system based models, many psychological theories and models of Pastoral Care and Counseling used in the United States and Europe tend to be based on individual intrapsychic understandings of human behavior. It may be that North American and European models of Pastoral Care and Counseling have adopted such individualistic approaches because of the historical concern of Protestant Churches for individual morality and salvation. One of the questions at hand is what happens when such models are imported to a culture, in this case Brazil, which tends to be family and relationship oriented and, at least historically, intimately identified with the natural world?

The metaphor used in the title of this presentation, *Planting Pastoral Counseling Seeds in Brazilian Soil,* is intentional. The seeds of Protestant Pastoral Counseling in Brazil were planted by North American missionaries beginning in the mid 1800s, and soon afterwards by missionaries from various European countries. What happened during the following century was that the seeds planted did not necessarily yield the fruits expected. Protestant missions in Brazil were generally, though far from exclusively, oriented toward the middle classes. These groups generally accepted imported understandings of Pastoral Care and Counseling, or it could be said that Historical Protestant Churches educated their members in terms of the identity and functioning of this ministry. However, as these Churches faced economic and social changes in Brazil, mainly in terms of industrialization and urbanization, and tried to reach beyond the middle classes traditional understandings of Pastoral Care and Counseling began to prove inadequate. Though a generalization it may be said that in Brazil the realities of poverty, oppression and powerlessness fundamentally challenged traditional notions of Pastoral Care and Counseling. This is particularly true of the period after World War II.

Metaphorically, the farmers that planted wheat began to notice that what sprouted was something they could not quite recognize. In some fields, such as in Historical Protestant Churches among the urban middle classes, what sprouted was very similar to the seeds planted. However, in many other fields, such as among the rural and urban poor, what sprouted was very different from the original seeds that were planted. It could be said that the current debate in Pastoral Care and Counseling in Brazil can be described as a discussion of what has sprouted, the value of these new plants, what to do with these new plants, and the relation between these new plants and the seeds originally planted. Given this context, this article will discuss the current status of Pastoral Care and Counseling in Brazil, and reflect on its uniqueness, challenges and opportunities.

GENERAL CONTEXT AND PERSPECTIVE

As will be discussed below in greater detail, the formal practice of Pastoral Counseling as a distinct discipline or practice is very limited, or quite different from traditional understandings, in Brazil. Pastoral Counseling understood as the more formal, structured and in-depth counseling offered by ministers or selected laypersons, is severely limited by the practical reality in Brazil that many Protestant ministers are part-time and frequently receive only basic training. They often work at secular jobs during the week and serve a local congregation one or two weeknights and on Sundays. While there is a desire for more full-time pastors, the economic realities faced by many Protestant congregations make this an unlikely occurrence in the near future. This economic, social and practical reality limits the possibility of local church pastors offering what is traditionally understood as Pastoral Counseling.

While Protestant ministers do very little traditional Pastoral Counseling they are involved in considerable short-term Crisis or Problem Solving Counseling. Pastors are also involved in considerable Pastoral Solidarity. In Brazil, Pastoral Solidarity is understood in much the same sense as, though broader than, Pastoral Care in the United States. Pastoral Solidarity describes almost every action that is oriented toward the cure of, care for or liberation of persons. As such, Pastoral Solidarity includes Pastoral Counseling, Education, Presence, Social Justice Work, Visitation, Evangelism, and, in some traditions, Liturgy, Music and Preaching. Key in this discussion are differences in how terms are used. While the division between Pastoral Care and Pastoral Counseling are relatively well established in North American and European traditions, the same is not the case in Brazilian Protestantism.

As will be discussed below, this article will only deal with Protestant religious traditions in Brazil. The reason for this is that I am not adequately familiar with Roman Catholic Pastoral Counseling and Pastoral Action to provide an informed discussion. One of the reasons that I am not well informed about Roman Catholic practices is that there is a wide gulf between Roman Catholic and Protestant Churches in Brazil. Protestant and Roman Catholic Churches exist in almost separate or parallel universes, and the Protestant Church is clearly in the numerical minority.

Brazil has a total population of approximately 157,000,000, with 70% identifying themselves as Roman Catholic and 8% as Protestant. While there is some ecumenical dialogue that takes place in Universities, in a few Theological Seminaries and between ecclesiastical authorities, interreligious discussions at the level of the local parish or congregation are rare. For these reasons, this article will deal almost exclusively with Protestant Pastoral Counseling and pastoral action in Brazil.

Another question that must be addressed is the meaning of the word "Protestant." In Brazil there is an ongoing debate as to what it means to be a "Protestant" Church. In general, Methodist, Baptist, Lutheran and Presbyterian Churches are self-identified as "Historical Protestant Churches." There are a variety of Independent Pentecostal Churches that also identify themselves as "Protestant" in that they share similar historical roots with "Historical Protestant Churches." However, differences in styles of worship, ministry and theology between traditional "Historical Protestant Churches" and "Protestant Pentecostal Churches" in Brazil are considerable. At times differences in styles of ministry are so great that it is difficult to see these Churches as "Protestant." There are also diverse "Neo-Pentecostal Churches" in Brazil that at times identify themselves as "Protestant" and at other times do not. These Churches are often so different in worship and ministry styles that there is very little similarity to "Historical Protestant Churches." The use of Theologies of Prosperity in these Churches also adds to the theological distance from "Protestant" theologies. In summary, it is not easy to define the term "Protestant" in Brazil. In general, this article will deal with Pastoral Counseling within "Historical Protestant Churches" and "Protestant Pentecostal Churches" in Brazil.

As has already been noted, perspective or context tends to greatly influence understandings of reality. In light of this, it is important to understand the social location of this author. I am not Brazilian. I am North American. I have lived in Brazil for eight years, and during that time have taught Pastoral Care and Counseling at the Methodist School of Theology in Brazil, and Practical Theology at the Graduate School of Religion of the Methodist University of São Paulo. I teach in Portuguese.

The Methodist School of Theology in Brazil offers a Bachelors Degree that is open to all students, but the vast majority are Methodists who have been sent by their ecclesiastical region to be trained as Methodist ministers. There are two required classes in Psychological Theory and two in Pastoral Counseling. Each Protestant denomination has its own seminaries, and sends its candidates for ordination to that seminary. There is very little, almost no, interdenominational exchange.

The Graduate School of Religion is one of three or four such schools in South America that is intentionally and actively interdenominational and ecumenical. At the graduate level, Roman Catholic students tend to frequent Pontifical Universities. Protestant students who are seeking Masters and Doctoral degrees have, in the past, generally studied in the United States or Europe. In terms of training in Pastoral Counseling there are only four or five graduate schools in South America that offer such programs. Training Institutes or Programs that specialize in Pastoral Counseling do not exist in South America. There are Protestant seminaries that have institutes or centers that specialize in Pastoral Counseling, but their function in generally limited to providing Pastoral Counseling to seminary students and, rarely, members of local churches.

I do brief Pastoral Counseling with students, faculty and a limited number of English speaking individuals and families who live in the community. I am also recently married to a Brazilian woman with two grown children and two grandchildren. So, I am in the process of learning a great many very practical lessons about family systems and intercultural relations. I am also an ordained Methodist minister, and serve as the pastor of a small Methodist church in a favela, or slum, on the outskirts of São Paulo, which is the third largest city in the world.

PROTESTANT PASTORAL COUNSELING IN BRAZIL

Presented below are some of the challenges and possibilities that mark Protestant Pastoral Counseling in Brazil. In reality, these challenges and possibilities often overlap. The challenges that Pastoral Counseling faces appear to provide the very space and wealth of ideas needed to give birth to creativity and development.

Challenges

1. *Pastoral Counseling is not well organized.* There are no equivalents of the American Association of Pastoral Counselors, Association for Clinical Pastoral Education, Association of Professional Chaplains or systematic training for Pastoral Counselors. There are two loosely organized national organizations that study the relationship between counseling and religion. One of these groups, *The Brazilian Counseling Association,* is largely composed of local church pastors who are interested in psychology. The larger group, *The Association of Christian Psychiatrists and Psychologists,* is mainly composed of psychologists and psychiatrists who are interested in religion. However, neither of

these groups has an identity that is defined in terms of Pastoral Counseling, though discussions of the identity and function of Pastoral Counseling are beginning to take place.

There are, to my knowledge, no Pastoral Counseling Centers and no Pastoral Counselors who claim that specific identity either within or related to local churches or within ecclesiastical structures. There are no private practice models for Pastoral Counseling. There are ministers who are both pastors and psychologists, but their identity is clearly as one or the other. The most frequent model is a local church pastor who is also trained in psychology. (To be licensed as a psychologist in Brazil requires a Bachelors Degree and passing a standardized test and interview.) However, the identity of these persons is as ministers who are also trained in psychology, and not as Pastoral Counselors.

2. *Pastoral Counseling theories and techniques are rarely generated within the Brazilian context.* Because Protestant Pastoral Counseling is neither recognized as a distinct field of study nor well organized very little intentional study or theory building takes place. Because of this vacuum, and due to historical traditions and attitudes, theories and techniques are generally imported from the United States and Europe. As noted above, in the past when a student wished to do advanced studies in the field of religion he or she, usually he, went either to the United States or Europe. This was also true in terms of the study of Pastoral Counseling. At present, the faculties in Pastoral Counseling of the two dominant, Protestant related, Graduate Schools of Religion in Brazil are composed of professors who are Brazilians trained in the United States or Europe, North Americans or Europeans. One implication of this is that the models of Pastoral Counseling used are predominantly North American or European.

There are a variety of introductory texts to Pastoral Care and Counseling that are available. However, these are almost always basic texts, tend to be very conservative, and are almost always translations of works from Spanish speaking countries, the United States or Europe. One of the best introductions to Pastoral Care and Counseling, written originally in Portuguese, was edited by a German professor of Practical Theology (Schneider-Harpprecht, 1998). Other texts that are in use in Protestant seminary classes come from the United States (Clinebell, 1987; Collins, 1984; Kelsey, 1998; Adams, 1970), Mexico (Hoff, 1996), Italy (Casera, 1985) and Holland (Faber and van der Schoot, 1973).

This fact is very revealing. It says that there is not a text originally in Portuguese that is available or as popular as these texts. While this reflects the reality that there is little writing being done in the area of Pastoral Counseling, it also reveals two deeper dynamics. First, there is a facet of Brazilian culture that believes, implicitly, that anything imported from the "First World" is superior to what is produced in Brazil. This applies to cars, refrigerators, clothes and ideas. Secondly, Portuguese speaking nations do not offer a large market for such texts. Since translation is an expensive process, there is very little translation of anything other that basic texts, except from Spanish, related to Pastoral Care and Counseling into Portuguese. As such, the study and practice of Pastoral Counseling in Brazil is limited by the lack of Portuguese resources and the implicit belief that theories and practices produced in the United States and Europe are automatically suited to Brazilian contexts. In summary, Pastoral Counseling is struggling to claim its identity and function in Protestant Churches in Brazil, and at the same time is trying to apply theories and practices imported from the United States and Europe, often without taking into account Brazilian social, cultural and economic realities.

3. *Pastoral Counseling is unsure of its identity or direction.* The cumulative effect of the above factors is that Pastoral Counseling is fragmented and uncertain of its direction. In terms of fragmentation, there is very little intentional study of the relationship between psychology and religion, or more specifically, between counseling, spirituality, religious identity and behavior. This tends to lead to a "use whatever works or is popular at the moment" attitude with little reflection on questions of "Why?" or the implications of specific practices or techniques. There is, then, very little dialogue between theory and practice, theology and psychology or form and content. As noted above, the two groups that do study Pastoral Counseling generally do so from either religious, *The Brazilian Counseling Association,* or psychological, *The Association of Christian Psychiatrists and Psychologists,* perspectives. There is not a sense of exploring the relationships between theology and psychology, or theory and practice, in terms of Pastoral Counseling. One group tends to explore how to apply psychology to the general practice of ministry, and the specific work of Pastoral Counseling, while the other group generally raises psychological questions about religion and religious practices.

The fact that most of the dominant models, theories and practices of Pastoral Counseling are imported leads to both conceptual and practical problems. Conceptually, this increases the sense that Pastoral Counseling is somehow not Brazilian. It is identified as European or North American, and this creates a sense of being artificial or imposed. Practically, many of the theories and practices that have been imported are based on individualistic, frequently psychoanalytic, models. Counseling is seen as helping the individual change unacceptable or destructive behaviors by incorporating unconscious content into consciousness. While Brazil has definitely accepted individualistic value systems, there is still a very strong sense of family and community where individuals are not seen as separate from their context. This is not always true, but it continues to be a characteristic of Brazilian culture. For example, Family Systems Theories do not have a strong presence in either the fields of Psychology or Pastoral Counseling. This is changing, but traditional understandings of personal sin and salvation in Historical Protestant Churches continues to dominate the psychological models used in Pastoral Counseling.

Pastoral Counseling in Brazil tends to be very Biblically oriented. Instead of expressing a dialogue between faith and psychological theory, Pastoral Counseling is usually seen in terms of stating what the Bible, or religious belief, says about a problem and then using psychological resources to guide the person along the Biblical or spiritual path. Confessional theology tends to dominate Pastoral Counseling in Historical Protestant Churches, and excludes psychological theories or practices that do not fit traditional theological formulations. Since traditional theological models in Brazilian Protestant Churches focus heavily on individual, original, sin and salvation, there is a tendency to value psychoanalytic theories over, for example, Client Centered Theories that see the person as either basically good or neutral or Family Systems Theories, that focus on systemic dynamics. Since confessional theologies tend to be very conservative in Brazil, creativity or growth in terms of integrating new theories and practices can be difficult.

Finally, informal Pastoral Counseling theory and practice ranges from psychoanalytic to magical, and this complicates dialogue and the formation of any unifying identity or direction for Pastoral Counseling. While formal confessional theologies are generally traditional and conservative, the theologies of many pastors and laypersons are a mixture of traditional Christian formulations and strong magical themes. An implicit belief in Magic permeates much of Brazilian traditional culture. Such beliefs are not explicit or universal, but are so much a part of Brazilian cultural and religious history that their presence continues to exert considerable influence. This may explain, to some degree, the popularity of various kinds of Theologies of Prosperity that are present, at least implicitly, in some traditional Historical Protestant Churches.

This tendency will be discussed below in terms of Pastoral Action in Brazil.

Possibilities

1. *Pastoral Counseling is diverse and dynamic.* The religious world in Brazil is incredibly complex and diverse. In the midst of this diversity there is also great richness in how Pastoral Counseling is done. While it is possible to criticize or critique these various, generally informal, models from an academic point of view, there is no doubt that they are genuinely grass roots visions that have their origins in specific religious traditions or specific religious communities. There are models that use predominantly psychological visions of the person, that use almost exclusively spiritual understandings of the person, that combine spirituality and magic, and that understand Pastoral Counseling almost exclusively in terms of acquiring financial success.

This richness of models and understandings obviously leads to questions of definition. What is the difference between Pastoral Counseling and Pastoral Care? What is the relationship between Pastoral Counseling and Exhortation? How are Pastoral Counseling and Spiritual Direction related? These questions are just beginning to be addressed, but the responses will without a doubt be different than those in other contexts.

This explosion of informal models appears to reflect both the social and economic realities of Brazil, and an underlying attitude regarding the relationship between theory and practice. Instead of relying on formal theory to inform or direct practice, there is a pronounced tendency to begin with practice and only much later build theory. While academic treatments of Pastoral Counseling often tend to begin with theory and then explore implications for practice, the many informal models or understandings of Pastoral Counseling begin with practice. This would seem to reflect a deeply practical, or pragmatic, attitude that reflects the needs and realities of both ministers and persons in local churches.

This also reflects the fact that most Protestant clergy receive only basic training or education, and are forced to deal with difficult circumstances the best they can. Lack of time, energy and resources demand creative responses on the part of individual clergy. Since limitations of time and energy, generally created by financial limitations, often excludes the possibility of offering long term Pastoral Counseling, Crisis or Problem Solving Counseling are the dominant approaches. Further, since there is very little interreligious dialogue or contact between theological traditions, local church pastors are generally limited to the theological resources of their faith communities. This results in an explosion of different theological understandings of Pastoral Counseling that respond to the beliefs of specific groups or communities.

However, this also often results in an attitude of "do whatever seems to work at the moment" with little reflection on questions of underlying meaning. It can also lead to very narrow understandings of what it means to be "Pastoral" and what "Counseling" means. As noted above, the dominant trend is to begin with Biblical resources and the beliefs of the community, and use counseling techniques to help believers return or adhere to accepted beliefs and behaviors.

In terms of the economic and social realities, this practice based model makes considerable sense. Though less true in the larger cities, many persons in Protestant Churches come from lower middle and poorer classes of society, and frequently have no more than a very poor High School education. Dealing with the spiritual and psychological needs of many persons in Protestant Churches is often dictated more by the availability of time and transportation than by the dictates of the delivery system. There is often very little time or energy for theoretical reflection or intrapsychic exploration. These factors added to the considerable power church members invest in pastors and in the Bible generally results in Pastoral Counseling that is based in Crisis Management and Problem Solving, which, in Brazilian contexts, are very creative responses to very real needs.

2. *Pastoral Counseling is slowly but surely moving away from models created in the United States and Europe.* As noted above, the creativity and diversity of possible models for Pastoral Counseling in Brazil offers considerable possibilities for generating new understandings of what it means to be "Pastoral" and what "Counseling" is. The relatively large distance between the practice of Pastoral Counseling and settings that promote theory building is also slowly diminishing as Protestant Churches come to appreciate the value of theological education. This is most clearly present in the growing number of discussions regarding the meaning of and how to do Pastoral Counseling. Most of these discussions take place either in the seminaries or in seminary sponsored continuing educational events. However, there seems to be a growing interest in the two national organizations that deal with religion and psychology in exploring what is distinctive about Pastoral Counseling.

In the past, Protestant Pastoral Counseling in Brazil, at least as taught in many seminaries, has been dominated by models which understand counseling as a process where the pastor enables or supports persons to make their own decisions, or resolve problems. However, Brazilian Protestant cultures generally give the pastor much more authority and responsibility when compared to North American churches. Further, these communities' understandings of, and beliefs in, the Bible and its ethical and moral demands are frequently taken very seriously. The pastor is the authority, and it is the pastor's responsibility to understand the problem and intentionally guide the person. Persons coming to a pastor in Brazil generally want and expect concrete guidance that uses Biblical and Spiritual resources as the final authorities. When a person does not receive this type of direct counsel or guidance, they often believe that the pastor is not truly "spiritual" or does not have the "spiritual" maturity or insight necessary to give such guidance. This tends to be very different from models used in the United States, which focus on enabling persons to make their own decisions and define their personal beliefs. This has often resulted in a conflict between what is taught and what various religious communities expect of their pastor. At present there is a profound rethinking of Pastoral Counseling that takes into account the various Brazilian religious contexts, and their beliefs in the authority of the pastor and the Bible. This collision of models is what currently defines discussions regarding Pastoral Counseling in Brazil, and appears to be a genuine effort to create understandings of Pastoral Counseling that are distinctly Brazilian.

Due to various cultural influences, Brazilian Pastoral Counseling is also moving away from fundamentalist or deeply conservative Biblical Pastoral Counseling that uses the Bible to reinforce oppressive social relationships. This is largely due to the influence of various Theologies of Liberation. This is particularly true in terms of marriage and family relations. There has historically been a tendency to accept so-called Biblical values presented by fundamentalist or deeply conservative evangelists from the United States.

As such, one of the signs of creativity in Pastoral Counseling in Brazil is the conflict and dialogue between imported models, which have often been uncritically accepted as adequate to the Brazilian context. This discussion is far from over, but appears to represents a genuine effort to create uniquely Brazilian models of Pastoral Counseling.

Another sign of creativity is the recognition that highly individualistic models of Pastoral Counseling are not adequate to this context. While Pastoral Counseling is definitely in the hands of the pastor, there is also a very real sense that the communities of the church and the family do Pastoral Counseling. Formal Pastoral Counseling is unquestionably in the hands of the pastor, but the church community and the family tend to take very active and intentional roles in the care of souls.

The extended family tends to be very active in everyday life, and does not see its role as motivating the individual toward independence and the creation of a separate or differentiated family. Families grow and extend much more than fragment and diversify. The family cares for its members in very active ways throughout the life cycle. Families also tend to live together longer, generally due to economic realities, and to rely on the extended family for support. New families are not so much seen as independent units, but as extensions of the family. As such, there is a sense that the whole family cares for its members, and is involved in their lives. This understanding or attitude carries over to the local church. The local church generally sees itself as a family, and takes on a very active role in caring for members of the church. Thus the family and the church community are very active in doing Pastoral Counseling, and this is an intentional identity. Once again, Pastoral Counseling in this context refers both to Solidarity and Crisis Intervention.

This reality is beginning to affect formal understandings of the nature and identity of Pastoral Counseling. Instead of understanding Pastoral Counseling as the Formal and intentional counseling done by pastors, a model that has been dominant in the past, new understandings are beginning to emerge. While systems thinking and models have not formally penetrated many Brazilian Protestant Churches there is a growing awareness that Pastoral Counseling is based as much in the community and family as in the formal ministry of the pastor. In Brazil, this awareness would not be called Pastoral Counseling. It would be understood as Pastoral Solidarity. However, the consciousness is that the church community and the family have a profound role in helping persons in their spiritual and emotional growth.

CONCLUSION

I am very aware that this presentation has often mixed the categories of Pastoral Counseling and Pastoral Care. This, however, is a reality in Brazil. The distinctions between these two modes of ministry are not as clear as in North American contexts. Further, I have not attempted to provide specific examples. This is, at best, a general introduction to Protestant Pastoral Counseling in Brazil. The primary goal of this article has been to describe Pastoral Counseling as it is understood and takes place in Brazilian cultural contexts, and thus to stimulate discussion regarding the identity and uniqueness of Pastoral Counseling.

Pastoral Counseling in Brazil is not a well defined profession or identity. It is highly fluid. This creates a wide variety of challenges, but also provides for immense possibilities. What is emerging from this complexity and diversity is in some ways similar to North American and European models and understandings of Pastoral Counseling, but in many ways radically different. This difference seems to be due to the influence of cultural context, and how Pastoral Counseling relates to the realities of given situations. As such, Pastoral Counseling in Brazil is much more influenced by context and practice than by theory.

Teaching Pastoral Counseling in this context is challenging. One of the ever-present temptations is to return to accepted texts, models and definitions. My students, either in the seminary or in continuing education classes, make this almost impossible. The stories they tell and the world they describe are different to what I am accustomed to hearing in North American contexts. The realities they face require different theories, models and practices. This awareness is the key to understanding Pastoral Counseling in Brazil.

REFERENCES

Adams, J., (1970). Competente a aconselhar. São Paulo: Nova Vida.

Casera, D., (1985). *Psicologia e aconselhamento pastoral*. São Paulo: Paulinas.

Clinebell, H., (1987). *Aconselhamento pastoral: Modelo centrado em libertação e crescimento*. São Paulo: Paulina.

Collins, G., (1984). *Aconselhamento cristão*. São Paulo: Edições Vida Nova.

Faber, H. and van der Schoot, E., (1973). *A prática da conversação pastoral*. São Leopoldo: Sinodal.

Hoff, P., (1996). *Pastor como conselheiro*. São Paulo: Vida Editora.

Kelsey, M., (1998). *Ministério profético: Psicologia e espiritualidade da ação pastoral*. São Paulo: Paulus.

Schneider-Harpprecht, C., (Ed.), (1998). *Teologia prática no contexto da América latina*. São Leopoldo: Sinodal.

Journeying on the Margins:
Moments in Pastoral Care and Counselling,
from the Inner City of Pretoria

Wilna de Beer, BA
Stephan de Beer, DD

SUMMARY. This article is written from the perspective of marginal people and places in the inner city of Pretoria, South Africa. Using a narrative-contextual approach to pastoral care and counselling, this chapter describes the socio-cultural context of ministry, and the story of a changing inner city community. The stories of the authors, their story of journeying with Siena–a young woman at-risk, and the emerging story of an ecumenical pastoral community, defining itself in relation to people and situations on the margins, form the soil for reflection.

Based on the different but overlapping stories, the nature and identity of pastoral care and counselling are described within a postmodern paradigm, proposing the pastoral worker as a facilitator, companion, or co-participant in a pastoral journey. It calls for a humbler approach to care and counselling, acknowledging the limitations of the pastoral worker, and that knowledge and meaning are co-constructed through relational conversations, and in communities of concern. *[Article copies available for a fee from The Haworth Document Delivery Service: 1-800-HAWORTH. E-mail address: <getinfo@haworthpressinc.com> Website: <http://www.HaworthPress.com> © 2002 by The Haworth Press, Inc. All rights reserved.]*

Throughout the article references are made between the text and the Story of Siena (corresponding numbers are used to illustrate specific points at the hand of this story).

[Haworth co-indexing entry note]: "Journeying on the Margins: Moments in Pastoral Care and Counseling, from the Inner City of Pretoria." de Beer, Wilna, and Stephan de Beer. Co-published simultaneously in *American Journal of Pastoral Counseling* (The Haworth Pastoral Press, an imprint of The Haworth Press, Inc.) Vol. 5, No. (3/4), 2002, pp. 253-294; and: *International Perspectives on Pastoral Counseling* (ed: James Reaves Farris) The Haworth Pastoral Press, an imprint of The Haworth Press, Inc., 2002, pp. 253-294. Single or multiple copies of this article are available for a fee from The Haworth Document Delivery Service [1-800-HAWORTH, 9:00 a.m. - 5:00 p.m. (EST). E-mail address: getinfo@haworthpressinc.com].

KEYWORDS. South Africa, inner city, pastoral counseling, poverty

INTRODUCTION

Stories are helpful in leading us to the heart of experiences. This chapter invites you, the reader, into a number of different stories. It tells the story of a city changing. It tells the story of two pilgrims in this city, with a desire to be part of the making of a better story. It tells the story of Siena, a young woman who found herself on the margins of the city, but with a persistence to re-story her life or co-author a better story for herself and her family.

These are different but overlapping stories. And throughout these different stories, another story emerges: the story of a pastoral community, seeking to establish a caring presence on the margins, wrestling with its own identity, dealing with its own baggage, and seeking for mutual liberation.

1. THE STORY OF PRETORIA'S INNER CITY AND PRETORIA COMMUNITY MINISTRIES

1.1 Our Social Context

Reading the social context of Pretoria's inner city, it tells a story of the dramatic socio-political transition after 1994, the challenge of our cultural diversity, and the increasing marginalization prevalent in inner city areas. It also invites the church to become co-author of a new (hi)story for Pretoria and its inner city.

Our ministry has started just before the political changes in our nation, with the dismantling of apartheid, and it is unfolding as a new city and a new nation unfold. It is happening at a time when the inner city is re-writing its own (hi)story, and we feel very proud and privileged to be part of this unfolding story. In many ways people like ourselves, who are residents and pastoral care workers in the city, are uniquely positioned to be co-authors with thousands of other people, of a new inner city. It is at the same time daunting, as we have the challenge and opportunity to write a better or preferred story to the previous one of apartheid and exclusion.

Since 1994, inner city neighbourhoods have changed to become the first multi-racial communities in the Greater Pretoria area. To a large extent the former white suburbs and black townships remained either black or white, until this day, with some exceptions. It is really in the central parts of our city where drastic changes occurred. When we moved into our current apartment building in 1995, there was only one black family on our floor.

For the past two years we are the only white family. In 1994 about 90% of the population in our inner city neighbourhoods was white, and today, only 7 years later, about 70% of the population is black. An increasing influx of people from Central and East Africa, speaking French and other indigenous languages from their own countries, complete the picture of diversity and change. Most of the large cities in the world have become completely heterogeneous and this has presented unique challenges to every institution and all urban dwellers. The specific history of South Africa has made the challenge of multi-racial living, integration and reconciliation, all the more interesting to observe, and to live with. The challenge to provide constructive meaning to this new reality has perhaps been even more vital as well in our context, as the eyes of many in the world are on our story, and we ourselves would like to see our "miracle" being completed.

We also face economic challenges. With racial changes in our neighbourhoods the same dynamics of North American and British cities occurred here, with white residents, business and even churches disinvesting from the inner city. At the same time a proliferation of informal businesses bring new life to town. The residents of our area themselves are quite diverse, ranging from homeless people, low-income working people and students, to lower-middle-class people and some emerging middle-class professionals. In many ways this is an ideal community, demonstrating co-habitation without many tensions. At the same time it is an at-risk community as economic forces are at work either to destroy or to enhance the fibre of our inner city neighbourhoods. And the active participation, or absence, of civil society and faith-based groups, would help determine the future of our neighbourhoods.

Another phenomenon is that inner city areas facilitate the entry of previously disadvantaged people into the city. In the past our cities were restricted access areas by law, which after certain hours of the day only allowed white people, while curfews and passes were required for other racial groups. Since our cities opened up, people grabbed the opportunities to be closer to the concentration of employment opportunities, urban housing and urban services. However, the lack of affordable housing and adequate employment opportunities, lead to people's frag-

ile hopes being shattered. Often, all that is left of their dreams are homelessness, unemployment, and various forms of urban exploitation.

1.2 Our Pastoral Challenge

Our pastoral challenge is varied, but themes such as identity, diversity, powerlessness, and marginalization, are important themes in our
daily pastoral praxis.

Firstly, the identities of individuals, groups and institutions have
been seriously challenged as South Africa has gone through its transition. We have to re-interpret our own roles as pastoral facilita-
tors/caregivers, we have to re-story being church in the city, and we
have to re-define our various and diverse cultural groups and expressions, in relation to each other. It is almost like a nation being born
anew, and we have to create new forms to give expression to this new
child.

That is why one colleague entitles his dissertation: "Co-constructing
Christianity in the local congregation" (Nienaber 2001)–the assumed
expressions and contents of Christianity itself are questioned, and people from diverse backgrounds in this (and many other) inner city con-
gregation(s), are invited to become co-authors of a process to construct
Christianity locally, in terms that give meaning to their collective and
individual lives and experiences.

Secondly, the inner cities of South Africa are increasingly places
where very poor people and victims of various forms of abuse, hope to
re-establish themselves. Thousands of people move from the periphery,
which might be rural areas or the urban periphery itself, to the centre
(inner city), hoping to connect with the perceived opportunities of the
city. This has led to the inner city increasingly becoming a place where
power and powerlessness stand in contrast, where the headquarters of
banks and corporations cast shadows over informal traders and street
dwellers sleeping on the pavements at night.

Vulnerability and risk have therefore become characteristic of many
inner city groups–the homeless, people living with HIV or AIDS, children on the streets, commercial sex workers (male, female and children), refugees, low-income women, and so forth.

Part of the church's journey towards constructing its own identity, is
on the crossroad between power and vulnerability, where the church has
to be clear about where it stands. It can decide (1) to condone the status
quo and the constructions of power, (2) to remain neutral (opting for

neither the powerful nor the vulnerable exclusively), or (3) to stand with those in places of vulnerability.

1.3 Our Emerging Pastoral Response

Pretoria Community Ministries (PCM) is an ecumenical community in the inner city of Pretoria, to which we have belonged since its inception in 1993. It was formed by 6 inner city congregations from different denominations, and has developed a diaconal model of pastoral care. PCM is intentional in seeking to combine pastoral care and social action, as it develops a presence between the margins and the public squares of the city. It is intentional in wanting to contribute to a new story for the city of Pretoria, a story that will include all people, whether black or white, rich or poor, women or men–a story that will heal the scars of the past and hear the voices of the present, as it writes its own future.

This ecumenical community is developing along two main pastoral thrusts:

- On the one hand it is intentional about the formation of small communities of solidarity/care/concern, in partnership with marginal, vulnerable and/or at-risk places or people, facilitating socio-pastoral projects and services that empower.
- On the other hand it engages in community organising, advocacy and lobbying, on behalf of and with marginal or at-risk groups, seeking for shalom not only in personal or individualised terms, but also in terms of structural change and the eventual creation of just communities.

The one thrust is playing itself out primarily in relation to marginal groups and in marginal places, and the other thrust is playing itself out on the "public squares" of the city–relating to local and provincial government, banks, local police stations, and so forth.

Both thrusts are essential elements of our emerging model of diaconal-pastoral care and action. They are extensions of our initial listening (pastoral) presence in communities. They flesh out the Word in terms that are concrete and visible. And they complement and correct each other continuously, holding the pastoral (priestly) and the prophetic in creative tension.

The following table is a summary of our diaconal-pastoral projects:

- street outreach programme: homeless people, teenage girls on the streets, commercial sex workers
- visitation & support programme: female juveniles in prison
- transitional housing: women (The Potter's House) & teenage girls at-risk (Lerato House)
- nurturing of life & social skills: conflict management, communication, HIV/AIDS, parenting, sexuality, employment preparation, etc.
- drop-in/support centres: homeless people, girls living and/or working on the streets
- social housing (Yeast City Housing)
- facilitation of community businesses (Tshepo)
- legal aid
- basic health clinics
- advocacy, lobbying & community organising
- day care centre for children
- development of community churches
- regular devotional times & community celebrations

These programmes are not developed in isolation, but in close partnership with other role players, local communities, a network of churches, and even local government structures.

Our own full-time pastoral team is multi-cultural and multi-disciplinary, which we consider to be one of our strengths. The team involves professional people and laity, complementing each other with different gifts, strengths, and functions.

Our professional expertise includes pastors and social workers on the full-time staff, and psychologists, legal professionals, property developers, financial managers, and health workers, on the volunteer team. We also understand the administrative staff to be an important part of our pastoral presence, as they provide not only the infra structural back up, but often also the face and first impression of the organisation.

Having said this, we often find that healing and growth take place in the spaces between individual conversations or specialised group work–in the moments of unexpected community and intimacy. PCM is intentional about be(com)ing a community of solidarity and care, inviting people to journey together, and we as pastoral workers are part of this journey. We are self-critical enough to know that we don't have answers and solutions for all the complex issues that people on the margins face in their lives. Often we can only walk with people, even in silence, since one word will be one word too many. And as we walk together, and converse, we all discover together, and hopefully we all are changed for the better.

We want to be a community where people are affirmed, and where people can experience being loved and cared for just for who they are. It is in inviting communities of unconditional acceptance that people are able to discover their particular gifts, where they can risk taking small responsibilities, where they can be helped to see that they too can contribute in smaller or bigger ways.

In walking together, without pastoral workers providing quick and easy answers, people often find the strength to discover new futures for themselves, and to shape their lives towards those futures. We therefore want to go beyond an individualist understanding of counselling and care, affirming the potential of inviting and caring communities, to facilitate healing and change.

2. OUR STORY OF PASTORAL COUNSELLING AND CARE: IDENTITY, NATURE AND DISTINCTIVENESS

We call this section *"Our* story of pastoral counselling and care." It describes, namely, the identity of pastoral facilitators, and the nature and distinctiveness of pastoral care and counselling, from *our* own local perspective and experience in the community of PCM.

Describing our pastoral journey with the people of the inner city, cannot exclude introducing ourselves as individuals. That would be contrary to our whole understanding of the pastoral journey, being a mutual journey of conversation, discovery, conversion and change. It might therefore be helpful for the reader if we tell our own stories, as they are not detached from the other narratives in this chapter. As we try to bring hope to others, they minister hope to us–we literally discover and *do* hope together.

In some ways our own personal stories qualified us for this particular journey into the city, and in other ways they hindered us. In many ways we have to construct, and deconstruct and reconstruct our identities, and ourselves as we continue journeying with others, as new questions arise continuously, and as we face ourselves in new ways time and time again.

On our journey we walk with many different people, who come from diverse racial and economic backgrounds. Most of the people that we are journeying with, however, are people who have landed on the margins of urban society. In many ways they have become our friends and our teachers, our guides into a city that is often not known, and into stories that are often not told. We cannot understand ourselves detached from the community/communities in which we find ourselves. These communities help shape and define us.

Wilna

My journey includes a wonderful family (three older brothers and two parents), life on a farm for some part of my life, being raised by black nannies that I loved very dearly, and a comfortable middle class education. I did not develop a social conscience until my student years. My parents wanted to protect us from the harsh realities of life–they would have preferred if I didn't study social work.

I was born in the middle sixties and was a student in the eighties, when the protests and political violence came to a climax. The shock of discovering the realities of apartheid caused me to lose faith in God, because the God I knew then, was the apartheid God of the Dutch Reformed church. I could not understand how my God who loved me so much, would always protect me, would never let me go from his/her hands, would at the same time allow so much oppression and injustice. My theology of that time could not handle the realities of other Christians who had to suffer because of the colour of my skin. I had to go on a journey of re-discovering God in the midst of suffering, before I could begin to understand God again.

This journey included the personal suffering of going through a painful divorce. In the healing process I discovered the wonder of community life, as I lived with Christians in community at that stage. I now find strength in ministry by remembering the way in which healing was brought into my life through community, and the commitment and love that others showed towards me during a time in my life when I couldn't have survived on my own.

I am excited about our new South Africa and am willing to spend the rest of my life dealing with the growing pains of new developments (especially in the church and ministry), together with everyone else from our rainbow nation.

Stephan

I grew up in an apartment building in the inner city of Pretoria, with my mother and sister. Although sole parent families were always, since I can remember, the dominant family structure around where I grew up, those who made the rules for society, and the church at-large, still preferred to marginalize and stereotype this reality, not knowing what to do with the women and children coming from these family structures. Hearing my mother's stories of anger and frustration at how the church has dealt with her, and us, made me sense something of how institutional and societal marginalization worked, and developed in me a very critical perspective on the church in relation to the city.

Whilst a theological student, I worked with children on the streets of Sunnyside, one of Pretoria's inner city neighbourhoods, where children experienced great harassment from local business people and the police. At this stage, Sunnyside was still an all-white neighbourhood. Eventually, early in 1992, a fire destroyed our shelter for boys, and killed 8 of the children. An investigation could not establish arson as the cause beyond all doubt, and up to this day the real cause of the fire was not established, although we have enough reason to believe that it was a deliberate attempt to close down this work (racially/politically motivated). The subsequent cover-up by the police and the failure of the justice system to deal with this matter decisively and truthfully helped me understand that pastoral care is taking place within a certain context where various forces are at work. We cannot develop an individualistic pastoral praxis, without recognising the death-dealing forces threatening those we are journeying with.

2.1 Identity of Pastoral Facilitators

For both of us, our current journey does not only facilitate healing for others, but is a way of being healed ourselves. It does not only help others towards constructing identities and realities that are meaningful to live with, but it is also helping us to define ourselves in relation to our context and other people.

Our Functions Differ

Stephan's focus is to help create the broader pastoral space in which to journey with urban people on the margins. It is done through project development, staff training, vision sharing with churches, advocacy and lobbying, organising of celebrations, and so forth.

Wilna's focus is on more direct journeying with people towards their healing and wholeness, through care, friendship and practical support, and through counselling and accompaniment, both individually and in groups. After walking with women in The Potter's House, a transitional residential facility for vulnerable women, for 7 years, she is now focussing her time in a community of young girls who come off the streets and who now live in Lerato House, a community of care.

Our understanding of pastoral care and counselling, is that it is *a journey of conversation and mutual discovery*. Pastoral facilitators are *fellow pilgrims or participants on this journey.* This is in line with Lowe's (1991: 45) ideas about post-modern discourse and therapy. He states that meanings are not pre-given and "found" through conversation, but are progressively made or fashioned through conversational action itself.

Wilna's position in the journey with Siena (cf. 3: The Story of Siena) is one of co-participant, who joins in conversation to co-construct a new reality with Siena. This helps to break down the modernist notion of subject-object, where the counsellor positions the individual as object of study. It also becomes liberating for the counsellor herself, being set free from having to have all the answers. At the same time it allows for conversations that might facilitate mutual discovery and change.

Gerkin (1991: 62) speaks about the limitations of counsellors and the challenge to become participants. He suggests ". . . that counsellors be spoken of as 'participant observers,' limited, finite and caught in their own subjective experiences of life."

You will note that we speak of pastoral facilitators, which means that we see our role as facilitating or creating space for conversation to take place between people, and between people and God. Such conversations might be in the form of individual therapy sessions, but we suggest that pastoral care and counselling need to go beyond that.

The pastoral facilitator (co-participant) is no longer the expert with all the knowledge, but a facilitator of a mutual process to exchange knowledge and experience, and to discover and construct new knowledge. In post-modern thought the *"relational nature of knowledge"* and the *"generative nature of language"* are emphasized (Anderson 1997: 36).

Postmodernism views knowledge as socially constructed, knowledge and the knower as interdependent . . .

In line with Lowe's suggestion of how meaning is constructed, Anderson (1997: 36) suggests that *"knowledge is evolving and continually broadening."*

We do not advocate an abandonment of all previous knowledge, but a new (and humbler) perspective on our "knowledge," even allowing for it to be challenged, deconstructed, and enriched, by new and other knowledge. The emphasis is on the relational nature in the conversational journey with others.

Such an approach to pastoral care and counselling, requires pastoral *engagement,* i.e., getting involved with our lives; becoming part of the stories of others; living with their stories and inviting others into our stories; engaging not only with the stories of individuals who come to us, but also with the larger narratives of their socio-cultural contexts, those very narratives that shaped their stories.

Julian Muller (1996: 24-25) differs from Louw (1993: 51), who speaks of "encounter" as the key concept for a pastoral model. Muller suggests that we rather think of "engagement" or "involvement," saying that *encounter* can be a very quick and rather superficial meeting between people, while *engagement* implies something more, something intentional, and something deeper.

In our community we try to move beyond simple methods and techniques of encounter, to embrace a journey of conversation and mutual discovery. On this journey pastoral counselling is embedded in a larger process of pastoral care and community building. Not only our professional staff, but our whole community, becomes part of the process of journeying, affirming, discovering, and change. Not only individual therapy, but the collective events of our community–skills training, celebrations, advocacy, protest meetings, common meals–become elements contributing to (or hindering) healing and liberation (*cf. Story: #10; #11*).

Likewise, we do not approach the city, urban challenges (or problems), or individual therapy, with fixed recipes of care and counselling. It is in the mutual journey with others that we discover moments and stories that liberate. As we become co-participants in conversation with others, participant observers living and doing with others, that we discover a way out of the negative story, and that we start to imagine what could be.

One could perhaps speak of our approach as a narrative-contextual approach to pastoral care and counselling. It is contextual in its insistence to consider the socio-cultural realities of our local context, and how these realities (and forces) impact upon local individuals, groups and communities. It is narrative in its invitation of the local stories of individuals, groups and communities, against the background of larger socio-cultural narratives.

2.2 The Nature and Distinctiveness of Pastoral Care and Counselling

In describing the nature of pastoral care and counselling from our perspective, we have drawn from theologies of liberation on the one hand, but our approach also corresponds with the approach developed by Gerkin (1991) in "Prophetic Pastoral Practise," or Larty (1997) in "In living colour." It places the activities of pastoral care and counselling in a broader socio-cultural, political or public context, recognising that we do not operate in a vacuum, but we are deeply affected by the realities where we come from, that we are in currently, and that we move toward.

Our understanding of pastoral care and counselling is highlighted by three themes running like threads through our pastoral journeying.

2.2.1 The Communal Nature of Pastoral Care and Counselling

We write about the nature of pastoral care and counselling, only as we are discovering it for ourselves in our own diaconal-pastoral community. Ours is therefore a very localised reading, but at the same time an unapologetic proposal for models of care and counselling that will recover the notion of community, rooted in a sustaining and listening presence, and focussing on empowerment and responsibility (cf. The process of pastoral care and counselling: 3.1-3.3).

Our understanding of the pastoral task is to help restore the original intended relationships of communion, between God and humanity, between human beings, and between humanity and the rest of creation. Wherever there is brokenness in the urban community, the church should be seeking for ways to facilitate healing and wholeness. Pastoral care and counselling should therefore have as its ultimate goal the shalom of God, which is a recurrent theme throughout the Old Testament.

It would be a contradiction to seek for wholeness (shalom) in the human community, if the process of pastoral care and counselling is not in itself embedded in a community of faith, that seeks to demonstrate signs of healing and shalom. We therefore seek for ways in which to locate our various caring ministries in communities of faith, where covenantal relationships of mutuality are envisaged, explored and (although not always) developed; where new stories are imagined, tested and practised, where hope is "lived" together (*cf. 3.2: Creating Communities of Concern*).

At the same time, it would be dangerous to develop models of pastoral care that is narrowly focussing within, and operating from, communities of faith as platform. There should be a dual concern with erecting signs of wholeness, both in the faith community, and in the broader urban community. We should continue to ask ourselves:

- What do the community and society in which marginal people have to re-establish themselves, look like? and

- How can we be facilitators of conversations that will help marginal/broken people to become co-authors of new stories–empowering stories helping them to re-enter life, but at the same time facilitators of conversations that will help transform the discourses of communities/societies, that have in the first place contributed to the marginalization of certain people?

It seems to require the dual task that Mary sang about in Luke 1: 52–"to bring down rulers from their thrones" (challenging dominant discourses), and "to lift up the humble" (inviting/affirming stories from the margins).

The tasks of pastoral care and counselling, in our understanding, need to include an intentionality about erecting signs of wholeness within the community of faith, as well as within the broader urban community; it should be a journey of mutual conversation between pastoral facilitators and individuals, but also between pastoral facilitators and the city itself.

2.2.2 The Social/Political/Public Dimensions of Care

We believe that pastoral care and socio-diaconic action can and should be married, or rather: that socio-diaconic action should form an integral part of any credible pastoral praxis. Such a holistic and inclusive pastoral praxis should be expressed both on the margins and on the public squares, as a sign of both responsible discipleship and an affirmation of our covenantal interdependence in the household of God.

Such an inclusive pastoral praxis will connect pastoral care and prophetic action. Care and counselling can no longer be done in a contextual void, but needs to grow out of critical analysis of the context in which people (and us as pastoral workers) find them(our)selves. In our context we journey on a daily basis with homeless people and young girls involved in commercial sex work. They face on-going harassment and various forms of abuse. Our individual journeying with them will lose all credibility, if it is not combined with appropriate social action, such as advocacy, participation in public or civil processes to shape policy, protest marches, and so forth.

In our own pastoral journeying with people and communities, we are therefore mindful of the threefold liberation that Gutierrez (1988: xxxviii) speaks of, namely liberation from personal sin (spiritual salvation), humanisation (human dignity, restoration of personhood, emotional and psychological healing), as well as socio-economic-political liberation. A lack of economic or social freedom often attacks people's notion of dignity or self-worth. People's perceptions or images of God are often constructions based on their existential experiences. And the lack of dignity or emotional wounds is often caused by social and structural sin, systematically destroying the soul of the city and the soul of its people.

Pastoral care and counselling, therefore, should mediate liberation/healing at all these levels, journeying with people towards

- personal freedom and meaningful conversations with God,
- dignity and worth within restored relationships and integrated into caring communities, and
- urban structures and systems (social, political and economic) that are inclusive, caring and life-giving

2.2.3. Care as a Common Journey, Nurturing a New Imagination and Way of Living

We understand the journey of pastoral care and counselling as a journey to help nurture a new or alternative imagination or consciousness of what could be, in the words of Walter Brueggemann (1978)–and walking with individuals, the church, communities, and the city as a whole, towards realising such an imagined future. Pastoral care and counselling becomes the journey of co-authoring together the stories of our lives, our living spaces, our communities, and our cities, into the preferred reality of our imagination.

Deconstructive, listening questions will help evoke new images of what could be, and the pastoral facilitator should consciously create the space for these images or preferred realities, to be explored and developed.

Muller (1996: 30) suggests that the telling of our stories can only be renewing and constructive, if the past story and the future story are brought in "congruency" with each other. And this happens only after repeated telling of the story. *Nurturing* implies patiently walking with others. To help nurture a new imagination of a preferred future reality, is not something that happens overnight, but only after repeated telling and re-telling of the old and the preferred story, and in affirmation as people start to live (in) the new story (*cf. Story: #1, #13 & 3.3: Invitations to Responsibility*).

The nurturing of a new imagination should happen not only at an individual level, but also at a community and a public level. As we walk with at-risk individuals (women from abusive relationships, young girls coming off the streets, homeless people, etc.) to help deconstruct destructive discourses and to discover new and preferred stories, we also get opportunities to ask deconstructive questions–critically questioning dominant perceptions and values where they are destructive–in churches, community forums and public meetings. We have found that many homeless people whom we are journeying with are keen to help re-author the story of the city, as we collectively participate in lobbying exercises, meeting high-ranking officials, and so forth.

Once again we are challenged to take pastoral care and counselling out of its narrow confines, and to practise it in the public arena-often those most at-risk and most wounded are the victims of these very public discourses. Therefore, pastoral counselling that is isolated from broader public pastoral action, will continue to offer a symptomatic service, without ever penetrating the roots of problems.

2.2.4. How Does God Fit Into Our Care and Counselling?

Does God fit into our pastoral care and counselling at all? This is, to us, what defines *pastoral* care and counselling–creating the space for conversations that might include God, that might facilitate new conversations with God, that might help to deconstruct patriarchal or other oppressive constructions of God, that might help to discover a caring and affirming and life-giving God.

Pastoral care and counselling also allows for an element of awe or surprise, inviting the Spirit of Comfort to breathe into the process of our mutual journey, so that healing and wholeness could break through, sometimes unexpectedly, sometimes quietly, sometimes dramatically, sometimes against all the odds.

So we would be inviting of the God-story or faith story, in our journey with people in the city. There seems to be hesitancy in some circles to invite such stories, and in other circles even a so-called pastoral praxis that is devoid of a clear spirituality. That is unfortunate, since it is probably a reaction to ways of pastoral care and counselling that sanctioned the status quo and affirmed destructive sociocultural discourses, using God in the process of doing so. But the very nature of a narrative approach, is to invite stories that will help deconstruct–even our mental constructions of God and church and faith–in ways that can be liberating and helpful to discover God and faith anew, through images and metaphors and relationships that truly transform (*cf. Story: #8*).

Being intentional about journeying in community, we also work hard on the development of rituals, such as celebrations and festivals, as expressions of our common life, as ways to "live the hope" recovered in the process of care and counselling, and as ways of creating space to re-construct our understanding of ourselves, of us together, and of us and God *(cf. Story: #10, #11)*.

Although ritual is not exclusively a religious or a Christian activity, we suggest that one of the distinctive marks of *pastoral* care and counselling should be the way in which we recover, re-interpret and re-create religious or spiritual ritual, to help facilitate healing and change.

I use ritual in the sense that Harvey Cox (1969: 70) suggested it, when he spoke about liberating ritual as "the form and the occasion for the expression of fantasy." He continued to say

> *It is through ritual movement, gesture, song, and dance that man (sic) keeps in touch with the sources of creativity.*

Ritual expression, practised in community, helps us to collectively imagine new patterns of living and sharing, while at the same time it becomes a way of re-storying our individual lives as well as our lives together.

One example in our community is the monthly celebrations. At this event people from our different small communities—women in crisis, teenage girls at-risk, homeless people, staff members, inner city residents, and some visitors—gather together. We come from different races, we speak more than ten mother tongues, and we probably represent more than ten church denominations. We also come from very different economic and social backgrounds.

Responsibility for the preparation of the celebration lies with a different pastoral community every month. It contains diverse elements, including music of praise and worship, introductions by name, the sharing of "Good News" stories, a short sharing of the Word, a common meal, intercessory prayers, play time with organised games, a song or two, and a benediction.

In these gatherings, we try to create the space for celebration (praise, play, common meal and prayer), commemoration (sharing good news, prayer and common meal) and contemplation (worship, sharing the Word, prayer). However, the structure is kept flexible to allow for spontaneous participation, rendering of items, and so forth. It is important that ownership is shared by *all* in the community, and not by one or two in leadership positions.

It has become a central event in the monthly programme, consolidating individual and collective journeys towards hope and healing.

2.2.5. Rooted in the Broader Christian (and Human) Community

Our pastoral community was created originally by a partnership of 6 inner city congregations from different denominations. We are therefore rooted in the larger story of the ecumenical Christian community in Pretoria's inner city.

It is important for us to remain accountable and connected to this community of Christ's body. Although we develop local theology and spirituality in relation to people and communities on the margins, and it might sometimes be in tension with the status quo, even of our partner churches, we are adamant to retain this relationship of accountability (which is sometimes also a relationship of creative tension). Not only does it help us not to fall into the traps of sectarianism, but also ensures that the voices from the margins and the streets are heard in the sacred spaces of the established (and emerging) church.

Part of our pastoral journey with people might include facilitating their re-connectedness to God and to a faith community in which they can root themselves (i.e., finding identity, meaning, community and symbols that they can relate to). Marginal people are often also on the margins of the established church. This is another important reason for our relationship to the inner city church community. Since we have relationships with a diversity of inner city churches, we can serve both as a kind of bridge for people into these churches, and a catalyst to help these churches become open towards people from the margins.

But we have conversations not only with the local Christian community in Pretoria. It is important for us to develop conversations with inner city Christians in other parts of South Africa, and with the urban church in other parts of the world. We are therefore participating in networks such as the Network for Urban Ministries in South Africa (NUMISA), the International Urban Associates, and others. We have learnt from urban pastoral models in places as diverse as Chicago, Amsterdam, Rotterdam, and Sao Paulo. We are also in conversation with groups who are interested in the kind of diaconal-pastoral model (or socio-diaconic pastorate) that we are developing, both in Germany and in Sweden.

We mention this basically to affirm the following: Although ours is a very local expression of pastoral care and counselling, responding to local contextual challenges, we are part of a global reality and a global church. And the global conversation remains essential, especially as globalising forces impact upon local realities.

Post-modern theory has asked critical questions of many of our previous assumptions in care and counselling. Our pastoral community is seeking to listen to these critical voices and in developing a narrative-contextual approach, we try to integrate the suggestions of people such as Gerkin (1991), Muller (1996) and Michael White (1999), with the voices of Boff (1986) and Gutierrez (1988), all of whom positions the process of care and counselling out of its narrow mold of individual healing, and emphasizing the context in which people were shaped and affected (sinned against), as well as focussing on the process of journeying with people towards a place of complete liberation-encountering God, being human again, and living with justice (cf. Gutierrez). Narrative models of therapy are providing constructive tools for appropriating the liberationist yearning for such complete freedom.

Although we are rooted in the broader Christian community, we are also in a dialogical relationship to the world (which is not exclusively Christian). In Marabastad, one of the poorest inner city communities in South Africa, most of the formal business people are Muslims. Yet, to discuss the future of Marabastad, all role players gather around the table collectively. This has led us into valuable relationships with diverse people, many of which do not share our faith convictions.

One previous example was when a young baby died prematurely. The chairperson of the Marabastad Development Forum, who is a Muslim man, went with me, a Christian pastor, to express our condolences with the family, a young husband and wife. When we got there and assessed that they were Christians, Mr. Dawood suggested I continue to take the lead, while he supported me. What is more, he even gathered some contributions from his Muslim business friends in the area, to pay for the funeral expenses–although the funeral was led by myself and the local Christian Fellowship that grew out of our presence in this area.

Similar relationships exist with Jewish and agnostic people, working in the city or in projects similar to ours, but with a "secular" base. It is possible, and mutually enriching, for pastoral communities to have dialogical relationships with people from other faiths or persuasions than our own–this is important in terms of our own journey and learning, in terms of developing credibility in the community, and in terms of ensuring the kind of long term partnerships that will facilitate the shalom/wholeness of the city.

2.2.6. *Searching for a Communal Spirituality of the City*

Besides being rooted in the broader Christian community, we seek to root our process of pastoral care and counselling within a broader search for a communal and story-telling spirituality of the city. In the process we were deeply influenced by the writings of people as diverse as Elizabeth O'Connor (1987), Jean Vanier (1989), Henri Nouwen (1971), Ray Bakke (1987; 1997), and Gustavo Gutierrez (1988).

Cities are often understood to be destructive, death-dealing places. Yet, millions have to create identity, meaning and family, within urban environments. As a pastoral community on the margins of the inner city, we have to be intentional about developing a spirituality that will make sense in, and speak clearly to (and from) this context.

There are certain themes that have become central in our common reflection and practise as a pastoral community in the inner city. These themes include notions such as calling, a Christian presence, nurturing community, God in the city, story-telling, practising a hermeneutics of suspicion, being in critical solidarity with marginal people/places, journeying with, empowerment, responsibility and ownership, and so on. We want to develop our pastoral praxis in ways that will reflect these key themes.

3. ENTERING THE STORIES OF OTHERS: THE PROCESS OF PASTORAL CARE AND COUNSELLING

We describe the process of care and counselling by way of three interconnected and interdependent moments that facilitate growth, healing and re-integration into society. These moments indicate how counselling cannot be separated from the broader concepts of pastoral care and social action. Somehow they belong together and we want to indicate how interwoven and essential these different dimensions of pastoral ministry are, how they complement, inform and correct each other, and how they can grow together into a credible and transformative pastoral presence.

Three distinctive moments of *presence, community* and *responsibility* (responsibility/vocation) are identified and described as a pastoral cycle of care, based originally on the pastoral cycle of Holland and Henriot (1984), and informed also by the cycle for social therapy that Larty (1997) suggests. This cycle (and the three moments) is by no means restrictive, but a mere "map" to guide us in our journey, and to keep the journey intentional.

- Different pastoral cycles

Larty (1997: 103-108) suggests a cycle of social therapy with the following components:

A. Recognition (self-awareness)
The first important aspect is for the pastoral facilitator to have a personal critical awareness.

"Where do I come from?"

"What are my issues?"

"What is the baggage that I bring into the pastoral space?"

B. Identification (people and issues)
The second component is to identify the people and issues to deal with pastorally. Larty (1997: 106) reminds us that we cannot deal with people in isolation from the issues that shape and impact upon them.

The struggle for change is personal and political.

This again emphasizes the importance of a broader critical analysis, and a proper reading of the socio-cultural text, if our pastoral care is to be appropriate.

C. Befriending–knowing and being known
Larty also implies a mutual conversation. It is not only for the pastoral worker to know, but *to be known*–and as we are known we can also change (cf. Parker Palmer 1983).

D. Working together in groups
Larty suggests collective action through working in groups as a next component, going beyond individualistic models of care and counselling, and affirming the notion of humanity as community, and Christianity as community of believers.

E. Acting together–symbolic, social, political
He works this out further by suggesting collective symbolic, social or political action. One example could be a protest march to advocate on a particular issue, such as homelessness or landlessness, which is simul-

taneously a demonstration of pastoral solidarity with this specific group.

We are finding these categories of Larty helpful and include them in our own approach.

However, most of the work in our community is based on the pastoral cycle of Holland and Henriot (1984), that suggests the four phases of insertion (description of experience), analysis (asking critical questions), theological reflection (utilising diverse resources) and planning for praxis (towards a new, transformed praxis). These phases also correspond with the pedagogical cycle for a liberational pastoral praxis, that Larty (1997: 94; 101-103) suggests. We will integrate the phases of Holland and Henriot in our discussion of the three moments of pastoral care and counselling.

The Story of Siena (and of Our Journey with Her)

Siena is in a volunteer programme at Lerato House, a residential facility for young girls at-risk run by our organisation. She is a relief housemother during weekends, does street outreach to young girls in prostitution, and is part of the team who visits juvenile girls in prison on a weekly basis. She has come back from Germany recently, where she worked as an Au Pair girl with a German family for one year (#1)

Who would have thought that this is the same girl who left a lifestyle of prostitution only two years ago? Siena took the first steps towards an alternative lifestyle when the South African Police Services did a raid on a hotel known for child prostitution. They found Siena and two other under-aged girls (under the age of 18 years) in the hotel and brought them to Lerato House. Very unwillingly, they agreed to stay at Lerato House. After a few days the two friends left, but Siena decided to stay (#2). This is how our journey together started . . .

Siena's life turned into a nightmare at the age of four years old, the day her stepfather moved in with her and her mother. He is an alcoholic and physically abused both mother and daughter continually. Two sisters were born and brought up under the same stressful conditions. When Siena was thirteen, he started sexually abusing her, and at age fifteen, she had to make the heartbreaking decision of either letting him continue to destroy her life for the sake of being with her beloved mother and sisters, or leave and try to survive on her own. She left and got caught up in a network of prostitution before long (#3).

Cities have become catch basins for youth at-risk in South Africa. Children who escape harrowing situations of poverty, abuse and neglect turn to the cities for help, and it is here that they encounter death or life. It is here that young jobless men, as well as older women, wait for the runaway girls to approach them for help. They know the entry points to the cities and recognize lost girls immediately. Young girls are lured into prostitution through threats and promises alike and soon find that there does not seem any way out of it. On the one hand the extreme shame that they experience prevents them from approaching anyone for help, and on the other hand they don't see or know about any alternatives.

This is the job of the street outreach team of Lerato House: to build relationships of trust with young girls in prostitution, to be caring, present and willing to journey with them (#4), to move with them from the dominant stories of their lives towards embracing alternative versions (#5). In the life of prostitution young girls learn to survive on their own. They cannot trust anyone, not even their friends sharing the streets with them, they live in a culture of disrespect where customers are ripped off wherever possible, where pimps abuse and society is shunned. The only way to survive is through an exterior of toughness–there is no space for vulnerability. Street outreach workers are therefore viewed with extreme mistrust in their first encounters with new girls on the streets, and treated with disrespect and affront continually by others who have been absorbed completely by the dominant story of prostitution (#6).

Siena was fortunate to be whisked away from the situation by the police to find a community living out the alternative story of life that she yearned for–a place of love and care, where everyone is treated with respect and no-one has to fend for herself on her own, but have the support of other girls and workers alike (#7). For other girls in prostitution the journey towards discovering the reality of an alternative story takes much longer and sometimes only becomes possible after something really drastic or tragic has happened that has forced them off the streets, e.g., becoming pregnant, being diagnosed HIV+, or being raped and assaulted by customers or pimps.

Initially it seemed as if Siena soaked in the love and care she experienced. She stuck to the rules of Lerato House, joined in every activity positively and never complained about a thing. Although she was pleasant and supportive to other girls, we were worried about her because she was very quiet and sometimes looked very sad. It was obvious that she suffered emotionally, and we tried to support her in every way possible. The hope of going back to school in the same year didn't become a reality because the schools didn't have space for her. She accepted this bravely and together we had many conversations about faith and the future. She embraced spirituality and believed that God loves her and will take care of her future (#8).

It was important to us that Siena understands her own past. We had discussions about the abuse in her home situation, as well as the reasons why she had to leave. Her own story was linked to the story of our society and how prostitution can sometimes be an extension of the abuse that a person experienced at home (#9). I think it was a liberating experience for her to understand how a dominant story in a person's life can lead to decisions which are motivated by one's understanding of life according to the dominant story, which in her case was a story that told her that her body was filthy and that she as a person had no worth in the world (#6).

Lerato House hopes to create a supportive, nurturing environment where young girls can experience a sense of belonging (#7). Love and discipline go hand in hand and decisions are made jointly, between girls and staff (#10). Young girls participate in a lot of community activities to give them a sense of being an important part of their society, and special occasions such as birthdays, school holidays, and Christmas times are celebrated together. Once a month our whole community has a celebration, where we join in music, sharing, play and a meal. The space is created for everybody to participate, and because Siena is musically gifted, she often led the other girls in a musical item, or worship songs. This probably helped to validate her worth and to affirm her inherent capacities (#11). Siena lived in Lerato House for one year and I believe that it was the community of concern that was formed around her during this time that facilitated healing and growth (#12).

As we couldn't place Siena in school, we decided to send her on a three week course in childcare (#1). She did very well and enjoyed it immensely. She shared her experience with the other children in the house by teaching them the songs she has learnt at the course, doing art programmes with them and helping younger ones with their homework (#13). Siena found pleasure in being helpful to others, and we realised that the childcare course was just the right kind of invitation to responsibility at the right time for her. She took it with both hands, and as we saw her success with the other children in Lerato House, we asked her if she would be interested to help in one of our other ministries. We have a shelter for women in crisis called The Potter's House, where mothers and children are supported through crisis situations until they are ready to live independently again. Siena worked at The Potter's House for three months, doing childcare in the mornings (#13).

As Siena experienced a bit of life at The Potter's House, she started to dream about her mother and sisters leaving her stepfather and coming to live in The Potter's House, in order to start a new life for themselves (#14). At this time we already had made contact with Siena's mother, Rosina, and had discussed Siena's situation together. Rosina felt happy that Siena left the streets and wanted her to go home with her. Siena never told her mother about the sexual abuse by her stepfather and obviously did not want to live with him in the same house again. She did not talk about this, but stood strongly on the point of his abuse of her mother and sisters, though, and told her mother about the purpose of the programme at The Potter's House, where abused women are welcomed and supported to start a new life for themselves and their children. Initially her mother was not willing, but after some time (and lots of prayers from Siena), she made the brave step to leave him.

To be reconciled with her mother and sisters was a real celebration for Siena, and it served an important purpose in thickening the alternative story of her life (#15). She now played her role as the older sister again, and had a sense of belonging again with her family (#16). We believe that it was the caring community of other young girls in Lerato House, and the privilege to be in close relations with her family again, that helped Siena to celebrate her new life, and not consider going back to the streets or into prostitution again. We believe that it is in community that hope is created, that a new reality is co-constructed between people who have experienced similar struggles in their lives, a reality that tells them a different story than the one they were subjected to before–the story that tried to destroy their lives (#17).

Siena's patience and courage during her first year with us as a young girl of Lerato House culminated in the wonderful opportunity to go to Germany as an Au Pair girl and live with a family for one year. This specific family knew about our work and asked if we would consider sending one of our girls that we believe would be able to make the most of the opportunity. We felt that Siena would be the ideal candidate, and the family offered to arrange the finances for this. She learnt German there, attended a computer course and grew in her Christian faith. On returning, Siena started to work as a volunteer with Lerato House (#1). Her mother is now a full-time staff member of our organisation. She works as a cleaner in one of the low cost housing buildings and she lives with her three daughters in our community (#18).

Although Siena has escaped a desperate life on the streets and found the courage to find life in a new way, she is still a struggling young person in the difficult socio-economic situation in South Africa. She has hope for her future, although finances for further educational opportunities for her are lacking and job opportunities few. In the meantime she is happy to work with us as we journey together and have hope together for a future for her in which she can be a useful and productive member of our society. It has been a privilege to witness her strength and courage and to become part of her life.

3.1 Establishing a Listening Presence

We believe in the vital importance of establishing a listening presence with people on the margins and people coming into one of our small communities of concern. In this moment–of intentionally establishing a listening presence–we are also intentional about applying the first two phases of the pastoral cycle (Holland and Henriot).

It is in the moment of *insertion,* that we try as best we could, to enter the world of the other person. But it is also the moment of critical and deconstructive *analysis,* where we explore the critical questions that will facilitate an appropriate, penetrating and transformative pastoral journey.

We suggest that the basic orientation of the pastoral facilitator in this initial moment, should correspond to the three basic attributes of the narrative approach, which are (i) a "not knowing" approach; (ii) active, responsive listening; and (iii) conversational/deconstructive questions (cf. Muller 2000: 68; Boyd 1996: 220).

The pastoral facilitator, in this approach, does not assume to have all the answers/knowledge, but enters into conversation to listen to the story of the other person/community, who knows best what they currently experience (*cf. Story: #4, #8, #9*).

> *Speaking first to be heard is power over. Hearing to bring forth speech is empowering.* (Morton 1995: 210)

It is a listening that empowers, as it creates the space for the other person in the conversation to speak as the "authority" of his or her own life story, without offering quick and superficial answers or solutions. At the same time it is active listening, that is engaging and participating in the story of the other. It is a listening that should lead to even more penetrating questions, in order to secure a credible, analytical and learning presence.

Both in our street outreach work, and in welcoming children at Lerato House, we seek to establish such a listening presence (*cf. Story: #4*).

The stories of our lives form us. Some stories are life giving and others destructive. Siena realised that the lifestyle she was pursuing (the stories of her life) would not benefit her future, and it did not bring her happiness. That is why she opted to become part of the community of Lerato House (*cf. Story: #2, #3*).

The ultimate goal of pastoral care and counselling should be to walk with a person/community from the story that is not helpful, that is dead-ended, or even destructive, towards embracing and living a new story. But first it is important to listen to the existing story, as told by the person/community (*cf. Story: #3, #5, #9*).

Bons-Storm (1996: 46) says that people's stories are micro-narratives within the structure of a broader narrative of life. In the process of listening, we have to invite people to introduce their own narratives or self-narratives, as Bons-Storm (1996: 46) defines it.

A self-narrative is a way of presenting a cohesive construction . . . of the way the self is experienced, telling stories about events that are seen as . . . for the experience of self.

Such a self-narrative is therefore not a chronological recording of events, but rather a selective sharing of stories, or an interpretation of stories that provides meaning to the self.

Important, however, is that the listening presence should also be seeking to uncover, or to deconstruct (using Derrida's ideas on deconstruction): to listen to what was not said; to take apart the interpretive assumptions in order to reveal the story behind the story (cf. Sampson 1989: 7, 8) (*cf. Story: #3, #6, and #9*).

Laird (1991: 437) and Bons-Storm (1996: 57) refer to the "unstory," i.e., those stories that are not told, that still need to be uncovered through the listening process. A painful or shameful experience often remains "unstories" or "unstoried" (Bons-Storm 1996: 57).

To put the experienced events into words and to tell another person the story would mean not only letting the experiences, but also the pain and the shame, out of the closet.

"Unstories" often contain gender roles that clash with dominant or "proper" roles as dictated by the larger socio-cultural narrative. Because of these clashes, it often remains "unstoried" (Bons-Storm 1996:

57). Such are the stories of abuse that eventually forced Siena to the streets. Instead of storying the abuse, the abuse led her into prostitution.

As suggested already, self-narratives are also affected by broader societal discourses, such as specific gender expectations or assumed gender roles.

Joan Laird (1991: 430; cf. also Bons-Storm 1996: 58) refers to these broader discourses as socio-cultural narratives. Socio-cultural narratives, she says, are explicit or implicit narratives ordering society, defining gender (and other) roles, and mirroring the values of society. Socio-cultural narratives are shaping people's self-narratives. Self-narratives have to be understood within their socio-cultural context. Freeman, Epston and Lobovits (1997:51) also talk about the complex relationship between the problem and wider social context (*cf. Story: #3, #6, #9*).

Because of this relationship between individual/problem and context, we have to move beyond naive listening, to a mode of listening that will be intentional about creating space for critical analysis. In individual therapy, and in walking with a group/community, people have to be assisted and encouraged to read their self-narratives against the dominant narratives of society, to explore how societal narratives have shaped them (for the good or the bad), and to assess such readings in terms of their own future.

Real conversations will help the pastoral facilitator to unravel the ways in which socio-cultural narratives impact upon people and communities, and also upon him/herself, as pastoral workers. It will deconstruct dominant discourses that are not helpful, and open the way for new interpretations, new imagination, and reconstructions.

One of the key elements of a narrative approach to care and counselling, is to ask conversational or deconstructive questions. That is a vital element at this point in the journey—asking questions that will facilitate the kind of conversation that will deconstruct narratives, expose the stories behind the stories, unravel the existing framework of meaning and the discourses in which it is rooted, and reveal their assumptions.

Deconstruction is vital in the pastoral journey, as we all know only partially. All our stories and our interpretations of our stories are subjective and coloured by our socio-cultural background. Similarly, our listening also screens and hears through our own socio-cultural lenses. Therefore we have to deconstruct the told narratives, and the broader socio-cultural narratives, as well as the assumed knowledge that we carry with us into the journey.

It was important to discuss different "knowledge," or ways of knowing with Siena, to open space for more perspectives and choices for action. It was important to introduce different perspectives on her life story and her interpreted story (*cf. Story: #3, #6, #9*).

Lowe (1991: 45) says that " . . . to know anything is to know in terms of one or more discourses." He defines discourses as

> . . . *systematic and institutionalised ways of speaking/writing or otherwise making sense through the use of language.*

Discourses are those broad-based socio-cultural narratives, that enough people ascribe to provide it dominance and ordering power in a society. It is these discourses that need to be deconstructed and evaluated for what they are.

In our context we have to consciously deconstruct dominant discourses on race, gender, culture and class. We have to deconstruct myths about the city and city people. We have to deconstruct even the very way in which we are church or pastoral, or pastoral workers. If the dominant discourses are destructive and exploitative, instead of healing and liberating, they need not only be deconstructed, but also replaced with liberating discourses providing new meaning.

Bons-Storm (1996: 149) speaks about this challenge in the context of women and patriarchy, and underscores the importance of good analysis.

> *Pastoral care and counselling have to acknowledge the hurt and the damage inflicted by patriarchy.*

Only then, Bons-Storm says, can pastoral care and counselling

> . . . *become a place where liberation and healing can happen in God/dess's name.*

In the process of journeying together we are intentional to listen in ways that will deconstruct dominant and exploitative stories about race or gender or class. And in a deconstruction of stories that were maintained over many years, people discover windows to new stories and preferred realities. On this journey the story of the city itself is deconstructed, and the stereotypes about cities and city people, about inner city decay and danger, are challenged and questioned.

But a committed pastoral presence on the margins, in conversation with people outside the ecclesial tradition, seldom leaves the church untouched. Our ecumenical journey on the margins also deconstruct notions of being church, of being pastoral, of being prophetic, of being community. On the margins new visions of community and church are often offered–free, but expensive.

A pastoral presence on the margins, confronted not only with new issues and challenges, but also with the fundamental deficiencies of the urban church and its models of pastoral care, at the same time becomes a prophetic presence. In conversation with those of the margins, new conversions take place, and sometimes include conversion from the church. It also includes conversion to new positions of economic and political exploration, as extensions of credible pastoral solidarity. And it therefore charges for a public presence that will be prophetic and critical.

3.2 Creating Communities of Concern

Deist (1990: 6) suggests that humanity can only be called good in close communion–that God's initial purpose for humanity was therefore community (cf. also de Beer 1999: 359). This is clearly expressed in Genesis 1 and 2, where

> . . . *life is mostly clearly expressed and experienced in the presence of close communion.* (de Beer 1999: 359; also Deist 1990: 6)

Maimela (1991: 11) refers to the traditional African vision of human beings being human only because of others, with others and for others. A loss of such communion will also result in a loss of life. To restore life, we have to restore community.

> . . . *the greatest effect of sin was not so much personal actions against each other, but the condition of estrangement from communion.* (de Beer 1999: 359)

Another African theologian, Thlagale (1991: 61), echoes this sentiment:

> *Total freedom and therefore total personhood, comes in the final analysis from communion with God and others.*

The next moment in our pastoral process is related to this notion: i.e., to establish and nurture communities of concern, based on our listening presence. This is vital as we choose for an approach that is not expert-driven and individualistic, but desires to move beyond profession-alism and individualism (cf. Nouwen), rather embracing community.

We want to explore and embrace the healing power of small commu-nities, as places that can mediate "total freedom and therefore total personhood" (Thlagale 1991: 61). At the same time small communities are inviting the diversity of God's people to become part of God's heal-ing work. This calls for models that are multi-disciplinary, inclusive of the laity, and focussing on healing within community. It is an invitation into a common journey of mutual discovery, learning and growth; mu-tual exposure, confrontation and change.

The notion of community links well with the narrative approach to pastoral care and counselling. In narrative therapy the term "communi-ties of concern" is used, stressing the importance of a person taking steps towards living an alternative story *together* with people who care and who can support and encourage you in your journey. We also speak about "communities of care," or even "communities of solidarity."

In this moment of our pastoral journey, the aspect of reflection (cf. the third phase of Holland & Henriot) also stands central, as we reflect together with an individual/community on that which has been related, either as self-narrative or socio-cultural narrative, but we also reflect on the possible alternative story. The space should be created at this point–through group work, devotional times, conversations, rituals, seminars, etc.–for various resources to help serve as catalysts for dis-covering a new story. Such resources might include reflection on per-sonal capacities (e.g., previous incidents of overcoming/resisting the dominant/negative story), support of friends and family members, re-trieving stories of faith and Biblical resources, drawing from music or art, and so forth (*cf. Story: #8, #11*).

We prefer to speak of moments of healing which occur not necessar-ily at any specific time in the pastoral process, but rather on the journey as a whole. That is why the cycle of care, or the various moments, is so important, since they complement each other. That which has been dis-covered in individual conversations, can now be practised and embod-ied in the community. Successes or failures in practising the new story in the community, can again be shared in the individual conversations. And step-by-step a person moves forward in embracing a new life story.

Let us say more about the purpose and importance of such a commu-nity of concern. Parks (1986: 33) says that

> *as human beings we seem to be dependent upon a network of be-*
> *longing ... We require a sense of connection with others who con-*

firm our being and provide a "home" which grounds or secures our sense of personal and corporate well-being.

Parks (1986: 41, 42) continues to highlight three purposes of a community:

- to be a "holding environment" in which life can come unravelled and be re-woven,
- "communities of confirmation" which affirm new being (strengthening the alternative story), and
- "communities of contradiction," where the dominant story of the individual's life, as well as that of society, is challenged.

Others also emphasize the need for such communities. Resistance to dominant discourses ("contradiction") should not be done alone, but needs participative, supportive communities (cf. Weingarten 2000: 389-402; de Beer et al. 2001: 38). Every person needs a community of listeners to help make small steps towards the new story possible ("confirmation").

Siena became part of a "holding environment" when she moved into Lerato House. The girls in the house became her community of concern, and assisted her to take the first small steps towards an alternative story *(cf. Story: #7)*.

The level of support among the children in Lerato House, also emphasizes the importance of communities as mediating places for healing and liberation *(cf. Story: #12)*.

White (1999: 23) emphasizes that there is a great deal of mutual care and support among children in their culture . . .

In Lerato House intentional attempts are made to nurture a community of concern. We encourage the young women to come up with creative ideas to support one another by creating space during meetings for enthusiastic plans to "inspire all of us." The young women come up with creative ideas to celebrate successes together, forgive one another and show practical love. These forms of love and care counter some of the problem-saturated stories that have ruled their lives before, such as not being loved, isolation and a lack of support as well as having to make it on their own (de Beer, Tumi & Kotze 2001: 38).

Instead of an approach focussing on the so-called "problem-saturated stories," we try to support people in affirming the preferred story for their lives, as they start to take steps towards *this* story.

Many of the practices of narrative therapy assist people to break free from the identity claims associated with the problem-saturated accounts of their lives . . . (White 1999: 7)

Other communities of concern also formed around Siena, namely her own family, as well as the community of staff in Pretoria Community Ministries, where she now worked as a volunteer (*cf. Story: #13, #14, #16*). These communities of concern further provided the "confirmation" and "contradiction" she needed to re-story her life (*cf. Story: #15, #17*).

These communities of concern are also communities of hope. As people are embraced in their journey towards a new story, hope is created in community (Weingarten 2000: 389-402). It is happening as people affirm and support each other, as people start to "do hope together" (de Beer et al. 2001: 40).

A person could be loved into hope when people who care, and who practise hope together surround the person (de Beer, Tumi & Kotze 2001: 40).

We believe that the communities of concern that developed around Siena, played a vital role (and still are) in her survival and growth. They managed to do hope together with her by thickening the alternative story of her life (cf. de Beer et al. 2001: 40). People walked alongside her and verified her preferred way of being (*cf. Story: #15, #17*).

In communities of concern people find ways to re-construct their lives into the preferred story.

A post-modern view of reality helped me to see that together people can construct their realities as they live them. This view does not deny the fact that specific realities are forced on groups of people in society who have no power and who have been discriminated against, people who have been marginalized. However, I have witnessed groups of marginalized and oppressed people deciding what reality they prefer and working towards that reality (de Beer, Tumi & Kotze 2001: 37).

As we try to create a listening presence with people who are marginalized and extremely vulnerable, where despair has long ago crept in and took away dignity and dreams of a better tomorrow, we are discovering the power of community. We find that small communities of concern can contribute greatly to affirm people in their new journey of re-creating hope out of despair, and of re-storying the newly imagined and alternative story of life.

Finally, we also sense that we cannot speak about Christ outside of community. Western Christianity has often misinterpreted the Biblical narrative, offering an individualistic, masculine and colonialist God, in whose name great destruction has been caused. We need (corrective and critical) communities of concern–close to the margins, humane, inclusive and nurturing–to mediate Christ anew. It seems to be precisely at the point where communities mediate dignity and healing and liberation, that people find it possible to reconnect to God, and to rediscover Christ in ways that deconstruct traditional images.

Maybe Bons-Storm's words (1996: 149) in this regard are most suitable:

> *The Christ lives as long as Christ like words are spoken and Christ like acts are done by women and men, as "gardeners." If the community of faith takes God/dess seriously, and God/dess's longing for a humanity that nurtures, and does not break others, then this community will become a place where people who have been hurt by others, hurt perhaps by the perspective of the Divine in traditional theology, can find liberation and healing in community with others.*

3.3 Invitations to Responsibility

At some point in the pastoral journey, people/communities need to be invited/encouraged to take responsibility–taking responsibility is a sign of empowered people ready to re-story their lives. At this point in the journey, the pastoral facilitator should consciously work to strengthen the imagined or alternative story.

Essentially we understand empowerment as assisting people to recover the notion of being created in the image of God, to accept and celebrate it, and to live accordingly. Empowerment is the process of re-storying one's life into the preferred reality. Empowerment is not about gaining power *over* others, but being empowered to live in the fullness of image-bearers of God, *with* others. In this third moment of empowerment to responsible living, people might also discover their vocation in life (cf. Gerkin 1991).

The nature of the responsibility that people take, might include responsibility for themselves and their families, for other people as good neighbours, for the community/city as good citizens, or to be co-workers with God as disciples.

There comes a point in the pastoral process when we are *inviting* people to responsibility. Siena's attendance of a child care course, her year in Germany, and her current volunteer work in Lerato House, all form part of such an invitation (*cf. Story: #1*). In our journey with her we tried to apply narrative principles of care. We aimed at being non-blaming in our approach, to be respectful, and to collaborate with her about her decisions. We had to make sure that we were not patronising her, but giving her space to move freely into becoming the person she prefers to be. She has to be the principle author of her new story. In doing so we encouraged her towards responsibility.

The invitation to responsibility corresponds with the three aspects that Jenkins (1990: 182) suggests, in inviting abusive men to take responsibility. We will briefly discuss it here.

3.3.1 Self-Responsibility

The one challenge is being able to attend to your own needs and own facing pressures. The fact that Siena was willing to make the decision to break free from the hold of street life and decided all on her own that she wants to live among others in a community, was highlighted by us as a capacity for responsible behaviour.

In Lerato House we encourage the young women to take as much responsibility as possible. Most of them come from abusive situations and have lost their sense of worth. It is thus important in the practical running of the house to invite responsibility by strengthening the girls' feelings of capacity. Besides participation in the household duties, they are encouraged to take responsibility for new children and for guests, by offering hospitality.

Active interaction among the young women, joint decision-making between staff and young women and the opening up of possibilities for these women to take responsibility for their own solutions and lives, are some of the principles guiding the work done in Lerato House (de Beer, Tumi & Kotze 2001: 37).

3.3.2 Other-Responsibility

Just as important is to develop sensitivity to the needs and feelings of others. In conversation with Siena, we dealt with the fact that living in community requires taking responsibility for others, caring for others in the house, not causing conflict, and doing your share of the work to make things easier for everyone. We looked back at how Siena took leadership when she lived in Lerato House and are still using stories we can remember to strengthen her self-construction of being a person who cares for others and who is able to live in/contribute to community with others.

Siena has also taken other-responsibility in the way in which she initiated and encouraged her mother and sisters to leave the abusive situation at home for a caring community.

Responsibility for others includes responsibility for our neighbours and for our community. Siena is acting this out as she does volunteer work with Lerato House, taking responsibility for girls in the house, for girls who are still on the streets, and for those girls who are in prison. In this way she shares her journey with others, thereby also taking responsibility for them, while at the same time it is still part of her own self-construction (*cf. Story: #13, #14, #16*).

3.3.3 Responsibility for Facing Consequences

In journeying with Siena from the streets and into Lerato House, she had to realise that basic rules must be obeyed, that there is a certain limitation on freedom for the sake of living in community (e.g., to do cooking, cleaning or washing up duties when it is your turn; to plan your day in order to be in time for programmes), and that one's actions always have consequences.

We supported her to think about the "rules" that she wanted to make for herself, that dealt with moral and lifestyle issues (how you want to live your life). We strengthened the decisions that Siena took herself, by retelling the stories that affirmed the kind of person she now preferred to be.

Living into the alternative story and breaking free from the dominant story, are simultaneous processes. In the case of Siena and her family, it became important to free them—as a family—from the influence of the dominant story of their lives (*cf. Story: #5, #14, #16, #18*). Morgan (2000: 80) feels that

> *. . . meetings with significant others are often extremely important in the course of the therapy. They engage people with a history to the alternative story that is linked to the lives of others in ways that powerfully contradict the problem-saturated account of their lives.*

Although we didn't have formal counselling sessions with them as a family, Siena's mother confirmed these alternative stories in informal discussions we had about Siena. We always felt it was important that

Siena heard her mother speak positively about her, and the effect on her was clearly very positive.

> *When we think about all these people we are associated with in the course of our daily lives, we could consider them as members of our "club" of life.* (Morgan 2000: 78)

As Holy Communion is a continuous reminder, strengthening the alternative story introduced by Christ, so we have to find ways to re-member people in community, and through each other, to the alternative story. We have to help them re-member to the significant others in their lives. Another example in our context is the prayer fellowship of landless people, meeting on Monday nights–winter and summer–in Marabastad in the open air and surrounded by informal shacks and squalor. The continuous re-membering conversations of these people living on the margins of the inner city, have started to bind people communally, and in their common faith, to the hope of the alternative story.

But this is not a quick or easy process. The pastoral facilitator almost acts as a midwife at this point, walking patiently with an individual or group or community, through the painful process of giving birth–re-authoring a new story for themselves, reconstructing their own lives or futures, re-creating meaning and hope.

This moment in the pastoral process obviously corresponds to the last phase in Holland and Henriot's cycle–planning. Although the pastoral process encourage that practical steps are (and should be) taken in terms of future life planning, and although good planning is part of taking responsibility, good planning alone is not adequate. The narrative approach is seeking for something more radical and liberationist, helping people not only to do good life planning, but to depart completely from destructive life stories, and to live/plan within a whole new understanding of their own lives in relation to the world, others and God.

The narrative approach wants to facilitate conversations that will liberate to conversion–turning from the destructive story and walking hopefully towards the alternative story.

- The place of spirituality in the moments of pastoral journeying

At this point one might conclude by asking where spirituality will fit into these moments of the pastoral process. Different people have indicated in different ways how spirituality functions in the pastoral cycle of Holland and Henriot (cf. Cochrane, De Gruchy & Peterson 1991:

75-83). On the one hand, we suggest that the cycle is taking as its point of departure a "lived faith" (Gutierrez 1988: xxxiv) which runs like a thread throughout the process. On the other hand, we suggest that every moment in the cycle should be rooted in a lived faith, open to the surprising presence of God, the comforting presence of the Spirit, and the liberating presence of Christ; open to meet Christ in the fellow traveller, and to be converted yourself (as pastoral facilitator) in the process of unfolding conversation.

We can say it differently: The listening presence find its theological roots in the incarnational Christ, the moment of community find its theological roots in the divine Trinity and in the unifying work of the Spirit, and the moment of invitation (empowerment) to responsibility find its theological roots in the notion of us all being made in the image of God. The pastoral journey is a yearning and an openness to recover the lost image of God, and the broken community, as we meet Christ in each other (sometimes surprisingly), and through our various conversations.

7. SPECIFIC CHALLENGES FROM OUR CONTEXT TO PASTORAL CARE AND COUNSELLING

7.1 Challenges from Our Social Context

Our social context presents us with various challenges. These might not differ much from other urban neighbourhoods globally. Issues of gender, race, abuse, questions of identity, power, marginalization and exclusion, and cultures of entitlement, are all dimensions of this challenge. These issues are not only to be found in the social context of our urban communities, but the very same issues are also plaguing the church in different ways.

Women, children and homeless people are affected by racial and gender bias, by systemic injustices and the lack of appropriate public policy, and by the way in which power is exercised to exploit and excludes. After 1994 questions of identity have become a reality, as many South Africans (if not all) have to reconstruct who we are in relation to ourselves, our own group and the diverse groups with whom we share the same land and national loyalties. At the same time an emerging culture of entitlement–claiming access to my rights without necessarily living up to the responsibilities going with these, or my individual rights weighing more than the collective rights of the community–have become pervasive and paralysing certain inner city neighbourhoods.

Pastoral facilitators need to be aware of these issues, deconstructing them in the pastoral journey, and in conversation with their fellow travellers. Some of these issues are embedded in historic socio-cultural narratives, but some have emerged as part of the socio-political transition in our country. There are not only negative narratives, however. Part of the challenge for our pastoral community is to strengthen the emerging alternative stories, to discover them where they are at work, and to lift them up for many to see (stories of women and children overcoming abuse, landless people constructing creative alternatives for themselves, racially divided neighbourhoods re-defining themselves in terms of newly found solidarity with each other, etc.).

7.2 Challenges Within the Praxis of Pastoral Care and Counselling

Besides the challenge from the social context that we need to hear and integrate into our pastoral journeys, there are also specific challenges to the praxis of pastoral care and counselling as such. Financial constraints (restricting access to "good" pastoral care to the middle-class), the exclusivist nature of most pastoral counselling models (our challenge is to develop multi-cultural and inclusive models instead), the lack of appropriate training opportunities (especially for the laity and poor communities), and the professionalism that lies behind this, are all challenges to the praxis of pastoral care and counselling. We suggest pastoral models that will go beyond professionalism (expert-driven) and individualism (focusing on individual therapy).

We suggest for local churches to work intentionally on the following:

- The pastoral challenge requires a more intentional effort from the church and theological institutions to provide training to the laity, that is both contextual and narrative.
- We also need to be intentional about establishing or nurturing pastoral *communities* that will help people to "live the recovering hope"–the majority of pastoral care models are still too individualist. Especially in the case of marginal people, healing can best be mediated in the context of communities of concern.
- We are adamant that the relationship between pastoral care, counselling, community development and social justice, need to be ex-

plored more, and the connectedness understood better, if we are to be credible companions on the journey (cf. Muller 2000).

- As part of a national process of redistributing resources, and of ensuring fair access to services that are affordable, the pastoral care and counselling community also needs to address the economic injustices inherent to their own field. Models of care and counselling that are elitist and profit-driven, ensuring nothing but the lack of access, need to be challenged.

In any situation where the poor and rich live side by side as we do in South Africa, pastoral facilitators, who claim to work in the name of Christ, need to create a presence among those without access, a presence that will transfer skills and empower communities, until local responsibility are fully taken.

8. CONCLUSION

The invitation to contribute this article has been a great privilege to us, as it is a way of journeying with the global pastoral community. We do not suggest that our struggles or challenges, or even suggestions, are unique. We do offer them as part of a local narrative, however, unfolding itself against the backdrop of a radically changed and still changing urban South Africa. We invite you to be part of this journey, as we would like to be part of yours.

QUESTIONS FOR DISCUSSION:

The purpose of these questions is to help the reader reflect critically, and to contextualise or appropriate the material presented here, to your own context/s.

Question 1: After identifying a marginal, excluded, or at-risk group in your local neighbourhood, discuss how you can go about to establish a listening presence with this group ?

Question 2: What are some of the sociocultural narratives that shape the people in your local church, and that shape the group you identified in discussion question 1?

Question 3: How can your local congregation be transformed to be(come) pastoral communities, that are open and inclusive to marginal people ? Or–if you are already such a community, how can you continue strengthen it ?

Question 4: Identify strategies through which the tasks and responsibilities of pastoral care and counselling can be shared with people of your local congregation/local neighbourhood (street outreach workers, housewives, caretakers, neighbours, hospitality workers, house managers, cleaners, etc.) ?

Question 5: What are the issues of social exclusion or exploitation that impact upon pastoral care and counselling in your congregation/neighbourhood ? In what way do you need to reconstruct your own understanding and/or praxis of care and counselling to address these issues meaningfully ?

REFERENCES

Anderson, H. 1997. Conversation, language and possibilities. A post-modern approach to therapy. New York: Basic Books.
Bakke, R. 1987. The Urban Christian. Downers Grove, Illinois: InterVarsity Press.
Bakke, R. 1997. A Theology as Big as the City. Downers Grove, Illinois: InterVarsity Press.
Boff, L. 1986. Wat is Theologie van de Bevrijding? Apeldoorn: Altiora-Averbode.
Bons-Storm, R. 1996. The Incredible Woman. Listening to women's silences in pastoral care and counselling. Nashville: Abingdon Press.
Boyd, G. E. 1996. Pastoral Conversation: A Social Construction View, Pastoral Psychology, vol. 44, no. 4, 220.
Brueggemann, W. 1978. Prophetic Imagination. Philadelphia: Fortress Press.
Brueggemann, W., Parks, S. and Groome, T. 1986. To Act Justly, Love Tenderly, Walk Humbly. An Agenda for Ministers. Mahwah, New Jersey: Paulist Press.
Cochrane, J. R., De Gruchy, J. W. and Peterson, R. 1991. In Word and Deed. Towards a Practical Theology for Social Transformation. Pietermaritzburg: Cluster Publications.
Cox, H. 1969. The Feast of Fools. A Theological Essay on Festivity and Fantasy. Cambridge, Massachusetts: Harvard University Press.
de Beer, S. F. 1999. Towards a Theology of Inner City Transformation. The Church, Housing and Community in the City. Pretoria: Unpublished DD Thesis.
de Beer, W. T., Tumi and Kotze, E. 2001. Inner-city talk, in Kotze and Kotze (Ed.), 33-46.

Deist, F. 1990. Genesis 1-11, Oppression and Liberation. Journal of Theology for Southern Africa 73, 3-11.

Freedman, J., and Combs, G. 1996. Narrative Therapy. New York: Norton.

Freeman, J., Epston, D. and Lobovits, D. 1997. Playful approaches to serious problems: Narrative therapy with children and their families. New York: W.W. Norton & Company.

Gerkin, C. V. 1991. Prophetic Pastoral Practice: A Christian vision of life together. Nashville: Abingdon Press.

Gutierrez, G. 1988. A Theology of Liberation. (fifteenth anniversary edition with a new introduction) Maryknoll, New York: Orbis Books.

Holland, J. and Henriot, P. 1984. Social Analysis: Linking Faith and Justice. Maryknoll, New York: Orbis Books.

Jenkins, A. 1990. Invitations to Responsibility. The Therapeutic Engagement of Men who are Violent and Abusive. Adelaide: Dulwich Centre Publications.

Kotze, E. and Kotze, D. 2001. Telling Narratives. (Spellbound Edition) Pretoria: Ethics Alive.

Laird, J. 1991. Women and Stories: Destroying women's self-constructions, in McGoldrick (Ed.)

Larty, E. 1997. In living colour. An intercultural approach to pastoral care and counselling. London & Herndon, VA: Cassell.

Louw, D. 1993. Pastoraat as Ontmoeting. Pretoria: Raad vir Geestesweten=skaplike Navorsing.

Lowe, D. 1991. Post-modern themes and therapeutic practices: Notes towards the definition of Family Therapy: Part 2, Dulwich Centre Newsletter (3): 41-52.

Maimela, S. 1991. Traditional African Anthropology and Christian Theology. Journal of Theology for Southern Africa 76, 4-14.

McGoldrick, M. (Ed.) 1991. Women and Familie: A Framework for Family Therapy. New York: Norton.

Morgan, A. 2000. What is narrative therapy? An easy-to-read introduction. Adelaide: Dulwich Centre Publications.

Morton, N. 1995. The journey is home. Boston: Beacon Press.

Muller, J. C. 1996. Om tot verhaal te kom. Pretoria: Raad vir Geestesweten=wetenskaplike Navorsing.

Muller, J. C. 2000. Reisgeselskap. Die kuns van verhalende pastorale gesprek=voering. Wellington: Lux Verbi. BM.

Nouwen, H. 1971. Creative Ministry.

O'Connor, E. 1997. Cry Pain, Cry Hope. A guide to the dimensions of Call. Washington, DC: The Servant Leadership School.

Palmer, P. 1983. To Know as We are Known. San Francisco: Harper Collins.

Parks, S. 1986. LoveTenderly, in Brueggemann, W., Parks, S. & Groome, T., 29-43.

Sampson, E. E. 1989. The Deconstruction of the Self, in Shotter J. and Gerkin, K. J. (Eds.), 7-8.

Shotter, J. and Gerkin, K. J. 1989. Texts of Identity. London: Sage.

Tlhagale, B. 1991. The Anthropology of Liberation. Journal of Theology for Southern Africa 76, 57-63.
Vanier, J. 1989. Community and Growth. Mahwah, NJ: Paulist Press.
Weingarten, K. 2000. Witnessing, wonder and hope. Family Process, 39 (4): 389-402.
White, M. 1999. Reflections on narrative practice. Essays and interviews. Adelaide: Dulwich Centre Publications.

AUTHOR NOTE

The process of care and counselling is described by suggesting three distinctive but overlapping moments, i.e., establishing a listening presence, creating communities of concern, and presenting an invitation to responsibility.

Complexity and Simplicity in Pastoral Care: The Case of Forgiveness

Archie Smith, Jr., MDiv, PhD
Ursula Riedel-Pfaefflin, PhD

SUMMARY. This article is about forgiveness and why it appears to us to be a central, yet complex, dimension of pastoral care and counseling. We argue that people cannot move forward if they do not experience forgiveness. The role of the witness in pastoral counseling is crucial in helping people to forgive and move forward. Forgiveness is not simply a matter of forgetfulness, repression or suppression. Rather, forgiveness presupposes repentance. It is complex and can be very difficult to achieve. Distinctions between pseudo-forgiveness, pre-mature forgiveness and mature forgiveness are made. In some cases of immeasurable human suffering, forgiveness may be impossible. The New Testament scriptures may shed only a little light on the complexity of the problem. We argue that forgiveness cannot stand alone. Forgiveness may be related to power, love and justice in concrete situations in order to be meaningful. When therapy and/or pastoral care fail to deal with power, love and justice, it will also fail to adequately deal with forgiveness. *[Article copies available for a fee from The Haworth Document Delivery Service: 1-800-HAWORTH. E-mail address: <getinfo@haworthpressinc.com> Website: <http://www.HaworthPress.com> © 2002 by The Haworth Press, Inc. All rights reserved.]*

KEYWORDS. Pastoral counseling, justice, love, forgiveness, repentence, power

[Haworth co-indexing entry note]: "Complexity and Simplicity in Pastoral Care: The Case of Forgiveness." Smith Jr., Archie, and Ursula Riedel-Pfaefflin. Co-published simultaneously in *American Journal of Pastoral Counseling* (The Haworth Pastoral Press, an imprint of The Haworth Press, Inc.) Vol. 5, No. (3/4), 2002, pp. 295-316; and: *International Perspectives on Pastoral Counseling* (ed: James Reaves Farris) The Haworth Pastoral Press, an imprint of The Haworth Press, Inc., 2002, pp. 295-316. Single or multiple copies of this article are available for a fee from The Haworth Document Delivery Service [1-800-HAWORTH, 9:00 a.m. - 5:00 p.m. (EST). E-mail address: getinfo@haworthpressinc.com].

If you, O Lord, should mark iniquities,
Lord, who could stand?
But there is forgiveness with you . . . (Psalm 130:3-4a)

. . . Forgive us our debts, as we also have forgiven our debtors . . .
(Matt. 6:12)

INTRODUCTION

This essay is about forgiveness and pastoral care in the context of systemic oppression and certain intercultural realities. Systemic oppression includes, but is not limited to, institutionalized racism, collective violence, rape, torture, persecution and historical discrimination. It may result in long-term suffering, demoralization, hopelessness and, possibly, death. The spiritual dimension of systemic oppression must also be recognized. It suggests that we have a relationship to God *and* to one another. Each violation of a living being, be it physical, psychical, emotional or social mistreatment, affects the divine-human relationship and is destroying the integrity of that being, her or his wholeness. This constitutes a spiritual problem and one that the practice of pastoral counseling ought to address.

We are writing this article because we believe that one of the fundamental underlying issues of pastoral care and counseling in various cultures has to do with issues of forgiveness. As such, we are not treating any one specific culture, but a dynamic that underlies pastoral care and counseling in many different cultures. Forgiveness defines a basic challenge world wide for pastoral care and counseling.

In his drama, *Death and the Maiden,* Ariel Dorfmann, raised the question: Is forgiveness really possible in the aftermath of rape and extreme experiences of torture? Forgiveness is not simply a matter of forgetfulness, repression or suppression. Forgiveness suggests a very complex relationship between victims, perpetrator and the system of persecution when placed in the context of torture or systemic oppression. There are several levels of relationship in a complex system of persecution. They include the relationship between: (a) the victim and the one who directly inflicts pain; (b) the agents of the pain and their positions in the line of command; (c) the agents' relationship to the system of persecution; (d) the relationship among the bureaucrats who maintain systems of torture; (e) all who are in positions of responsibility even if they are far removed from carrying out the torture; (f) the host society that tolerates it; (g) the relationship of the victim to her or himself, to the past and present, belief and trust of the god within; and (h) the role of the witness. The witness is one who listens to and acknowledges the experience of the traumatized individual(s). The witness encourages the human capacity for resiliency, enables and supports the injured person through a healing process. Forgiveness may entail all of these levels of relationships. Hence, forgiveness is not a simple matter of letting go or repression.

A few years ago, on a flight back to San Francisco from Denver, Archie and his seat partner got into a conversation about forgiveness. His seat partner was a medical doctor, philosopher and Jewish. He was born in Vienna in the early 1940s and left for the United States just before the Nazis took control. He commented that the Christian concept of forgiveness made no sense to him. After Auschwitz, it was impossible for him to believe in or pray to a personal god. He appeared a bit agitated as he said this. He threw his hands in a downward direction as if in disgust or to denounce something. He said, "I am not unreligious. I am just areligious or non-religious." He repeated that "forgiveness" did not make philosophical sense to him. He then gave the following statements as an illustration of his thinking.

If ten years ago a tragic event happened and the perpetrators were aware of their part in it but were not asking or seeking forgiveness, then what is the point of saying, "I forgive you"?

If ten years ago a tragic event happened and the perpetrators were not aware of their part in it and were not asking or seeking forgiveness, then what is the point of saying, "I forgive you"?

If ten years ago a tragic event happened and the perpetrators were asking forgiveness because they were a part of the general history (i.e., German guilt in the Nazi atrocities), but those seeking forgiveness never participated in specific acts of torture and extermination, then what is the point of the victim saying, "I forgive you"? How does this help the victim?

If ten years ago a tragic event happened and the perpetrators were asking or seeking forgiveness, but they were not doing anything to correct the behaviors that led to the tragic events in the first place, then they are basically the same people today and would do the same again should similar circumstances materialize. What good does it do for the victims to say, "I forgive you"?

If ten years ago the perpetrator was asking or seeking forgiveness and has been doing things to correct the behaviors that led to the first tragic event, then the perpetrator has already changed and is not the same person today. What is the point of the victim saying to the changed perpetrator,

"I forgive you" when the person who is seeking forgiveness today is not the same person who committed the tragedy ten years earlier?

Archie's seat companion, then said, "You see . . . forgiveness makes no philosophical sense to me." Archie did not challenge him. Raf, the drowned in his book, *Survival in Auschwitz*. The drowned is "an emaciated man, with head dropped and shoulders curved, on whose face and in whose eyes not a trace of a thought is to be seen."[1]

Such a person has been reduced to silence by forces of oppression from without and from within. Forgiveness is improbable for persons in such a state of extreme demoralization. Although Levi was describing the faces he saw in a Nazi death camp, his composite image was representative of the cumulative forces of human evil etched upon the tortured of our time. The drowned are both sign and symbol of those who have lost the capacity for anger, protest or hate. They are the women, men and children who "suffer and drag themselves along in an opaque intimate solitude, and in solitude they die or disappear, without leaving a trace in anyone's memory."[2] Archie's seat partner did not describe this extreme situation of systemic oppression and improbable forgiveness, but he believed he could have. In situations of collective violence where human suffering is immeasurable, this level of trauma is horrifyingly normal. How is forgiveness possible?

We have thought about Archie's seat partner's complex way of framing the issue of forgiveness. He did not make it a simple matter. Indeed, he said, it was impossible to believe in this idea of forgiveness as a concept related to justice and as a viable way to be human. His analysis was from the point of view of the victim whose act of forgiveness would release the perpetrator from responsibility and guilt. It would not address the shame and humiliation of the victim or bring justice. Hence, forgiveness is a meaningless gesture, he claimed. What sense does it make for the victim to forgive when perpetrators are not seeking it, lack comprehension of their deeds, are essentially the same people today and would do the same if the opportunity were to present itself again?

We shall consider the relevance of these questions and ideas of forgiveness by drawing on vignettes from different cultural and international contexts. Ursula Riedel-Pfaefflin will reflect upon her experiences in Germany as therapist and professor of pastoral theology and care. Archie Smith, Jr. will reflect upon experiences in Great Britain and the United States. The vignettes below will add dimension to the questions of forgiveness as we consider it across different cultures.

VIGNETTE 1:
DRESDEN:
RACISM, VIOLENCE AND FORGIVENESS?

In her introductory class on theory and practice of pastoral care and counseling, Ursula asked her students to take a narrative approach and interview a person or a family, and report on the interview in class. Students were asked to listen to the life-story and evaluate it by asking for indications of dominating knowledge, underprivileged knowledge, preferred ways of living and sources of power in their own lives.

One student, whom we shall call "K," interviewed an old man whom we shall call Mr. F. He had recently returned to Dresden from Russia. Mr. F told his life story.

Mr. F was a youngster when the Nazis took over in Germany. One law after another was introduced. These laws diminished the rights of certain persons. Those especially affected were Jews, homosexuals, Sinti, Roma and psychiatric patients. The latter were labeled: "Life not worthy to live." The people of Dresden stood by. They did not protest or intervene as the rights of these citizens were diminished. One of the laws promoted racism by demanding that every German family trace their family of origin for several generations and show proof of their roots in the Arian race.

Mr. F's family originally came from Rumania. His mother was able to trace back her origins according to the law. His father could not find the ethnic and racial roots of his relatives. Thus, a Nazi administration officer inscribed his passport: "Jew!" This fateful act changed his life forever. It led to a series of events that seem unbelievable and had disastrous consequences for his entire family. They were forcefully deported to Poland together with many other Jewish families from Dresden. There, they were brought to the Ghetto in Warsaw. It had been emptied when Polish Jews were sent to concentration camps and murdered. The new arrivals were told that they would get their belongings by train. Their friends managed to send their belongings. But when the train arrived at Warsaw, the Nazis bombed the city that very night. Their belongings were destroyed. While in Warsaw, Mr. F heard about the possibility of work in the USSR. This was appealing. He was young and adventurous. He applied and was transferred to the Soviet Union where he was employed. He worked hard. But during the war he was under suspicion of being a German spy. The Soviets put him in jail for several years. When he got out of jail, he was transferred to another region and started a new life.

Anti-Semitism was soon on the rise again. He became the object of persecution having the J already inscribed in his passport. He was jailed once again, and for many years. He was eventually released and once again started a new life. He married, established a new home, and had a family. He maintained a friendly disposition. He got to know tourists and visitors from East Germany and had good conversations with them. When East and West Germany were reunited in 1989-1990, a new law encouraged former German Jews to return to Germany from Russia. Returning Jews were promised compensation. He responded positively to this encouragement to return to his homeland. But new problems arose around his identity when he returned to Dresden, where he was born. Unwittingly, he was able to convince the post Nazi administration that he never was Jewish in the first place, and that his inscription as a Jew was due to Nazi terror. The new Dresden administration saw in this a new opportunity and now conveniently withholds his compensation because he is not recognized as a returning Jew. He now struggles to survive with very little money and in an economy that has grown very expensive. He cannot afford the rising cost of housing and general increase in the cost of living.

This vignette about systemic oppression mirrors how racism, militarism, economic interests and violation of human rights were intertwined. Mr. F was experienced by the student as a lively, cheerful man who still invests in life. He has many contacts and is able to share his story with others. In spite of systemic forms of injustice such as racism, violence, separation from his father and mother, friends and families, the trauma of several dislocations and long years of innocent imprisonment, he somehow remains buoyant. He appreciated the willingness of the student who listens to him without much interruption. She became a witness and gave voice to his experience and his family's experience of systemic and systematic racism, violence and injustice.

This vignette leads to many questions about forgiveness. If forgiveness presupposes repentance, then who is to repent? How can forgiveness be meaningful in this situation? We extend the questions raised by the Jewish Doctor Archie met on his plane ride. If no one has acknowledged wrongdoing, apologized, offered or made restitution, then what sense does forgiveness make? Who can forgive in a life journey where so many people participated in different acts and levels of violence, injustice and racism, knowingly and unknowingly? What happens when injustice is inscribed and experienced in many ways at different times and places? Injustice becomes a characteristic way of life, inscribed upon society itself. This vignette suggests that systemic injustice and racism is everywhere. The good in life is intertwined with evil and affects victims and perpetrators disproportionately–regardless of ethnicity, personal attributes or political background.

VIGNETTE 2:
DRESDEN:
SEXISM, POWER AND JUSTICE–
AN INTERNATIONALLY CHALLENGING PROBLEM

A student/social worker from Dresden narrated her experience with a married sixty-five year old woman who came to a local women's shelter. The sixty-five year old woman had been married fifty years and lived in a village with her husband. The couple owned a large house. The husband, now seventy-three, had been mayor of a neighboring village. Jealousy played a big role in their relationship. The wife had been suffering his abuse for the past fifteen years. The situation worsened and came to a head when he forced her to drive to a place where he wanted to convict her of an alleged offense. But he was unable to do so. The husband was not able to "prove" his wife's guilt. She was innocent. On the way home he made her leave the car. She walked home alone. Upon arrival she discovered that he had locked all the doors to the house. She sought help from a neighbor who, in turn, brought her to the women's shelter. The sixty-five year old woman told the student/social worker that her husband had weapons in the house. Since she did not bring any clothes with her to the shelter, it was necessary to go to her home under police escort to get her clothes. Police escort to the house of the abused woman was arranged. Everything was planned by both systems, the women's shelter and the local police. Yet, there was another police from another city involved. He had not been a part of the conversation that led to a plan between the women's shelter and local police. The special task of the police from the other city was to search for the weapons. The husband was held in the police car in order to protect the wife and the social worker. The wife was told to get the most necessary things and return from the house so a weapons search could be conducted. It was here that differing interests collided. The police officer who was commanding the weapon search spoke harsh and threatening words to the social worker. The officer felt that the woman was taking too long to gather her things and he wanted to begin the weapon search right away. The social worker felt caught in the middle of the woman's need to gather her belongings and the harsh words from the police. The social worker felt overwhelmed. She grew anxious, paralyzed and unable to act according to her professional wishes.

What was going on? The social worker/student felt disrespect from the police officer and wondered how she could deal differently and professionally in the future with a similar situation. Why would she be so paralyzed?

Where is the issue of forgiveness in this situation? There were implicit issues of whether to forgive or to withhold forgiveness. Three general areas that are relevant to the vignette include: (1) the wife's relationship to herself and to her future. It will be important for her to gain help in clarifying her relationship to herself and to her life of abuse, weapons in the home, where "home" will be, and what to do next; (2) the gender and power issues of professional abuse, the women's shelter, and harsh treatment of the social worker by police authority. How can professional women who run a shelter for abused women, ask male members of the police department to apologize? Are professional women, who run a shelter, expected to forgive automatically other professionals who treat them disrespectfully? If no wrong doing is acknowledged by the commanding police officer, would forgiveness have any meaning?; (3) the role of witness that the social worker played by hearing the sixty-five year old woman's experience of abuse, and the role of witness played by the group of students who observed and acknowledged the painful experience of their sister student. Can she forgive herself for feeling professionally "paralyzed"?

VIGNETTE 3:
THE UNITED KINGDOM:
STEPHEN LAWRENCE:
AN EXAMPLE OF SYSTEMIC OPPRESSION

On April 22, 1993, a young black teenager, Stephen Lawrence was murdered while waiting with a friend, Duwayne Brooks, for a bus in southeast London. A gang of five white youth approached assaulting them with racial slurs and attacked Stephen and his friend. Duwayne Brooks managed to escape, but Stephen Lawrence was knocked to the ground, kicked, and beaten. He died from his injuries. His murderers were never charged for the murder. The Metropolitan Police's investigation into the murder of Stephen Lawrence was described by a High Court Judge as fundamentally flawed and marred by a combination of professional incompetence, institutional racism, and a failure of leadership by senior officers. Little would have been done about the murder or the police investigation had it not been for the out cry of the black community, the quest for justice, support of the family's minister, and the efforts of Stephen Lawrence's parents who pressed for an investigation of the police's handling of their son's murder. As a result of their persistent effort and the investigation of a High Court Judge, Sir William Macpherson, a report was issued. It called for wide spread reform in government and social institutions. It defined racism as "the collective failure of an organization to provide an appropriate and professional service to people because of their colour, culture or ethnic origin. It can be seen or detected in processes, attitudes and behaviour which amount to discrimination through unwitting prejudice, ignorance, thoughtlessness and racist stereotyping which disadvantage minority ethnic people."[3] Six years later, *The Guardian* newspaper reported, "Any parent faced with the death of their son in such circumstances would have been devastated. But for Stephen's parents, Doreen and Neville Lawrence, their sense of despair has been compounded by the failure of the criminal justice system to deliver them justice to secure the conviction of those responsible."[4]

The unprovoked and racist attack that lead to Stephen Lawrence's death is not an isolated or singular event. It is a part of the black experience in Britain, and an established way of life. Racism can be "seen or detected in processes, attitudes and behavior" which result in harm to non-white people.

Another example—On 4 June 2000, fourteen-year-old Christina was the victim of a racist attack by a gang of four white youth near her home. She lived with her widowed father, Jan Marthin Pasalbessy, age forty-eight, a former merchant seaman from Indonesia. Because of head injuries from the attack, Christina's father took her to the nearby hospital. There Christina and her father ran into members of the same group who attacked her. This time they verbally attacked Mr. Pasalbessy. According to news reports they called him, "black bastard," punched and kicked until he fell to the ground. They continued the attack while his daughter, Christina looked on helplessly. Mr. Pasalbessy died of injuries the next day, leaving his daughter an orphan. The gang members who attacked Mr. Pasalbessy were all convicted of his murder. At the trial the prosecution told the court that the attack upon Mr. Pasalbessy was unprovoked, gratuitous violence.[5] "The murder of Christina's father was one of at least eight killings in Britain with a racist element since the publication two years ago of Sir William Macpherson's ground-breaking report into the botched Stephen Lawrence murder inquiry."[6]

Racism is systemic–an entrenched, institutionalized pattern which will be with us for a long time to come. Given this, what does forgiveness mean for the individual, for society and for our sense of justice? It seems improbable that forgiveness of the perpetrators by the victim's survivors will bridge the gap between them, especially where the perpetrators have not admitted to any wrong doing and are not seeking forgiveness. How can Stephen Lawrence's parents forgive when no one has confessed or been held responsible? How can fourteen-year-old Christina forgive those who attacked her and then took her father's life, leaving her an orphan? Was there no one at the hospital to witness this event or who could have restrained the attackers? How can malicious acts and institutionalized patterns of racism be forgiven?

VIGNETTE 4:
THE UNITED STATES:
RACISM, FORCE AND FORGIVENESS?

It was the counseling session just after the fourth of July holiday weekend. My counselee was a black man in his early twenties. He appeared a bit agitated as he entered my office. He sat down and blurted out the phrase, "This was a rough weekend!" "What happened?" I asked. It was Saturday night and he was returning home from a gig in San Francisco. He was a musician and his jazz combo had just finished playing for a dance. After he had gotten off the underground train on his way home police cars converged on him. One officer forcefully pushed him to the ground and held a cocked pistol to the back of his head, saying, "I know you are the one who did it." My client asked, "Did what? What are you talking about?" He tried to explain where he had been and that he was heading home from work. He had an underground train ticket to verify his sortie. A police officer said in reply that anyone can grab an underground train stub for an alibi. He was shoved into the police car and jailed.

A store had been robbed, unknown to my counselee. The storeowner came to the police station and identified my counselee as the one who robbed his store. My counselee was roughed up. He called a friend and asked him to go to his bank and get out a large sum of money for his bail. The friend did this, and my counselee was released. After examining the film of the robbery taken by the camera in the store, the police concluded that my counselee was not the one who committed the robbery. My counselee asked for the return of his moneys. He was told that was not possible. He went to his attorney who informed him that police always make mistakes like that. You just have to get over it and chalk it up as one of those experiences in life that happens.

This was not the first harsh encounter my counselee had had with the police. This experience reflects a typical experience of young black men with the law and so called justice system. They are expected to grin and bear it, but not to retaliate when they are wrongfully accused and harshly handled. My counselee said, "I understand how Rodney King[7] felt about those police officers who beat him." Rodney King was another black man who was beaten by the police and arrested. News of his arrest ignited rioting in Los Angeles, California.

This experience of brutal police force is commonplace for young black men. It may be viewed as an incident of racial profiling. Racial profiling is defined here as the practice by police to stop motorists or a pedestrian and interrogate them because they appear to be a member of a racial or ethnic group that officers believe are more likely than others to commit certain types of crimes. This practice has been enforced for a long time and is viewed as widespread in the United States, and in Britain, especially among young black men.

Is forgiveness relevant to this situation of racial profiling and injustice? Archie's counselee was falsely accused and forcefully arrested. When he turned to his attorney for help, a representative (or witness) of the justice system, he was told to 'forget about it, overlook the offence and get on with the rest of your life.' Here, social and political issues of racial injustice were interwoven with traumatic and emotional experience. The victim was made to pay twice (once when he was falsely accused, forced to the ground, and jailed, and secondly when he posted bail to gain his freedom). His perpetrators were never held accountable. They never apologized. They were not seeking forgiveness. They were not interested in making restitution. They were merely going about their job. What sense does forgiveness make in the context of this experience?

We have asked many questions about forgiveness, when and where it is relevant. All of the above vignettes raise forgiveness issues. If no one has acknowledged wrong doing, apologized, repented, offered or made restitution, then what sense does forgiveness make? Who can forgive in a life journey where many people participated in different acts and levels of violence, injustice and racism, knowingly and unknowingly? Holocaust survivors, fifty years after the horrendous events, may or may not be able to forgive. But their grandchildren, who never experienced the atrocities first hand are not in the position to forgive either. They were not victims and never knew the perpetrators. How can past collective violence and institutionalized patterns of racism be forgiven? How can women with little power (as in a shelter for women) forgive men with much greater power (police authority)? The vignettes come from societies that are influenced by Western and Judeo-Christian values. There are in these societies (Germany, the United Kingdom, and the United States) a generally shared and Christianized democratic ethic that people should love, forgive and bear one another's burdens. This ethic may also be vaguely stated in the golden rule: 'Do unto others as you want them to do unto you.' It underlies a sense of fair-play or justice. There are different conditions for the expression of this ethic, different interpretations of what this may mean and variations within each of the societies, and different interpretations of who is included in neighbor love and who is not. Not everyone accepts this ethic. Christianity is not the only force that shapes a complex value system in each of these societies. There are other influences and interests such as nation building and recovery from war experiences, cultural development, the spirit of capitalism and socialism, equality. The history and infrastructure of these societies are very different from each other. And so goes the experience of forgiveness. Experience with abuse, degree of trauma and demoralization will influence understandings of forgiveness and whether or not one can or ought to forgive. Forgiveness or withholding forgiveness will vary and depend upon whether or not one is able to resolve mistrust, despair, demoralization and begin to build a new life. These capacities will depend upon the individual's beliefs and capacity for resiliency and available therapeutic resources that will vary in different cultural contexts. What role can spirituality, our sacred texts, and theology play?

FORGIVENESS–A BIBLICAL PERSPECTIVE

The Judeo-Christian tradition professes a belief in a forgiving God. The Old Testament describes those in covenant with God and details their faithlessness, rebellion, disobedience, repentance, and God's offer to deliver them. The backdrop for this cycle is God's faithfulness; God is ever ready to forgive. Forgiveness involves sorrow for offenses committed, repentance and intention to live an upright life. If there is no sorrow, repentance or change, then there is no divine pardon. "Even though a man pays another whom he has insulted, he is not forgiven by God, til he seeks forgiveness from the man he has insulted. That man, if he does not forgive the other, is called merciless."[8] Repentance and forgiveness become ways for God to cleanse the people from all sins committed against God and one another. In the New Testament the word *aphesis* (forgiveness) is almost always that of God.[9] To this extent, the concept is the same as that in the Old Testament. But in the New Testament there is a new and specifically Christian feature evident. The community realizes that it has to receive from God the forgiveness which is offered through the saving act of Jesus Christ.[10]

While the word *aphesis* enjoys secular usage as well, in the New Testament the word is used thirty-six times, always meaning pardon for sins as if this were a technical term reserved for religious use.[11] "It first occurs on the lips of Zechariah in his description of the goal of John the Baptist's ministry, namely to give to the people the knowledge of salvation through the forgiveness of their sins."[12] Baptism is a means of realizing this conversion and its goal is a washing, the remission or forgiveness of sins.[13] In the covenant sealed by Jesus with the institution of the Eucharist, the new covenant is shed for the remission of sins.[14] Thus *aphesis* is the fundamental element of redemptive work. It is connected with pardon, sanctification and salvation.[15] In the preaching of Peter at Pentecost and throughout the book of Acts, this forgiveness depends on faith in the person and power of Jesus; it is universal so that everyone can benefit from it.[16] God's power of forgiveness is creative and on going. We are continuously offered the possibility or opportunity to forgive or to withhold forgiveness.

In the synoptics this is a forgiveness to which humanity is constantly referred; it is a forgiveness that can be received as long as one is willing to forgive others (Mt 6:12,14; 18:21-35; Lk 17:3; Mk 11:25).[17] Derived from the central theme of the oneness of God and humankind, and the inseparability of loving both God and neighbor, is the understanding that forgiveness given by God and to others are intimately related. "Forgive us our debts as we forgive our debtors and do not bring us to the time of trial, but rescue us from the evil one. For if you forgive others their trespasses, your heavenly Father will also forgive you, but if you do not forgive others, neither will your Father forgive your trespasses" (Mt 6:12-15. NRSV).

It is this imperative "to forgive" that is potentially destructive and dangerous in a diverse and complex world. When the understanding of forgiveness is to give unconditional pardon, to forget, to repress, to overlook an injury, to condone, or to excuse the perpetrator from responsibility, then forgiveness is shallow, premature and potentially harmful to the one forgiving. This form of premature forgiveness (or unconditional pardon) is what Archie's seat partner referred to when he said, "If ten years ago a tragic event happened and the perpetrators were aware of their part in it but were not asking or seeking forgiveness, then what is the point of saying, 'I forgive you'?" Or "if they were asking or seeking forgiveness, but they were not doing anything to correct the behaviors that led to the tragic events in the first place, then they are basically the same people today and would do the same again should similar circumstances materialize. What good does it do for the victims to say, 'I forgive you'?" To require forgiveness under these circumstances is premature and destructive. On the one hand, it is destructive because it traps the victim in a false sense of guilt and shame. This imperative to forgive is destructive when it serves to devalue the victim, fails to recognize her or his integrity and contributes to her or his humiliation and lack of self-esteem. It may also be a destructive form of rationalization, i.e., 'they did not intend to harm me,' or 'I was wrong to provoke them.' It is a destructive form of rationalization when it serves as a defense against self-blame, anger, depression, feelings of aggression or as a doomed attempt to combat hopelessness. On the other hand, it is destructive when it serves to enshrine the unrepentant perpetrators in self-righteous attitudes, legitimate their harmful behavior and support its repetition. When this happens it furthers oppressive practices and weakens, if not helps to destroy, the social fabric of which we are all a part.

True, there may be specific situations where an injured party might say, "I forgive you," *before* wrongdoing has been admitted. The source of injury may be an event or it may be an agent. In such instances, the party who says, "I forgive you" is not under the "imperative to forgive" in the sense that we have talked about it above. They are exercising choice. The injured party may have come to a decision about the injury or worked it through and is ready 'to let it go,' 'release' themselves from it or 'let it be' and 'leave.' They may have mourned the injury and have recognized their own need to move forward with their own lives. To find an acceptable way to move forward implies the work of meaning integration and overcoming the separation within the self that the injury may have helped to create. Where a specific agent is involved, he or she may recognize that the perpetrator is incapable of or may never admit to having done wrong. But the injured party is ready to move on. Readiness to move on is a sign of self-growth and a form of self-release, rather than a pardon of the perpetrator. The unrepentant perpetrator is still accountable for his or her behavior. The injured party, however, may have worked through the meaning of the injury and is ready for something new.

The Christian imperative to "forgive" (i.e., pardon) must be understood within the context of repentance, divine justice and mercy. Both repentance and mature forgiveness are acknowledgements that we live in an imperfect world and that human beings commit grievous errors. When they regret such errors, repent and seek amendment of life then meaning in life is redeemed. To repent, seek forgiveness and work to amend life is a way to bring renewal and healing, insight, greater freedom and wider justice, into situations that might otherwise become enshrined in self-righteous attitudes, repetition of harmful behavior, and oppression. Repentance and mature forgiveness can help strengthen the social fabric, the links between people and the ties that bind them.

Pastoral care providers recognize that repentance and forgiveness can be the means through which injured relationships can be restored. It can be experienced as the recreative power of God released and clothed in the speech and activity of the common people. The difficult challenge, then, in every human encounter is to come to a decision about whether to forgive or withhold forgiveness, to acknowledge the depth of our involvements and injuries, and stand before God in faith and openness to the transforming power of forgiveness. This is a difficult challenge, because human forgiveness may not be possible or desirable in all situations and especially in situations of extreme prejudice, where wrongdoing has not been acknowledged, forgiveness is not being sought, and the offender is not seeking peace with justice. Pastoral caregivers may ask: When is the offering of forgiveness premature? When is it not warranted? Under what conditions can forgiveness be destructive? What is mature forgiveness?

It is when forgiveness is seen in relationship to power, love and justice that it is mature. It is healthy, holistic and potentially redemptive when it is mature. This kind of forgiveness is necessary for spiritual and psychological development. It is related to the important processes of recognizing the injury, appropriate expression of anger, seeking information, and finding appropriate resolution. For those who hold fast to a tradition that asks that they forgive, helping them to see forgiveness in this new and expanded light can itself be a redemptive process.

For the purposes of this paper we define "forgiveness" as the redemptive activity of the divine that works in and through human activity. It can be a creative form of release when it emerges from awareness of our own on-going experiences with forgiveness, our on-going human capacity for injuring others and to be injured by them (intentionally or unintentionally). Mature forgiveness is manifest through a process of discernment where responsible forms of power are recognized and one comes to decide how to hold others and oneself accountable. Mature forgiveness requires that justice with compassion is served, healing is possible and our lives can move forward with integrity and faith in God's redemptive purposes.

Theologically, forgiveness cannot stand alone. It needs to be framed in terms of an ontological analysis. The full scope of such an analysis is beyond the aims of this essay. The word, 'ontology' is evoked here to suggest that power, love, and justice are essential qualities of existence, or Being. Power, love and justice are sometimes contrasted in such a way that love is identified with a resignation of power and power with a denial of love and justice with absolute exactness. But this way of contrasting the relationship between power, love and justice is in error.[18] Power is the drive in every living thing to realize itself with increasing intensity and extensity. It is the self-affirmation of life that seeks to overcome non-existence. Love is the drive for meaningful connection, the overcoming of separation and alienation. "And the greatest separation is the separation of self from self."[19] Justice is the drive for adequate forms of fairplay in concrete situations. "Justice can be reached only if both the demand of the universal law and the demand of the particular situation are accepted and made effective for the concrete situation."[20] In every human encounter these qualities, power, love and justice are present in varying degrees. Forgiveness cannot be adequately thought about apart from the unity of power, love and justice. Human encounters require that they work together if human life is to be healthy, sane and balanced. This is to say, that forgiveness can be further explored from a pastoral Christian theology perspective and in relationship to an understanding of the unity of power, love and justice. What follows are idealized descriptions of mature forgiveness when the unity of power, love and justice are considered and what they might entail for our vignettes.

POWER AND FORGIVENESS

Power requires that forgiveness become a dynamic, life-affirming force in the self and in the community. The danger is that forgiveness, as a form of personal, social and political power, may fall into the trap of becoming destructive, especially where there is a lack of power or voice. In the women's shelter, for instance, forgiveness must not be used as a pretext to further diminish their effective work. If women offer pre-mature forgiveness, when the perpetrators have not acknowledged wrongdoing, then it becomes expected. This is destructive. In important ways, each victim could, rather, work to balance more helpfully systems of power in the following ways:

- Mr. F.–forming support groups and educating those in his age group to use the power of the ballot to hold elected and appointed officials responsible for the mandates on which they were elected.
- The sixty-five year old woman–seeking a new life that would honor her remaining years. Her work to encourage others in situations like her own involves eliciting their stories and the formation of new structures of accountability.
- The parents of Stephen Lawrence–crying out for justice until the murderers are held accountable for their crime.
- The black man from the United States–staying alert to the ways that legal and law enforcement systems often collude to thwart justice in order to advocate just practices among the police and legal system.

LOVE AND FORGIVENESS

Love is, by nature, giving. It seeks to overcome alienation and make connections where there is separation. However, love can be destructive when it becomes narcissistic (self-absorbed), sentimental (uncritical), gives away too much, that is to say, becomes one-side sacrificial and helps to erode self-esteem. It can be used to control and disempower others. Healthy forms of love require mutuality, reciprocity and that forgiveness join self-love and self-healing with care and concern for others in building up responsible forms of community. The forgiving self (or selves) that have been violated must struggle with self-acceptance, and find fulfillment in forms of self-healing and in responsible service with others in the following ways:

- Mr. F.–acknowledging all of the feelings of anger and hatred he may harbor toward his country might express his outrage at a cruel system of violence and aid a process of healing by breaking the silence and speaking out about the memories of persecution that he experienced and witnessed under Nazi rule. Love would be experienced as self-integration, self-acceptance and part of a process of mature forgiveness and self-other relatedness.
- The abused sixty-five year old woman from Dresden–acknowledging her feelings of powerlessness and lack of hope, expresses

her feelings of self-blame and inadequacy and is led to healing and mature self-relatedness. Her healing work leads her to decide whether forgiveness is appropriate or not. Healing leads her to assist others in voicing their pain and come to a mature decision about forgiveness.

- The parents of Stephen Lawrence–mourning their loss acknowledges a sense of guilt or self-blame that a parent may feel for not having protected their child from irreparable harm. They reach out in concern and support of other parents who have lost loved ones through racial violence and encourage the support of social and religious agencies that reach out to the voiceless and powerless.
- The young black man from the United States–expressing his shock and outrage toward the way he was accosted by the police and using this knowledge and sensitivity to witness for the other countless young black men and women who are profiled, falsely accused or attacked by the police and other agents of social control.

JUSTICE AND FORGIVENESS

Justice is carried out when forgiveness has found adequate form for fulfillment in specific or concrete situations. There exists the possibility for the injured party or parties to condone, overlook or release the perpetrators from responsibility without acknowledging or confessing any wrongdoing. When this happens, then it is likely that the victim will blame self for the violation and negotiate forms of settlement that only aggravates the original injury, thereby leaving the victim in a state of trauma, and a set-up for additional trauma. This was the case of the student social worker who felt abused by the power of a police officer, doubted herself, and felt blamed for the abuse she was receiving. Adequate forms of justice protect, restore and maintain the dignity of the violated ones and holds perpetrators accountable to retributive, restorative or distributive responsibility. Justice and mature forgiveness work in the following ways:

- Mr. F.–seeking to express his wisdom about systemic violence and oppression and sense of fair play in appropriate organizational forms and curb its abuse.
- The sixty-five year old woman–helping to form organizations that strengthen women's rights and capacities to define and defend themselves with integrity.

- Mr. and Mrs. Lawrence–working with others to expose the abuse of unilateral forms of power and working to increase relational forms of power where respect for difference is valued; decrying a society that is unable to protect the human rights of certain of its citizens while protecting or making it possible for others to hide behind their privilege and abuse of power.
- The young black man from the United States–using his understanding of justice, experience of coercive power and brute force, works with others to expose the limits of unjust power as a basis for building up community. He might seek alternatives to brute force in private and public life and use his knowledge and voice to articulate the greater power that is released when people freely co-operate and use their creative talents for human betterment.

The unity of power, love and justice sustains the work of mature forgiveness. Together, they contribute to a developing capacity for self-affirmation in relationships that renew and restore a sense of intrinsic worth for self and others.

PASTORAL CARE IMPLICATIONS

Pastoral caregivers can enable mature forgiveness as a redemptive force in the therapeutic process when they work from the theological premise that we have a forgiving god and we are called to forgive others. We must acknowledge that our common understandings of forgiveness are not adequate when they condone evil, contribute to further trauma, fail to hold perpetrators accountable, or inappropriately release them from responsibility. These are among the fruits of pseudo and pre-mature forgiveness. They thwart God's redemptive activity. As already suggested, there are practical reasons for holding theological forgiveness together with psychological explanations in a therapeutic process. Clients who come from Christian or other religious traditions and hold guilt feelings because they are unable or not yet ready to forgive, or may have a shallow understanding of their faith and tradition, will need to grow into a mature understanding of their faith. This becomes possible when the theological and psychological explanations are kept together.

Coming to terms with forgiveness, then, is challenging work. In the context of popular culture forgiveness may be seen as morally irrelevant, or as an inept response to injustice. When wrong is done, the focus

314 INTERNATIONAL PERSPECTIVES ON PASTORAL COUNSELING

may be on revenge, 'get mad,' 'pay the perpetrator(s) back or make them pay,' 'even the score,' 'an eye for an eye!'. When we have been the innocent party or victim of violence, we want justice from our systems of law. This is what we would want for Mr. F in our first vignette. He was an innocent victim of systemic injustice and will live with the trauma of his experience for the rest of his life. This is similar for the sixty-five year old woman. Who knows of the humiliation and abuse she endured behind closed doors? Institutional racism, a miscarriage of justice and trauma continue to be experienced by the family of Stephen Lawrence. Trauma and systemic injustice was the case with the young black man in the vignette from the United States. We want those responsible for injuring us to apologize, we want to live in safety, and we want perpetrators of violence to be held accountable. In the case with the parents of Stephen Lawrence from the United Kingdom forgiveness may be negatively interpreted as forgetfulness or repression, overlooking the injury, condoning, excusing, letting the perpetrators off the hook or releasing them from responsibility. This would be pseudo-forgiveness.

Mature forgiveness is an essential element in mental health and a central virtue of the religious life. It is necessary for spiritual and psychological development. From a perspective of mental health, the inability to forgive may be related to an increase of anger, depression, anxiety, paranoia and schizophrenia. On the other hand, mature forgiveness may be marked as the ability to forgive when related to repentance, processes of recognizing the injury, appropriate expression of the anger, seeking information, and finding appropriate resolution. There are tensions to be faced. In the societies that we have identified (Germany, the United Kingdom, the United States) the tensions may include the polarities of depression vs. hope, expressed anger vs. denial of anger, judgment vs. overlooking, condoning the violation or excusing the perpetrators. The tensions will vary from culture to culture depending upon normative definitions of what is "mental" and what is "health." Further tensions may include guilt and shame vs. self-acceptance, information seeking vs. not wanting to know anymore, a decision to forgive vs. withholding forgiveness, humility vs. humiliation. These are among the tensions that may be expressed in the counseling and/or pastoral care context. The manner in which they are expressed or communicated depends upon the beliefs of the victim, surrounding cultural or intercultural realties, the therapeutic space, training, orientation and cultural competence of the caregivers.

Issues of forgiveness are linked to everyday problems of living that are close at hand. Forgiveness issues flood the daily news and show up

in the office of pastoral caregivers. In the context of everyday life forgiveness is often construed in personal terms and fettered with hurt or
pride, ambition, anger, hatred and hostility or harmful deeds we have
committed. These issues of forgiveness must be linked with systemic
awareness of patterns of abuse in the wider society. They in turn must
be connected with self-recovery, self-integrity, self-acceptance, and
self-knowledge in healing relations with others. In this way, pastoral
caregivers can enable mature forgiveness as a redemptive force in the
therapeutic process. When they enable mature forgiveness it can be an
unmatched resource for building a strong sense of self and communal
relationships when repentance and justice are a part of a healing process. Pastoral caregivers can help create healing rituals which enable
traumatized persons to fully face the range and depths of their experience–deception, betrayal, physical violence, shame and humiliation,
self-blame and depression; to express anger, rage, hate; to confront the
offender and address the issues of pseudo-forgiveness and pre-mature
forgiveness. Where the perpetrator or offender is incapable of or refuses
to recognize the offence or is not seeking forgiveness, then adequate
forms of pastoral care will support the recovering individual in creating
safe boundaries and finding appropriate ways to establish distance from
the offender and offending situations. An important task for the pastoral
counselor in international and intercultural contexts is to witness. A witness is one who hears the story of the traumatized ones, acknowledges
their demoralization, and enables them to face the depths of their experiences. Most therapists and counselors who work with victims have indicated the importance of listening to the reports of victims themselves
and to the reports of eyewitnesses, and to acknowledge their experiences no matter how strange they may sound. We learn when we witness to, recognize and respect the integrity of persons across cultures
when we take into account the cultural contexts that shapes the meaning
of violence and violation in their lives.[21] The role of witness is at the
heart of pastoral care and counseling, and so is the work of forgiveness.
The witness encourages the human capacity for resiliency, enables and
supports the injured person through a healing process. In this way, pastoral care and counseling can be effective for those who can participate
in the creation of a relationship (individual and/or group) where unconditional acceptance is possible and where witnesses are able to hear and
assist the sufferer to face the depths of their horrendous suffering. There
may also be those who cannot participate in this form of counseling
care. Adequate forms to meet the needs of those who cannot participate
in counseling care will need to be found or created. Pastoral counselors

then will be challenged to find alternative and adequate resources for witnessing. And they will be able to do so when power, love and justice informs the witness, the context and the work of mature forgiveness.

NOTES

1. Primo Levi, *Survival in Auschwitz: The Nazi Assault on Humanity.* New York: Published by Simon and Schuster, 1996: 90.

2. Ibid, p. 89.

3. *The Guardian,* Thursday, 25 February 1999.

4. *The Guardian,* Wednesday 24 February 1999.

5. *The Observer,* Sunday, 18 February 2001.

6. Ibid.

7. Rodney G. King was a young black man, age twenty-five, who was beaten by police officers at a traffic stop in South Central Los Angeles on March 3, 1992. He was hit between 53-56 times by officers wielding their batons. The bones holding his eye in its right socket were broken, and he suffered 11 broken bones at the base of his skull. The police officers reported that King appeared to be on PCP. However, subsequent tests showed that King had neither PCP nor alcohol nor any other drug in his system. The attack on Rodney King was deemed as racially motivated by the Mayor, Tom Bradley, and civil rights leaders because of the "bigoted remarks" of the officers and because the beating fit the pattern of abusive behavior by police toward blacks. The Los Angeles police officers and supervisors downplayed the level of violence used against King claiming that he suffered only cuts and bruises of a minor nature. Source: *Los Angeles Times,* Tuesday March 19, 1991. Page A20. "A Perspective on the Rodney King Incident."

8. C.G. Montefiore and H. Loewe. Edited. *Rabbinic Anthology.* New York: Schocken Books (1974) 462.

9. *Theological Dictionary of the New Testament.* Edited by Gerhard Kittel. Translated by Geoffrey W. Bromiley. Volume 1. Wm B. Eerdmans Publishing Company: Grand Rapids: Michigan/London, 1964, pp. 511.

10. Ibid.

11. *Theological Lexicon of the New Testament.* Ceslas Spicz, O.P. Translated by James. De. Ernest. Volume 1. Hendrickson Publishers: Peabody, Massachusetts, 1994, pp. 242.

12. Ibid.

13. Ibid.

14. Ibid.

15. Ibid.

16. Ibid.

17. *Theological Dictionary of the New Testament,* Op. cit., p. 511.

18. See, Paul Tillich, *Love, Power and Justice.* New York: Oxford University Press, 1960.

19. Ibid, p. 25.

20. Ibid, p. 15.

21. See, Inger Agger, *The Blue Room: Trauma and Testimony among Refugee Women.* A Psycho-Social Exploration. London: Zed Books, Ltd., 1992.

Pastoral Counselling
in Multi-Cultural Contexts

Emmanuel Y. Lartey, PhD

SUMMARY. This article explores ways in which pastoral counselling reflects cultural preferences. By reference to Western, Asian and African contexts it shows how culture affects what is accepted and practised as counselling. Four views of multi-cultural society are presented and critiqued. An trinitarian, inter-cultural approach to pastoral counselling is proposed that promotes respect for the universal, cultural and unique aspects of all persons. Each of these three elements needs attention and must be held together in creative, dynamic tension. *[Article copies available for a fee from The Haworth Document Delivery Service: 1-800-HAWORTH. E-mail address: <getinfo@haworthpressinc.com> Website: <http://www.HaworthPress.com> © 2002 by The Haworth Press, Inc. All rights reserved.]*

KEYWORDS. Pastoral counselling, Asia, Africa, intercultural

Pastoral counselling means different things in different communities. As such in order to undertake an adequate exploration of pastoral counselling in multi-cultural contexts it is necessary firstly to seek some

---

An earlier version of this article was previously published.

[Haworth co-indexing entry note]: "Pastoral Counseling in Multi-Cultural Contents." Lartey, Emmanuel Y. Co-published simultaneously in *American Journal of Pastoral Counseling* (The Haworth Pastoral Press, an imprint of The Haworth Press, Inc.) Vol. 5, No. (3/4), 2002, pp. 317-329; and: *International Perspectives on Pastoral Counseling* (ed: James Reaves Farris) The Haworth Pastoral Press, an imprint of The Haworth Press, Inc., 2002, pp. 317-329. Single or multiple copies of this article are available for a fee from The Haworth Document Delivery Service [1-800-HAWORTH, 9:00 a.m. - 5:00 p.m. (EST). E-mail address: getinfo@haworthpressinc.com].

317

understanding of the nature and meaning of pastoral counselling in different cultural contexts. It is important to realise that the roots of pastoral counselling in very many cultural contexts lie in the healing and restorative rituals and arts practised by priest-healers within their traditions in the past and to some extent, the present. The traditional healer often combined the roles of priest and physician. He or she was the one to whom folk went in times of difficulty. The expectation was of words and rites grounded in culture, world-view and belief that were deemed efficacious in bringing relief and restoration to functioning order. The traditional healer had to be knowledgeable concerning a wide range of physical, emotional, social and cultural phenomena.

Modern day western pastoral counsellors may appear very different from their historical predecessors. The understanding of what it is they are engaged in may also be radically different. Nevertheless, it is true that the needs, expectations and desires for relief of anxiety that propel people into counselling relationships today, share several similar features with those in the past. It is also the case that in virtually all areas of the world currently, people seek out others they believe have some knowledge, expertise or power that they understand might help them in their quest for relief, well-being or meaning in life. In this article we first examine some understandings and meanings of pastoral counselling in different cultural settings. We then examine different forms of pastoral counselling in multi-cultural contexts. The essay ends with a proposal of an intercultural approach that I believe might offer helpful insights for pastoral counsellors. Since most of us work in situations where we are called upon to interact across cultural boundaries such an approach offers an orienting principle that might facilitate our work.

PASTORAL COUNSELLING IN GLOBAL PERSPECTIVE

Pastoral counselling can and has been understood in a variety of ways. I have elsewhere presented five distinct understandings that appear in western contexts (Lartey,1997, pp. 73-78).

(1) There is a secular usage in educational settings in Britain in which 'pastoral' counselling focuses on the welfare or well-being of students and the personal, social and moral developmental issues faced by pupils in school. Pastoral tutors in schools and colleges seek, through counselling and other means of communication, to facilitate the personal

growth and welfare of their students. (2) There is the exclusive focus of the term upon the counselling work of ordained clergypersons. Here, pastoral counselling refers only to what the clergy do when they offer guidance or counsel to parishioners or others who seek their help. (3) Pastoral counselling may also refer to counselling with a broadly religious frame of reference or counselling which unlike other forms does not equate religion with pathology but rather seeks to take into account clients and counsellors religious sentiments. (4) Pastoral counselling is also seen as counselling offered within or by a community of faith. On this view, groups or individuals within or else representing a particular faith community, work with individuals or groups in accordance with the beliefs of their community's faith. An example of this would be Christian counselling or counselling which seeks to base its theory and practice exclusively on the Bible and the tenets of evangelical Christianity may also be described as a form of pastoral counselling. (5) When counselling focuses on the whole rather than specific aspects of a person's experience (e.g., emotions or cognitive functioning) then the qualifier 'pastoral' in pastoral counselling refers to the whole person. Here the pastoral counsellor is concerned for the total well being of a person mentally, physically, emotionally, spiritually and socially. Such a person would not, of course, offer everything on his or her own. They often work alongside others and have recourse to referral as a means of enabling attention to specific needs. Their overall aim is for holistic health that ignores or minimises no aspect of this.

Wicks and Estadt (1993) edited a book entitled *Pastoral Counselling in a Global church: Voices from the field* in which the work of pastoral counsellors from ten different countries, namely Venezuela, Panama, Kenya, Malawi, Zambia, Ghana, Thailand, Korea, Australia and the Netherlands, is presented. What is clear in this text is that all the writers have found it necessary to modify the western-based training they have received with its assumptions and presuppositions in order to relate in culturally different contexts. Ghanaian pastoral theologian Ghunney, for example declares,

> After completing the Masters Program in Pastoral Counselling at Loyola College in Maryland, where I learned many theories in counselling, I returned home to Ghana in West Africa with the hope of practicing the theories I had learned in the West. I realised, however, that though the theories I learned were good ones, most of them were not practicable in Ghana. The only way I could succeed in the coun-

selling situations there was to contextualize and graft what I had learned with the Ghanaian culture. (in Wicks & Estadt, 1993, p. 82)

Counselling which has developed in the west, by and large, is individualistic, rationalistic and promotes the self (ego) above all else (Lambourne, 1974; Wilson, 1988; Halmos, 1965). This is in line with a system of thought that is essentially materialistic which places the highest value on the acquiring of measurable objects. Colin Lago and Joyce Thompson (1996) in a useful book entitled *Race, Culture and Counselling* attempt to assist counsellors understand the different underlying philosophies that inform non-western approaches to helping and counselling. They (p. 86) argue that western forms of knowledge have tended to be external, the result of counting and measuring with the knower distancing themselves from the object to be known. On the other hand, Asian conceptual systems tend to emphasise cosmic unity and place much value on the cohesiveness of the group. Both inner and external ways of knowing are important and the aim is the integration of body, mind and spirit that are considered to be different aspects of the same oneness (1996: 86).

African systems are often based on a spiritual (or supernatural) and pragmatic ontology that places value on relationality. Knowledge is acquired through intuition and revelation that comes through ritual, symbol and rhythm. The focus of African healing and counselling then is the relationship between and among persons whose intrinsic worth is to be found through the network of spiritual and familial relationships within which they are embedded. With regard particularly to African and Caribbean contexts reference has been made, within the context of pastoral counselling, to the pervasive nature of religion and transcendence in all of life. There is little or no separation between a 'sacred' and a 'secular' realm. All of life is both sacred and secular. These beliefs are expressed most clearly in rituals that are meant to foster and enhance harmonious relations between humans and with the unseen world of ancestors, gods and spirits. Rites and rituals emphasise the importance of symbolic representation and celebration. This is evident also among African Americans and other diasporan African communities (Smith, 1997). For most traditional African and Caribbean peoples, dreams have great significance because they may be avenues through which the really important issues of life may be communicated to persons. Attention within this context is paid to a plurality of practitioners of the healing arts that include traditional priest-healers, herbalists, ritualists as well as diviners, dancers and creative artists. All creative performers are seen as having a part to play in the processes of healing. The pastoral counsellor is seen as part of a community of healers. Life as such is experienced and conceptualised in holistic and synthetic ways (Lartey, 1993; Mulrain, 1995).

Masamba ma Mpolo (in Masamba & Nwachuku, 1991) argues that illness in Africa may be thought of as having spiritual or else relational causes. This is in line with cosmologies that emphasise the inter-relationships between the seen and the unseen world. As such illness may be ascribed either to bewitchment, the anger of mistreated and offended spiritual forces, possession by an alien spirit or to broken human relations. Masamba therefore suggests that spiritual means including 'through ecstasy, rituals and symbolic representations' (p. 28) need to be adopted in helping people deal with their emotional and psychological needs.

Berinyuu (1989) attempts to be deeply rooted in the therapeutic practices and interpretations of the peoples of Africa while dialoguing critically with and attempting to integrate western forms of healing. He defines a pastoral counsellor in Africa as a 'shepherding divine who carefully guides a sheep through a soft muddy spot' (p. 12). Berinyuu's model of the pastoral counsellor is essentially that of one who is adept at harnessing the African 'spirit-filled' universe as well as culturally recognizable symbolic forms of interaction such as storytelling, myths and proverbs, dance, drama and music, in the quest for appropriate responses to the exigencies of life. Such a view could be said to be representative of, in broad terms, an essentially African picture of a pastoral counsellor.

Clearly then, the inclusion of spiritual and cultural resources as pivotal to the work of the counsellor is a distinguishing feature of pastoral counselling. Moreover, in different geographical areas and contexts what is needed is the freedom to recognise what is of value in their historic traditions, to reject what after careful contextual and contemporary examination proves ineffective, and the skill to initiate new syntheses out of the blending and clashing of the different cultures which make up most of contemporary societies.

It is as such true that all forms of counselling are inseparable from cultural assumptions and biases. Different cultural systems appropriately find expression in different therapeutic styles and approaches. In view of this it is reasonable to argue that effective pastoral counselling practice involves reflection on the significance of both the counsellor's and the client's cultural world for the therapeutic process. In what follows we will critically examine a number of different models of multi-cultural society and the form of counselling that emerge on those assumptions.

MODELS OF PASTORAL COUNSELLING
IN PLURALISTIC PLACES

Monoculturalism

Basic maxim: 'We are all really the same.'

The monoculturalist basically claims to work in a 'colour-blind, culture-free' way. For such a counsellor little or no attention is paid to differences that arise from cultural or social background. The overriding assumption is that all human persons in a given situation are basically the same. Most often what such workers accept are the presuppositions of the particular theoretical position that under girds their approach to counselling. They proceed on the basis of these presuppositions often with little critique or question. Seldom do they raise the question of cultural 'fit.' As such they unwittingly insist upon the core values and cultural norms of the particular class or social group represented by the theory they espouse.

Monoculturalism therefore in spite of suggestions to the contrary is not neutral. Two aspects of this unwitting non-neutrality are apparent. Firstly, it universalises particular sets of norms, values, cultural beliefs and practices. Everyone regardless of preference or background is assumed or expected to function in accord with these universals. In this regard the 'white western' and sub-cultures akin to it is regarded as the norm to which all must conform. In terms of pastoral counselling the 'tried and tested' person-centred values of humanistic counselling baptised with healthy doses of liberal western theology become the underlying premises upon which the practice of universal pastoral counselling is based. Secondly, it at best, denies and at worst suppresses cultural expressions that do not appear to conform to this mould. Difference is equated to deviance and is denied, suppressed or forced into conformity. An example of this would be any form of counselling that appears directive. Such would be seen as inappropriate, oppressive or outdated. Practitioners of such abominable arts as 'advising' or 'informing' are shunned or else offered courses in counselling skills.

Pastoral counselling in a monoculturalist framework has tended to take the form of an insistence upon privacy, intimacy, confidentiality and surrogacy. Such counselling usually takes place in one-to-one sessions held in the privacy of the 'pastor's office.' It is premised upon the ability of clients and counsellors to self-disclose and to be articulate, autonomous, independent and self-directing–the predominant values of secular western society. The point is that these values are assumed to be normative in all 'civilized societies.'

While pastoral counselling as described is of value for many in western society it must not be assumed to be so for all in multicultural societies in the west. The next approach to be described takes cultural difference more seriously.

Cross-Culturalism

Basic maxim: 'They are totally different from us'

Pluralism is the credo of the cross-culturalist. Cross-cultural work in counselling based on cross-cultural psychology. The latter sought, from its inception in the 1960s and early 1970s, to study and respond to cultural variations in behaviour in a bid to validate or replicate generalisations about human behaviour based on white European or American studies. Studies undertaken in Europe or America were suitably modified and then undertaken in other parts of the world in order to ascertain the extent to which these generalisations were valid.

Cross-culturalists recognise cultural difference. Such difference is located in social groups that are constituted on the bases of identifiable physical, geographical or cultural characteristics. There are three sets of ideas that seem to be uppermost in the thinking of those who take this approach to the multi-cultural reality. Firstly, the very fact of *difference*– namely the recognition that real difference exists between groups of people in a society. That we are not all the same. Secondly, the view that the *boundaries* around groups are *fixed,* unalterable and to a degree impenetrable must be taken into consideration. Third, that each group has an *identity* that is shared by all who belong to the group. Identity is viewed as a bond that associates all who share it. It ties members together in a collective unity of homogeneity. Every member so identified is like everyone else within the social bond.

One of the pioneers of cross-cultural pastoral counselling is American Mennonite David Augsburger. In a very useful book entitled *Pastoral Counseling across cultures* (Augsburger, 1986) he argues for the need for 'culturally capable pastoral counsellors' who have the 'ability to join another in his or her culture while fully owning one's own' (p. 19). Augsburger's aim is to assist in training culturally able counsellors who are at home on the boundary, able to cross over effectively into another culture with deep 'interpathic' understanding and then return to their own. Howard Clinebell, in the Foreword to the book captures this vision clearly:

> Crossing over to another culture with openness and reverence and then coming back is the spiritual adventure of our time, according to David Augsburger. In his view, crossing over with this mind-set and heart-set enables one to return to one's own culture enriched, more aware, more humble, and more alive. In a real sense, the power of this book is that it can enable us as readers to cross over, experience a stunning array of diverse cultural realities, and then return home with the treasure and growth-in-personhood that comes from interpathic caring in different worlds. (p.10)

Augsburger offers much that is of value and use in the encounter across cultures. However there is a fundamental problem that emerges when one adopts this mentality. The difficulty is that it encourages a 'them' and 'us' mentality that creates problems in any pluralistic society. It is *we* (invariably the dominant, white European/American) who cross over to *them* (the 'rest') and then return. We do things to them. *We* learn about them. *They* are different from *us*. The unconscious assumption is that the counsellor belongs to the dominant majority and the client/patient to the other. The problem is highlighted for me as a Black African pastoral counsellor in Britain–am I part of the 'we' or the 'them' on such reckoning?

Moodley and Dhingra (1998) have recently commented usefully on the complexity of the relationship between counsellor and client when the counsellor is of ethnic minority extraction. Bearing in mind McLeod's (1993) reminder that counselling remains a predominantly white occupation with relatively few ethnic-minority counsellors they explore the client's choice of counsellor. 'For white clients the appearance of a black counsellor may unconsciously evoke certain prejudices and stereotypes which could lead to the rejection of the counsellor but be interpreted by the client as not having a right to choose' (Moodley and Dhingra, 1998, p. 296). They examine white clients' strategies in accepting black counsellors and black counsellors' strategies in managing the relationship. By exploring the questions of 'race' in therapy and facing up creatively to issues of difference, perception and expectation, they argue that white client and black counsellor 'can develop a rich environment for effective and creative therapeutic outcomes' (p. 299).

A very real danger in the cross-cultural approach is the encouragement of division through the *essentialising* of cultural difference. Essentialising occurs when we make particular characteristics the only true or real expressions of a people. The assumption is that there exists an *authentic* African, Asian, African-Caribbean or Black other who is totally different from the dominant one's own cultural experience. The 'exotic' other only exists in the imagination and fantasy of the person within the dominant culture. This way of thinking leads to stereotyping and is related to the over-emphasis of cultural difference. It fails to recognise the mutual influence of cultures within multi-cultural societies.

In terms of pastoral care, the identity and difference of the 'other' is recognised as sacred and advocated for by carers and counsellors from the dominant culture. These brave souls become the 'experts' on 'the Asian community' or the Black community. They then become spokespersons for these cultural groups and inform the rest of the dominant group, relieving them of any responsibility to get involved themselves in the difficult business of cross-cultural encounter. In one sense these cultural informants vicariously bear the vulnerabilities of members of the dominant culture who leave them to get on with it. From time to time members of the subaltern groups who successfully manage to cross over in the other direction become incorporated as token representatives of their cultures and evidence of the liberalism, kindness and tolerance of the dominant group.

Cross-culturalism represents a serious and valuable critique of monoculturalism's presumption of universal values. Nevertheless it operates on the basis of a flawed overemphasis on the identity, difference and homogeneity of other cultural or ethnic groups. While cross-culturalism over-emphasises difference, educational multi-culturalism, which we will now discuss, over-simplifies cultural difference for the purpose of quick and easy encounter.

Educational Multi-Culturalism

> Basic maxim: 'Aren't they interesting: We need to learn as much as we can about them.'

The fundamental premise upon which this approach is based is the need for accurate and detailed information to provide the basis for relevant policy and social action. If appropriate services are to be provided for a multicultural society, it would make sense for the nature and needs of the various cultural groups to be properly understood. Healthy 'race-relations' within any community must be based on knowledge and information about the groups constituting the community. The approach to the multi-cultural society favoured here is that of 'facts and figures' as providing the necessary tools for effective action. As such an attempt is made to build profiles of the various ethnic communities in the society which seek to give information about, for example, social customs, religious rites, food habits, leisure activities, family patterns, gender roles, education and housing within each group.

In Britain of the 1990s ethnic monitoring questionnaires represent, in a crude form, this approach to the multicultural society. It certainly goes some way in providing information. However, the information generated in such ways is too often understood in a reductionistic and individualised way. It thus becomes fuel for cultural, ethnic, religious or other forms of stereotyping. Stereotyping involves perceiving and treating any particular individual member of a cultural group as bearing the presumed characteristics of that group. Stereotyping homogenises groups creating expectations of sameness among all who are classified as belonging to a group. Some attempts at multi-cultural education for counsellors and pastoral carers in an attempt at informing them about 'ethnic minority clients' perpetuate stereotypical myths concerning, for example, the angry underachieving Caribbean male; the Asian young woman's oppressive cultural role; the aggressive Muslim or the problems of the Asian extended family system.

Along with categorising often goes placing in hierarchical order. Cultural groups are tacitly or at times explicitly placed in order of preference or value on particular characteristics. In such rankings the social or cultural group to which the one classifying belongs usually comes out on top. Moreover there is an accompanying presumption that particular cultures are fixed or in some sense static.

Educational multi-culturalism then adopts a commendable information-based, scientific-data oriented approach to the multi-cultural. However, like cross-culturalism, it fails to avoid stereotyping, reductionism, individualising, placing groups in hierarchical order and perpetuating myths that where imbibed can induce self-hatred within the sub-dominant groups. Educational multi-culturalism is often led by media, consumer, tourist, quick fix or market considerations. Busy pastoral counsellors wish to be able rapidly to obtain the information they need to enable them visit or counsel their ethnic minority clients. So they turn to these manuals of information as they would to tourist guides. The problem is the gross oversimplification of the cultural that can mislead and distort any real human relationships to be found therein.

Pastoral counsellors who operate on such premises are often sensitive and caring persons who seek as much information as they can obtain in order not to offend or act inappropriately with the cultural other. However what is lost in a dependence on this information is the spontaneity and sensitivity that is a *sine qua non* of genuine human interaction. 'For pastoral care to be real it has to arise in the midst of genuine human encounter where carer and cared for are both vulnerable and open.' (Lartey, 1998, p. 49).

Intercultural Pastoral Counselling

> *Basic Maxim: 'Every human person is in some respects (a) like all others (b) like some others (c) like no other.'*

In order to gain a fuller understanding of human persons within the global community, it is necessary to explore the ways in which culture, individual uniqueness and human characteristics work together to influence persons. Kluckholn and Murray's (1948) phrase quoted above captures these three spheres of influence that act simultaneously in the experience of every human person. By 'human characteristics' (we are all *like all others*) refer to that which all humans as humans share such as physiological, cognitive and psychological capabilities, with all the common human variations. The 'cultural' (we are *like some others*) refers to characteristic ways of knowing, interpreting and valuing the world which we receive through the socialisation processes we go through in our social groupings. These include worldviews, values, preferences and interpretive frames as well as language, customs and forms of social relationship. The 'individual' (like no other) or personal indicates that there are characteristics–both physical (e.g, finger-print and dental configuration) and psychosocial–which are unique to individuals.

These spheres of human experience interact constantly in living human persons who continually learn, grow and change. Intercultural pastoral counsellors seek to work with persons in the light of these pre-suppositions and realisations. In any pastoral counselling encounter three kinds of issues are attended to by the intercultural pastoral counsellor. Firstly, there is an attempt to inquire what of the common experience we all share as human persons is to be found in the particular situation in question. The attempt here is in recognition and affirmation of the fact that all human beings are created in and reflect the image of God. The assumption therefore is that in spite of variations, ambiguities and differences there will be evidence of humanity in all pastoral counselling encounters. Second, there will be an attempt to figure out what in the experience being dealt with is the result of social and cultural forces. Attention will need to be paid to specific socio-cultural views and practices relevant to the social group the counselling partner recognises as their own. Carter's 'Racially Inclusive model of psychotherapy' offers many useful insights in this respect (Carter, 1995). What would need to be encouraged would be an affirmative as well as self-critical and open exploration of these cultural views and practices in an attempt to discover their influence upon the issue being examined. Within multi-cultural environments, the influence of other cultures than one's own will need to be investigated. Questions of power, domination, benefit and suffering are of particular poignancy here. Third, in intercultural pastoral counselling attempts will be made to investigate what in the experience could be said to be uniquely attributable to the personal characteristics of the counselling partner.

At various moments in any pastoral encounter one or other of these aspects of our humanity will be the focus of attention. Nevertheless, intercultural pastoral counselling will always have the other aspects in view and seek to hold all three in creative and dynamic tension. On such a Trinitarian and communitarian view and vision the relational character of the three Persons of the Godhead is never lost sight of. As such the 'universal,' the cultural and the personal in all human persons are attended to on their own while also being seen as in creative and dynamic interaction with each other.

REFERENCES

Augsburger, D.W. (1986) *Pastoral Counselling Across Cultures*, Philadelphia: Westminster.
Berinyuu, A.A. (1989) *Towards Theory and Practice of Pastoral Counselling in Africa*, Frankfurt: Peter Lang.
Carter, R.T. (1995) *The Influence of Race and Racial Identity in Psychotherapy*, New York: John Wiley.
Ghunney, J. (1993) 'Ghana' in R.J. Wicks and B.K. Estadt, (eds), *Pastoral Counselling in the Global Church*, Maryknoll, NY: Orbis, pp. 82-104.
Halmos, P. (1965) *Faith of the Counsellors*, London: Constable.
Kluckohn, C. and Murray, H. (1948) *Personality in Nature, Society and Culture*, New York: Alfred Knopf.
Lambourne, R.A. (1974) 'Religion, medicine and politics,' *Contact*, 44: 1-40.
Lartey, E.Y. (1993) 'African perspectives on pastoral theology,' *Contact*, 112: 3-12.

_____ (1997) *In Living Colour: An Intercultural approach to pastoral care and counselling*, London: Cassell.

_____ (1998) 'The Fernley Hartley Lecture-Pastoral Care in multi-cultural Britain: White, Black or Beige?' *Epworth Review* 25(3): 42-52.

Masamba ma Mpolo and Nwachuku, D. (eds) (1991) *Pastoral Care and Counselling in Africa Today*, Frankfurt: Peter Lang.

McLeod, J. (1993) *An Introduction to Counselling*, Buckingham: Open University Press.

Moodley, R. and Dhingra, S. (1998) 'Cross-cultural/racial matching in counselling and therapy: White clients and black counsellors,' *Counselling*, 9(4): 295-9.

Mulrain, G. (1995) 'Bereavement counselling among African Caribbean people in Britain,' *Contact*, 118: 9-14.

Smith, A. (1997) *Navigating the Deep River: Spirituality in African American families*, Cleveland, Ohio: United Church Press.

Sue, D.W. and Sue, D. (1990) *Counselling the culturally different*, New York: John Wiley.

Wicks, R.J. and Estadt, B.K. (eds) (1993) *Pastoral Counselling in a Global Church: Voices from the field*, Maryknoll, NY: Orbis.

Wilson, M.J. (1988) *A Coat of Many Colours*, London: Epworth.

Index

Numbers followed by a "t" indicate tabular material.

A Spiritual Strategy for Counseling and Psychotherapy, 141
A Theory of Multicultural Counseling and Therapy, 88
A third look at Jesus, 22
AA. *See* Alcoholics Anonymous (AA)
AAPC. *See* American Association of Pastoral Counseling (AAPC)
Abesamis, C.H., 22
Abesamis, C.H., 21
Abineno, J.C., 153
Abuse, child, pastoral counseling related to, 35-36
Acquired immunodeficiency syndrome (AIDS), pastoral counseling for, in Asia Pacific region, 106-107
Adams, J., 86,145
Addiction(s), pastoral counseling related to, 42-44
Adlerian, 15
Aguiling-Dalisay, G., 39
Aguinaldo, Pres., 9
AIDS. *See* Acquired immunodeficiency syndrome (AIDS)
Alcoholics Anonymous (AA), 44
Alejo, A., 27
Alliance Biblical Seminary, 24,45,121
Alves, R., 202,205
American Anthropological Association, 128-129

American Association of Pastoral Counselors (AAPC), 59,78, 92
American Psychological Association (APA), 141
Anderson, H., 182,228
Andres, T.Q.D., 39
Anitos, 25
Anthropological viewpoint, of pastoral care in Latin America, 199-202
APA. *See* American Psychological Association (APA)
APECA. *See* Association of Psychological and Educational Counsellors in Asia (APECA)
Aquino, B., 10
Aquino, C., 36
Aragon, J.G., 22
Arbularyos, 25
Arevalo, C., 21
Asante, M.K., 141
Asia, pastoral counseling in
  clinical contexts of, 88-91
    cultural contexts of, 87-88
    cultural landscapes of, 77-97
    overview of, 78-80
  educational contexts of, 83-85
  historical contexts of, 80-82
  societal contexts of, 82-83
  supervisory contexts of, 92-93
  theological contexts of, 85-87

Asia Graduate School of Theology, 45
Asia Pacific region, pastoral care and
    counseling in
  in community, 107-112
  future landscape of, 99-118
    AIDS, 106-107
    globalization, 104
    growth of technology, 104
    introduction to, 100-101
    knowledge explosion, 104-105
    new economy, 105
    poverty, 106
    violence, 105-106
  helping communities to cope with
    change, 112-114
  reconciliation in, 114-115
Asian Clinical Pastoral Education
    Association, 23
Asociación de Seminarios y Institutos
    Teológicos del Cono Sur, 203
Assimilation, 138
Assmann, H., 231
Association of Psychological and
    Educational Counsellors in
    Asia (APECA), 15
Association of Psychological and
    Educational Counselors of
    Asia-Pacific, 48
Association of Theological Institutions
    of the South Cone of South
    America, 203
Augsburger, D.W., 17,18t,28,88,
    323-324

Bakke, R., 271
Baltodano, S., xi, 2,191
"Barkada," 39
Basic Christian Communities (BCCs)
  described, 207
  pastoral care with poor through,
    206-215
Basic Law, 132
*Basic Types of Pastoral Care and
    Counseling,* 86,171

Basic Types of Pastoral Counseling,
    86,154
Basilio, N., 50
Bautista, V., 29,42
Baxter, R., 180
"Bayanihan," 12
Becker, E., 108
Behavior modification, 15
Bellah, R., 110
Beltran, B.P., 22
Benzenhafer, P., 50
Berger, P., 108
Berinyuu, A.A., 321
Berne, 203
Bloch, E., 236
Body of Christian Psychologists and
    Psychiatrists, 203
Boff, C., 192,206,214,232
Boff, L., 192,206,211,215,270
Bond, M.H., 11
Bons-Storm, R., 278,280,285
Bonthius, R.H., 206
Bowen, 32
Boyagan, F., Fr., 50
Boyd, D., 10
Bradshaw, J., 34-35
Branqueamento, 198
Brazil, pastoral counseling in, 239-252
  context of, 242-244
  introduction to, 240-241
  perspective of, 242-244
  Protestant, 244-251
    challenges facing, 244-248
    possibilities for, 248-251
*Breaking the silence: The realities of
    family violence in the
    Philippines and
    recommendations for change,*
    36
Brief therapy, 15
Brueggemann, W., 266
Bubbod, L., 50
Burke, J., 112

Cabrera, A., 23,50
Calpotura, V.S., 27
Canada
    Chinese immigrants in, cultural
        adjustments of, and pastoral
        counseling, 137-139
    Chinese in, historical background
        of, and pastoral counseling,
        134-136
Canadian Pacific Railways, 134
Carandang, M.L.A., 36
Carino, F., 20-21
Caritas, 212
Carnadang, M.L.A., 15
Carter, R.T., 328
Catholic church, in pastoral care in
        Latin America, 204-206
Catholic Theological Union, Chicago,
        Illinois, 228
CEDEPCA (Centro de Estudios
        Pastorales en Centro
        America), 204
CEDI (Centro Ecuménico de
        DocumentaÇao e
        InformaÇao), 204
CELEP (Centro Evangélico
        Latinoamericano de Estudios
        Pastorales), 204
Center for Family Ministry, Ateneo
        University, 32,45
Centro de Estudios Pastorales en
        Centro America
        (CEDEPCA), 204
Centro Ecuménico de DocumentaÇao
        e InformaÇao (CEDI), 204
Centro Evangélico Latinoamericano de
        Estudios Pastorales (CELEP),
        204
Cervera, V., 43,50
Cheatham, H., 140
Cheun Lee, S.Y., 2
Child abuse issues, pastoral counseling
        related to, 35-36
Chinese church, pastoral counseling
        considerations in, 144-148

Chinese cultural contexts, pastoral
        counseling in, 119-149
    case study, 125-126,129-130
    described, 126-130
    introduction to, 119-121
    in multicultural perspectives,
        139-144
    philosophical perspective of,
        121-126
    socio-historical background of
        Hong Kong and, 131-134
    case study, 133-134
    sociological perspective of, 130
    special considerations in Chinese
        church, 144-148
Chinese Exclusion Act, 134
Chrisitans, C., 233
Christian Counseling, 86
Christian Medical Commission of
        World Council of Churches,
        155
Chuen Lee, S.Y., 119
Church, A.T., 16
CLAI. *See* Consejo Latinoamericano
        de Iglesias (CLAI)
Clinebell, H., xi,xix,86,154,156,171,
        324
Clinical Pastoral Care Association of
        the Philippines (CPCAP), 23
Clinical Pastoral Education (CPE), 78
Collins, G., 86
Communal spirituality, in pastoral care
        in Pretoria, South Africa, 271
Community(ies), pastoral counseling
        in, in Asia Pacific region,
        107-112
Competent to Counsel, 86
Conference on Pastoral Care and
        Counseling, 23
Conflict resolution, pastoral counseling
        related to, 69-70
Confucius, 122,123
Consejo Latinoamericano de Iglesias
        (CLAI), 204
Conversation(s), "exculpatory," 186

Corpo de Psicólogos e Psiquiatras
    Cristaos, 203
Counseling
    directive, 15
    "nonuthetic," 145
    third-party, in Philippines, 30-31
"Counseling for Peace," 18
Counseling in the Asia Pacific Region,
    102
Counseling the Culturally Different:
    Theory and Practice, 88
Counselor(s), pastoral, training of,
    45-48,46t,47t
CPCAP. *See* Clinical Pastoral Care
    Association of the
    Philippines (CPCAP)
CPE. *See* Clinical Pastoral Education
    (CPE)
Critical prophetic approach, 213
Cross-Cultural Counseling, 168
Cross-culturalism, in pastoral
    counseling, 323-325
Cuen Lee, S.Y., xii
Cultivating Wholeness, 166
Culture, defined, 152

Dalton, A., 23
Dangawan, S., 50
Dangerous Drug Act of 1972, 42-43
Dangerous Drug Board, 42-43
David, R., 104
de Beer, S., xi,2,253
de Beer, W., xi-xii,2,253
de Paula Cavalcante, E.V., 203
de Santa Ana, J., 202
Death and the Maiden, 296
Decenteceo, E.T., 18
Deficit-based approach, vs.
    strength-based approach, in
    pastoral counseling, 185-186
Deist, F., 281
dela Rosa, Fr., 33
dela Torre, E., 21

Dellosa, R., 50
Department of Corrections, 43
Department of Social Welfare, 36
Depression, pastoral counseling related
    to, 44-45
Dhingra, S., 324
Directive counseling, 15
Divorce, pastoral counseling related to,
    41-42
Doctor of Pastoral Studies Program, of
    South East Asia Graduate
    School of Theology, 153-154
Donne, J., 107
Door of Hope Counseling Resource
    Center, 50
Dorfmann, A., 296
Drucker, P., 231
Duan, C., 123
Dumalagan, N.C., 23

Economy, effects on pastoral care and
    theology, 225-237
    analysis of, 229-232
    context of, defined, 227-229
    introduction to, 226-227
    pastoral-theological agenda in,
        232-236
Educational multi-culturalism, in
    pastoral counseling, 325-327
Egan, G., 164
EIRENE, 203-204
Emmaus Road Counseling Center, 23
Empathy, in pastoral counseling,
    162-165
Empowerment, defined, 285
Enriquez, V., 16,17
Escape from Evil, 108
Essentialising, defined, 325
Estadt, B.K., 319
Estrada, J., 10
Ethnic identity, 138
Ethnicity, as factor in pastoral care in
    Latin America, 196-199
"Exculpatory" conversations, 186

Faber, H., 180
Faith and the Future, 233
Family(ies), pastoral care of, in
        Philippines, 31-32
Family Code of 1987, 38
Family problems, pastoral counseling
        related to, 35
Family systems, pastoral counseling
        related to, 68-69
Family violence, pastoral counseling
        related to, 35-36
Farris, J.R., 1,2,239
Feminism, in Philippines, 37
Filipino culture, distinctiveness of,
        11-14,13t
Filipino psychology, emerging, 14-20,
        17t-19t
Filipino religious psychology, 26
"Filipino time," 31
Fiorenza, F., 233
Floristan, C., 213
Foregiveness, in pastoral care, 310-313
Forgiveness, in pastoral care, 295-316.
        See also Pastoral care,
        complexity and simplicity in
*Foundations for a Practical Theology
        for Ministry,* 167
IV Women's Conference, 196
Frankl, 203
Freud, S., 107,203
Fromm, E., 108,203

Galdamez, P, 212
Galdamez, P., 207
Galilea, 213
Gaudium et Spes, 204
Gender, as factor in pastoral care in
        Latin America, 196-199
Gender issues, pastoral counseling
        related to, 37-39
Gerkin, C.V., 262,270
Gestalt therapy, 15,140
Ghunney, J., 319-320
Giglio, K., 108

Gingrich, F.C., xii,2,5
Girard, R., 231
Glasserians, 171
Globalization, of pastoral counseling,
        in Asia Pacific region, 104
God, in pastoral care in Pretoria, South
        Africa, 267-269
Gorospe, V., 21
Graham, L., 235
Greenhills Christian Fellowship's
        Pastoral Care and Counseling
        Ministry, 23
Grief, loss and, pastoral counseling
        related to, 71
Griswold, W., 110
Gutierrez, G., 236,270,271

Haley, A., 203
*Handbook of Psychotherapy and
        Religious Diversity,* 141
Harper, G.W., 20
Harperians, 171
Haug, I.E., 47
Hayes, R., 229
Head Tax, 134
Health-orientedness, in pastoral
        counseling, 185-186
Hechanova, L., 22
Henriot, P., 271,273,288-289
Hermeneutics, and cultural
        anthropology, 168-169
Hiltner, 86
Hinkelammert, F.J., 195
"Historial Protestant churches," 243
"Hiya," 16
Ho, D.Y.F., 124
Ho, M.K., 126
Hoch, L., 203
Holand, J., 271,273
Holistic health care movement, in
        Indonesia, 154-156
Holland, J., 288-289
Hommes, T., 153,154

Hong Kong, socio-historical
    background of, and pastoral
    counseling in China, 131-134
"Hunger for God, Hunger for Bread,
    Hunger for Humanity: A
    Southern Perspective," 230

"In living colour," 263-264
*Indigenous psychology and national
    consciousness,* 16
Indonesia
    location of, 151-152
    pastoral counseling in, 151-173
        academy-based, 161-162
        bases of, 158-159
        case studies, 159-162
        chruch-based, 160
        cultural anthropology in,
            168-169
        empathy in, 162-165
        evaluation of, 171-172
        future of, 173
        hermeneutics in, 168-169
        historical background of,
            152-154
        holistic health care movement
            in, 154-156
        holistic model of, 171-172
        hospital-based, 161
        office-based, 162
        psychology of, 170-171
        skills involved in, 162-165
        sociology of, 169-170
        terminology related to, 156-157
    population of, 151
Indonesian Association for Health
    Services, 154
Indonesian Christian Association for
    Health Services, 155-156
Integrating Spirituality into Treatment,
    141
Intercultural pastoral counseling,
    327-328

International Christian Peace
    Movement, 227
International Congresses on Pastoral
    Care and Counseling, xv
International Pastoral Care Network
    for Social Responsibility,
    xv-xvi
Interpersonal relationships, pastoral
    counseling related to, 67-68
Invitation to Sociology, 108

Jakarta Theological Seminary, 153
Jen, 123
Jenkins, A., 286
Jubilee Consultation 1996, 235
Jung, C., 107
Jungian, 15
Justice, in pastoral care, 312-313

"Kaibigan," 30
"Ka-loob," 27
"Kapwa," 16
KASP. *See* Korean Association of
    Spirituality and
    Psychotherapy (KASP)
Katigbak, M.S., 16
KBE. *See* Knowledge-based
    economies (KBE)
KCICP. *See* Korean Christian Institute
    of Counseling and
    Psychotherapy (KCICP)
Kim, T.C., 11
King, R., 305
Kluckhooln, C., 327
Knowledge-based economies (KBE),
    105
Koininia Theological Seminary, 50
Korea Association of Pastoral
    Counseling, 85
Korea Christian Institute of Counseling
    and Psychotherapy (KCICP),
    91

Korean Association of Christian
    Counseling and
    Psychotherapy, 92
Korean Association of Pastoral
    Counseling, 92
Korean Association of Spirituality and
    Psychotherapy (KASP), 92
Korean Association of Clinical
    Pastoral Education, 92
Korean Association of Family
    Therapy, 92
Korean Christian Institute of
    Counseling and
    Psychotherapy (KCICP), 87
Korean Counseling Association, 92
Korean Counseling Psychology and
    Psychotherapy Association,
    92
Kornfeld, M.Z., 61-62,166
Koyama, K., 20
Krisetya, M., 154
Kwan, K-L.K., 127

Lago, C., 320
Laird, J., 278,279
Lake, F., 177
Lala, A., 165
Lamang lupa, 25
Lapuz, L.V., 37,38,39-40
Lartey, E.Y., xii,2,263,271,272,273,
    317
"Las Brisas del Bogota," 193
Latin America, pastoral care in,
    191-224
    anthropological viewpoint in,
        199-202
    Catholic work in, 204-206
    described, 193-194
    ethnic viewpoint in, 196-199
    gender viewpoint in, 196-199
    introduction to, 192-193
    Protestant theological institutions
        in, 202-204
    protestant work in, 202-204

socioeconomic viewpoint in,
    194-196
through Basic Christian
    Communities, 206-215
towards liberating pastoral care to
    poor, 215-217
Latin American Council of Churches,
    204
Legally law, 36
León, J.A., 203
Lerato House, 261,273,274,275,276,
    278,283,285-286,286-287
Leslie, 88
Lewis, O., 199
Li, 123,124
Liberating Pastoral Care (LPC), to
    poor in Latin America, 215
Liberation Theology, 206
Life Innovations, 146
Listening presence, in pastoral care in
    Pretoria, South Africa,
    277-281
Logotherapy, 15
Loss and grief, pastoral counseling
    related to, 71
Louw, D., 263
Love, in pastoral care, 311-312
Lowe, D., 262,280
Loy, D.R., 228-229
Loyola School of Theology, Ateneo de
    Manila University, 23
LPC. *See* Liberating Pastoral Care
    (LPC)

ma Mpolo, M., 321
Macapagal, D., 9
Macapagal-Arroyo, G., 9,10,36
MacArthur, D., Gen., 9
Mackerras, C., 113
"Made in Hong Kong," 135
"Made in Taiwan," 135
Maidment, R., 113
Maimela, S., 281

Maldonado, J.E., 203
Mandela, N., 115
Mao, Chairman, 131
Marabastad Development Forum, 270
Marcos, F., Pres., 10
Marital problems, pastoral counseling
    related to, 35
Marital separation, pastoral counseling
    related to, 41-42
Marriage, pastoral care of, in
    Philippines, 31-32
McLeod, J., 324
McLuhan, M., 107
Medina, B.T., 38
Meeks, D., 234
Meeks, L.M., xii-xiii,2,57
Meeks, M.D., 229
Mehta, K., 110
Menchu, R., 198-199
Mercado, L.N., 20,26
"Merit System," 134
Metanoia Psychological Foundation,
    23-24
Methodist School of Theology, in
    Brazil, 243
Metz, J.B., 233
Michal, Y., Rabbi, 64
Miller, 167
Miller-Mclemore, B., 235
Minuchin, 203
Moltmann, J., 234-235
Monoculturalism, in pastoral
    counseling, 322-323
Moodley, R., 324
Morais, R.J., 12
Moral Man and Immoral Society, 108
Morgan, A., 287
Muller, J.C., 263,266,270
Multi-modal therapy, 15
Murray, H., 327

Nacpil, E., 21
Nambu, T., 50

National Council of Churches, in
    Philippines, 21
"Neo-Pentocostal churches," 243
Network for Urban Ministries in South
    Africa (NUMISA), 269
Neuro-linguistic programming, 15
Niebuhr, R., 108
No Future Without Forgiveness, 115
Not-knowing position, in pastoral
    counseling, 184
"Nouthetic" counseling, 145
Nouwen, H., 271
Novak, M., 231
Noyce, G., 180
NUMISA. *See* Network for Urban
    Ministries in South Africa
    (NUMISA)
Nunos, 25
Nurturing, defined, 266

O'Connor, E., 271
OFW. *See* Overseas Filipino Workers
    (OFW)
Openmindedness, in pastoral
    counseling, 184
Ornstein, R., 112
Ortigas, C.D., 15
Overseas Filipino Workers (OFW), 35

PACERS. *See* Philippine Association
    for Counselor Education,
    Research and Supervision
    (PACERS)
"Pagdadala," 18
Pambansang Samahan ng
    Sikolohiyang Pilipno (PSSP),
    15
Paniagua, F.A., 142,143
PAP. *See* Psychological Association of
    the Philippines (PAP)
Parenting issues, pastoral counseling
    related to, 36-37

Parks, S., 282-283
Pastoral care
  bases of, 158-159
  in Brazil, 239-252. *See also* Brazil,
    pastoral counseling in
  complexity and simplicity in,
    295-316
    Biblical perspective on, 306-310
    case studies, 299-306
    forgiveness in, 310-313
    implications in, 313-316
    introduction to, 296-298
    justice in, 312-313
    love and, 311-312
    power in, 310-311
  economy effects on, 225-237. *See*
    also Economy, effects on
    pastoral care and theology
  in Latin America, 191-224. *See also*
    Latin America, pastoral care
    in
  in Pretoria, South Africa, 253-294.
    See also Pretoria, South
    Africa, pastoral counseling in
Pastoral care and counseling in Asia:
    Its needs and concerns, 23
Pastoral counseling
  in Asia, cultural landscapes of,
    77-97. *See also* Asia, pastoral
    counseling in, cultural
    landscapes of
  in Asia Pacific region, future
    landscape of, 99-118. *See*
    also Asia Pacific region,
    pastoral care and counseling
    in, future landscape of
  bases of, 158-159
  in Chinese cultural contexts,
    119-149. *See also* Chinese
    cultural contexts, pastoral
    counseling in
  Chinese in Canada and, historical
    background of, 134-136
  cross-culturalism in, 323-325

    educational multi-culturalism in,
      325-327
    global issues in, 57-75,62-66
    global perspective of, 318-321
    holistic model for, 165-171
    in Indonesia, 151-173. *See also*
      Indonesia, pastoral
      counseling in
    intercultural, 327-328
    meaning of, 60-62
    method for, 169-171
    monoculturalism in, 322-323
    in multi-cultural contexts, 317-329
    new Canadian Chinese immigrants
      and, cultural adjustments of,
      137-139
    in Philippines, 5-55. *See also*
      Philippines, pastoral
      counseling in
    in pluralistic places, models of,
      322-323
    in Singapore, 175-189. *See also*
      Singapore, pastoral
      counseling in
    sociology of, 169-170
Pastoral Counseling, 86
Pastoral Counseling Across Cultures,
    323
Pastoral counseling model, theology
    for, 167-168
Pastoral Counselling in a Global
    Church: Voices from the
    Field, 319
Pastoral counselors
    described, 157-158
    training of, 45-48,46t,47t
Pastoral critico-profética, 213
Pastoral Popular, 204-205
Pastoral solidarity, 242
PCGA. *See* Philippine Guidance and
    Counseling Association
    (PCGA)
PCM. *See* Pretoria Community
    Ministries (PCM)
Pedersen, P., 123

"Pendampingan," 159
Philippine Association for Counselor
        Education, Research and
        Supervision (PACERS), 15
Philippine Association of Christian
        Counselors, 48-49
Philippine Guidance and Counseling
        Association (PCGA), 15
Philippine Journal of Psychology, 15
Philippines
    cultural mosaic of, 10-11
    described, 11
    feminism in, 37
    Filipino culture in, distinctiveness
        of, 11-14,13t
    National Council of Churches, 21
    pastoral counseling in, 5-55
        addictions, 42-43
        challenges facing, 48-50,49t
        child abuse, 35-36
        context of, 24-27
        cultural contrasts in, 6-7
        culture in, 7-8
        depression, 44-45
        dynamics of, 27-31,29t
        emerging Filipino psychology
            in, 14-20,17t-19t
        family problems, 35
        family violence, 35-36
        family-related, 31-32
        gender issues, 37-39
        historical background of, 22-24,
            24t,26t
        historical context of, 8-10
        issues in, 57-75
            case studies, 72-74
            conflict resolution, 69-70
            family systems, 68-69
            interpersonal relationships,
                67-68
            introduction to, 58-60
            loss and grief, 71
            referrals, 71-72
            spirituality, 70-71
        marital problems, 35

        marital separation and divorce,
            41-42
        marriage-related, 31-32
        parenting issues, 36-37
        problems related to, 33-45,34t
        sexuality issues, 39-41
        shame issues, 33-35
        suicide, 44-45
        theologizing in Filipino context,
            20-22
        third-party counseling, 30-31
        training of pastoral counselors,
            45-48,46t,47t
    population of, 11
Philippines Association for CPE, 67
Philippines Association for Pastoral
        Care, 67
*Planting Pastoral Counseling Seeds in
        Brazilian Soil,* 241
Poling, J., 167,214
Popular Pastoral Care, 204-205
Poverty
    culture of, in Latin America,
        199-202
    pastoral counseling for, in Asia
        Pacific region, 106
Power, in pastoral care, 310-311
Prasantham, 154
Preface to Pastoral Theology, 86
Prepare-Enrich Inventories, 146
Pretoria, South Africa
    described, 254-259
    pastoral counseling in, 253-294
        in broader Christian community,
            269-270
        case studies, 260-261,271-289
        challenges facing, 256-257,
            289-291
        as common journey, 266-267
        communal nature of, 264-265
        communal spirituality in, 271
        creation of communities of
            concern in, 281-285
        described, 259-271
        distinctiveness of, 263-271

God in, 267-269
introduction to, 254
listening presence in, 277-281
nature of, 263-271
pastoral facilitators in, 261-263
pastoral response to, 257-259
questions related to, 291-292
responsibility in, 285-289
self-responsibility in, 286
social context of, 254-256,
 289-290
social/political/public
 dimensions of care in,
 265-266
Pretoria Community Ministries (PCM),
 257,284
"Prophetic Pastoral Practise," 263
"Protestant Pentocostal churches," 243
Protestant theological institutions, in
 Latin America, 202-204
Psicologia Pastoral, 203
PSSP. *See* Pambansang Samahan ng
 Sikolohiyang Pilipno (PSSP)
Psychological Association of the
 Philippines (PAP), 15
Psychology
 Filipino, 14-20,17t-19t
 of pastoral counseling, 170-171
Puebla, 213

"Querida," 42
Querijero, M., 50
Quezon, M., 9

Race, Culture, and Counselling, 320
"Racially Inclusive Model of
 Psychotherapy," 328
Raiser, K., 235
Ramos, F., 10
Rational-emotive therapy, 15,28
Reality therapy, 15,28

Reconciliation, helping communities in
 experiencing, 114-115
Referral(s), pastoral counseling related
 to, 71-72
*Religion and the Clinical Practice of
 Psychology,* 141
Respectfulness, in pastoral counseling,
 184-185
Responsibility, in pastoral care in
 Pretoria, South Africa,
 285-289
Richards, B., 108
Riedel-Pfaefflin, U., xiii,2,3,295,298
Rieschick, J., 11,14
Ro, B.R., 21
Rogerians, 171
Rogers, C., 185,203
Roldan, A., 42
Roy, D.E., 59
Ruiz, L., 228
Ruiz, N.R., 19
Rustin, M., 108

Salazar-Clemena, R.M., 18,19,48
Samekto, G., 163
Santosa, P., 155
SAR. *See* Special Administrative
 Region (SAR)
Satha-Anand, C., 227
Sathler-Rosa, R., xiii, 2,3,225
Satya Wacana Christian University,
 154,163
Schak, D., 113
Schipani, D., 203
Schoot, E., 180
Schreiter, R., 228,230
Secretariat of Family Pastoral Care,
 204
Secretariat of Women and Children,
 204
Self-responsibility, in pastoral care in
 Pretoria, South Africa, 286
Separation, marital, pastoral
 counseling related to, 41-42

Sexuality, pastoral counseling related
to, 39-41
Shame issues, pastoral counseling
related to, 33-35
Shim, S.S., xiii,2,77
"Sikolohiyang Pilipino," 16
Sin, J., Cardinal, 27-28
Singapore, pastoral counseling in,
175-189
  exploratory approach to, 183-184
  health-orientedness in, 185-186
  not-knowing position in, 184
  openmindedness in, 184
  personal response to, 187-189
  perspective of, 178-179
  proposal for, 179-181
  respectfulness in, 184-185
  strength-based vs. deficit-based,
  185
  systemic and multi-perspectival
  orientation in, 186-187
  therapeutic conversations in,
  181-189
SIR. *See* "Smooth Interpersonal
Relationships" (SIR)
Skinner, B.F., 203
Smith, A., Jr., xiii-xiv,2,3,295,298
"Smooth Interpersonal Relationships"
(SIR), 13,17
Sobrino, J., 205
Social/political/public dimensions of
care, in pastoral care in
Pretoria, South Africa,
265-266
Socioeconomic viewpoint, of pastoral
care in Latin America,
194-196
Sociology, of pastoral counseling,
169-170
Solomon, R., xiv,2,3,99
Sonh, C.S., 20
South African Police Services, 273
South East Asia, pastoral counseling
in, 175-189. *See also*

Singapore, pastoral
counseling in
South East Asian Graduate School of
Theology, 159
Special Administrative Region (SAR),
132
Spirituality
  communal, in pastoral care in
  Pretoria, South Africa, 271
  pastoral counseling related to,
  70-71
Stamateas, B., 203
Strategic family therapy, 32
Strength-based approach, vs.
  deficit-based approach, in
  pastoral counseling, 185
Sue, D., 127
Sue, D.W., 88,127,140
Sui, P.Y., 21
Suicide, pastoral counseling related to,
44-45
Sung, J.M., 230,231,232
Survival in Auschwitz, 298
Susabda, Y., 154

Tagalog, 33,37
Tambalan, 25
Tan, S.Y., 29-30,31
Tano, R.D., 21, 22
Tanseco, R., Fr., 23,45,46t,50
Teilmann, G., Rev., 176
The Afrocentric Idea, 141
*The Association of Christian
  Psychiatrists and
  Psychologists,* 244-245,246
The Axemaker's Gift, 112
The Brazilian Counseling Association,
244-245,246
*The Christology of the inarticulate: An
  inquiry into the Filipino
  understanding of Jesus
  Christ,* 22
"The Cult, The Crowd, and The
  Community," 109
The Denial of Death, 108

The Family Code of the Philippines,
    37-38
The Filipino elderly, 36
"The Future Landscape of Pastoral
    Care and Counseling in the
    Asia Pacific Region," 100
The Guardian, 303
The handbook of Chinese psychology,
    11
"The Living Human document," 168
*The Mental Health of Asian
    Americans,* 128-129
The Potter's House, 261,275-276
The Reformed Pastor, 180
The Skilled Helper, 164
The Theology of Conquest, 22
Theologizing, in Filipino context,
    20-22
Theology of Struggle, 21
3rd Theory Building Conference of the
    International Pastoral Care
    Network for Social
    Responsibility, 109
Third-party counseling, in Philippines,
    30-31
Thlagale, B., 281
Thompson, J., 320
Transactional analysis, 15
Trinity Theological College, 176,177
Truth and Reconciliations Council,
    115
Tutu, D., Archbishop, 115
Tyndale Theological Seminary, 121

UKIT University, in Tomohon, 159
Universidad Biblica Lationamericana,
    204
University of Santo Thomas, 15
"Utang na loob," 16

van Beek, A.M., xiv,2,88,151
van den Blink, 64

Vanier, J., 271
Villar, I.V.G., 15,16,17
Violence
    family, pastoral counseling related
        to, 35-36
    pastoral counseling for, 105-106

Wat, B., 32
Wesley Methodist Church, 176
White, M., 270
Wicks, R.J., 319
Wiryasaputra, T., 157,163
Wise, 86
World Bank, 235
World Trade Organization, 132

Yeo, A., xiv,2,175
Young, K.P.H., 146
Young, R., 108

Zea, L., 197